African Beads

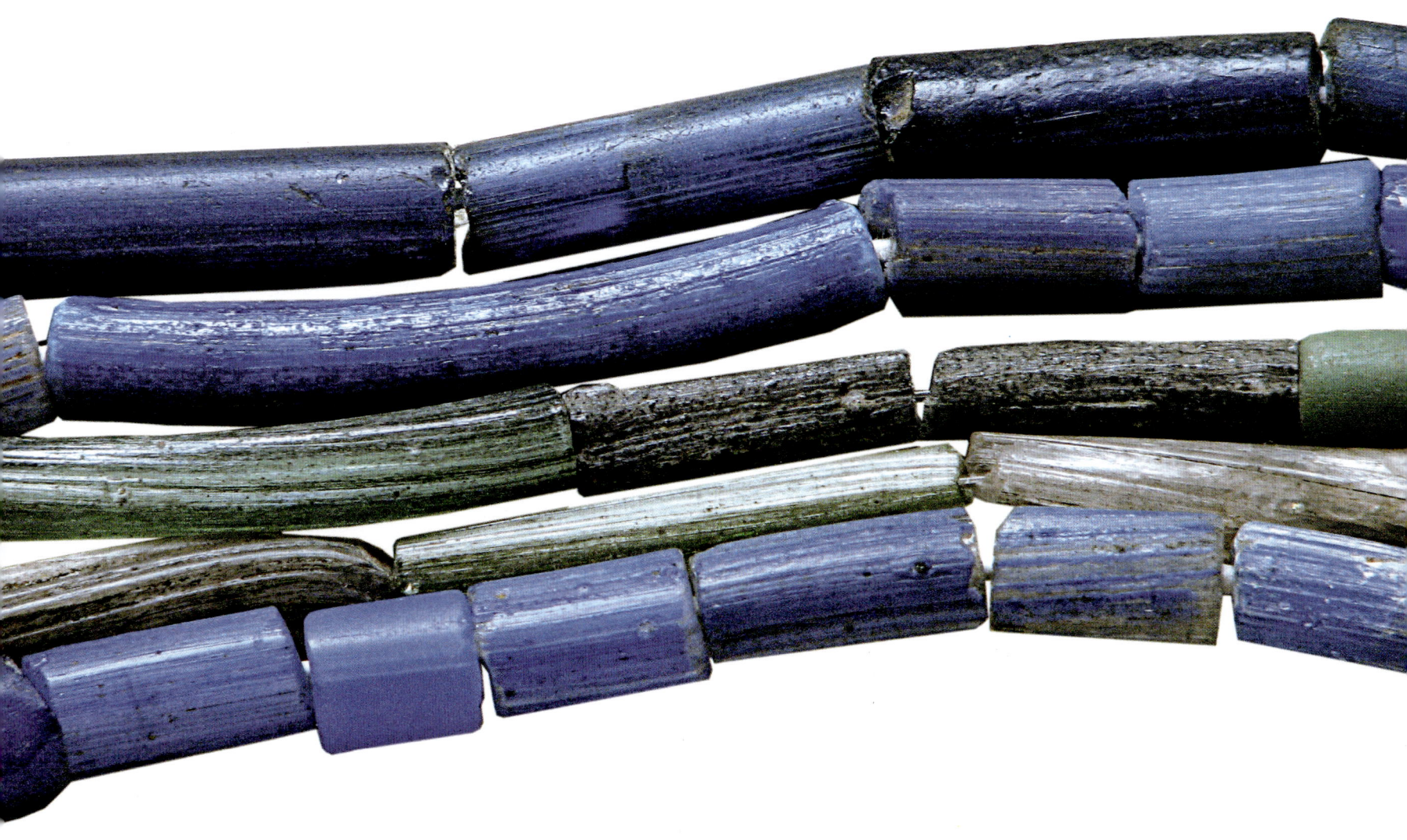

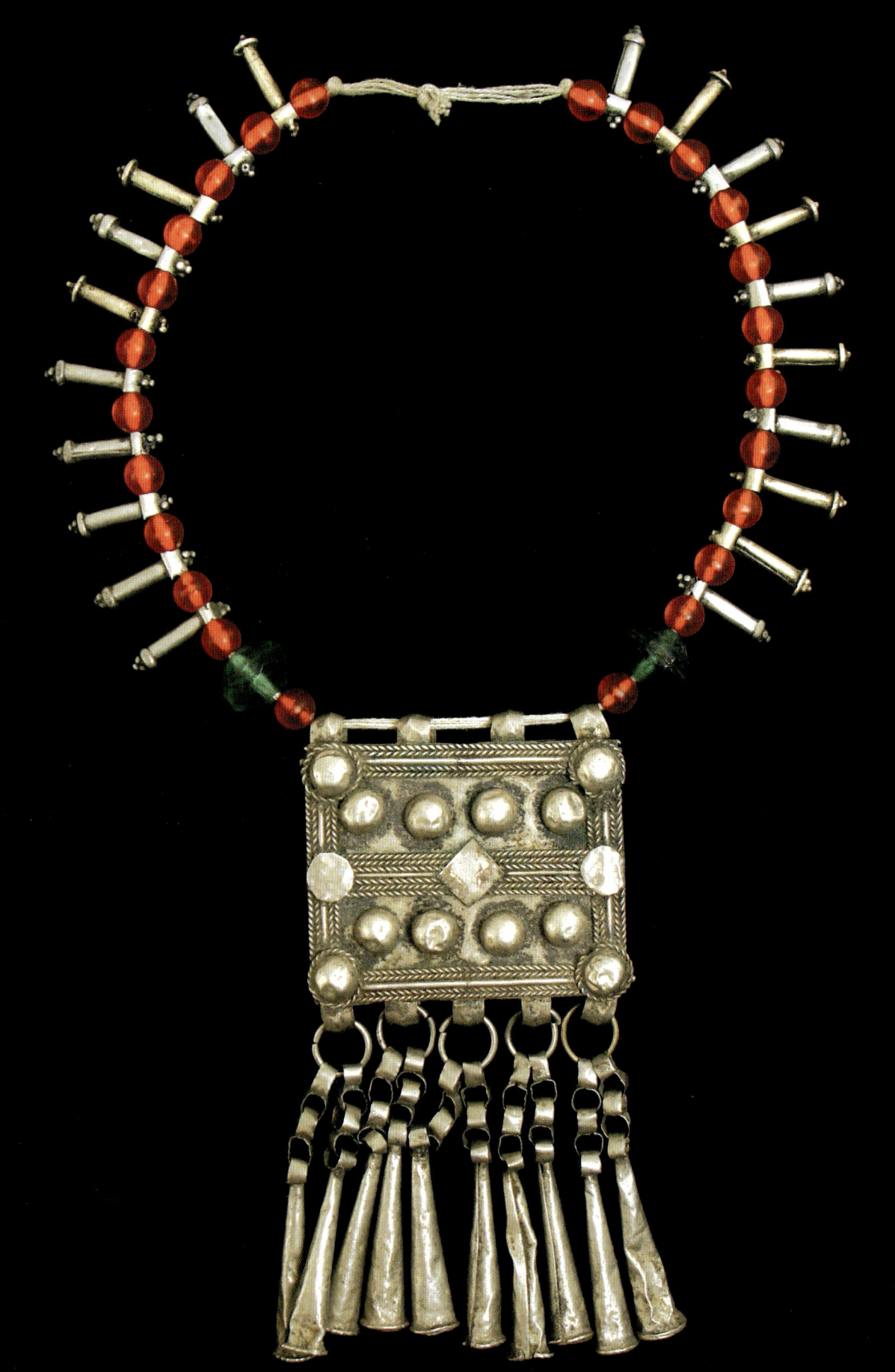

African Beads
Jewels of a Continent

Evelyn Simak
with Carl Dreibelbis

and an introduction by
Lois Sherr Dubin

Photography by Mark Donato

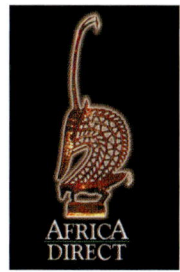

Copyright © 2010 by Africa Direct, Inc.
All rights reserved.

No part of this book may be reproduced in any form beyond that copyright permitted by Sections 107 and 108 of U.S. Copyright Law and except by reviewers for the public press, without permission from the publisher.

Photography by Mark Donato
with additional photography by Evelyn Simak, Hiram Yates, Adam Line, Floor Kaspers and Thomas Mercer
Art direction and jacket design by Jacob Liechty
Text design by Mayapriya Long, Bookwrights Design

ISBN: 978-0-9816267-2-7
Library of Congress Cataloguing Number: 2009907618

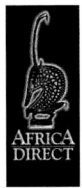

Published by
Africa Direct
Denver, Colorado
www.AfricaDirect.com

Printed in The United States of America

Contents

Foreword 13
Introduction 15

Bones, Teeth, Claws and Shells 23
    Ostrich Eggshell Beads 23
    Heishi: How They Are Made 26
    Shells 26
        Clam 26
        Giant African Land Snail 26
        Cowry 26
        Shell Currencies 28
        Conus 36
        Arca 36
        Coral 36
        Benin 36
        Morocco 37
        Imitations 38
    Bone 38
        Beads, Pendants and Charms 38

Snake Vertebrae	42
Fish Vertebrae	43
Antelope Bones	43
Batik Bone Beads	44

Teeth and Claws 44

Ivory 46

Amber, Clay and Beads Made from Plant Materials 53

Amber 53

What Is Amber? 53
Broken Amber Beads 54
Medicinal Properties 57
Copal 57
Testing Amber 57
Phenolic Resins and Other Amber Imitations 57
Amberoid 57
Bakelite, Resolan and Novalak 57
Phenolic Resins 57
Bernat 58
Celluloid 58
Casein 58
Horn, Bone and Glass 58
African Amber 59

Clay 59

What Is Clay 59
History of Clay-working in Africa 59
Clay Artifacts of Djenne 63
Clay Spindle Whorls 66
Clay Beads 66

Wood, Seeds, Nuts and Other Plant Materials 67
Wood 67
Seeds, Seed Pods and Nuts 67
Sea Beans 67
Kekeore 67
Job's Tears 67
Rosary Pea 67
Coconut Palm 73
Scented Paste Beads 73
Tunisia 73
Algeria 76
Morocco 76
Mauritania 76
Mali 76
Senegal 76
Nut Grass Corms 77
Recycled Plastic Beads 77

Stone Beads 79
The First Stone Beads 79
Granite and Gneiss 80
Dogon Ancestor Stones 81
Bauxite (Abo) 82
Jasper (Lantana) 86
Jasper in the Kingdom of Benin 87
Amazonite 88
Serpentine 88
Quartz 88
Pietersite 88

Metal Beads 89

History of Metalworking 90

African blacksmiths 90

Mande 90
Bamana 92
Wolof 92
Hutu 92
Dogon 92

Iron 92

Dogon 92
Yoruba 97

Gold 97

Ashanti 97
Akan 99

Silver 102

Tuareg 102
Berber 107
Silver in Ethiopia 109
Oromo 109
Maria Theresa Thaler 109
Telsum 110
Mergaf 113
Pendants and Amulets 114
Musbaha 114
Coptic Crosses 115
Falasha 115

Brass 116

Brass in Nigeria 116
Yoruba 117
Fulani 118

Tiv	120
What Is Lost Wax Casting?	122
Brass in Ghana	122
Ashanti	122
Brass in Ivory Coast	122
Baoule	122
Other Brass	122

Copper 124

Aluminium 124

Glass Beads 125

History of Glass Beads 125

Drawn and Lapidary Beads 127

Kori Stones 127
Kori Beads 127
Kori Bead Imitations 130
Lapidary Worked Glass Beads 130

Powder glass beads 131

History 131
Powder Glass Beads in Ghana 131
Dipo Ceremony 131
How Powder Glass Beads Are Made 132
Krobo Powder Glass Beads 134

Powa 134
Miti Metee 134
Gige 135
Tsakati and Okata 138
Ologo 138
Terrazzo 139

- *Mue Ne Angma* 139
- *Cedi* 139
- *Art Seymour* 139
- Bodom Beads 139
  - *New Bodom* 145
- Akoso Beads 145
  - *New Akoso* 148
- Ashanti Powder Glass Beads 148
- Yoruba Powder Glass Beads 151
  - *Keta Awuazi* 151
  - *Niusisi Koli* 151
  - *Tehe Koli* 151
- Powder Glass Coral Imitations 152
- Kano beads 153
- Mauritanian Powder Glass (Kiffa) Beads 156
  - *History* 156
  - *Technique* 156
  - *Purpose* 156
  - *Styles, Shapes and Decorative Patterns* 157
  - *New Kiffa Beads* 158
  - *Indonesian Kiffa Bead Imitations* 162
  - *Krobo Kiffa Bead Imitations* 162
  - *Other Kiffa Bead Imitations* 164

Wound Beads 164
Bida beads 164

Ceramic Beads 164
Kazuri Beads 164
Prosser Beads 166
Faience Beads 166

History of Trade in Africa from Antiquity to the Present Day 169

- A 20th Century African Bead Trader's Story 169
- Antiquity 169
- The Trans-Saharan Trade 172
- The West-Atlantic Trade 174
- The Pilgrim Routes 176
- 19th Century 176
- African Bead Traders 176
- 21st Century Bead Business 179

Notes 181
Bibliography 193
Index 199
Acknowledgments 213
Publisher's Note 215

Foreword

Peoples of all cultures have used beads since ancient times, be it for personal adornment, for protection against evil powers, or as symbols of status and wealth. Jewelry and ornaments made of precious metals such as gold and silver, feathers, leather, bones, shells, wood, ceramics, glass, hair, brass, copper and iron have been worn in the form of crowns, necklaces, pendants, ear and nose rings, hair ornaments and waist belts since times immemorial. Some of the oldest known beads, 37,000 years old and made of ostrich egg shells, were found in the Enkapune Ya Muto rock shelter in the Rift Valley of Kenya. Shells, seeds, nuts, wood, bones and stones that could be found in the natural environment were ground, carved, drilled and polished, and threaded on strips of wool or leather to adorn and protect early man. In sub-Saharan Africa, the complex technology of ironworking was discovered 2,500 years ago. Natural glass has existed since the beginnings of time and according to the ancient Roman historian Pliny (23-79 BCE), Phoenician merchants became aware of its existence by accident when transporting stone in the region of Syria around 5000 BCE. The oldest fragments of glass vases date back to the 16th century BCE and were found in Mesopotamia.

Beads became objects of trade, and particular types of beads attained such well-established values that they were used as currencies in pre-colonial Africa. In West Africa, this development was accompanied by a proliferation of kingdoms and city-states, the most important of which were ancient Ghana (1200-1300 CE), Mali (1300-1400 CE), Songhai (1400-1600 CE) and Kanem-Bornu (750-1075 CE). Among the items that were exchanged by trade were iron, salt, cowry shells, brass rods, palm oil, gin, gold dust, cattle, goats, sheep, brass bracelets, copper rods, muskets, powder, shot, slaves and beads, with one of the accepted currencies being shell money.

Beads were being made in West Africa long before trade with Western civilizations brought imported beads into the region. In the 19th and 20th centuries, a great variety of glass beads were manufactured by the flourishing European bead industries of Venice, Italy, and Bohemia-Czechoslovakia, especially for export to West Africa. Ever since the 1960s—when the bead was discovered as a collectible item—these so-called African Trade Beads have been made available to American, European and, more recently, Asian clientele by African bead dealers who spend many months of the year traveling throughout West Africa and beyond to source their merchandise. Several centuries after their manufacture, whole strands comprised of European-made glass beads are now returning to their countries of origin, accompanied by a variety of beads produced by African industries.

Because of the abundance and desirability of European-made beads in West Africa and among non-African collectors alike, it is easy to forget that West African cultures such as the Krobo and Ashanti of Ghana and the Yoruba of Nigeria have long traditions of bead making of their own. Sadly, many of these bead industries have ceased to exist. While traditional techniques such as wax-casting, employed in the manufacture of brass beads and ornaments, are still practiced, and while the Ghanaian industries have been very successful in developing ever more colorful and interesting styles of powder glass beads, the art of making Mauritanian powder glass Kiffa beads appears to have become extinct with the passing on of the last bead makers in the 1970s. Only recently could it be established that certain types of glass beads ascribed to the European or Middle Eastern industries were in fact manufactured by the Yoruba almost a thousand years ago.

When speaking of African beads, the bead types that usually come to mind are Millefiori and Chevron beads, which were brought to Africa from European countries. Apart from a few exceptions, beads manufactured in Africa, by Africans, are often considered less attractive and interesting than the so-called African Trade Beads, and many African-made beads are currently misunderstood, misidentified and undervalued. With its presentation of beads manufactured by and unique to West African cultures, including descriptions of the techniques employed in their manufacture, "African Beads: Jewels of a Continent" pays homage to the beads, and to the craftsmen and women of Africa for whom bead making still is a way of life.

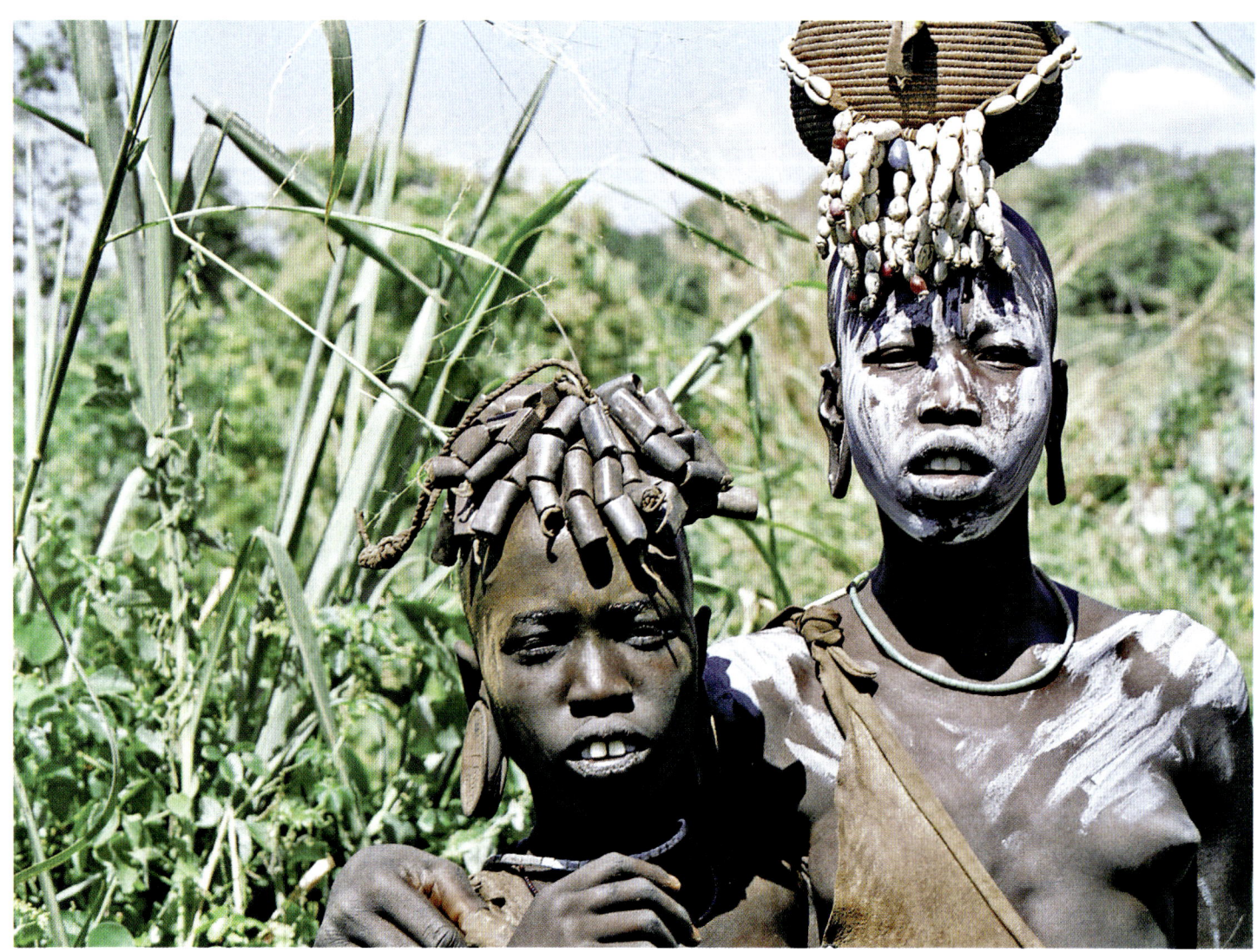

ABOVE *The Mursi people of Ethiopia's Omo Valley are semi-nomadic and live in remote areas. In recent years, however, tourists have begun to take an interest, showing a particular fascination with the Mursi custom of wearing large ear-disks, lip-disks and metal (probably aluminum) hair beads like those shown here.*

Introduction

African-Made Beads: The Matter of Materials

BY LOIS DUBIN

To understand African art, "it is necessary" says African philosopher Anthony Appiah, "to see things with an African eye… the eye is trained differently in Africa [than] in the West."[1] African aesthetics cannot be comprehended apart from the sacred. Art, whether it be sculpture or adornment, was, and still is created to represent spiritual values that are basic to the survival of the community. Art is made to express what people know and believe rather than what they actually see.[2]

Most Africans conceive of the visible world of the living as analogous to the invisible world of the spirits and ancestors. The whole of creation is imbued with powerful spiritual energy. Artisans use materials from the natural world to provide a link with the supernatural. It is believed that these materials contain forces, which, when properly employed may offer protection, healing or leadership. Although decoration for the sake of beauty exists in Africa as elsewhere, appeasing sacred forces is the fundamental reason for adorning the human body with paint, tattoos, masks, clothing, jewelry, amulets and beads.

Beads are connected with every aspect of African existence. They are an integral part of a multilayered communication system among all groups. Through their materials, colors and arrangements, beads communicate cultural values as clearly as the spoken or written word. This is as true for the hunting-gathering peoples of the southern Kalahari Desert as for the wealthy Nigerian and Ghanaian villagers. A particularly marvelous example of beads as a visual language occurs with the Luba of Zaire, who string shell and glass beads into necklaces that are literally read as history books. Called "chains of memory," the arrangement of the beads recalls historic facts, important persons and the hierarchy of authority within the royal court. The necklace is a microcosm of the Luba society.[3]

It was, in fact, during a trip to Kenya in 1982, when I observed the Maasai and Samburu in their layers of beaded jewelry, that I envisioned the concept for my book, "The History of Beads." The idea was to present beads within the context of the people who made and wore them; to understand beads as a microcosm of the macrocosm. Twenty-five years later, I am even more deeply convinced that beads are the DNA of adornment, most particularly in Africa.

The plethora of African beads reflects the enormous range of raw materials that has long been available to African bead artisans. For thousands of years, each group has crafted beads from local and accessible resources —seeds, shell, clay, stone, minerals and metals— as well as from exotic substances introduced via long distance trade— Mediterranean coral, Baltic amber, Islamic and European glass. Yet, although much attention has been focused on imported European glass beads, little information is available on beads made by the African peoples themselves. "African Beads: Jewels of a Continent" fills that void. It is the first comprehensive overview of African-produced beads. Organized by medium, the book points to a particularly intriguing feature: that specific materials (shell, ivory, coral, iron, copper and brass) were important to Africans in the past and remain so today. Beads are a central component of a fascinating adornment narrative that extends far back into African prehistory. There is, for example, the persistence of wearing beads made

---

1 Appiah 1984:17
2 Vogel 1981:9

3 Roberts p. 29, 97. *See the necklace of Chief Kifwa Kaula Kisangani wa Nyemba, collection of the Zairian National Museum, Lubumbashi. (in Roberts, plate 87)*

of white shell. At Grotte des Pigeons, in Morocco, North Africa, archaeologists recently excavated a cache of perforated *Nassarius* shell beads stained with red ochre. These beads, recovered at archaeology levels dating to 82,000 years ago, substantiate the dates of similar ornaments from other African sites (see page 26). Most significantly, they not only confirm early bead-making, and suggest the existence of long distance exchange systems, but, as these African beads predate Upper Paleolithic shell beads in Europe by at least 40,000 years, they offer interesting possibilities for the origins of modern human behavior in Africa.[4]

We have no way of knowing what these shell beads meant to their Middle Paleolithic owners, nor why they were covered with red pigment. Nonetheless, as noted by the archaeologists, "The choice, transport, coloring and long-term wearing of these items was part of a deliberate, shared and transmitted non-utilitarian behavior.... To be conveyed from one generation to another over a very wide geographic area, such behavior must have implied powerful conventions that could not have survived if they were not intended to record some form of meaning."[5] The Grotte des Pigeons beads further hint at a remarkable cultural continuum, as shell beads continue to occupy a special position within African adornment.

The huge ostrich eggshell, used for beads since 37,000 BCE[6], is coveted in East and Southern Africa where the raw and durable material is still found. Ostrich eggshell beads are treasured by the !Kung San of the Kalahari Desert above all other ornaments. White discs cut from the eggshell are filed, strung and worn in layers around the neck. Traces of red clay, used cosmetically by many East African tribes, often remain between the discs, bringing to mind the ancient association of the Paleolithic *Nassarius* shell beads stained with red ochre.

Within the Western world, beads created of organic substances such as shell, bone, wood, stone and clay, have typically been thought to have little monetary worth and were thus considered the "small change" of a culture. However, for many Africans, objects produced from these materials often convey a connection to the sacredness of the larger cosmos as well as their immediate surrounding world: the plants, creatures and minerals. Objects embedded with beads of sacred materials play a major role in rituals celebrating birth, circumcision, marriage, warriorhood, kingship and death.

Ritual and Regalia: Regalia, the major form of visual artistic expression among all African societies, is a complex assemblage of body decoration, clothing, masks and ornaments that comes alive through ritual and dance. All the elements form an elaborate system of correspondences that gives order to what is significant in each group's world. Therefore, while viewing the beads displayed in "African Beads: Jewels of a Continent," remember that they are only one part of the total ensemble. Anthony Appiah reminds us that when seeing African jewelry out of context, "we are moving away from the wholeness of vision of traditional culture. To see these objects properly, we must imagine them adorning the body."[7]

Envision the regalia of a Luba king, or chief, as he is transformed from an ordinary mortal into a sacred ruler during investiture rites. "Eventually, the chief bursts forth [out of the house] dancing and prophesying, supposedly under the inspiration of the spirits of his forefathers." The assemblage may include "an enormous red [parrot] feather headdress, a shell necklace, a bead necklace, a leopard skin, a belt made of twisted hippopotamus or elephant hide, a bone or ivory bracelet, a spear, a staff, a stool, a bowl for *pemba* [white chalk], a receptacle for the cranium and genitalia of the last ruler, an ax, a knife, iron bells and a drum."[8]

Or picture the golden splendor at the Ashanti kingdom's lavish ceremony held in 1995 to honor the twenty-fifth year of rule of King Otumfuo Opoku Ware II. As photographed and described by Carol Beckwith and Angela Fisher in "African Ceremonies," "The Asantehene, his royal court and numerous paramount chiefs of Ghana displayed the most extravagant collection of golden regalia to be seen anywhere in the world.... Sitting in state, [the Asantehene's] arms are so heavily laden with gold jewelry that when he moves they must be supported by a special attendant. His ankles are circled for protection by gilded leather talismans and his feet rest on a footstool that prevents evil spirits from entering his body from the ground.... Female court dancers... [are] adorned with gold belonging to the royal treasury, among which are large breast-shaped plaques.... Bracelets are made from hollow-cast beads threaded together with ancient glass beads which are even more valuable than the gold."[9]

Prior to the public appearance of the Ashanti king, priests throughout Ghana gathered together to call upon the gods to ensure the well-being of the kingdom. Wearing

---

4 Bouzouggar et al. 2007: 9964
5 ibid, 9969
6 See text, page 23

7 Appiah 1984:19
8 Burton 1961 and in Weydert 1938 in Roberts and Roberts 1996:64
9 Fisher and Beckwith 1999: vol. 1:352-382.

adornment of leather, shells, iron and medicine charms, the priests covered themselves with charcoal, red clay or white chalk powder (kaolin), a medicine that is considered to be "food for the spirit" and is used to obtain the sacred spirit's power.[10]

The concept of assemblage ranges from adornment of the body to adorning an artifact. An elder from the Dinka tribe of the Sudan displays a necklace, known as a "gift of God" made of snake vertebrae, white glass beads and cowry shells.[11] In Namibia, a young Himba bride is beautified with red ochre and butterfat, iron beads and a conus shell pendant.[12] A Zulu shaman's necklace, a powerful assemblage within itself, is composed of twigs, tortoiseshell, seeds, snake vertebrae, teeth, glass beads and leather and glass beaded amulets.[13] Kuba masks combine skins, raffia cloth, glass beads, cowries, feathers and seeds for rattles. (See plates, right and next page)

Materials: Despite the wide contrasts of the adornment materials worn at the Luba investiture, Ashanti royal extravaganza and the Ashanti priestly ceremonies—as well as those exhibited by the Dinka elder, Himba bride, Zulu shaman and Kuba masked dancer—every substance has sacred content. African artists do not arbitrarily choose their materials. Each plays a specific aesthetic and symbolic role when used for objects of adornment. Careful selections purposefully determine what will be transformed into a tool of communication with the supernatural.[14]

Coral, ivory, brass and gold—all durable, expensive and exclusive—are associated with Africans of privilege. Shell adornment is more egalitarian. Yet the Western distinction between secular and religious within all these materials is less absolute in the African context. Precious materials enhance the prestige of their owner. At the same time, many of these materials are used for healing and protection when they are thought to contain spiritual forces with curative and protective powers. A North African Berber necklace— one of the most visually impressive African objects of assemblage—must contain at least one shell, amber or coral bead in order for it to have the therapeutic qualities integral to the Berber cultural belief system. Otherwise, the necklace

---

10 Fisher and Beckwith 1999: vol. 2:167
11 Dubin 1987:121
12 Fisher and Beckwith 1999: vol. 1:286
13 Dubin 1987:120
14 Herreman 2003:9

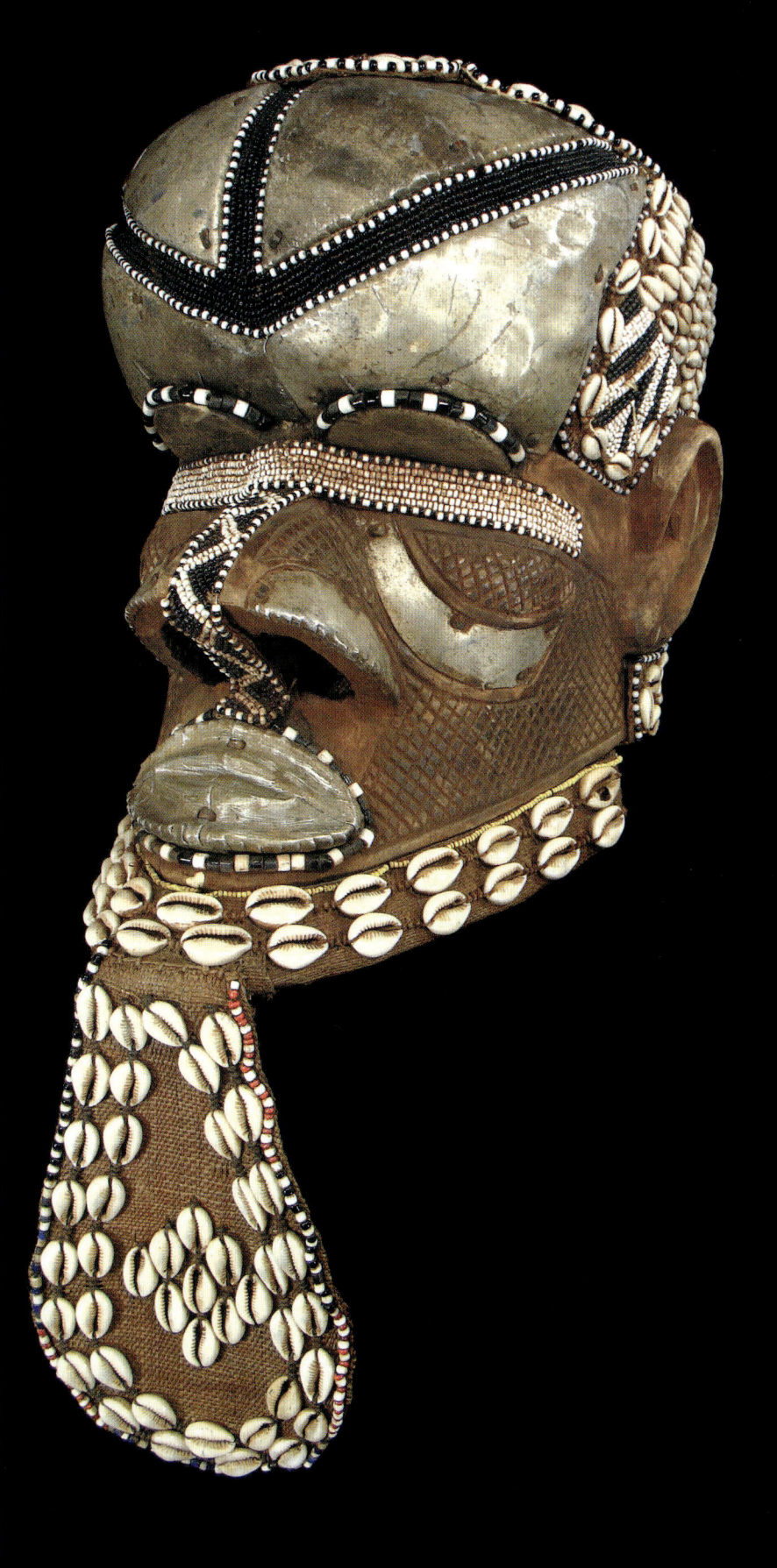

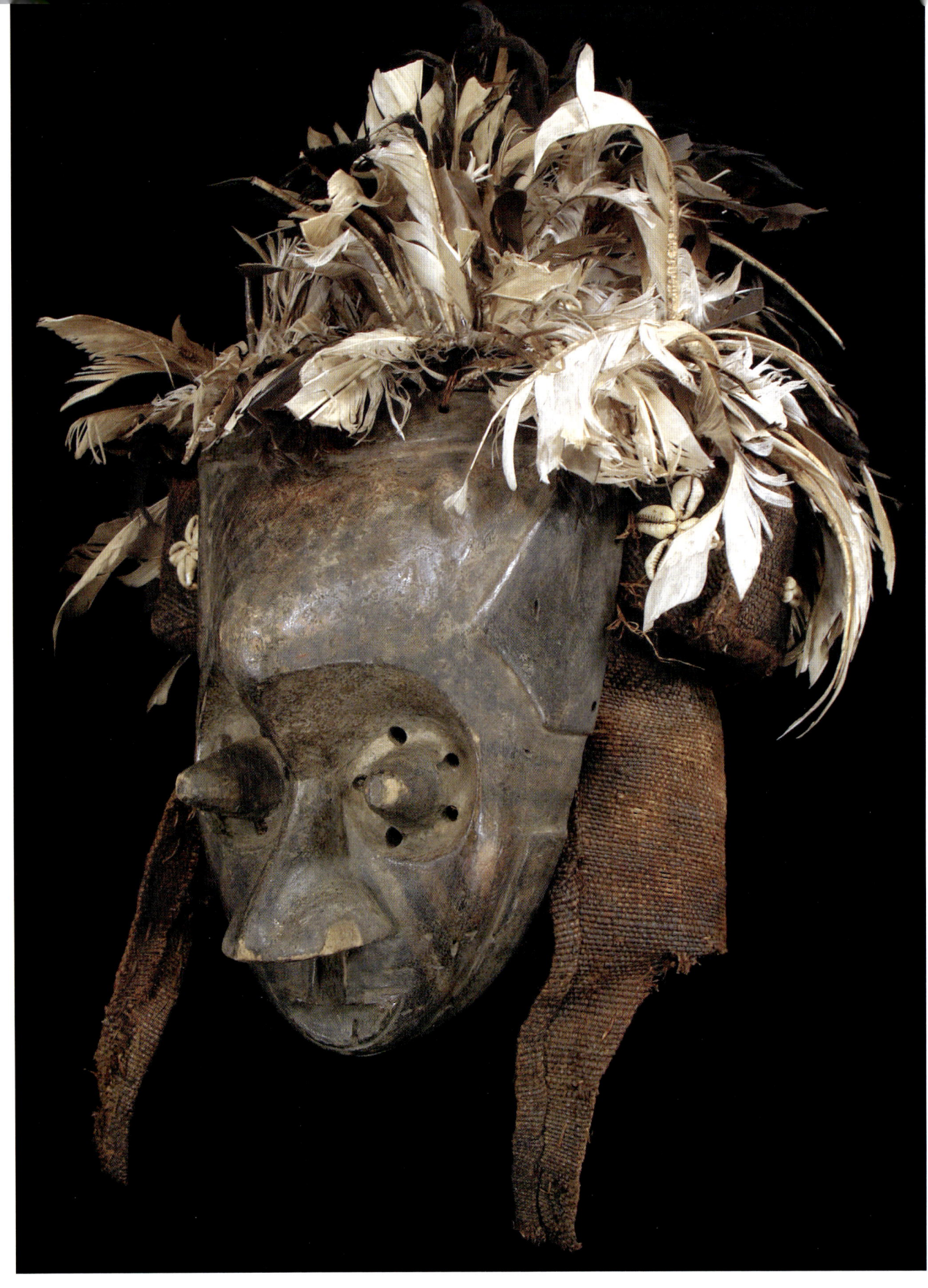

has no perceived status or power. Silver is extolled by Allah and adored by the Berber who use it for numerous amulets, talismans and beads.[15]

Shell: Africans accord a sacredness to shells that has never been equaled by any other material. The use of cowry shells is particularly ubiquitous, which, perhaps owing to their shape (resembling the eye and female genitalia), has long been associated with the fertility of both women and the land.[16] Among the Booran Oromo, desert pastoralists from Kenya and Ethiopia, cowry shells symbolize the mother-child relationship through their color: white, like milk—the daily sustenance. Cowries are worn by very young Oromo, and boys privileged to have been selected as future spiritual leaders.[17]

Many girls, such as the Senufo from the Ivory Coast, wear strings of cowry shell beads during initiation rites.[18] For the Mende people living in the central Niger Valley in West Africa, cowries are valued because their shape, suggestive of female sexuality, relates to the "aesthetic and social value of the woman herself; their structure and color recall bones and the human skeleton, thus equating the shell with man (both being the most beautiful of earth's creations); and the brilliant whiteness of the cowry evokes the color of yet unborn beings from the invisible world."[19]

"Luba chiefs of the most ancient royal lineage at Kabongo still have necklaces made from cone shells," wrote anthropologists Mary Nooter Roberts and Allen F. Roberts. "The symbolic relationship between cone-shell disks and political authority is based on the shell's whiteness and interior spiral. 'White' for Luba people is the color of bone, chalk, purity and the spirits. The link with the other world is fundamental to sacred royalty.... Luba associate the spiral inside the cone-shell disk with the rainbow. The rainbow stands for the primeval king Nkongolo Mwamba, who, after being killed by his nephew, was transformed into a enormous red serpent. The rainbow is the breath of this aquatic and subterranean creature, joining the living to the dead. The symbolism of the serpent is so powerful that some Luba chiefs are forbidden from viewing the striations of the shell, which they must wear in such a way that only the reverse side is exposed."[20]

Coral: Coral beads are items of immeasurable value to the Edo people of Benin and Nigeria, and have been so for hundreds of years. They are cherished for their aesthetic and spiritual significance. Even some names given to children at birth are connected to coral beads: "Ivie" (coral beads) is a common name for female children connoting something "priceless."[21]

Although most descriptions focus upon the elaborateness of the coral bead ceremonial regalia displayed by the Edo ruler (*Oba*), the regalia, too, has a dense secular/sacred duality. "Wealth must not hide," wrote author Alate Fubara-Manuel, a Kalabari of Nigeria. "A chief must be wealthy to fulfill his obligations to himself, his people, his town and his national deity."[22] African court art assists the state by providing noble symbols of power. There is believed to be a spiritual connection between the well-being of both the king and the people of the Benin kingdom. The Oba—an embodiment of the legendary founder of the kingdom—is a supernatural being: the conduit through which divine forces are made available to his subjects.[23]

A king must look dignified and prosperous, as befits the entire lineage's prestige: to please the spirits, honor the ancestors and reflect pride into the present. For the Oba of Edo, this means an impressive display of coral beads which benefits the entire community. As, for example, when, during a yearly ceremonial, the Oba's coral bead regalia—composed of robes, crowns, a high collar, shoes, necklaces, wristlets and anklets—is rinsed in sacrificial blood to protect the fertility of the land.[24] Benin scholar S.U. Ebeigbe explains:

> *"Red coral beads are extensively used for these items.... The bright red coral (Ivie ebo) is considered to have an inherent spiritual essence.... This indeed... accounts for the reverence accorded these items and the special way they are handled and treated. The beaded regalia of the Oba is credited with metaphysical powers; hence the beads of the Oba are periodically strengthened and rejuvenated during the Ugie ivie ceremony... an important ritual performed exclusively for this purpose. The application of sacrificial blood and various medicinal substances spiritually charges the beads. Thus, they are imbued with magical powers, which transmute them into formidable phylacteries capable of providing physical and spiritual projection onto the Oba."[25]*

---

15 Jereb 1989:40
16 Sciama 1998:15
17 Kassam and Megersa 1989:28
18 Fisher and Beckwith 1999:volume 1:76-7
19 Zahan 1984:23
20 Roberts and Roberts 1996:92

21 Ebeigbe 2004
22 in Eicher 1998:106
23 Vogel 1981:196
24 Fisher and Beckwith 1999: vol. 1:320
25 Ebeigbe 2004

Ivory: Ivory, associated with political and social power, has a particularly complex symbolism. In most cases, ivory was owned by the rulers and high dignitaries and carved by a specialist. The massive elephant is respected for its size, strength and long life expectancy. The qualities of the material—hard, strong and enduring—parallel the animal from which it originates. Prior to the use of firearms, hunting elephants required exceptional skills and daring. In sub-Saharan Africa, elephants were traditionally hunted for subsistence purposes; their ivory tusks were not the focus. Many tribes mollified the spirit of the dead elephant with song and ritual offerings.[26]

Since early times, the elephant has been linked with "important matters," powerful persons, wisdom and majesty. The elephant—the chief or leader of all the creatures—is an apt metaphor for high stature. Both elephants and rulers are mighty; big signifies greatness and prestige. Ivory, representing the elephant, evokes these concepts. Privileged persons—diviners, leaders and elders—symbolize their powerful positions with ivory regalia.[27] The fact that ivory is more frequently used for objects of social prestige than for religious purposes is due to its cost. Nonetheless, the rulers of the ancient Benin kingdom wore miniature ivory masks on their belts, and the Yoruba use ivory in divination regalia. Splendid figurative pendants from the Pende people of Zaire and Angola also have a protective function.[28]

Metal: Metal is prominent in African myth and ritual. Evelyn Simak informs us that "In African society, the mystical and mysterious powers of transformation are associated with status and authority. Blacksmiths, with their ability to create and shape pieces of metal through the metamorphosis of heating iron ore and forging it into new shapes, became respected and feared for the powers they possessed.... Due to their importance, blacksmiths were associated with divine kingship and with spirituality.... Blacksmiths of the Dogon people of Mali were the only persons permitted to create objects for use in Dogon rituals." The forged iron and stone necklaces produced by Dogon blacksmiths are worn by the *Hogon*, their spiritual leaders. Dogon myths of creation identify the blacksmith as having been one of the first primordial beings.

For the Oromo, iron—representing strength, resistance and divine power—is thought to be of meteorite origin and "fell from heaven."[29] The first sacred Luba king, Kalala Ilunga, taught the people how to smelt iron. Subordinate lineages were subsequently sent a forge or bellows with instructions on their use, and many still claim that this event signaled the origin of their chieftaincies.[30]

The Ashanti king of Ghana is considered sacred. He is seen as Earth's representative of the sun. His soul, imbued with the sun's power, is regarded as the source of all life and blessings within the kingdom. Gold, his sacred metal, is abundant in regalia; gold dust is strewn on his royal body during important ceremonials.[31]

Gold production involved rituals. In the Bambuk and Bure regions during the opening of a new mine, red kola nuts were distributed, prayers and Koranic verses were recited, and a goat, bull or red fowl was then sacrificed. The Akan too would summoned a fetish priest before opening a mine. He also sacrificed a fowl, poured a libation on the earth, and prayed to the earth spirit and to the ancestors.[32]

Gold beads and pendants made from local gold deposits by the Akan people of Ghana were described by a French Huguenot trader in the seventeenth century as "things sacred" to the Akan.[33] A nineteenth century necklace of 108 gold beads contains a rich mixture of spiritually significant forms including seeds, kola nuts, cotton husks, corn cobs, shells, crab claws, canine teeth, weaver-bird nests, stars and cowry shells. Such an assemblage is called a ***suman*** (talisman or amulet), indicating that it once was regarded as protective.[34]

Throughout sub-Saharan Africa, iron and copper, the earliest metals traded into the region, were used for adornment. Copper was esteemed for its scarcity, malleability, and, apparently, its symbolically significant red color.[35] Brass (an alloy of copper and zinc) was coveted more than gold. A preference for brass among the peoples of Benin was reported by a German traveler in 1603-4: "They do not care for gold, nor for silver. Brass, however, they value highly, and also everything red."[36]

The linking of copper, brass and red exposes a fundamental—and seemingly ancient—color symbolism that was important not only in Benin, but in much of Africa, and is beautifully expressed within African adornment.

Color: Color, and its associations, play an equal, if not even more important role than materials within Afri-

---

26 Ross 1992: 60.
27 Drewal 1992:188, 190-1, 207
28 Burssens 2003:60
29 Kassam and Megersa 1989:26

30 Roberts and Roberts 1996:62, 64
31 Fisher and Beckwith 1999:vol. 1:318)
32 Garrard 1989:116
33 Ibid, 64
34 Ibid
35 Roberts and Roberts 1996: 51
36 Ben-Amos Girshick 2003:106

can adornment. Africans, on both religious and aesthetic grounds, usually divide their chromatic universe into three basic colors—white, red and black—into which all other colors are reduced. Each of the three colors defines the phases of life—white represents the beginning and end phase of life, red the intermediary, black the final phase—as well as the character or quality of things, persons and divinities. The Bantu BaRanga people compare a human being with a piece of pottery. Both are white, soft and fragile at the beginning of their existence; they become red and hard when fired (pottery by the real fire of the kiln, man by the metaphoric fire of his life in society); and finally black when they have acquired, respectively, the real or symbolic patina that comes from use.[37]

Although specific meanings of color vary within each group, in general, white is the color of the realm of the dead, of their bones, of the heaven from which it is believed that children come and to which the departed return. Red is the color of blood and the symbol of life. Black can mean night, and the ambiguity of relationships between the dead and the living.[38]

Each color of the white-red-black triad includes a range of hues as well as various values (shades or tints) and intensities. For example, the Bambara of Mali and the Bassari of Senegal and Guinea regard all green or blue objects as black, those that are dark yellow and orange as red, and bright yellow ones as white. The Ndembu of Zambia consider blue as if it were black; shades of yellow and orange are red.[39] For the Igbo of Nigeria, light colors stand for the beautiful and/or the good, while darker tones represent the feared and the ugly.[40]

It is significant that the majority of the beads featured in "African Beads: Jewels of a Continent" are white, red or black. White is the color that occurs most frequently in African adornment, due to its associations with the two extremes of human life (birth and death) and also with moments of intense religious emotion. It is the color of joy, celebration and the holy. White is fully-attained growth which undoubtedly explains the characteristic white ornaments—metal, beads or shells—of, for example, the Bassari elders. These are the "strong men, the preeminent adults who have passed through all the stages of initiation to become integrated into society by proving their self-mastery; those who can face their own death in war and that of others."[41]

When worn as ornament, white plays still another role: it emphasizes the black color of the body it adorns. In traditional Africa, ones own black skin becomes a "living canvas, on which the energy that typifies life may be read." White as the color identifying a human's beginning yields to red and then to black.[42]

The white-red-black triad is common in body art and jewelry. Among the Samburu warriors, red ochre from the Aedare mountains mixed with mutton fat is rubbed over the face, neck and chest skin and accented with ivory ear plugs and lower lip ornaments.[43] The Karo men who live on the Omo River in southwestern Ethiopia paint their faces and bodies in white chalk and red ochre, while their clay hair-buns are embellished with black and white ostrich feathers.[44] Ashanti priests, covered in charcoal and red clay, wear necklaces of white stone and white shell beads, carnelian beads and iron chain.[45]

In Benin belief, the lustrous red surface of copper, "offers glimpses into the dangerous world of gods and spirits, *erinmwin*," explains Margaret Blackmun. "Its shining red evokes the magnificent power of Olokun, god of wealth and of the sea, with whom the Oba is closely associated. Like red coral beads (*ivie*), scarlet cloth (*ododo*) and the kingly leopard (*ekpe*), copper is "hot" with creative energy and the threat of death. Through mysterious fiery processes, copper must be wrested from stone and shaped or cast into objects that endure for generations."[46] Copper also has a magical transformative quality: it turns green in humid air, or becomes black if heated red hot in the presence of oxygen. The Bambara and Dogon people thus associate copper with the Water Spirit. They believe that copper is the excrement of this spirit, which accounts for its high religious and aesthetic value.[47]

Luminescence: Africans recognize the importance of another property of color: luminescence or brilliance, which ties into their acceptance of glass beads, as glass itself unites hardness, color and brilliance. For many Africans, the nature of the luminous sources in their world corresponds to the white, red and black chromatic triad, which neatly translates into beads of glass. The stars (sun and moon) are the source of white, fire of red, and night of black.[48] According to a Coniagui legend, glass beads came from heaven,

---

37 Zahan 1984:21
38 ibid
39 ibid:20
40 Burssens 2003:29
41 Gessain 1984:52

42 Zahan 1984:21
43 Kasfir 1992:321
44 Fisher and Beckwith 1999: vol 2:37, 43-44
45 Ibid: 166-167
46 Blackmun 1992:164
47 Zahan 1984:23
48 Zahan 1984:22

while relatives of the Coniagui, the Bassari, believe that white rings of shell or glass are stars fallen from the sky.[49]

In Mauritania, "glass beads, as do all things that shine—glass, metal, as well as shells, carnelian, coral, amber and mirrors—have the power to ward off the evil eye," wrote Jacques-Meunie.[50] Furthermore, "the secret of their fabrication was handed down from the prophet Souleiman, which adds to this noble bead a benefic origin," noted Jean Gabus.[51]

Throughout the Muslim world, glass is thought to reflect envy, a component of belief in the Evil Eye. Eye motifs—an important design on Mauritanian glass beads—are used to thwart evil spirits. The triangular bead shape represents a stylized eye. Colors are often combined with shapes in order to express complex beliefs. Evelyn Simak relates that when designing a bead, it was the Mauritanian bead maker's intention to express her beliefs to the best of her knowledge and craftsmanship. "Every line, dot, circle and triangle mirrored the bead maker's personal interpretation of the universe. Magic, as well as happiness and other emotions, were incorporated and infused in the process of making a bead, always accompanied by a ritual of prayer and incantation. Mauritanian women strongly believed in this magic which offered them powerful protection from the "evil eye," illness and other mishaps. They also considered their beads to be objects that transmitted emotions such as joy and tenderness."[52]

Yoruba beadwork (though outside the scope of this book, as the glass beads are imported from Europe) should nonetheless be mentioned. The Yoruba have created a glass bead art form of remarkable conceptual depth based on the white, red and black chromatic grouping. Even their stringing of beads has symbolic content. Henry John Drewal tells us that for the Yoruba, "beads stand for unity, togetherness and solidarity…. Encircling parts of the body (i.e. head, neck, arms, wrists, legs, ankles, toes) with beads literally and symbolically 'tie up,' seal in, protect and enclose unseen forces that make up the inner, spiritual essence of persons and things. In a sense, the body is 'threaded' with pierced forms—bracelets, necklaces, etc.—that proclaim the powers of transcendence and the interconnectedness of spiritual and worldly realms."[53]

The Continuum: Africa's cultural continuum rests upon a dual foundation of aesthetics and spirituality. Spirituality is, however, ultimately responsible for the intrinsic quality of creative activity. Today's Africans remain deeply spiritual, and artistic expression continues to be woven into the fabric of daily life. The pragmatic connects to the sacred and the artifact to the belief system. African-made beads, such as coral, ivory and particularly shell beads, continue to communicate important cultural values. African adornment enhances the wearer, says Anthony Appiah, by being "sometimes moral (fitting), sometimes technical (well made), and sometimes aesthetic (beautiful)."

A question remains: what draws those of us outside of the culture to African-made beads? There is always the humanity of their origin. Who can own or wear these beads without recalling the people who made them? Nevertheless, the universal appeal of materials and colors encompassed within the patina of ivory, the radiance of coral and the warmth of shell is certainly another very basic reason. For, as Anthony Appiah so perceptively remarks, to appreciate art "we must always remember that it is the pleasing of the mind through the pleasing of the eye that is at issue."[54]

---

49 Gessain 1984:52
50 Jacques-Meunie 1989:34
51 Gabus 1958:47 in Simak 2006
52 Simak 2006:52-53
53 Drewal 1998:18
54 Appiah 1984:19

Bones, Teeth, Claws and Shells

Ostrich Eggshell Beads

Adornment of the human body predates all written history, and exact dates pertaining to the ages of beads are difficult to establish. Some of the oldest beads on record, dating to approximately 37,000 years ago, were excavated by Stanley Ambrose of the University of Illinois, in the Enkapune Ya Muto rock shelter in the Rift Valley of Kenya. These beads were made from fragments of the shells of ostrich eggs. Nearly six hundred shell fragments and thirteen undamaged whole beads were found. Their shapes revealed that the disks were formed individually, as the bead maker

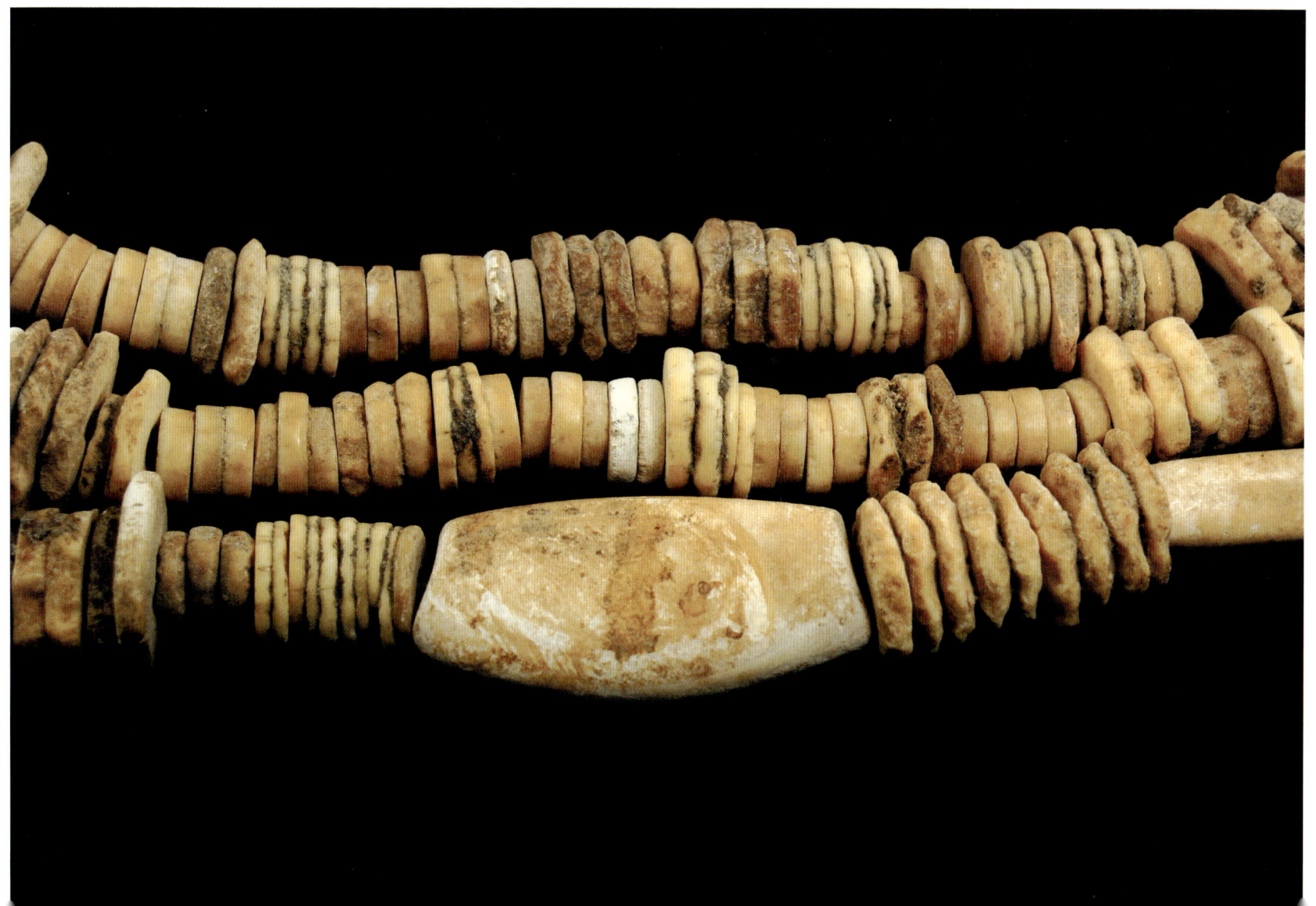

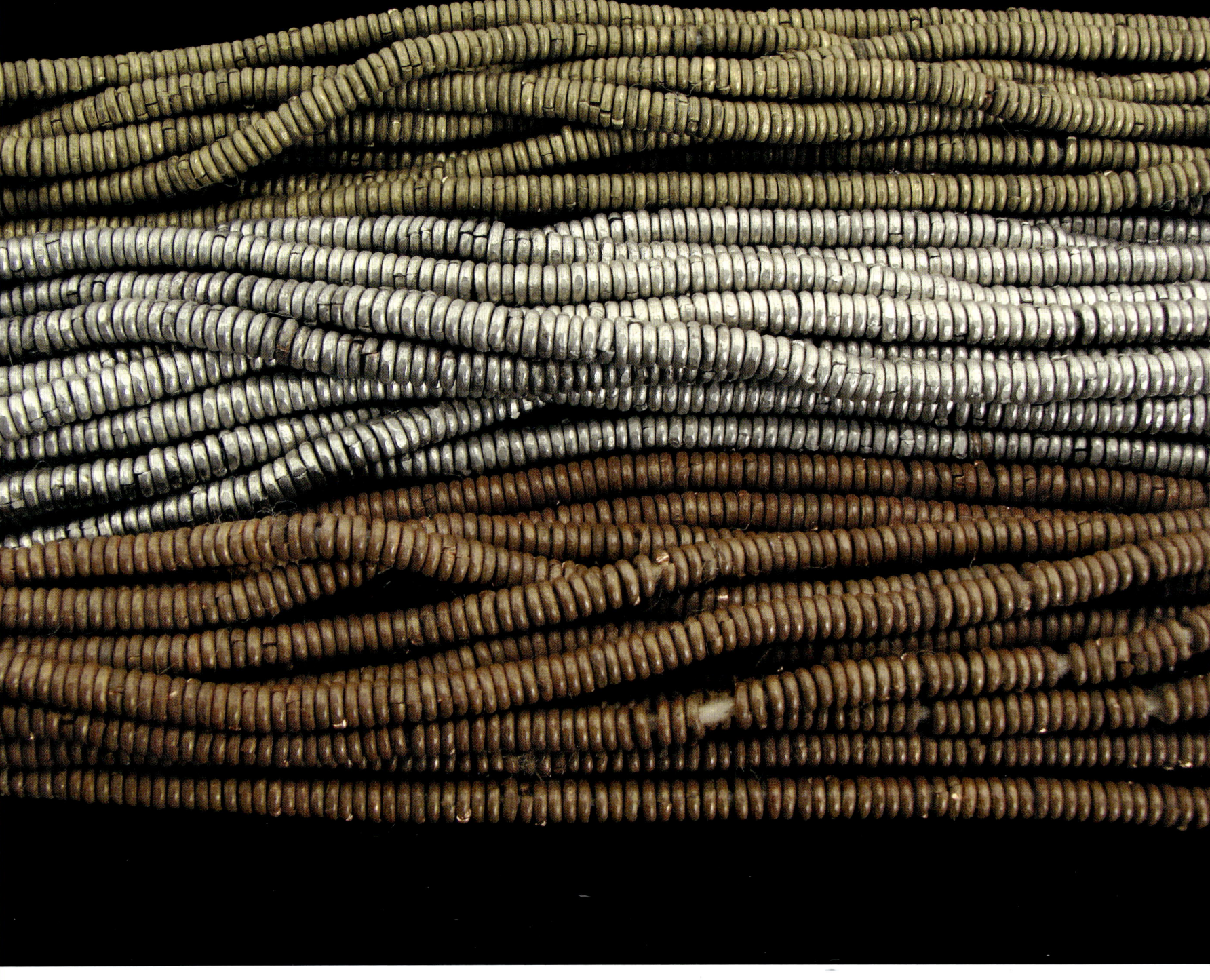

PREVIOUS PAGE *The first beads known to have been used in rituals and for adornment were fashioned from materials that could be found in early man's natural environment, such as marine or land shells, stones, animal bones and teeth, wood and seeds, and, where available, shell fragments of ostrich eggs.*

ABOVE *Thin, disk-shaped metal beads, similar in appearance to heishi but made instead from brass, aluminum, copper or other metals, are often described as heishi although their method of manufacture is entirely different.*

Bones, Teeth, Claws and Shells

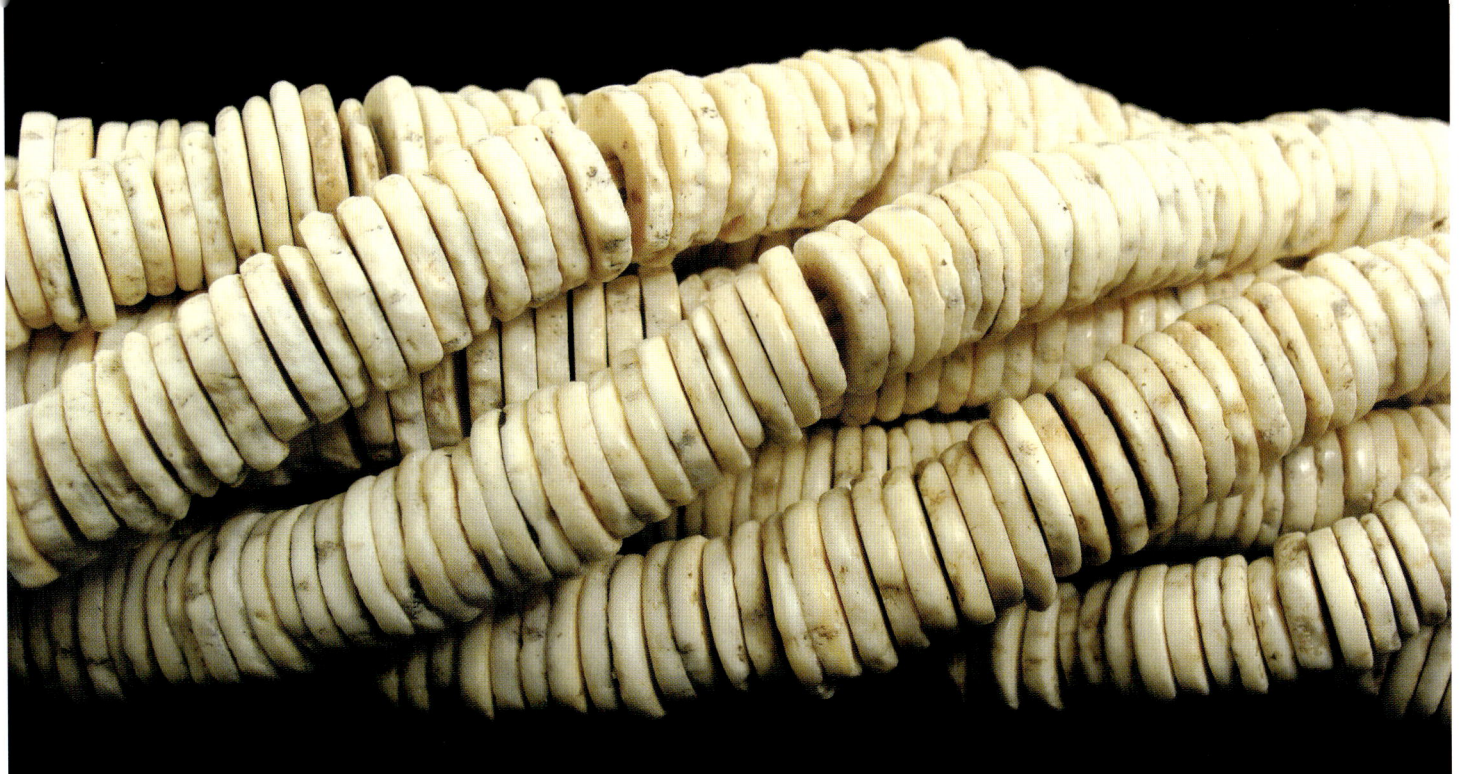

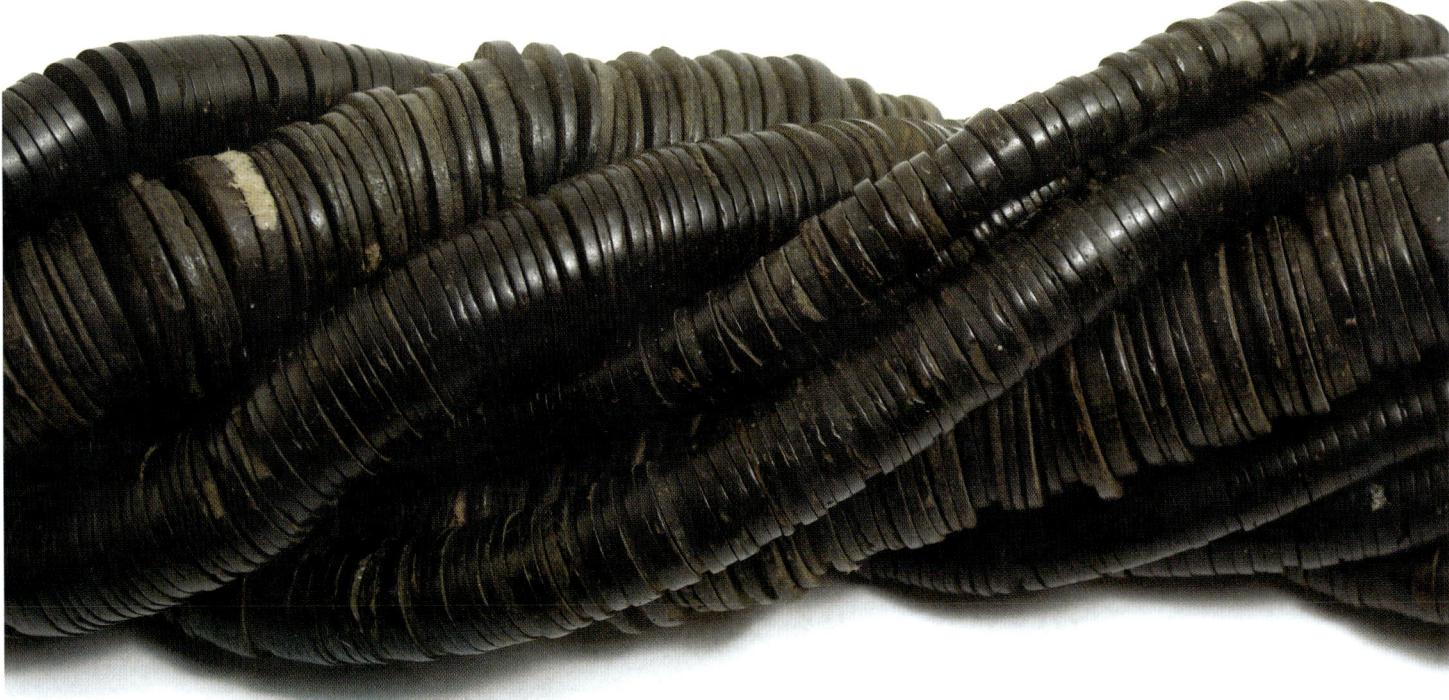

TOP It is likely that the oldest beads on record were made from the shells of ostrich eggs. The eggshell fragments were painstakingly shaped into individual disks by carefully evening out and breaking off any irregularities. A later technique allowed for the finishing of several beads in one step by drilling and threading the rough fragments onto a wire and using a grinding stone for smoothing and polishing uneven edges. Beads made in this manner are called heishi.

BOTTOM The term "heishi" was originally used to describe shell disks made by the Santo Domingo and San Felipe Pueblo Indians of New Mexico. Over time, the term has also been adopted to refer to beads of a similar appearance, manufactured from a variety of other materials, using the same technique or process applied in the making of shell disks. Today, heishi (pronounced hee-shee) has come to refer to hand-made, thin, disk-shaped beads made of any natural material, such as the coconut shell heishi depicted here.

Bones, Teeth, Claws and Shells

carefully broke the shell between his or her fingers, probing for already existing fracture lines. Close examination of the bead fragments showed that the entry point for the perforation in each bead was first marked on the inner side and then reamed out from the convex or outer side with a thin blade or a pointed tool. The reaming of perforations was accomplished by rotating a borer in alternating directions, resulting in oblong perforations. By gripping the perforated shell between two fingers and pressing the convex side against a stone surface, excess material was trimmed off. The shell was then ground into its final round shape on a grinding stone, usually made from sandstone. [1]

Ethnographic records show that modern hunter-gatherer groups still commonly use similar pieces of jewelry for trading and for other forms of social interaction. In Africa, ostrich eggshell heishi were commonly worn in combination with white body paint. Thin disks manufactured from broken ostrich eggshell were the most favored bead style among Bushman cultures, where they were also used as currency.

Heishi: How They Are Made

The first examples of ostrich eggshell beads were shaped individually, as has been noted. Chinese and Indian bead makers may have developed a similar process, producing a number of uniformly shaped disk beads in one step by applying the "heishi technique" some 20,000 years ago. The term "heishi" derives from the Santo Domingo and San Felipe Pueblo Indians of New Mexico and means "shell bead." In order to manufacture heishi, fragmented pieces of shell or other natural materials with irregular shapes are drilled at their centers and threaded onto a length of wire. The threaded raw fragments are then shaped into round disks by repeatedly moving short segments of the described assemblage against a grinding stone, until all fragments on the strand are round and uniform in shape and size, and their outer surfaces are polished and smooth. [2]

Shells

Clam

The oldest existing examples of art from Africa are beads fashioned from the shells of mollusks and snails. Sediments adhering to one of two pierced, pea-size Nassarius shells excavated during the 1930s in Skhul Cave on the slopes of Mount Carmel, Israel (and now in storage in the London Natural History Museum), have been dated to 100,000 years ago using chemical and element analyses. Flint tools (possibly used for perforating shells) found in the same layers as another perforated Nassarius shell bead suggest that this bead specimen might be up to 90,000 years old. These findings come from the Qued Djebbana site in Algeria, which was excavated during the 1940s and whose treasures have recently been rediscovered at the Musée de l'Homme in Paris. Similar beads, dated to some 75,000 years ago, were discovered in 2004 in the Blombos Cave in South Africa. [3]

Clam shells are one of the natural resources used for making heishi. Clams are shelled marine or freshwater mollusks belonging to the class Bivalvia. In general, the term refers to a bivalve (a mollusk whose body is protected by two symmetrical shells) that is not an oyster, mussel, or scallop, and that has an oval shape. Alternatively, it can refer to a freshwater mussel.

Giant African Land Snail

The shell of the giant African land snail (Achatina spec.), cut into disks with large open centers that functioned as holes for stringing, was used as currency in Benguella, Portuguese West Africa (now Angola). The disks were also worn as beads. Heishi was produced from smaller shell fragments, while whole shells were used to adorn Congo nkisi power figures, which were believed to offer protection from harmful forces. The giant African land snail is very large, with adult specimens reaching a length of twenty centimeters or more.

Cowry

Cowries are among the most important shells that were used (and still are being used) as adornments. When used to embellish a mask or a modesty apron (cache sex), the back side of the shell was removed. The Kuba of Zaire and the neighboring Lele used cowries to decorate their mask headdresses. Perhaps the most ornate use of cowry shells is in the Kuba royal regalia. The Hausa people adorn their wedding baskets with cowry shell ornaments and the Yoruba use cowries for decorating eshu staffs and other ritual objects. Cowries were applied to some Congo nkisi power figures and are also used in the divination rituals of the Dogon of Mali, the Masaai and the Senufo. [4] Cowries are rarely

RIGHT *A selection of shell and other pendants, Kuba in origin, from the collection of Dr. J. Walter Mason. The spiral-shaped pendant at the top right of the photograph would have been worn by the Kuba King or other dignitaries on the front brim of a hat or headdress. The pendant at the bottom center is etched with a decorative pattern known as lantshoong, as are the two pendants on the top left, which are known as malekma-pyeem.*

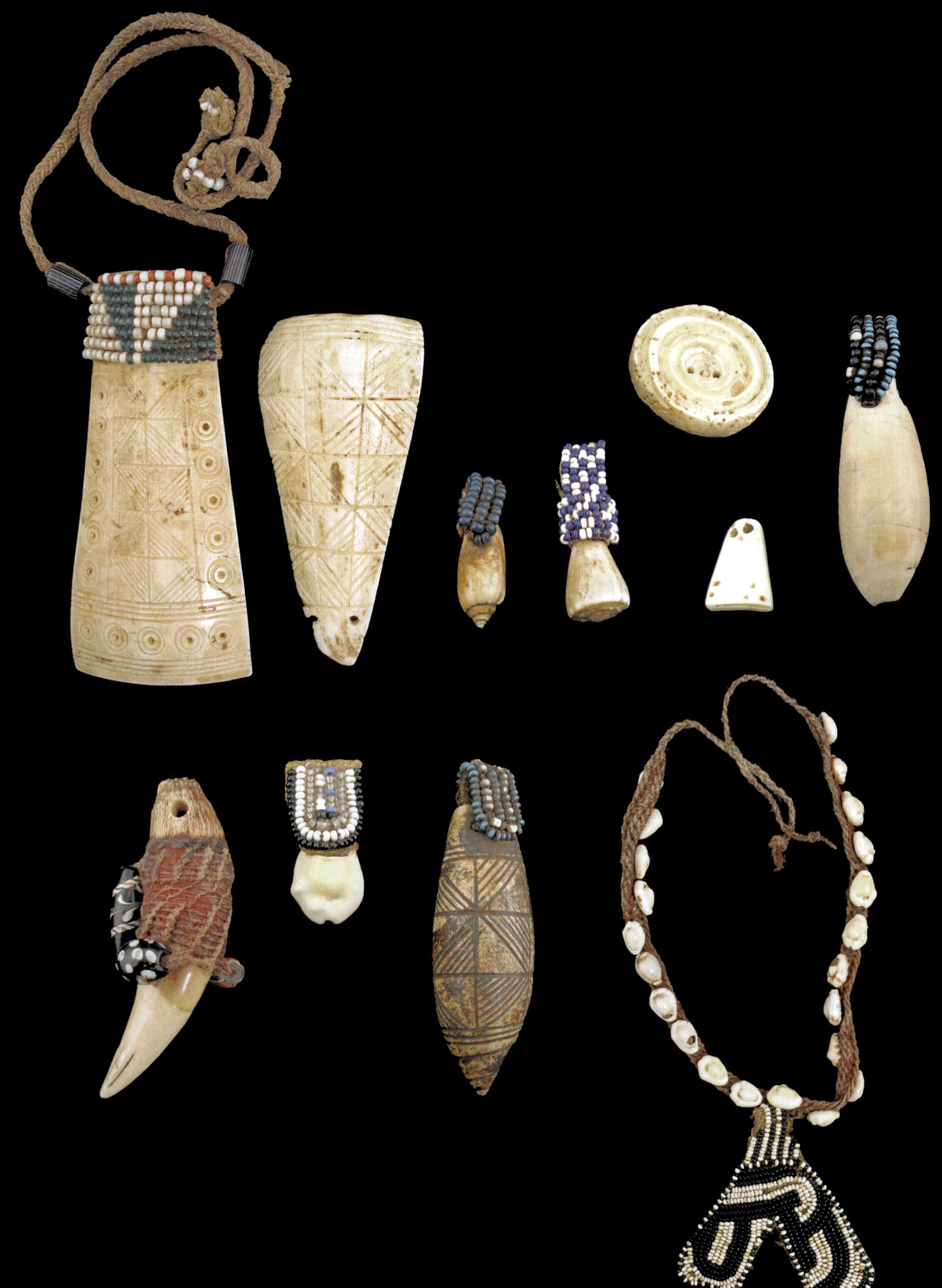

RIGHT *Igbo maskette, elaborately decorated with cowries, ostrich eggshell heishi and brass bells.*

found strung like beads, although it has been documented that Fulani men and women in Upper Volta wear necklaces comprised of cowry shells and that the Dinka also use cowries in their jewelry.

The most common cowry species is the ring cowry (C. annulus), which can be found from southeast Africa to the Cook Islands. The true money cowry (C. moneta) is found mostly around the remote Maldive Islands.

The English name "cowry" derives from the Hindu "kauri", a term widely used for seashells in general. The scientific name of the cowry is Cypraea, a word which shares its roots with the name for the Mediterranean island of Cyprus, the birthplace of Venus or Aphrodite, the Goddess of Love. Marco Polo (1254-1324), born in Venice and one of the first Europeans to travel through Asia, called them porcellana.

Cowries are considered to have powerful properties in ensuring female fertility, and they are believed to protect against the "evil eye" because of their eye shape. Real and imitation cowries were used in China as beads and as currency for thousands of years, and cowry beads made of gold were worn in ancient Egypt. It was Arab traders who brought cowries to East Africa. By the 14th century, the shells had been introduced to West Africa, via North Africa and the Sahara. Cowry shells did not arrive in great quantities, however, until the start of the Portuguese cowry trade in 1515, when ships returning to Europe from India were authorized to carry cowry shells as ballast.

Shell Currencies

The idea of money is believed to have arisen from the ritual of giving presents, a feature of many primitive societies. Accumulating objects of value was important, both as evidence of status and prestige, and also as a personal source for gift-giving. Cowry shells were deemed to be of markedly high value. They were found most abundantly in the lands bordering the Indian Ocean—the Maldive Islands,

Bones, Teeth, Claws and Shells

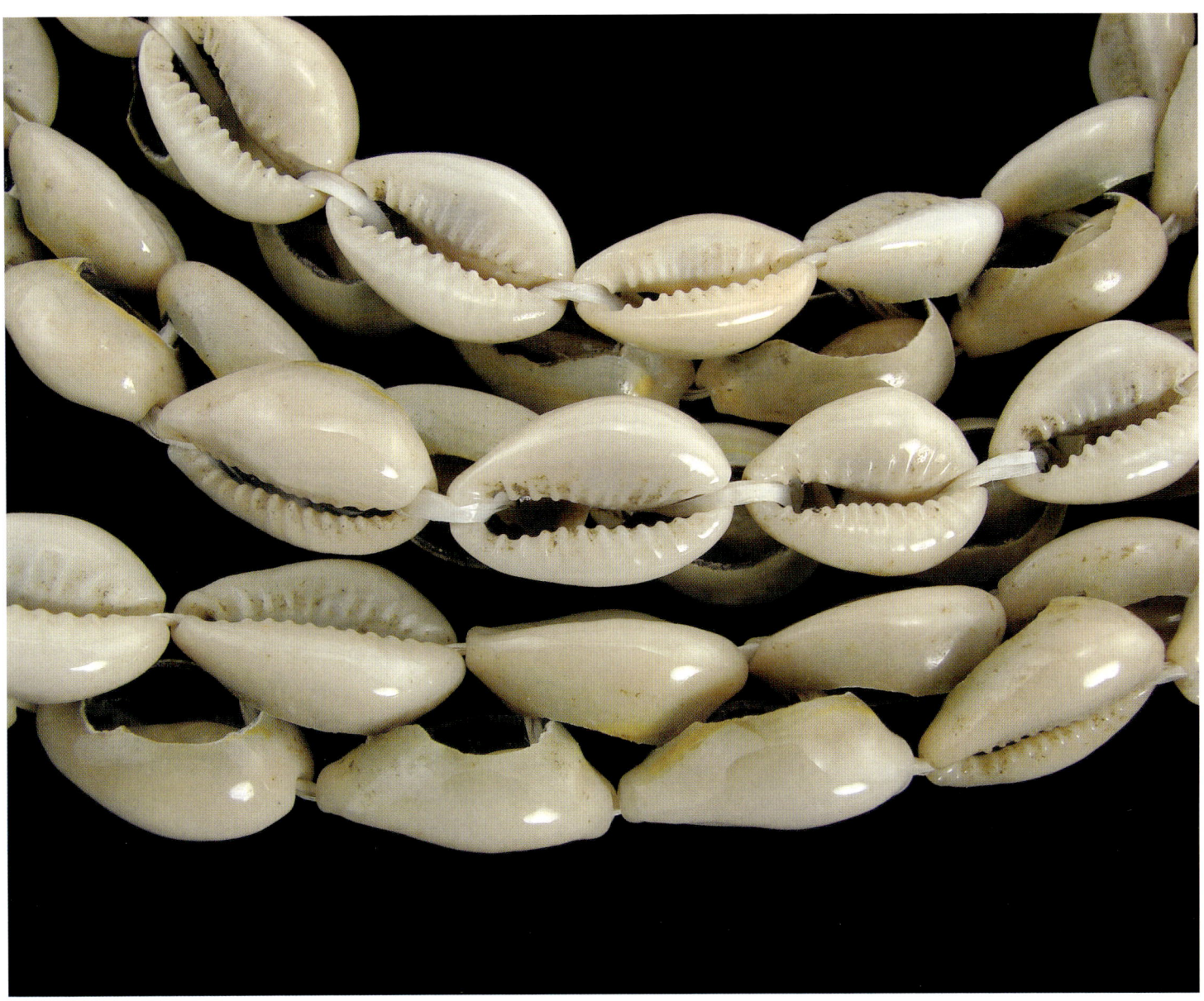

ABOVE *Cowries are perhaps the most important and most commonly used shells for ornamentation and adornment. The backs are sometimes removed for easier threading onto necklaces. For pendants, perforations are created by drilling one end. Because they were deemed to have magical properties, cowry shells were often used for decorating cache sexes, masks and fetishes.*

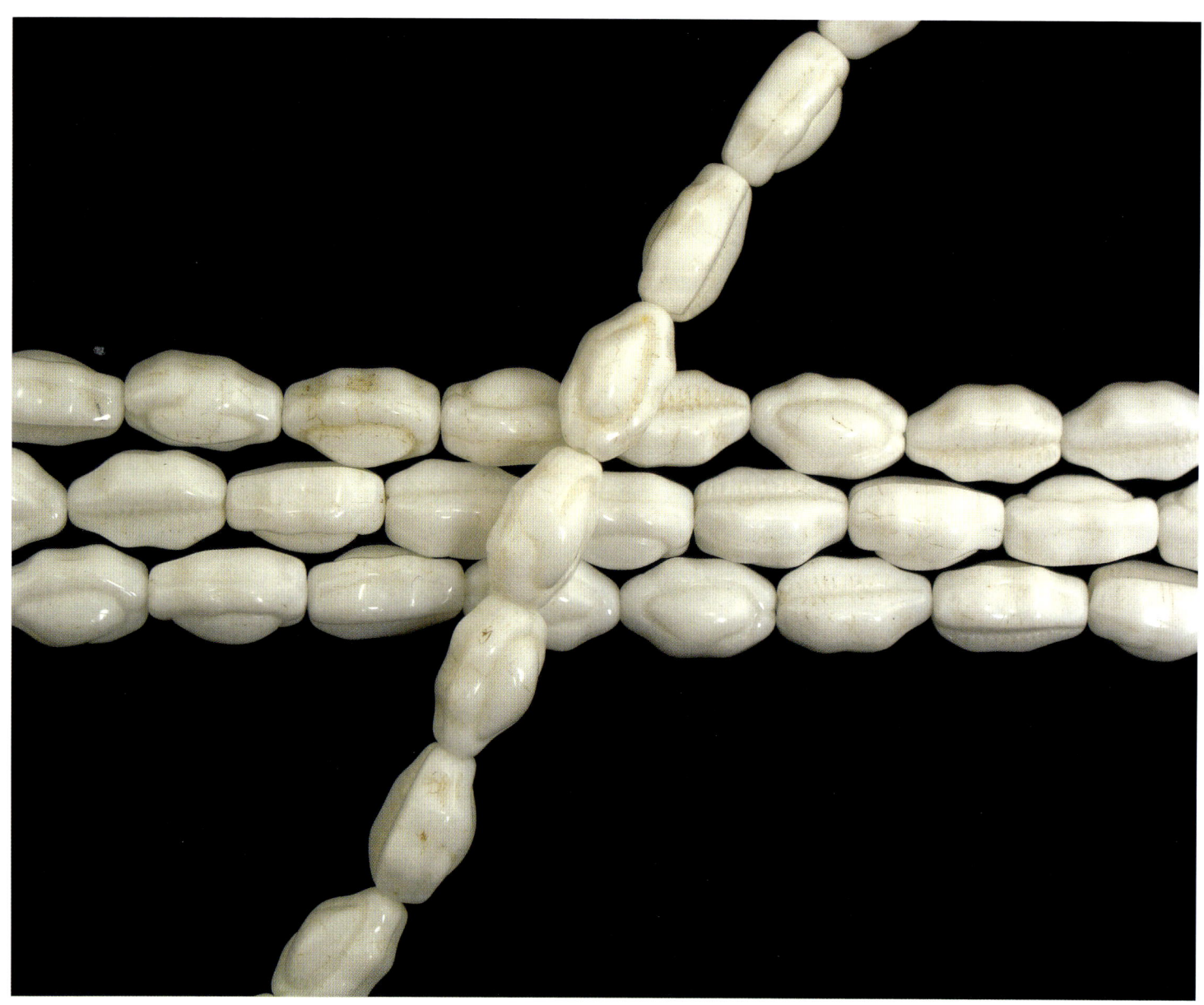

ABOVE *During the first half of the 20th century, Czechoslovakian bead makers manufactured glass imitations of cowry shells for export to West African countries.*

Bones, Teeth, Claws and Shells

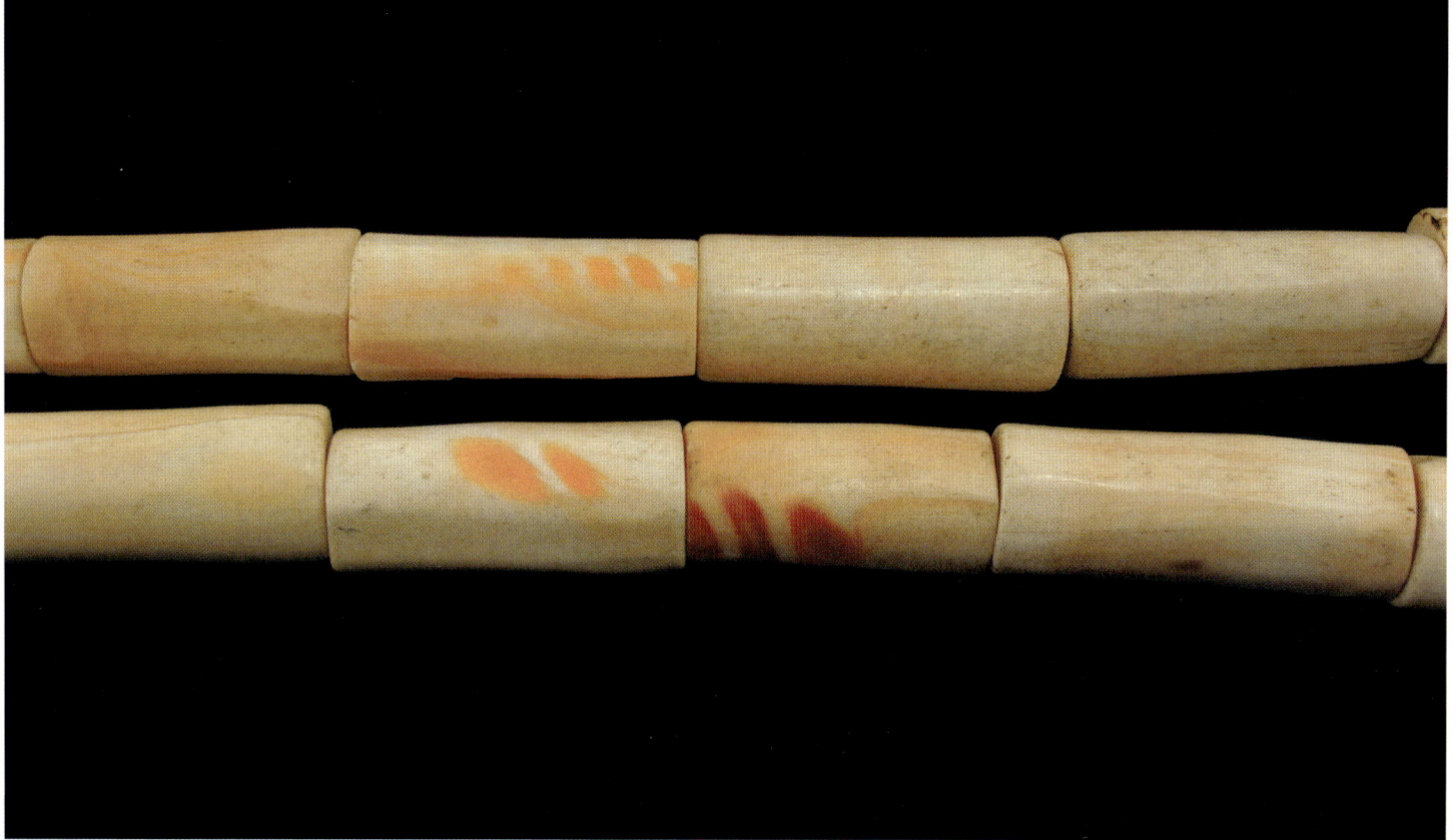

ABOVE *Commonly referred to as "white coral," the materials used for making these beads actually come from marine shells of the Conidae species.*

Sri Lanka, the Malabar Coast, Borneo and other East Indian islands—and along the African coast from Ras Hafun to Mozambique. The desirability of cowries as gift objects, such as offerings for bridal and burial ceremonies, led to large accumulations. These stores gave rise to the practice of having cowry shells serve as currency to be used in barter (the exchange of goods of equivalent value). Barter is still in widespread use around the globe for small trading purposes, and "money cowries" still function as currency in parts of Africa.

As cowries were considerably more valuable in West Africa than in the regions from which they were obtained, the cowry trade was extremely lucrative: in some cases the gains are said to have been five hundred percent. The use of cowry currency gradually spread inland in Africa; in 1850 the German archaeologist Heinrich Barth found such currency in Kano, Kuka, Gando, and even Timbuktu. In Bornu—an empire that once encompassed much of present-day Chad, parts of southern Libya, northeastern Nigeria, eastern Niger, and northern Cameroon—the King's revenue was estimated at thirty million shells. Every adult man in the kingdom was required to pay an annual head tax of one thousand shells, plus one thousand for every pack-ox, and two thousand for every slave in his possession.

The rise of the slave trade had a marked impact on the supply of cowry shells. Prior to the 16th century, most of the human beings sold into slavery were shipped from East Africa to the Arabian peninsula. But during the 16th century, Europe began to outpace the Arab world, shipping enslaved Africans to the Americas in ever larger numbers. Initially this slave traffic was carried out by the Portuguese, followed by the Dutch and British East India Companies from the early 17th century onwards. Since prevailing winds obliged the East India trading ships to sail far out into the Western Atlantic as they headed for European ports, cowries from the Indies, stored in large bags, were first shipped to European markets such as London and Amsterdam. There they were repacked in wooden barrels and purchased by slave merchants who transported them to West Africa. Cowry imports into Africa averaged 110 tons per year during the 18th century. Without doubt, it was the expansion of the slave trade that accounted for these record levels: during this period an average of 61,000 slaves were exported from Africa each year. According to Jean Barbot (1655-1712), who made two voyages on French vessels trading slaves and other commodities in Guinea, and who as a commis (agent) for the French Compagnie du Senegal was able to observe details of the coastal trading and the conveyance of the slaves, a male slave could be bought for forty thousand to fifty thousand cowries. By the 1770s, prices had increased and the price

Bones, Teeth, Claws and Shells

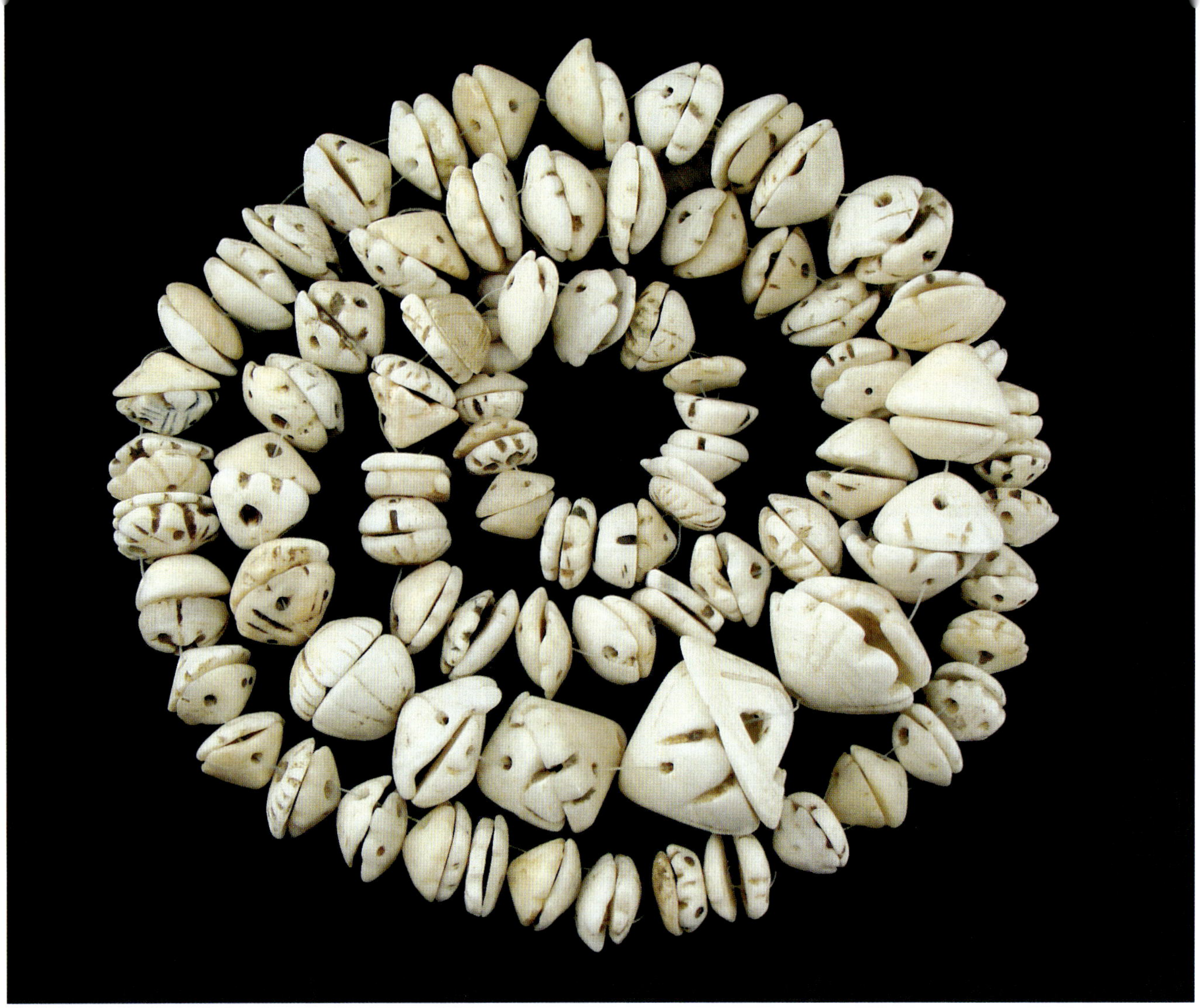

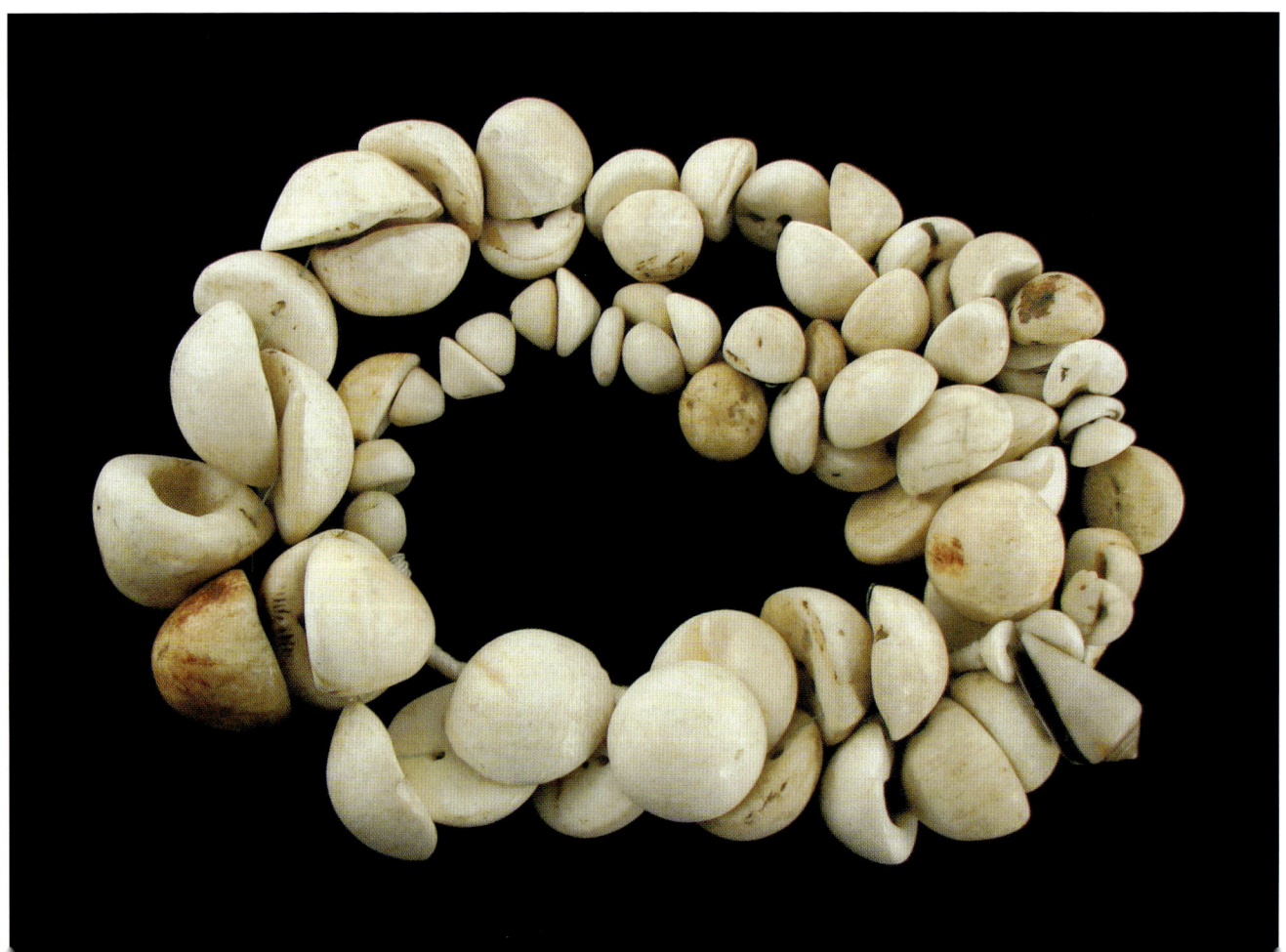

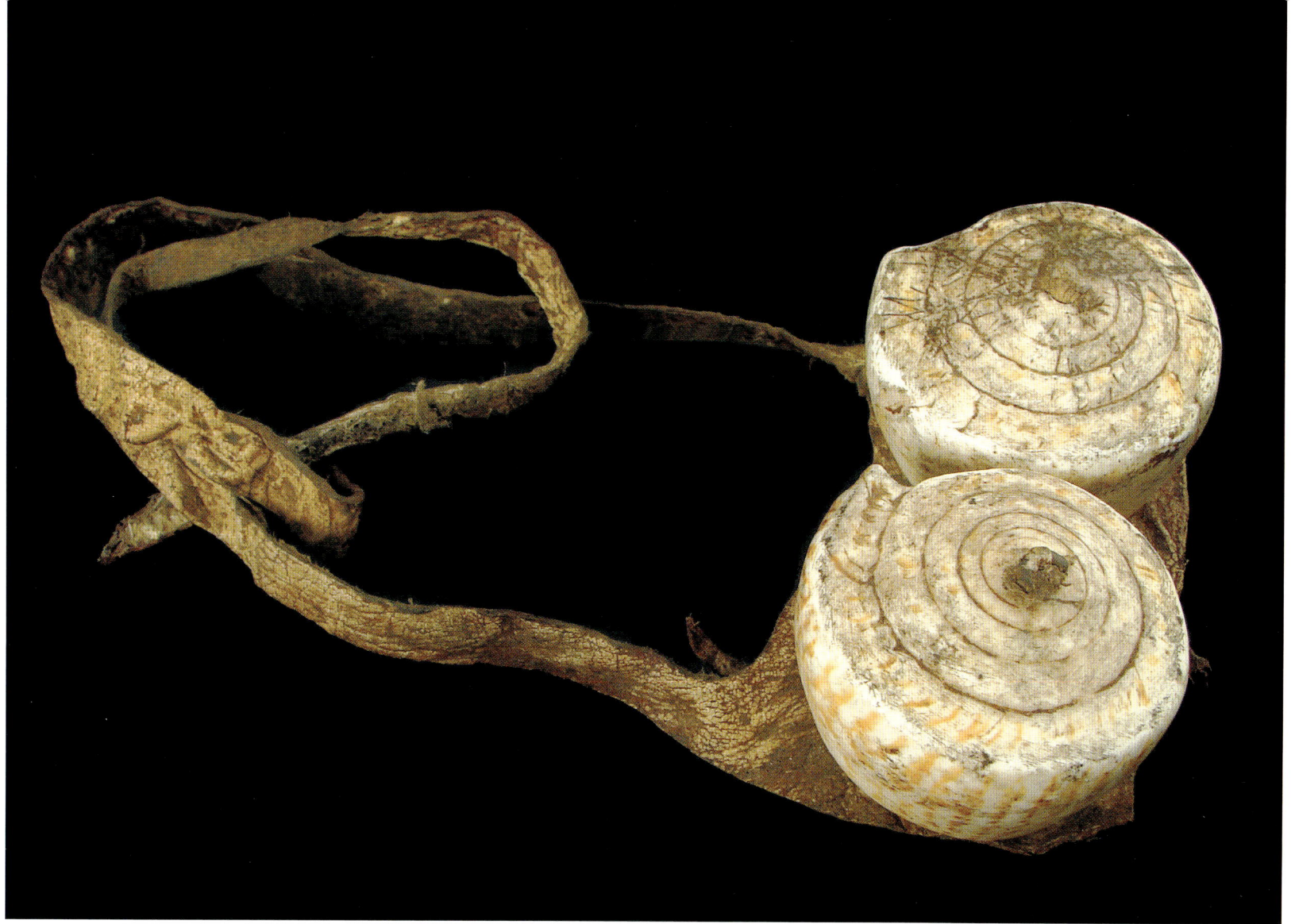

ABOVE *Two conus shell spires attached to a square piece of leather. Worn in necklaces they served both as ornamental and amuletic objects.*

LEFT TOP AND BOTTOM *Although whole conus shells can sometimes be found threaded and used as beads, the more common practice is to remove and discard the whorl or body of the shell and use only the remaining spire. This method produces fat, disk-shaped beads with one open end displaying the internal spiral. Used since antiquity, conus shell spires are worn by women in Mauritania, who plait them into their hair or wear them attached to hairpieces, often in combination with elaborately carved conus shell pieces and glass beads.*

for a male slave had risen to 160,000 to 176,000 cowries. Payments commonly consisted of a mixture of trade goods and currencies. Cowries constituted only a proportion of the total, although it has been documented by the Royal Africa Company that the shells usually made up at least one third of the purchase price along the 1,000 km stretch of coastline from the Volta River to east of the Niger delta, encompassing the notorious slaving ports of Ouidah, Lagos and Benin.

Shells which had once been used as currency in China and in India now served as currency in Benin, Yorubaland and on the Slave Coast. In the slaving kingdom of Dahomey, cowry shells were the only currency. By the mid 16th century, the Portuguese merchant ships were transporting as many as 130 million cowries to Africa per year, and they were soon joined by the Dutch, the English and the French. In 1773, one 260-ton French slave ship carried thirty-five million strung cowries to Whydah (Ouidah, the slave capital). From 1700 to 1790, the Dutch and the English together shipped more than ten billion cowries to West Africa. The

Bones, Teeth, Claws and Shells

English alone brought 5.5 billion cowries from 1800 to 1850. By the time the slave trade ended, European ships may have disgorged a total of fifty billion shells.

In the countries along the coast, it was the practice of Arab traders to pierce the cowries with a nail and fasten them together in strings of forty or one hundred, which were called bouges. Strings of forty were called toques in Portuguese, and cenre in the local language. Five of these toques were called fore. In the interior, however, the shells were laboriously counted, one by one or five by five. The Igbo appear not to have strung them but were unique in counting them in sixes. Bunches of two hundred, one thousand, two thousand and four thousand cowries became standard units of accounting. Most of the Yoruba counted cowries in multiples of twenty, rather than forty, and put them in bags of four thousand which had a convenient head load of approximately fifty pounds and were called alcoves. One alcove was equivalent to twenty galinas, which in turn had a value of fifteen bars of iron. [5]

In western Africa, cowry money was common tender until the second half of the 19th century. Until the abolition

BELOW *Necklace of Arca shells, cut into large rectangles and separated by red trade beads. Beads like these are sometimes erroneously described as "Hippo Tooth" beads.*

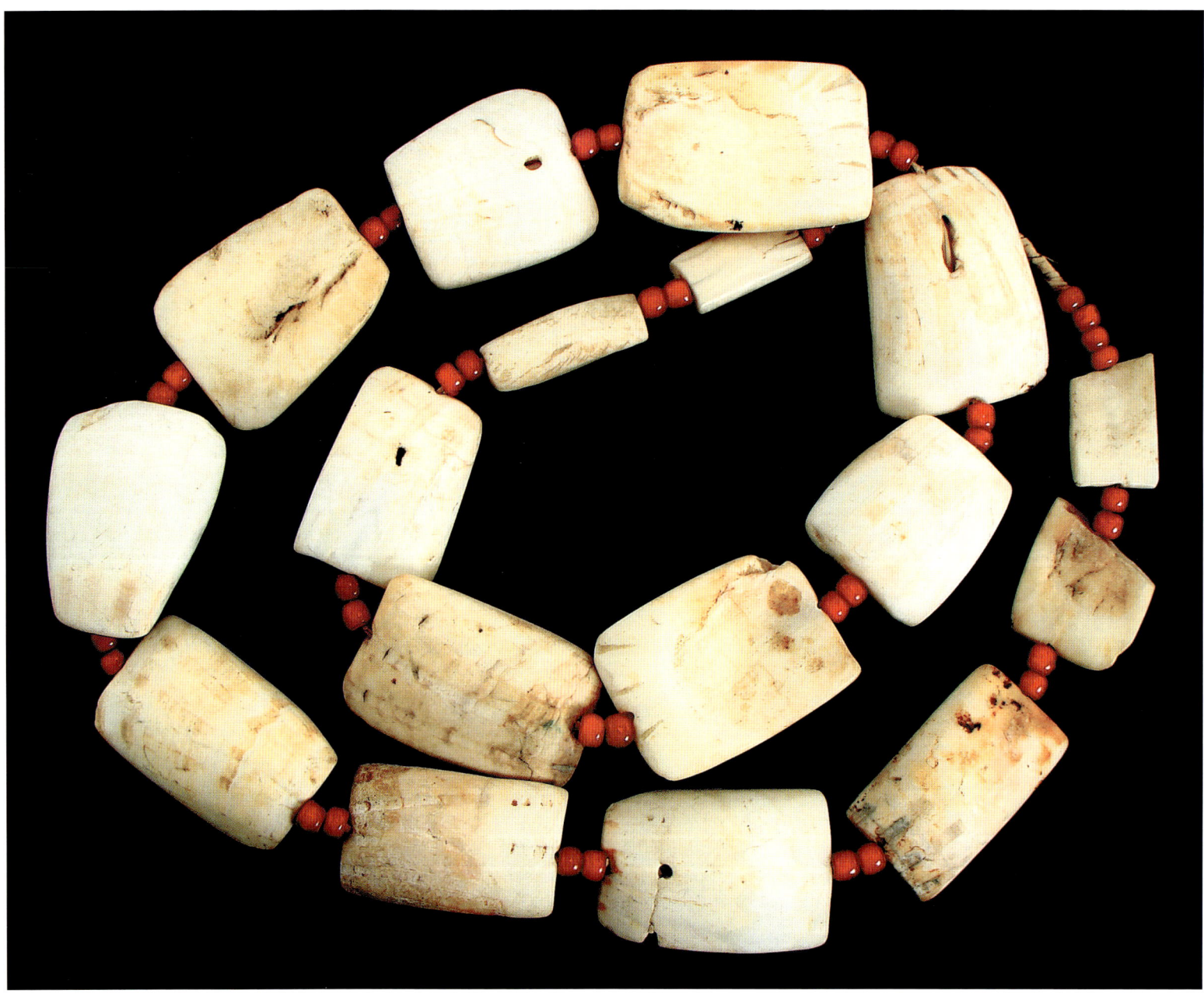

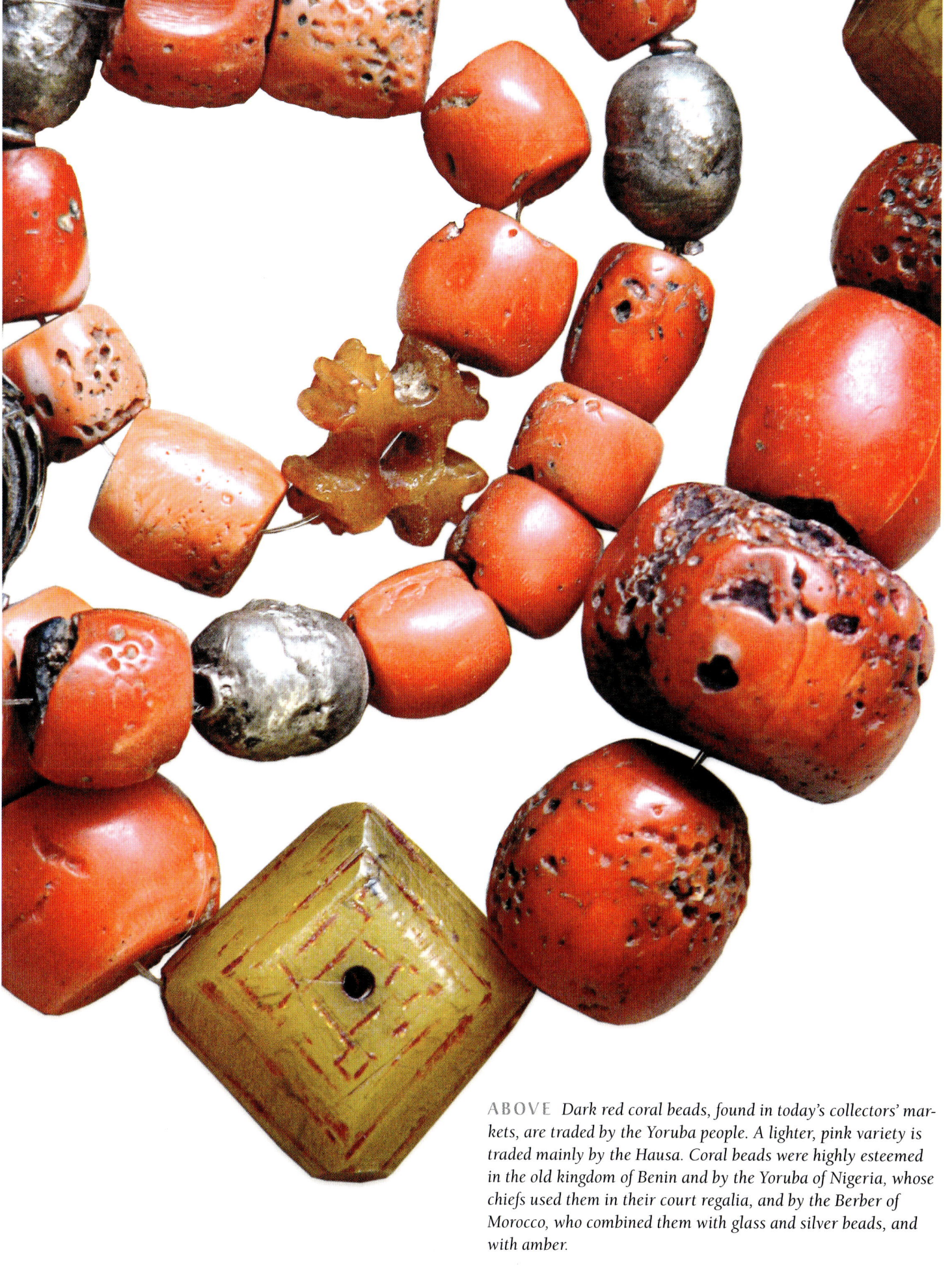

ABOVE Dark red coral beads, found in today's collectors' markets, are traded by the Yoruba people. A lighter, pink variety is traded mainly by the Hausa. Coral beads were highly esteemed in the old kingdom of Benin and by the Yoruba of Nigeria, whose chiefs used them in their court regalia, and by the Berber of Morocco, who combined them with glass and silver beads, and with amber.

Bones, Teeth, Claws and Shells

of the slave trade, large shipments of cowry shells were still being carried to English ports, intended for reshipment to the Slave Coast. In the more remote parts of Africa, cowry money was used into the early 20th century. The Bamun of Cameroon to this day use the word "mbuum," meaning "cowry," when speaking of money. Cowry shells are still official currency for bride price among the peoples of northeastern Ivory Coast, southern Burkina Faso and northwestern Ghana.

Apart from its historic use as money, the cowry shell also served as ornament. In 1853, the German explorer Heinrich Barth, only the second European traveler to return from Timbuktu alive, observed that while cowries were not used as currency in the Chari-Baguirmi region, they were still being brought in by Arab traders. Large quantities found their way to neighboring countries not yet converted to Islam, where the women used them as adornments, primarily to wear around their waists, or for decorating specific types of hats that adorned the heads of their dead. [6] Another shell documented to have been used as a local currency is the shell of the giant land-snail, Achatina monetaria. Cut into disks, it was used as currency in Benguella, Portuguese West Africa (present-day Angola). Also, disks cut of conus shell were used as currency in Malawi and Zimbabwe, especially by Arab slave traders. [7]

Conus

Conus shells (Conidae) are marine snails found in reef environments throughout the world. Their name derives from the shell's shape, which resembles two cones joined at the base. Conidae prey upon other marine organisms, immobilizing them with a unique venom. There have been 30 recorded cases, some fatal, of human poisoning from eating conus shells. Precautions must be taken when working with conus shells in order to prevent ingestion and inhalation of toxic particles. The toxins in conus shell venom possess pharmacological qualities, however, and are valuable tools in medical research.

When the British abolished slavery in the late 19th century, conus money was largely destroyed. Czech porcelain copies were commissioned in 1892 to be used in place of the conus, since the populace had rejected wood or metal tokens. Some of the first porcelain copies had serial numbers. Other, later specimens were almost twice the size of natural cowries. During the late 19th and early 20th centuries, the Czech-Bohemian bead industries also produced molded glass imitations in a variety of colors, which had no resemblance to real shells. Pre-1900 copies of conus shells, made of ivory, have been documented in Zambia. [8]

Arca

Pendants were manufactured from a variety of marine shells, including the shell of a West African species called Arca. The shell was cut into large rectangles, and a perforation was drilled near one end so that the pieces could be strung. Due to their superficial resemblance to teeth, the pendants are at times erroneously described as "Hippo Tooth" beads. Very realistic glass copies were manufactured in Czechoslovakia during the early 1900s. Large, curved, diamond-shaped shell beads found in the deserts of West Africa, mainly in Mali, are believed to have been fashioned from similar shells. [9]

Coral

Coral is a marine animal of the class Anthozoa that includes sea anemones. Red Mediterranean coral is the most valued coral; it is favored worldwide for its hardness, beauty and hue. It is harvested from the sandy bottom of Mediterranean coastal regions, including the Gulf of Naples, coastal areas of Genoa, Algiers and Tunis, and the waters of Sardinia, Corsica, Catalonia and Provence. Black coral is particularly good for carving and molding because it becomes flexible when heated. Once abundant in the Persian Gulf, it is also found in the Mediterranean.

The Romans believed coral to be a potent charm and hung it around the necks of their children to protect them from harm. Pulverized and mixed with wine it was used for medicinal purposes. During the Middle Ages, coral was used as a cure for sterility and as a charm against the "evil eye."

Benin

Coral was introduced to the west coast of Africa by Portuguese merchants plying the slave trade. Some of these specimens are believed to be 400 years old. During the early 1500s, the Portuguese traded gold, coral, glass beads and cowries for Korisa, presumed to have been Kori beads. [10] Coral beads are highly esteemed in West African societies, where they still play a significant role in court regalia. For example, the regalia worn by the Oba of Benin include a ceremonial cap, called erhu ivie, and a vest, both made entirely of coral beads and weighing about nine kilograms. The Benin name for coral is eshugu. On occasion of the annual festival called Ugie ivie (Festival of Corals), the royal coral beads are ritually cleansed and washed in blood, a ceremony that is believed to renew the beads' properties of fertility, wealth and power. [11]

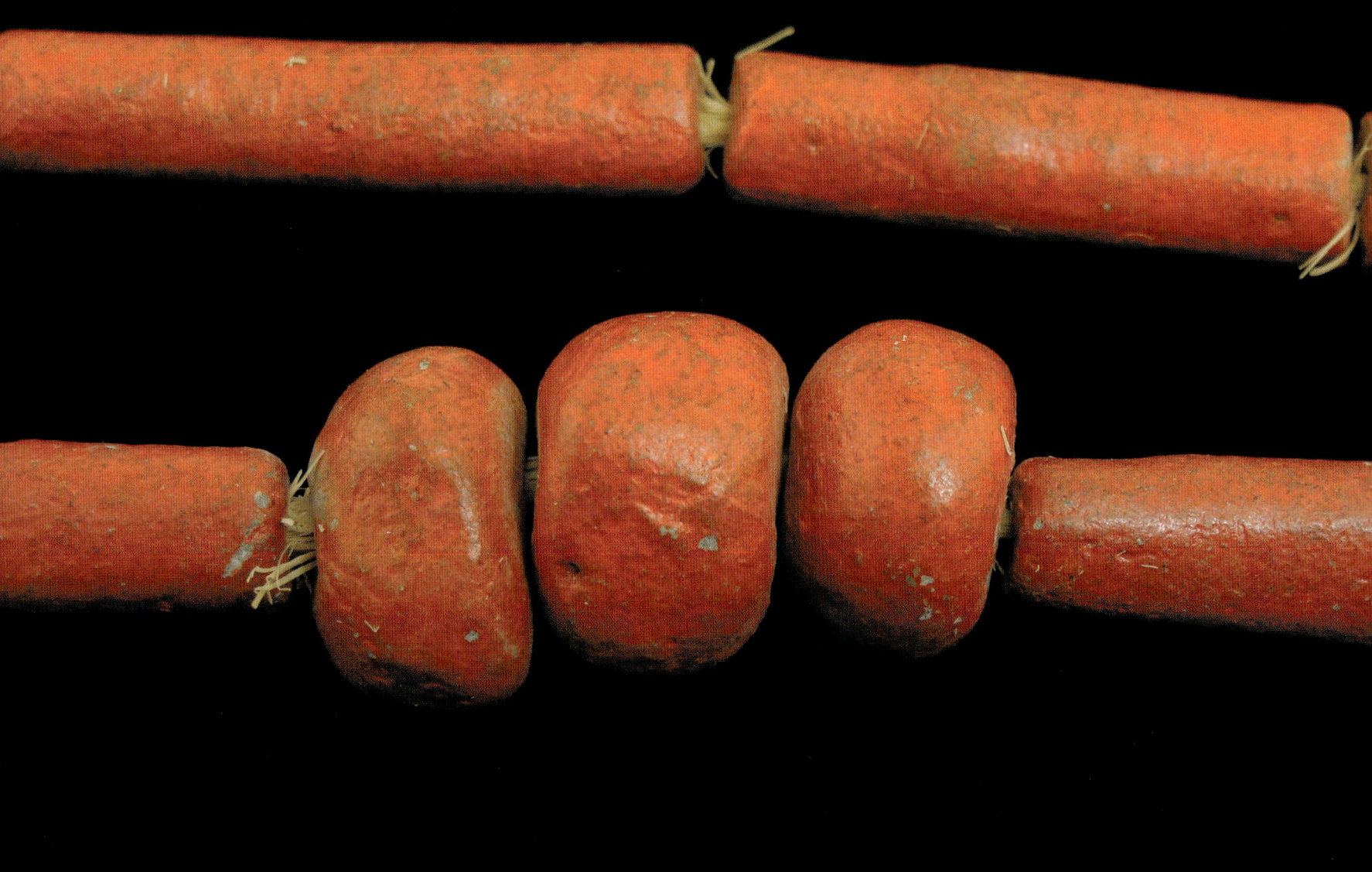

ABOVE *Coral bead imitations were made from a variety of materials, including glass, shells, plastics, vulcanized rubber and powder glass. The beads depicted here were fashioned from clay, painted a coral red hue.*

Morocco

Morocco is another region where coral beads are highly valued and often incorporated into necklaces and other items of jewelry. Branch coral, found along the Algerian coast, is believed to protect children. Every female child receives a necklace comprised of glass beads, branch coral stems, and old coins and silver amulets. Branch coral can also be found attached to doors of Berber dwellings. It is believed that coral possesses the power to ward off the "evil eye," and protect against lightning and tidal waves. Mothers wear coral to ensure a flow of milk and men wear it in the shape of horns to make them fertile. Round corals imported from Italy are believed to have fewer powers. Berber women from the Draa Valley in southern Morocco decorate their long plaited hair with rings of silver, agate and glass, and hang bunches of branch coral, shells and old silver coins from the tips. Women of the Ait Atta pastoralists, who inhabit the central High Atlas Mountains, wear adornments composed of coral, amber, copal and its imitations, wood, glass beads, and shells. These are usually worn at temple-height in two complementary sets. The women of the Ait Baha tribe also use Mediterranean coral in their necklaces. [12]

RIGHT *Crocodile teeth are believed to have special healing powers, and to protect the wearer from poisoning. The crocodile teeth depicted here were decorated with circle-dot motifs for additional protection from the "evil eye."*

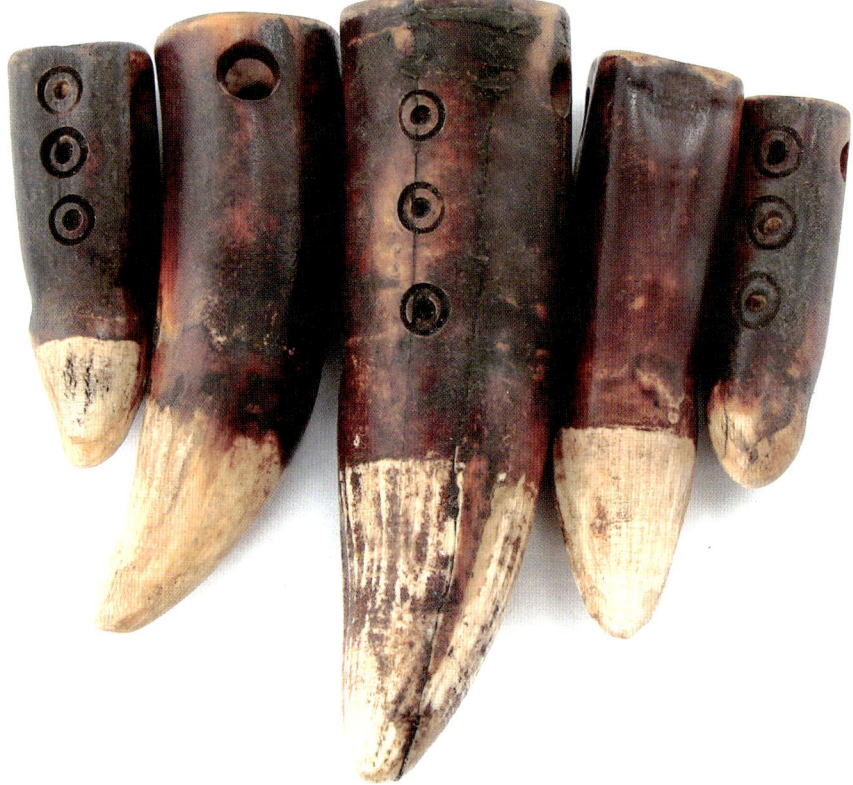

Imitations

Due to the scarcity and cost of genuine Mediterranean coral, as well as the fact that by tradition coral was reserved for royalty, African bead makers have manufactured many coral imitations, using a great variety of materials. Some were fashioned from clay or wood, painted red. There are powder glass coral imitations, as well as plastic (one of which is highly flammable). Probably the most recent imitation is that produced by a cooperative of Hausa women in Ghana from recycled plastic, derived from worn out plastic basins and other household paraphernalia. Both the Czech-Bohemian and the Venetian glass bead industries produced very realistic imitations during the early 1900s, for export to West Africa. [13]

BELOW *The teeth of predatory animals considered to be strong, powerful and cunning—such as lions, leopards or crocodiles—were worn by chiefs and diviners and held in high esteem for their amuletic properties. Their powerful magic could be further enhanced by adding meaningful symbols, as observed on this canine tooth of a lion from the Congo. Lion teeth from West African countries were so coveted that the Czech bead industry manufactured very realistic molded glass copies for export.*

Bone

Beads, Pendants and Charms

Amulets appear to have been in use in Africa from an early period. In ancient times they were made from materials found in the natural environment such as animal bone, shells and rock. One of the earliest known charms was made of bone. It was found in the Sudan and has been dated to the Neolithic period (ca. 5000-3000 BCE). There is speculation among ethnologists that this particular relic is a type of fertility charm comparable to those still used by the Fulani. Pendants attached to fetish necklaces worn by priests and shamans often contain the bones of birds, chickens and other small animals, to give protection and add to the power of the wearer.

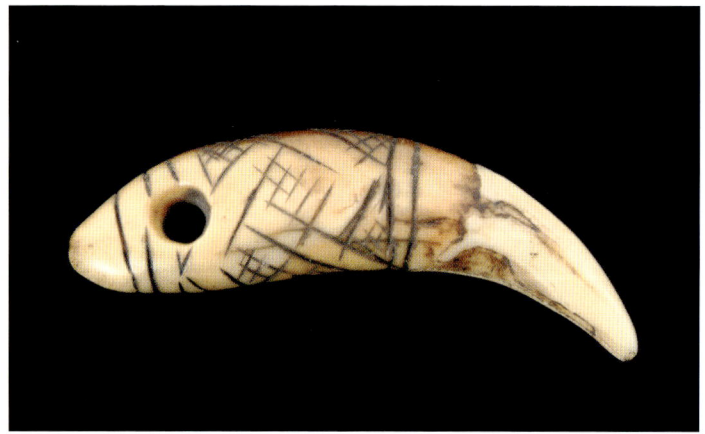

RIGHT *Cultures all over the world use amulets and talismans to symbolize power. Talismans are considered to be magnets, attracting luck, love, health, success, power and wealth. A profusion of protective objects, including mirrors and a multitude of other small fetish packets—filled with contents unknown—may be observed on this hunter's jacket from Mali. It was believed that they would transpose good luck, power and prosperity onto the wearer and protect him from evil forces.*

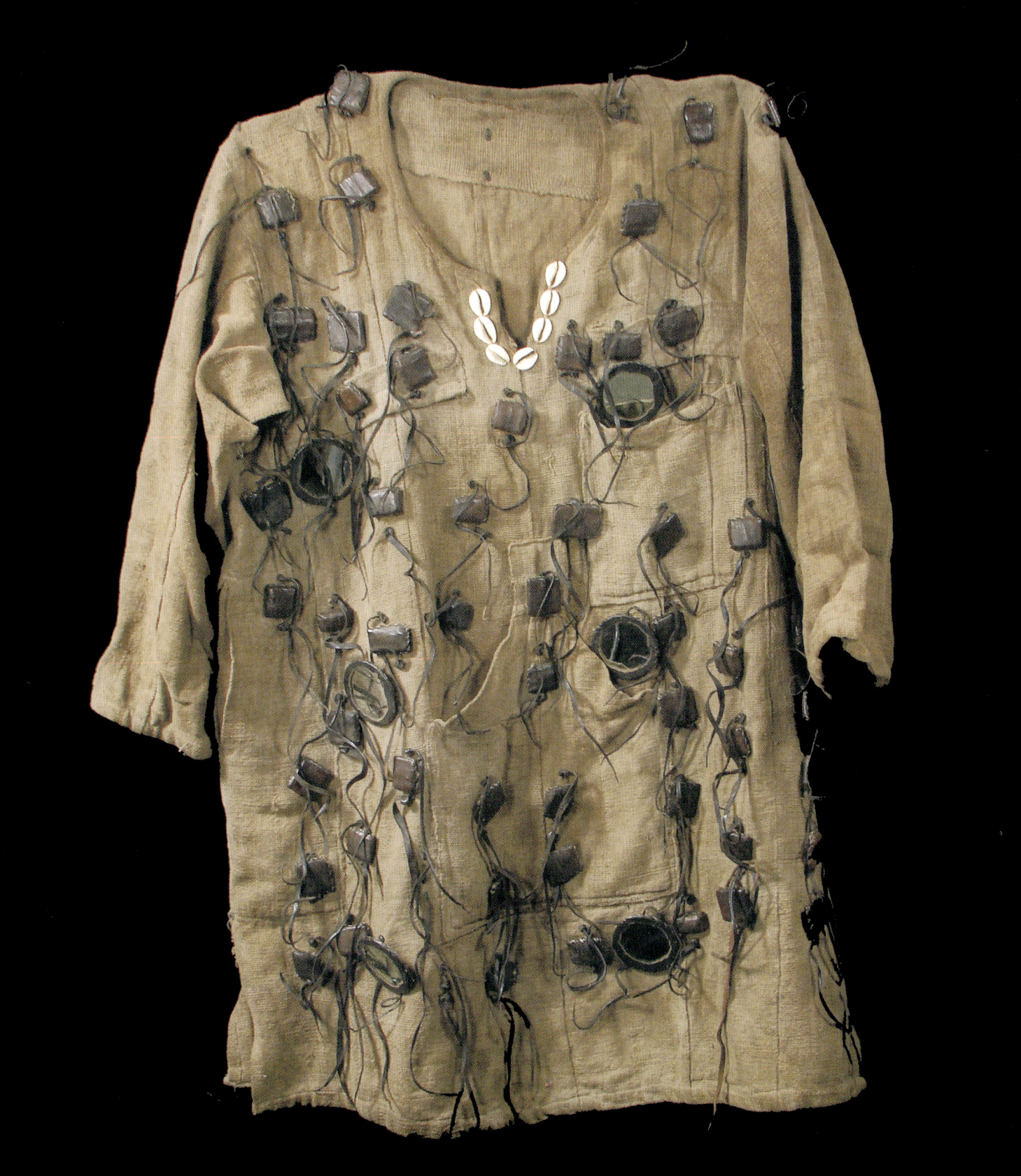

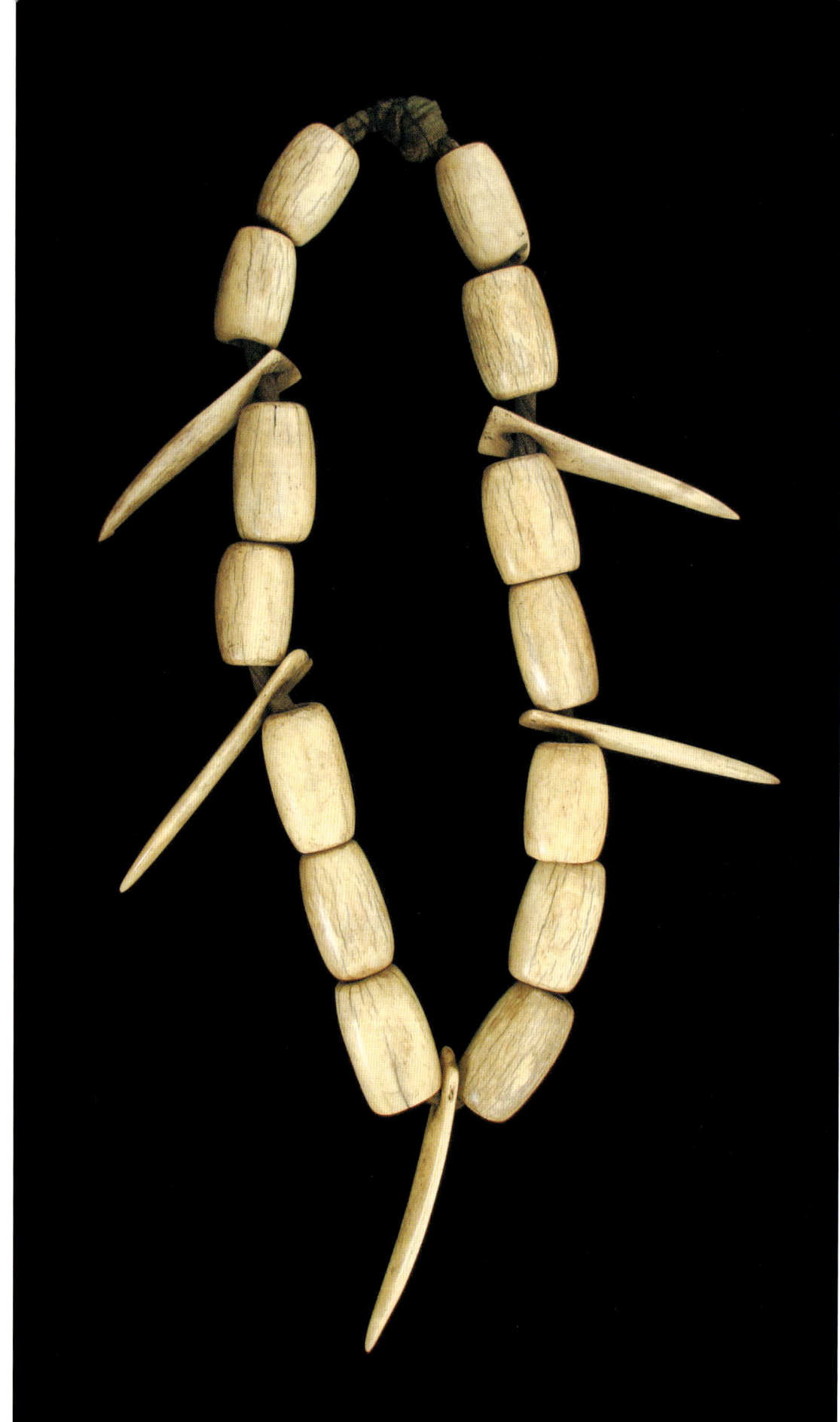

RIGHT *A necklace comprised of barrel-shaped bone beads and claw-shaped pendants, designed to symbolize status and power and to protect the wearer.*

Bones, Teeth, Claws and Shells

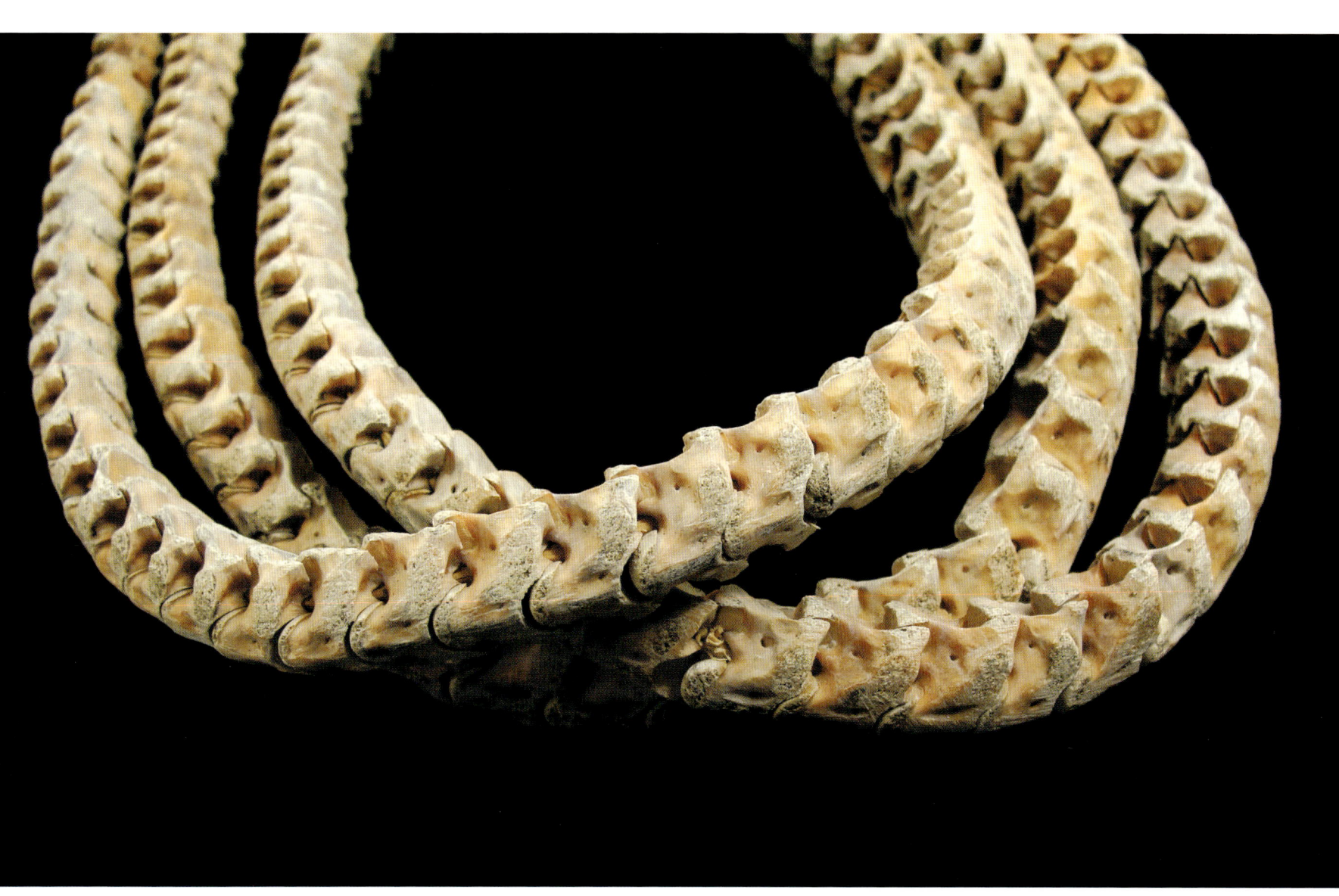

ABOVE *Whole snake vertebrae were strung on strands and worn as necklaces, as in this example.*

Bones, Teeth, Claws and Shells

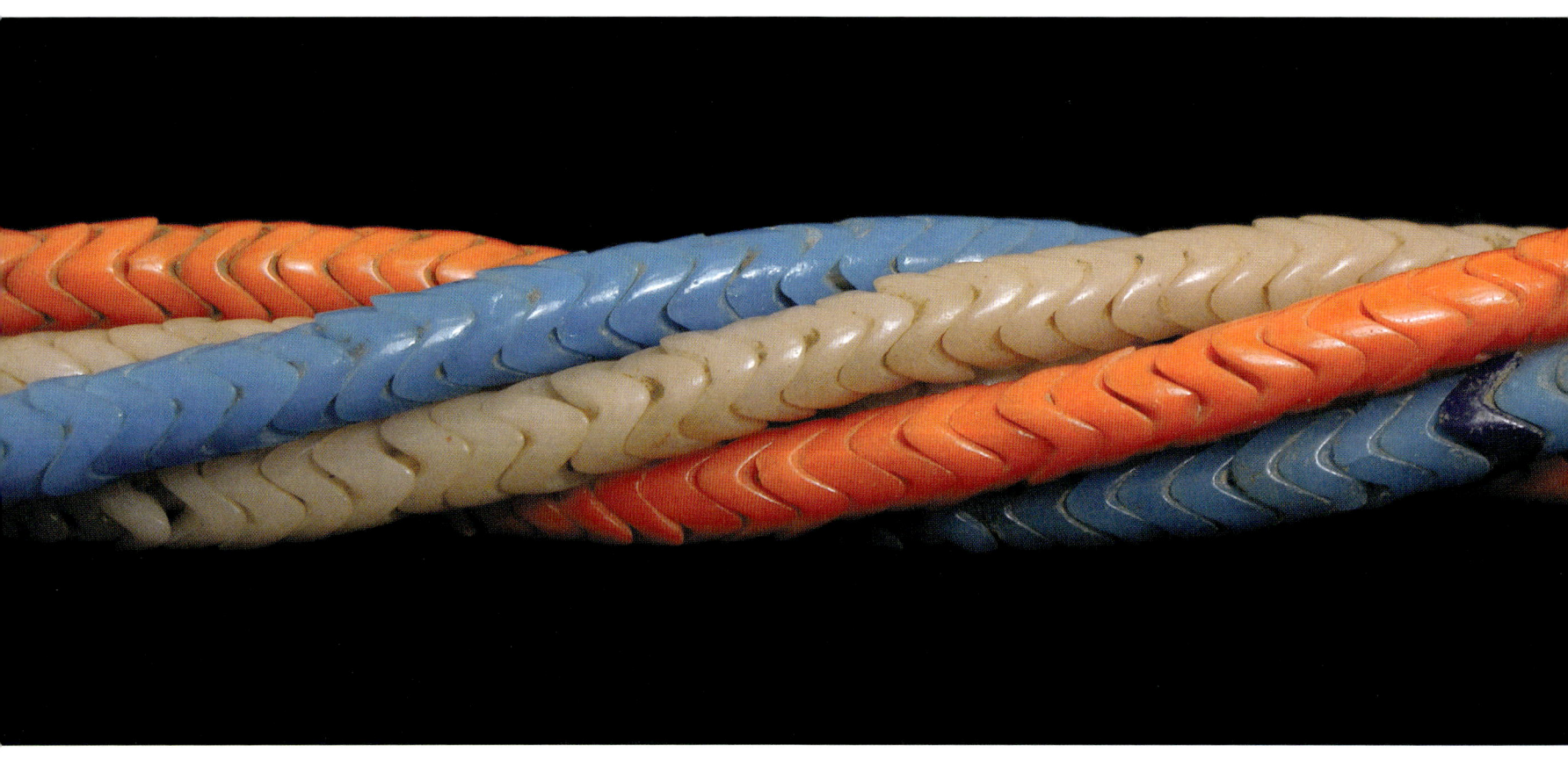

ABOVE *Molded glass snake bead necklaces like this one were not colored realistically, but they did interlock like real snake vertebrae.*

Often a talisman has protective qualities and acts both passively as an amulet, and actively as a talisman. The wearer's choice of a talisman or an amulet depends on local belief structures and superstitions. Sometimes the object is inscribed or engraved with symbols representing the forces of help or protection. Amulets are deemed to provide defense against demonic or negative forces or hostile powers of any kind. Many amulets are made specifically to combat the "evil eye" or to protect against poisonous animals. Charms to enhance the luck of the hunter were important in many African societies and were often sewn onto hats or shirts. Sometimes they would take the form of the animal that was being hunted to give protection during the hunt or to prevent the spirits of dead animals from causing harm. This practice continued in regions of South Africa and Nigeria until well into the modern era.

Many of these charms, talismans and amulets were made of bone or ivory. Bone beads were commonly fashioned from the bones of animals whose meat was used for human consumption, from shark and other fish, or from snake vertebrae (the latter being more highly prized than fish vertebrae). [14] Bone beads of more recent production are commonly manufactured from camel bone. In Morocco, beads derived from the long bones of domestic sheep and goats or from camels are often dyed yellow with locally grown saffron to make them look like amber.

Snake Vertebrae

Snake vertebrae are believed to protect the wearer from snake bites. Whole snake vertebrae can be found strung as necklaces, often ground to varying degrees of smoothness.

Elders of the Dinka from Sudan are known to wear necklaces comprised of a combination of snake vertebrae, glass beads and cowry shells, and snake vertebrae necklaces are also worn by the Luo and the Kikuyu of Kenya. Royal executioners in Ghana wear necklaces made of python vertebrae.

Imitations of snake vertebrae were manufactured by the Czech-Bohemian glass bead industries, mainly for export to West African countries. Examples of molded snake beads produced by the Bohemian Redlhamer Brothers in the early 20th century can be seen on some of their bead sample cards. The beads were made in a variety of colors, none of which resembled the color of real snake vertebrae. They did, however, interlock like real snake vertebrae, fitting together smoothly. [15]

Fish Vertebrae

Shark and other fish vertebrae were made into separate necklaces, or were added to necklaces made of beads of other materials. Certain styles of Mauritanian scented paste necklaces and waist belts also incorporated shark vertebrae for additional protection.

Antelope Bones

One unique type of bead is that made from the phalanges (toe bones) of antelopes. The Turkana and Sambara people of Kenya, who inhabit the western shores of Lake Turkana near the borders of Sudan and Ethiopia, incorporated these beads into belts. The Turkana represent the largest ethnic

BELOW *Several strands of fish vertebrae. Such vertebrae were valued for their protective properties.*

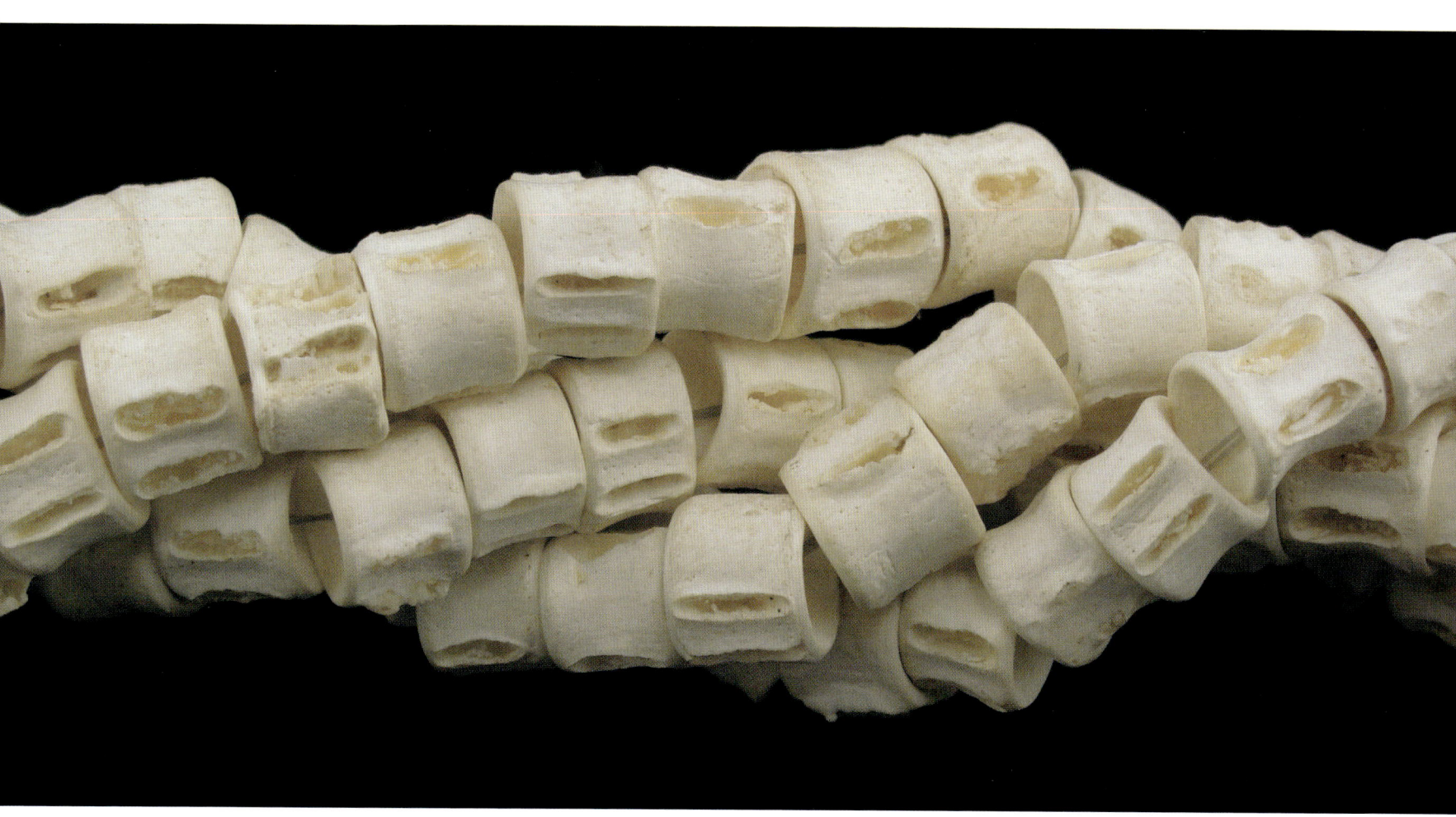

Bones, Teeth, Claws and Shells

group of the Ateger-speaking peoples and are Nilotic in origin. Turkana and Sambara women are known to wear belts comprised of antelope phalanges and other small bones, interspersed with blue and red glass beads. Necklaces, pendants and belts comprised of animal bones, and occasionally other animal body parts, may have had properties similar to the rabbit's foot, which was believed by European cultures to bring good luck, good crops, many children, prosperity, and protection from misfortune. [16] Interestingly, a necklace comprised of deer phalanges is on display in the Pearsall Collection of American Indian Art at the Florida Museum of Natural History.

Batik Bone Beads

In recent years, Kenyan craftsmen and women have produced a great variety of decorated bone beads using a technique similar to batik, in which they apply wax onto the bleached bone in the desired patterns and then dip the bone into a thick black dye made from boiled tree sap. [17] When the wax is removed the dyed patterns remain. Primarily fashioned from cattle bone, the beads often have designs that closely resemble the patterns of traditional East African textiles. The hollow centers of large bone beads are filled with carved plugs made from soft wood. A hole is drilled in the center of this wooden plug to make the bead perforation.

Teeth and Claws

As noted, the use of charms, amulets and talismans has been well documented in Africa, and the practice still plays a major role in many African societies. The difference between an amulet and a talisman is that an amulet is said to protect its wearer from bad influences while a talisman attracts good influences.

Animal teeth and claws are commonly believed to transfer to their wearer the esteemed attributes ascribed to the animal they are derived from, such as power, strength, endurance and speed. They also are believed to protect against evil powers such as the "evil eye." Teeth and claws are commonly worn as pendants, in their natural state and with their larger end encased in metal. The possession of a lion's tooth was believed to gain its wearer greater popularity, especially when the tooth was taken from the right side of the beast's mouth. It also symbolized cunning and strength. In Nigeria, iron bracelets with a leopard's tooth attached are believed to be powerful protection against all harm. The Mangbetu and the Lego people of Zaire wear necklaces comprised of leopard teeth and make ivory imitations of leopard teeth. Podokowo women of the Mora Massif of Cameroon wear leopard teeth necklaces on festive occasions. Crocodile tooth pendants or whole necklaces comprised of crocodile teeth are worn in the belief that they possess the power to heal the body and counteract poison. Alligator teeth (and alligator feet) are regularly used in African-American mojo bags to increase gambling luck. In societies such as the Mangbetu of Zaire and their neighbors, the Azande, men wore the teeth of their slain enemies around their necks. [18]

Imitations of leopard teeth made of forged iron have been documented in Liberia, Sierra Leone, Ivory Coast and Guinea. Among the cultures of this large region, the leopard is regarded as an animal of courage, great strength and cunning—traits also ascribed to chieftains and other power figures, such as priests and diviners. Necklaces comprised of forged iron leopard teeth and other animal teeth were worn as symbols of authority or as indicators of magical powers in ritual ceremonies and at other special occasions. The forged iron leopard tooth necklace was a special symbol of prestige; it marked the wearer as a person of substance and authority who could control the forces of nature and had the wherewithal to commission a blacksmith to make such a necklace.

Tooth-shaped pendants were produced in the lost wax casting technique, and imitations of animal teeth and claws can also be found in a variety of other materials such as bone and wood.

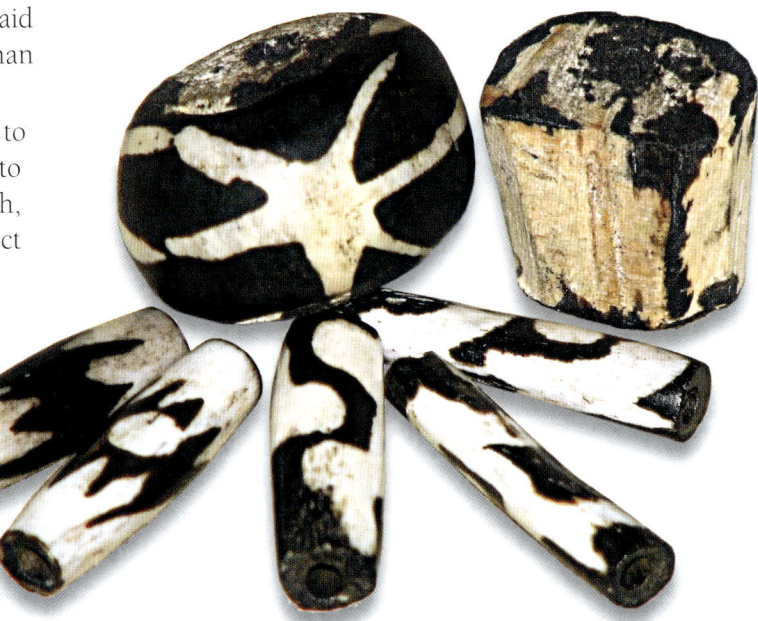

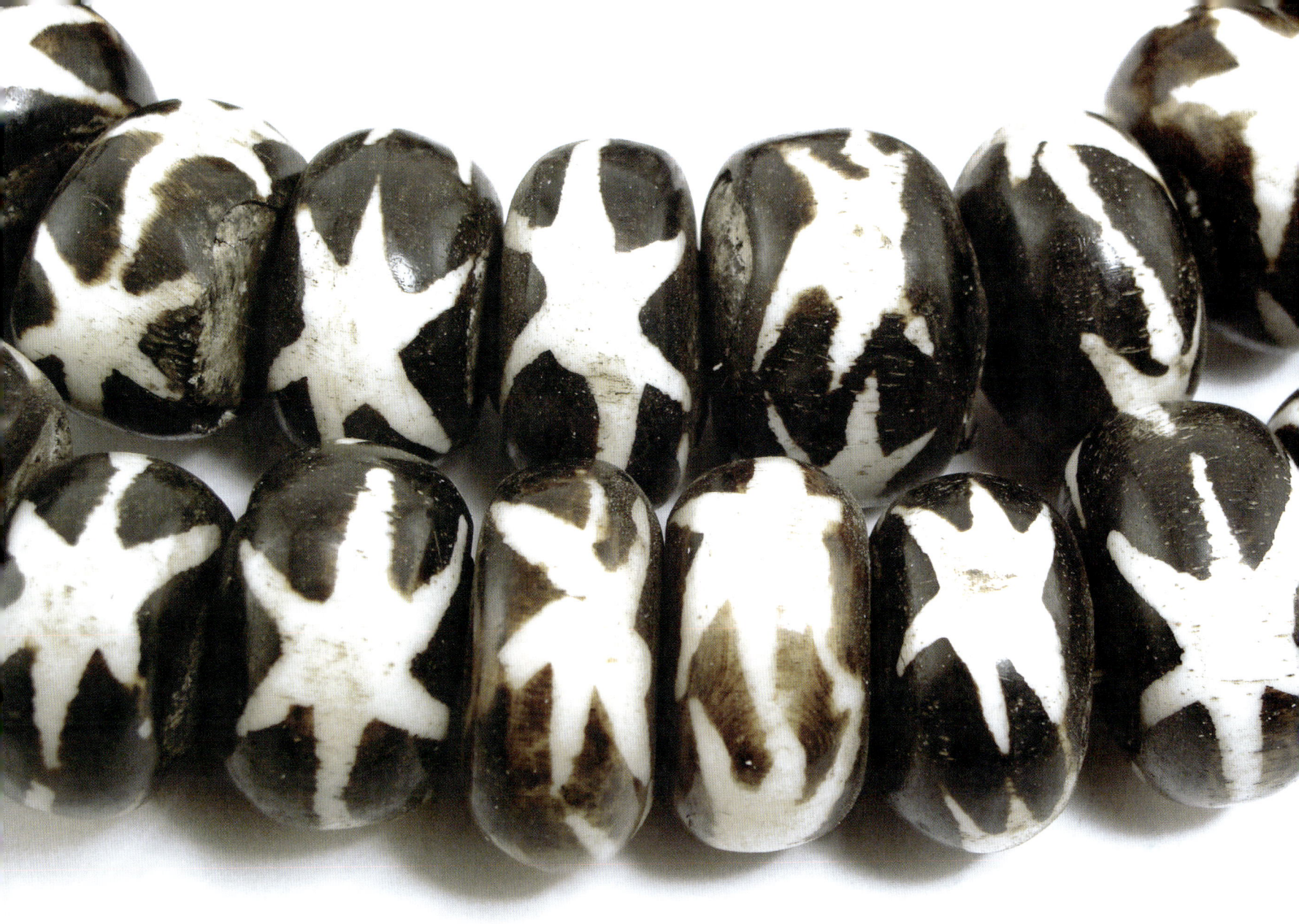

ABOVE AND LEFT *Batik bone beads from Kenya are produced in a variety of styles, shapes and sizes, with decorative designs resembling those found in traditional East African textiles. The hollow centers of the larger beads are filled with plugs of soft wood for easier threading, as depicted to the left. Next to the large oblate bead with the star pattern, which has a wooden plug as its center, a wooden plug can be seen on its own.*

Realistic glass copies of animal teeth were manufactured by the Czech-Bohemian bead industry during the early 1900s, as were stylized imitations of animal claws in several sizes and colors.

Ivory

In equatorial West Africa, ivory has long been valued for its association with status and wealth and its supposed magical powers. For the Igbo of Nigeria, status was measured by material wealth, and ornaments made of ivory conferred prestige by their weight alone. Married women wore ivory anklets and bracelets consisting of cross sections of large elephant tusks that were purified by special rituals, then cut and fitted by the smith around their arms and legs. The ivory was neither carved nor decorated and the smith's only skills involved the manipulation of these pieces onto the limbs. Despite the protracted and painful procedure, women esteemed these pieces, as they entitled them to the highest social status. [19]

Chiefs and kings patronized specially appointed ivory carvers, who designed and manufactured ornaments to be worn by court and religious officials and others of high standing. Surplus ivory could be traded for other goods. Ivory was widely available in southern Nigeria, Cameroon and Zaire, but as trade developed and hunting decimated the elephant population, substitute materials such as hippopotamus teeth and warthog tusks replaced true ivory. These were deemed less valuable because they were smaller and possessed a higher density, making them more difficult to carve.

In the kingdom of Benin, the tusks of every elephant killed were the property of the Oba, the Divine Ruler, who retained one tusk for his own use and offered the other one for sale. The Oba supported a guild of carvers who designed belts, masks, bells, amulets and a variety of other ornaments in both ivory and wood for the royal court.

Even today, among the Pende of Angola and Zaire, elders continue a custom in which they carve small ivory masks known as minyaki. Initiates wear these masks as amulets while they undergo rituals that prepare them for adulthood. The Luba of Zaire wear pendants that commemorate dead relatives on their belts or bracelets, or hidden in an armpit. Luba pendants are carved from hippopotamus or warthog tusks, simulating ivory. In Cameroon, fetish priests used to wear figural pendants of ivory depicting religious predecessors of particularly high repute. These pendants were deemed so powerful that they could answer questions and advise on important issues. [20]

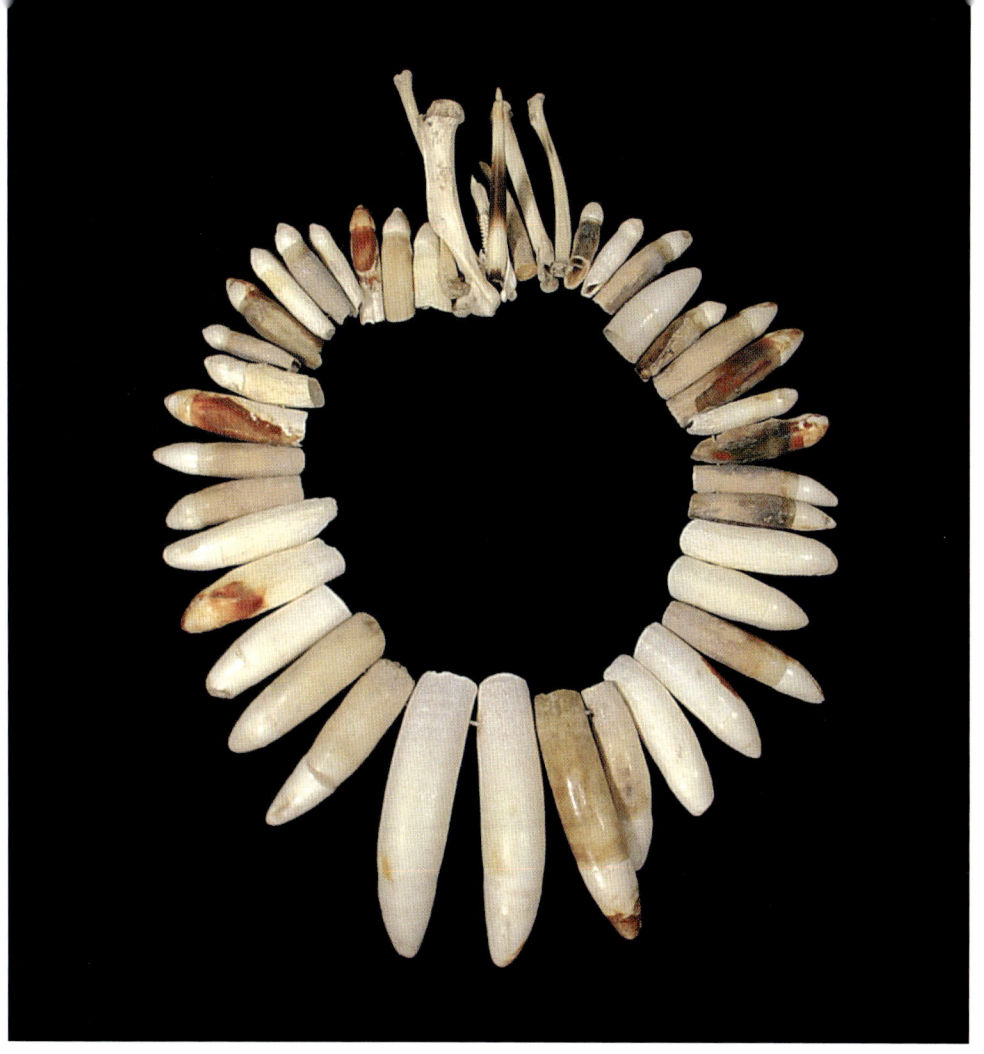

LEFT *In addition to protective properties, necklaces comprised of crocodile teeth are believed to have healing effects and to protect their wearer from bodily injuries and poisoning.*

BELOW AND NEXT PAGE *In the Congo, whole necklaces of lions teeth, or of lions teeth combined with highly valued Venetian chevron beads, were worn as symbols of authority and power, mainly by high ranking members of the community such as chiefs and diviners.*

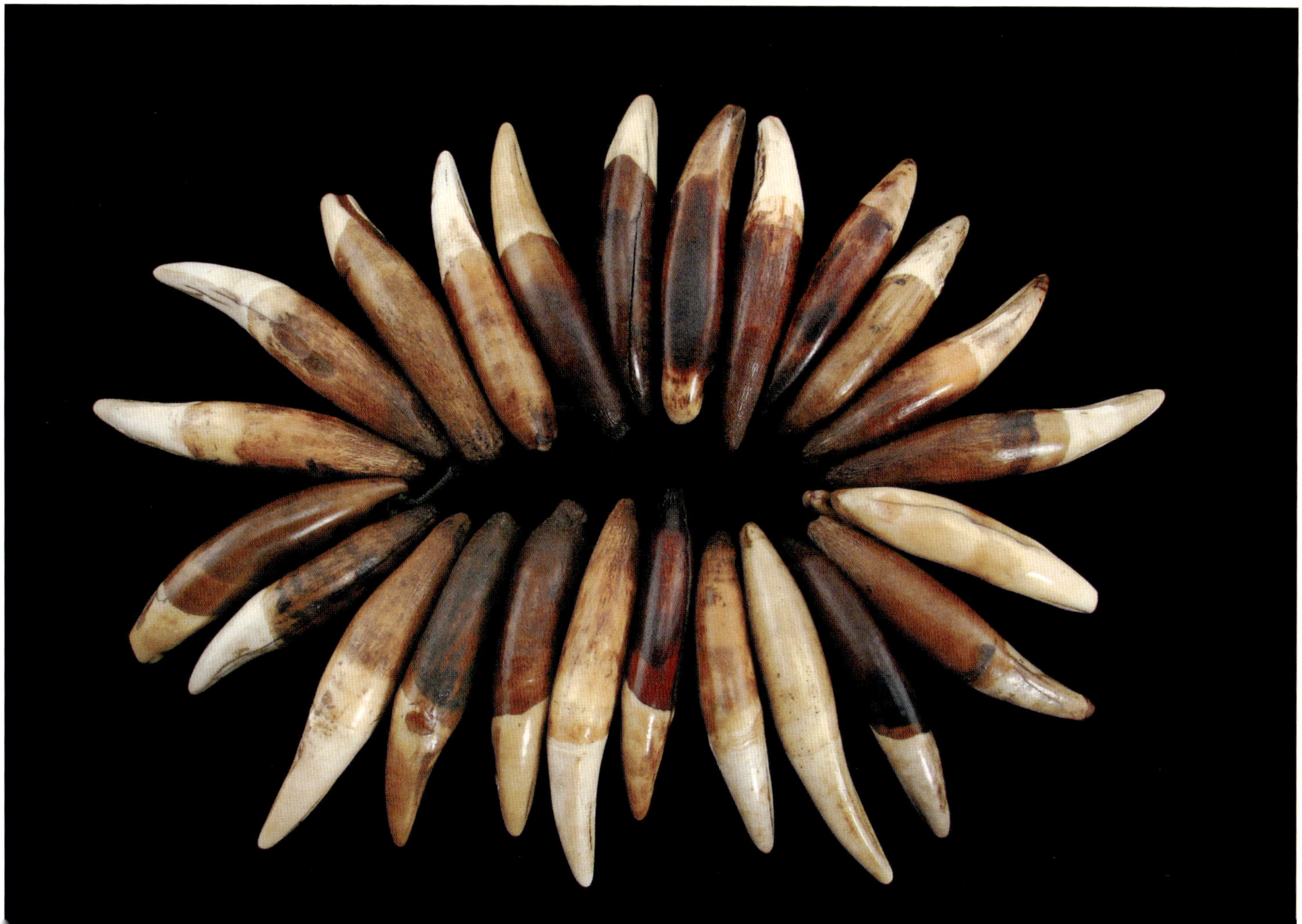

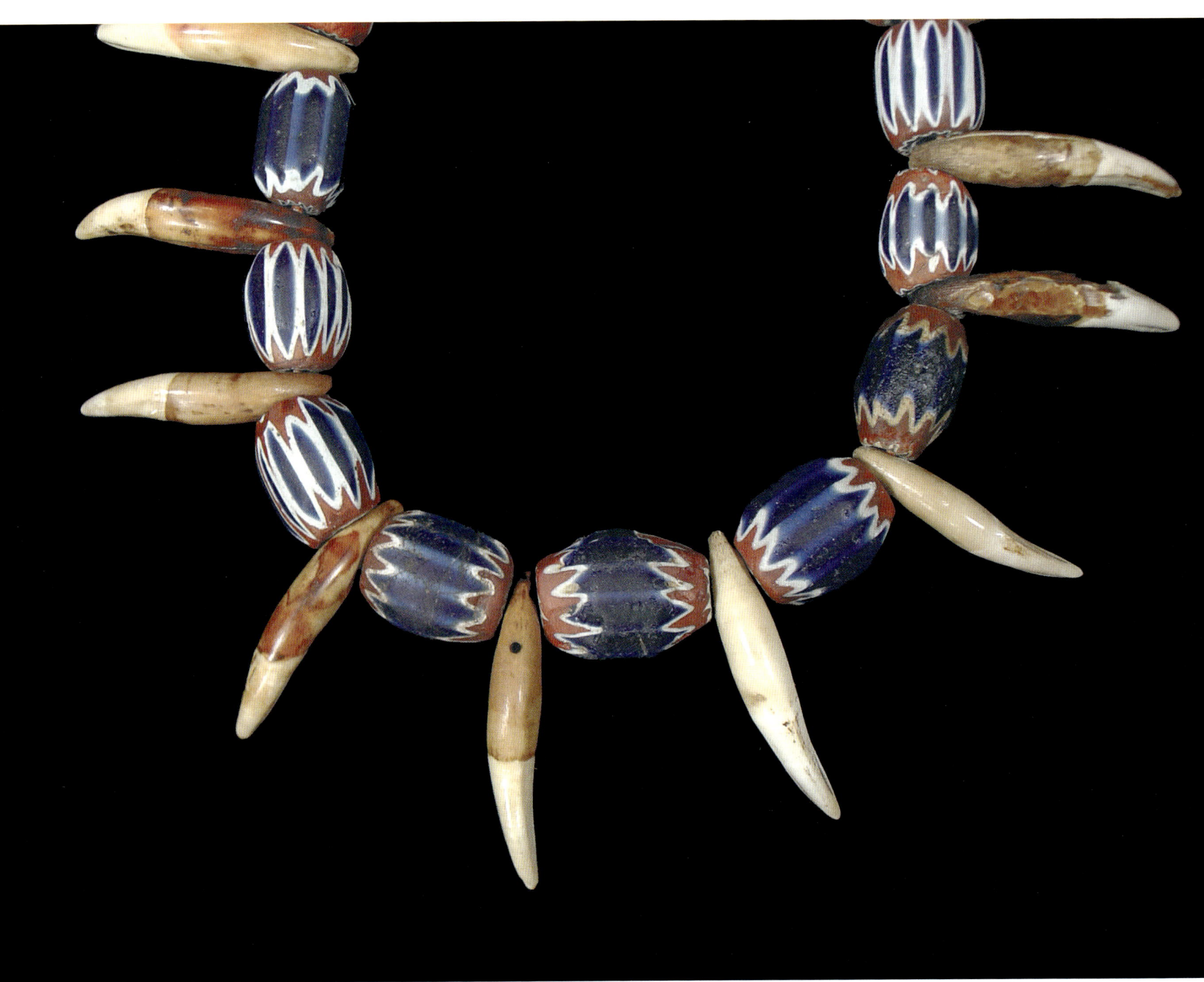

48 ◆ Bones, Teeth, Claws and Shells

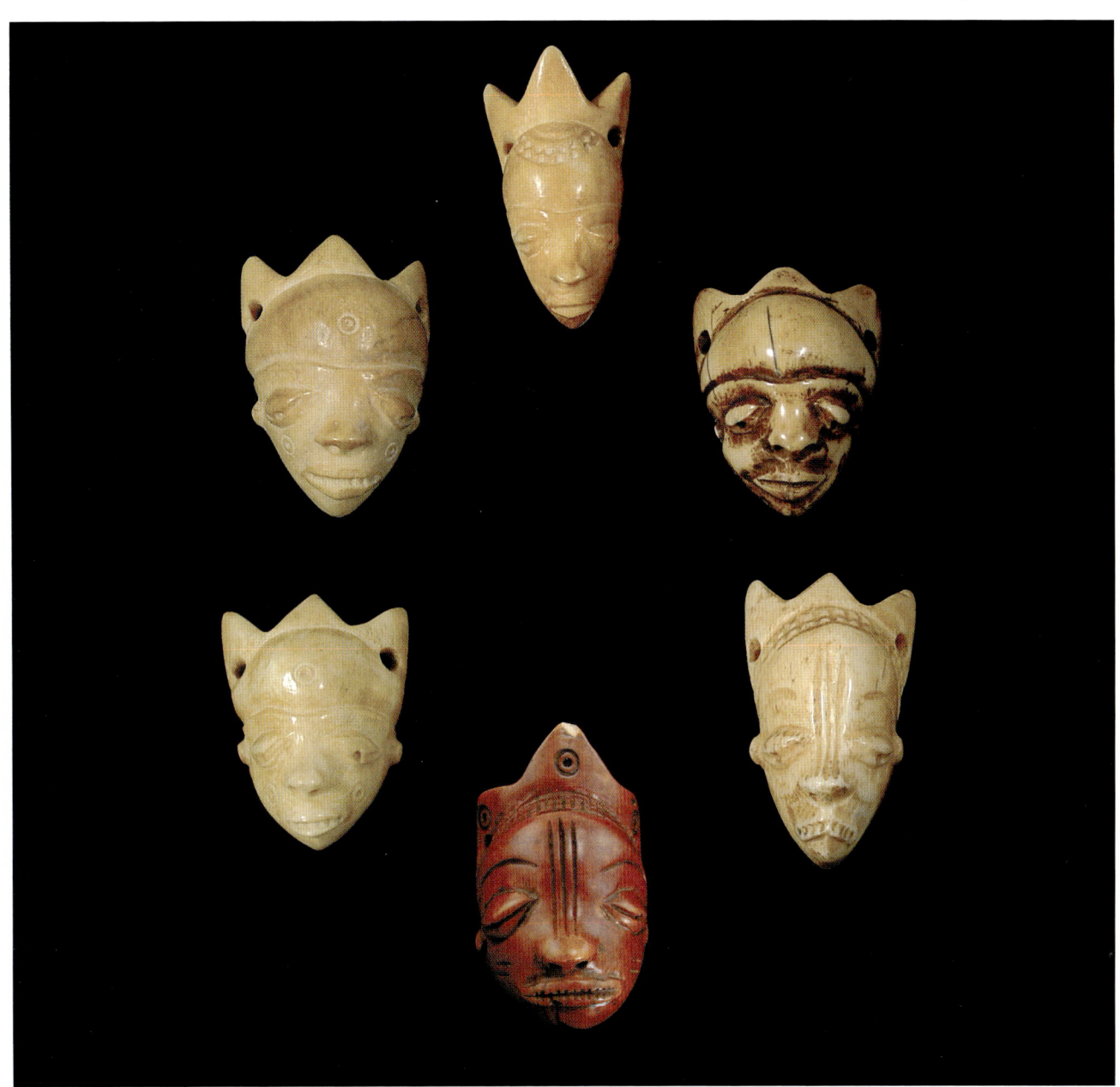

ABOVE *Ivory was associated with status and wealth and was highly esteemed for its magical powers. The materials used for the carving of amuletic pendants were often derived from elephant ivory. When ivory was unobtainable, hippopotamus ivory and warthog tusks were substituted.*

Bones, Teeth, Claws and Shells

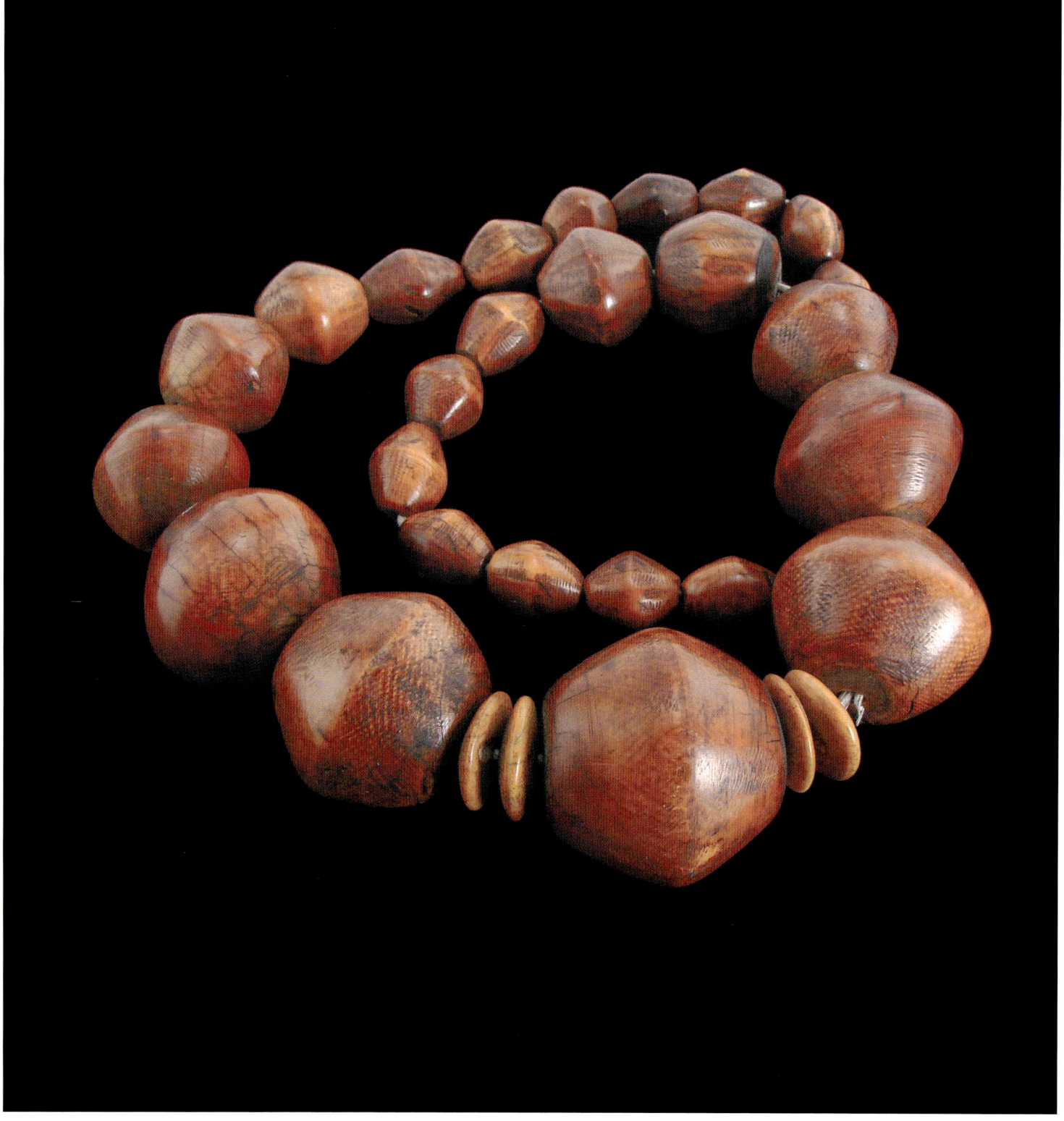

ABOVE *Necklace from Ghana comprised of very large bicone-shaped ivory beads with a particularly rich brown patina. The crosshatched pattern observed on the surface—called Schreger Lines or Lines of Retzius—is a characteristic of elephant ivory. Chiefs and individuals of high status would have worn necklaces of this style.*

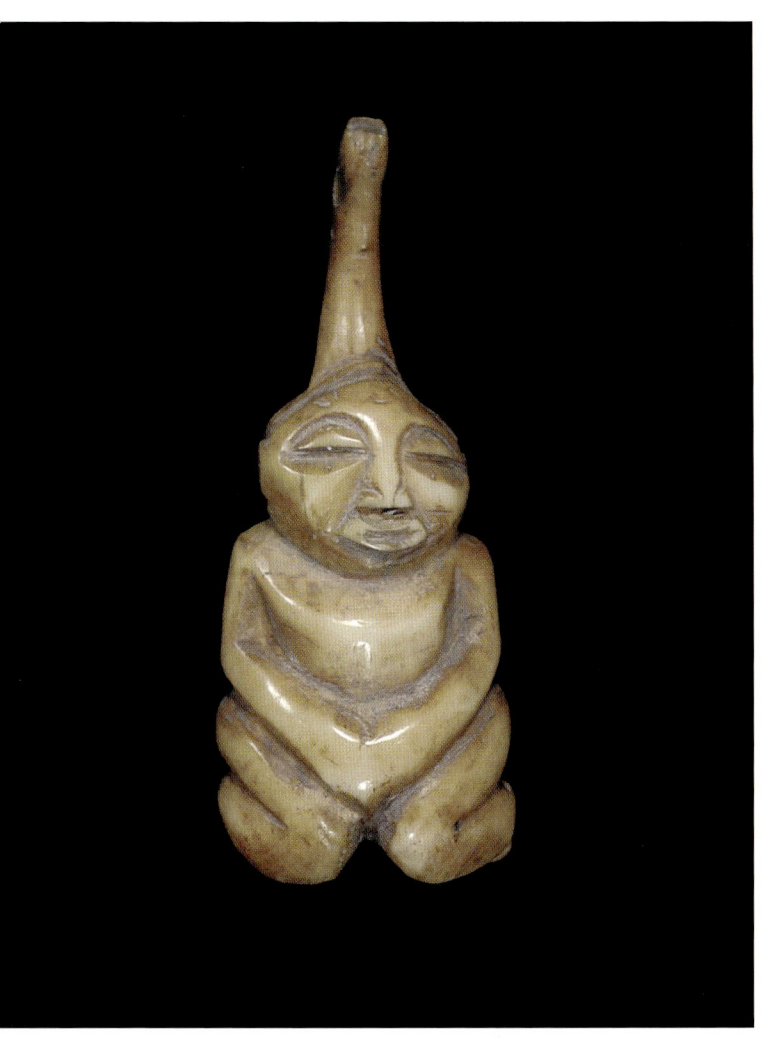
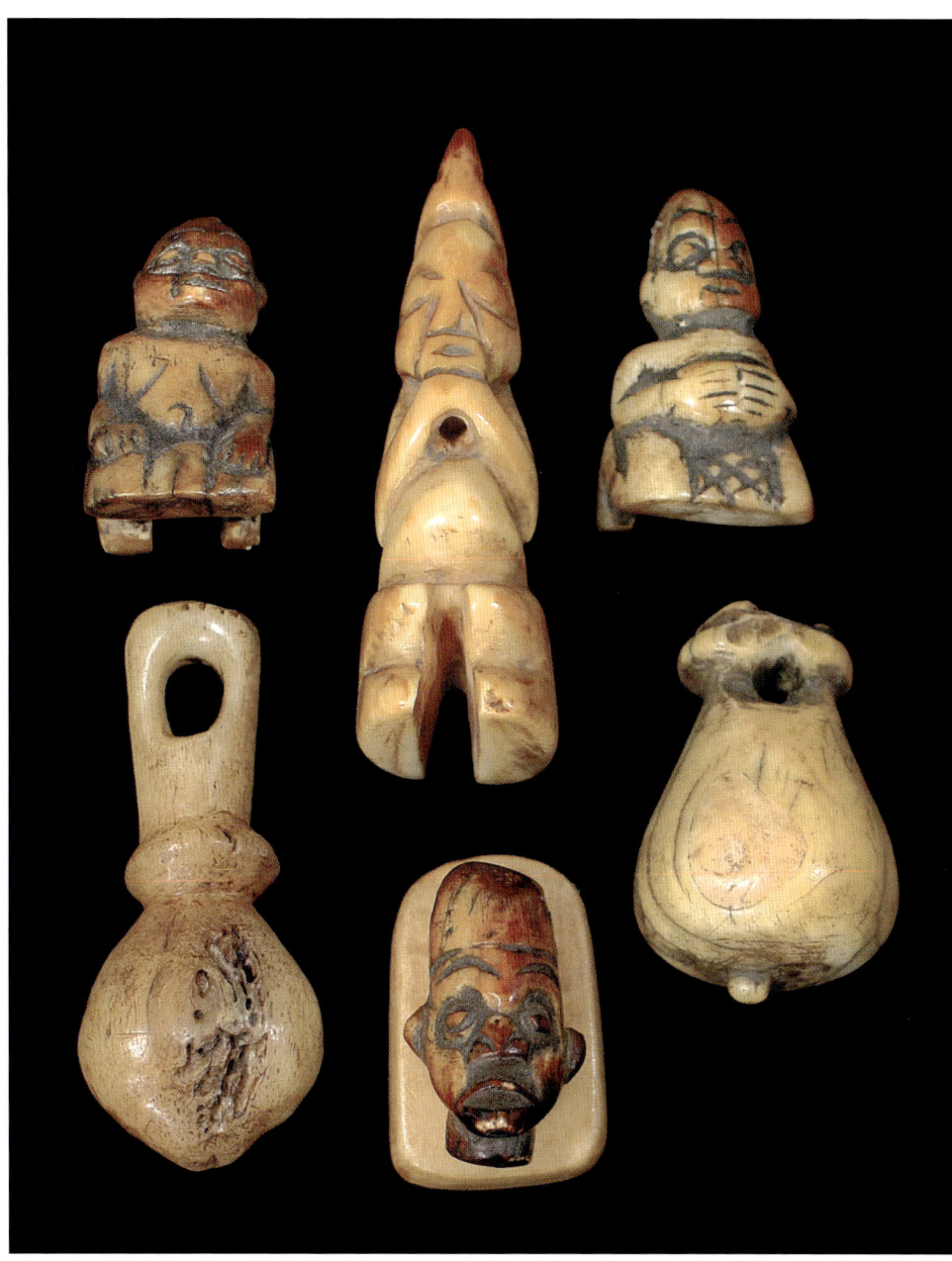

ABOVE (LEFT & RIGHT) AND NEXT PAGE
Specially appointed carvers, often organized in guilds, were employed by the Oba (the Divine Ruler of Benin) for the manufacture of pendants of special importance, intended to be worn by individuals of high standing or to be used in ritual ceremonies.

Bones, Teeth, Claws and Shells ◆ 51

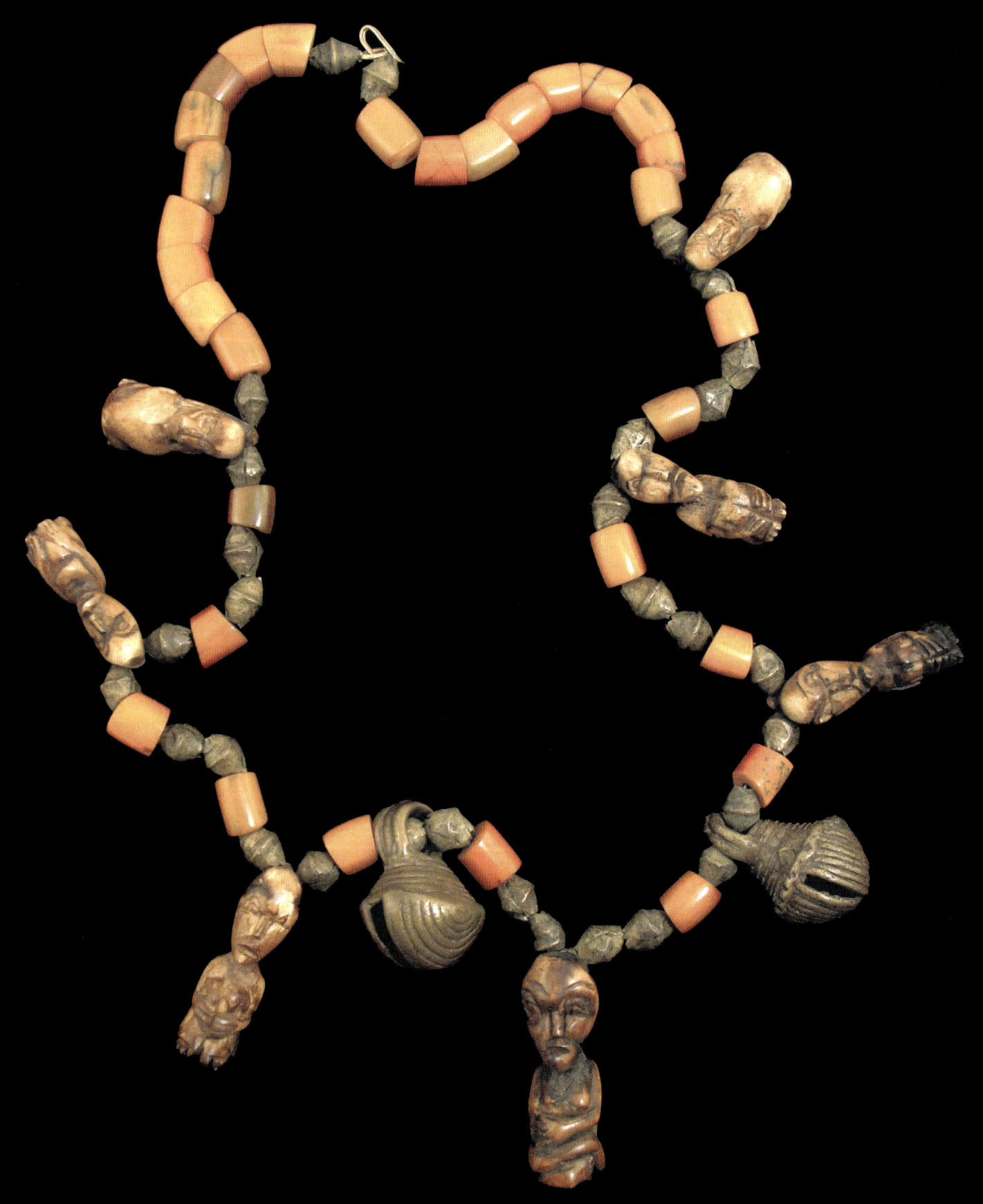

Amber, Clay and Beads Made from Plant Materials

Amber

What Is Amber?

Ever since the Bronze Age (2500-500 BCE), amber has been used for creating jewelry. The name is derived from the Arabic word "anbar." For thousands of years, amber has been valued for its amuletic properties: its ability to prevent disease, ward off bad luck and give the wearer courage. Hippocrates (470-410), the Greek mathematician who made such an impression on medical history that his name is still associated with the field, considered amber a cure for gonorrhea, earache, poor sight, fevers and hysteria. In Greek mythology, amber was believed to be the solidified tears shed by the Heliades as they mourned the death of their brother, Phaeton.

The principal source for amber since ancient times has been the area around the Baltic Sea; and Germany, Lithuania, and Latvia continue to produce great quantities of amber every year. The Dominican Republic has also been a major source for amber since the time of Christopher Columbus. Other fossil amber localities are located throughout the world, some yielding a younger form of amber, called copal. In 2006, an Australian fisherman found the first amber ever documented on that continent, while he was walking on a beach on the remote coast of north Queensland one evening. Another fairly recent discovery of true amber, named Amekit, has been documented in southeastern Nigeria. The source is located in the Eocene clay sandstone deposits of the Ameki Foundation, which gave this amber its name. The name of the tree species from which it is derived has not yet been established.

Amber comes into existence by a slow process, which begins with the fresh sap, called resin, oozing from a tree. The resin decomposes when left exposed to the atmosphere. Molecules of resin, carried by moving water and deposited in the sediments of an oxygen-poor environment, cross-link with one another over millions of years. There is a continuum of the kinds of amber that form during this process. Copal is a substance from an intermediate stage. It is not as hard and durable as amber and is said to age differently. Both amber and copal are produced not by one kind of tree but from a wide variety of conifers and tropical broad-leafed trees.

In its final form, amber is a hardened resin derived from tree sap—usually from an injured or scarred deciduous or coniferous tree—and is composed primarily of carbon, hydrogen and oxygen. It can also be a fossil. It has been found in sedimentary deposits as old as the Pennsylvanian period (325 to 286 million years ago) and as recent as the Miocene (twenty-five to thirteen million years ago). The oldest fossil resins found derive from seed ferns (pteridosperms) and date back 320 million years. Unlike other fossils, in which minerals replace the original organic structure, the chemical compositions of amber remain virtually unchanged. For this reason, perfectly preserved insects, leaves and small animals such as lizards and frogs can often be observed within it, having been trapped and encapsulated when the amber was in its sticky resinous stage. The oldest ambers found with such inclusions come from the early Cretaceous period, in Lebanon.

Amber is transparent to semi-translucent, with some cloudy amber being virtually opaque because of the presence of gas bubbles. Cloudy amber can be clarified in an oil-bath: the oil fills the numerous pores which cause the turbidity. Brown amber that has been heat-clarified, however, sometimes loses the outer coating responsible for its acquired dark brown appearance and becomes much lighter

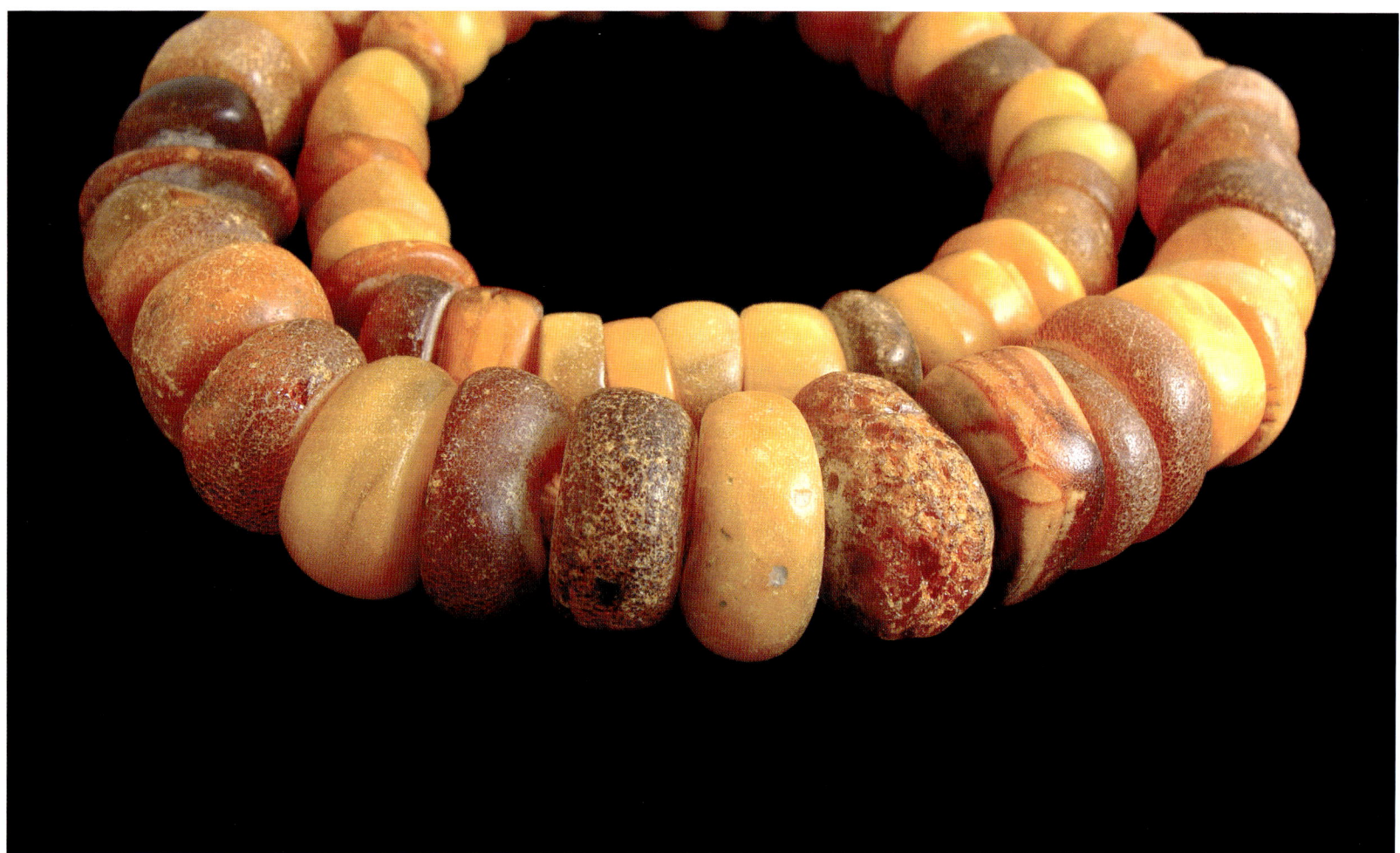

ABOVE *Amber beads can be translucent or opaque, and range in color from brown and orange to honey-yellow. The beads on this strand show just part of the spectrum.*

TOP RIGHT *When amber is unobtainable, the Berber of Morocco use horn as a substitute. Formed into the desired shapes under the influence of heat, the beads are dyed with locally grown saffron until they have acquired a hue similar to genuine yellow amber.*

BOTTOM RIGHT *Broken amber beads are often elaborately repaired and valued as highly as intact pieces. Depicted above are several broken and repaired genuine amber beads that were found in Mauritania. Several short lengths of corrugated silver wires, shaped like the figure eight, are holding the fragments together.*

in color when exposed to strong light. The hues of amber range from nearly colorless to light- and honey-yellow; orange; reddish, greenish or bluish brown; and, rarely, to red, white or black. The color of yellow amber can change to an orange-red hue after a relatively long period underground. The colors of amber can be enhanced by heating, dyeing, varnishing or embedding it within materials such as plastics. Another treatment, called "spangling," involves heating amber in oil until cracks appear in its surface, then introducing a dye, commonly red or green in color, into the cracks.

Broken Amber Beads

Amber in its various forms and imitations is highly esteemed throughout West Africa. Broken beads are never discarded and repaired pieces are often valued even more highly than unblemished specimens. Silver, copper or brass wires are wound around the equator of damaged beads in order to keep broken pieces in place or to stabilize fractures. Short lengths of preformed corrugated silver, copper or brass wires are heated and inserted into the bead to hold together adjoining fragments. Missing chunks are filled in with pastes that harden and can also act as "glue." The in-

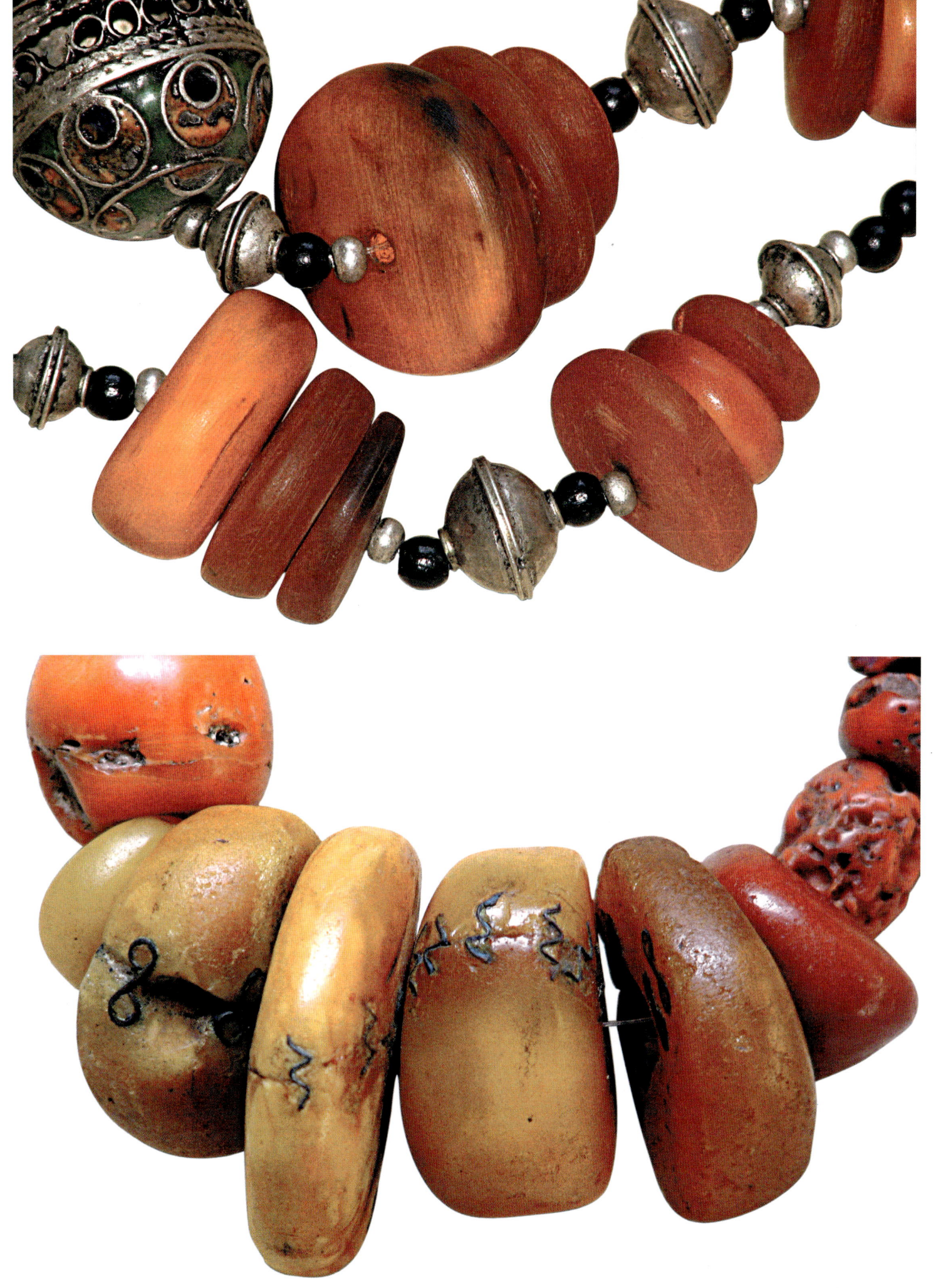

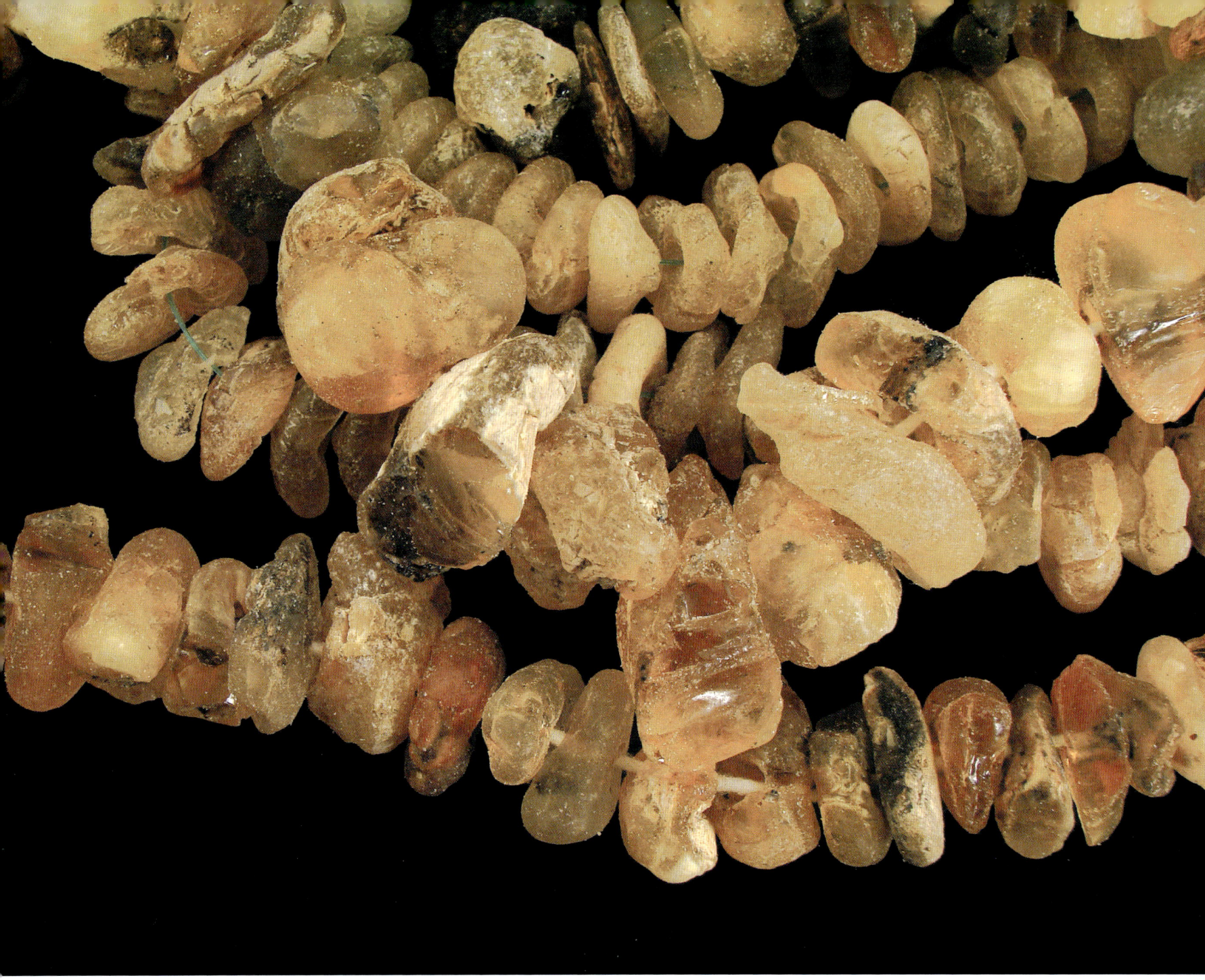

ABOVE   The literature related to Africa from before the 1970s suggests that African peoples are familiar with, and made beads from a native, local variety of copal. Because it can be found in rivers, it is called "River Amber" or "Ocean Amber." Deposits of "River Amber" have been documented in Zanzibar in East Africa, in Sierra Leone, and in Guinea-Bissau.

gredients of these pastes are closely guarded secrets. The suggestion that camel dung may be one of the components could not be verified. Elaborately decorated metal caps are sometimes found inserted into worn-out perforations.

Medicinal Properties

In Morocco, amber is highly prized not only for its color but also for its medicinal powers. In southern Morocco, amber is one of the ingredients of a sticky ointment of grayish color called "lunar paste." It is highly recommended by talebs (healers) for specific beneficial or destructive purposes. Amber is also highly valued in Somalia for its colors and its supernatural powers, and by the women of Harer in southeast Ethiopia, who on formal occasions wear bright head cloths adorned with strings of amber beads and silver pendants. Men often prefer their prayer bead necklaces to be comprised of amber beads not only because of their special talismanic powers but also for their light weight. Because amber is known to retain body temperature, women favor it in the belief that it will protect against chills. [21]

Copal

Semi-fossilized resin or sub-fossil amber is called copal. Copal looks very similar to amber but it is not as old, not as polymerized and not as hard as true amber. [22] It also has a lower melting point, melts rather than burns, becomes sticky when heated and emits a different odor than amber. The two do share many properties, however. Like amber, copal often encapsulates small creatures from long ago, species which may now be extinct. The word "copal" is derived from "copalli," which means "incense" in the old Mayan Nahuatl language. Many indigenous cultures in Mexico still use fresh copal as incense. Copal deposits in Africa are one of the natural sources for making beads. They are found in Congo, Madagascar, Kenya, Tanzania and Zanzibar.

Testing Amber

The ancient Greeks called amber "elektron" because it produces static electricity when rubbed against wool cloth. Since charged amber attracts particles of dust, small pieces of paper, feathers, etc., this property served as a test to determine whether a material was genuine amber. Since the introduction of amber imitations made from phenolic plastic in the mid 1920s, however, the rub test has become obsolete, in that the plastic imitations also take a negative static-electric charge when rubbed.

There are other methods to determine whether an object is made from amber, from copal, or from some other material. For example, amber shows no reaction when a drop of isopropanol or ethanol is applied to its surface, whereas with copal, the polish is removed and the surface becomes sticky.

Another test involves touching the material with a hot needle to produce a puff of smoke. Smoke from amber will have a slightly acrid, resinous smell, while copal will give off a sweeter resinous smell, and many fake materials will produce an acrid, plastic-like odor.

Since amber and copal have a lower specific gravity than saturated salt solution, they will float whereas other substances will sink. (To make a saturated salt solution, stir seven heaped teaspoons of salt into a half pint (284 milliliters) of water and stir for a few minutes until the salt has dissolved.)

When rubbed for at least a full minute, amber will emit a pleasant odor reminiscent of pine resin; phenolic plastics will discharge an unpleasant, acrid, carbolic odor.

Phenolic Resins and Other Amber Imitations

Amberoid

A number of materials are commonly used to make imitation amber, including glass, phenolic resins, phenolic and other plastics, Bakelite, synthetic resins, celluloid, horn, casein, polyester, polystyrene, bone and glass.

One method of producing imitation amber involves heating small fragments of genuine amber with the exclusion of air, then compressing them into a uniform mass with intense hydraulic pressure. The resulting material is known as "amberoid" or "pressed amber."

Bakelite, Resolan and Novalak

Bakelite, resolan and novalak are synthetic resins (phenoplasts) that were used to produce amber imitations on a large scale in German factories in Prussia and in the Free City of Gdansk between the two world wars. These plastics, however, are no longer used for the manufacture of amber imitations.

Phenolic Resins

Phenolic resins were also widely used for the production of amber imitations and were the most common material for making fake amber beads. At the beginning of the 20th century, necklaces of deep, dark cherry color imitating the reddish hue of museum artifacts were referred to as "antique amber" for this reason. Most often, these beads are oval in

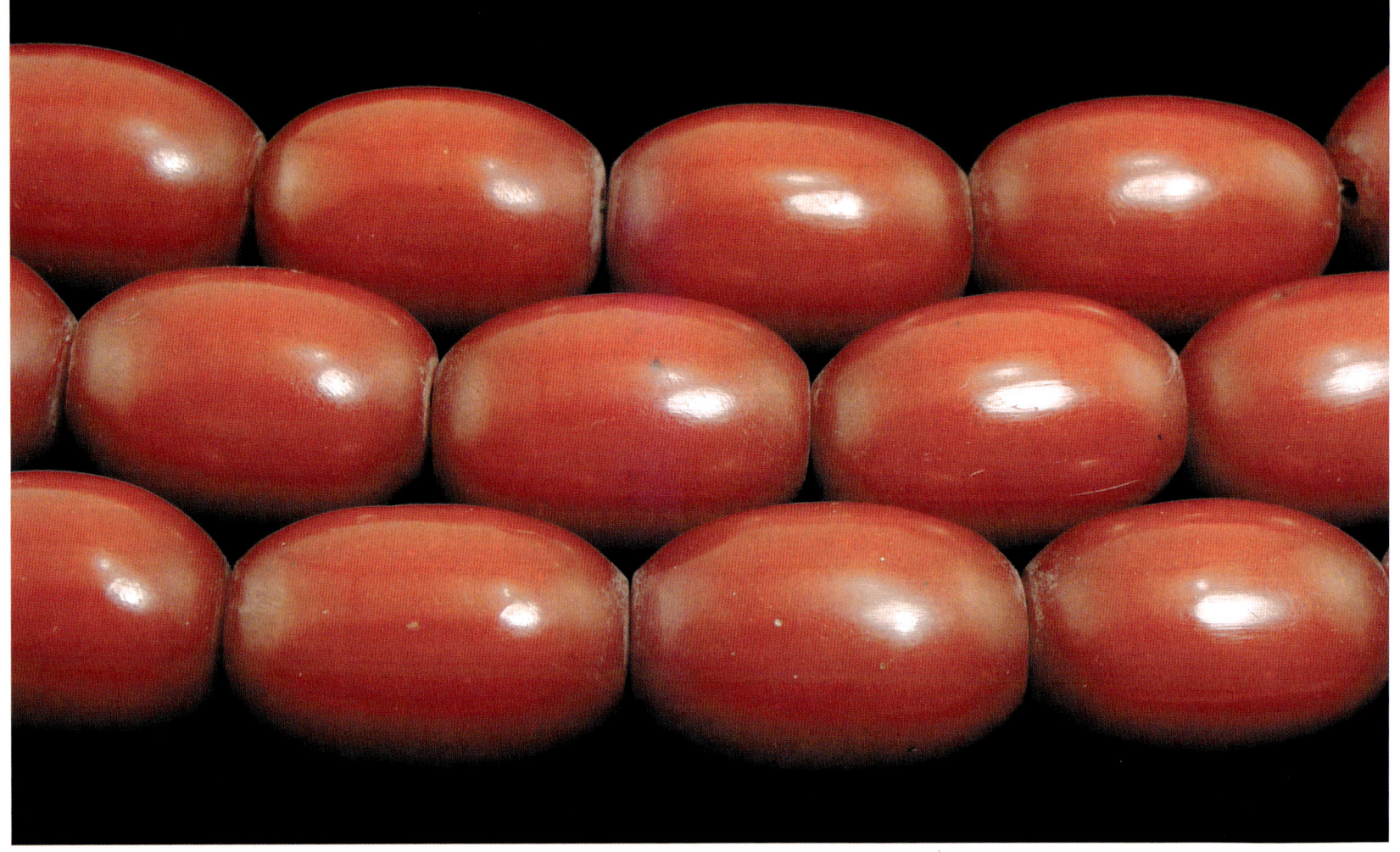

ABOVE *The so-called "Cherry Amber," which is highly esteemed in Ethiopia, is made from dark red phenolic plastics.*

shape and graduated in size. The predominant color is a dark red, but tan or yellow beads (transparent or opaque) were also manufactured. Phenolic resin is slightly denser than amber.

Bernat

Bernat is an amber-colored polyester resin developed by Gebhardt Wilhelm. It has a characteristic glittery appearance and a higher specific gravity than amber.

Celluloid

Imitation amber made from Celluloid (cellulose nitrate) is usually yellow in color and cloudy. It is slightly denser and more flammable than amber. The English patent for Parkensin, a cellulose nitrate, was issued in 1855. Celluloid was patented in 1870 in the United States of America. Significantly improved plastics based on cellulose have come to replace the earlier cellulosic plastics.

Casein

Casein is a plastic made from milk. Imitation amber beads made from this material are cloudy, opaque and a dirty yellow in color. Casein is slightly heavier than amber and will sink if placed in a saturated salt solution.

Horn, Bone and Glass

Amber imitations have also been made from glass and from horn—either dyed a dark brown or, as is the custom in southern Morocco, a honey yellow color derived from locally grown saffron. Strands of beads made from horn—which was heated until pliable and pressed into round and oblate shapes to resemble the shapes of "African Amber" beads—have in recent years been documented in Ghana. Horn is softer than amber, it scratches easily and emits a characteristic odor when burnt. Differences in the density and heat conduction of glass and amber prevent attempts to sell glass amber imitations as authentic amber. [23]

African Amber

So-called "African Amber" is manufactured from a variety of plastic materials, produced mainly in Germany during the early 20th century for export to West African countries. Occasionally these beads were decorated locally by carving into their surface magical patterns such as the circle-dot motif. Cross-perforated beads are highly valued by Mauritanian women, who wear them as hair ornaments.

In a study conducted by J.D. Allen, where eighty bead samples—originally described as amber or copal—were submitted to various tests, only seventeen percent of the examined beads could be established as amber and five percent as copal, while the balance was made up of plastics of various types and some other materials such as horn. [21]

Clay

What Is Clay?

Clay consists of a variety of phyllosilicate minerals, which include variable amounts of structural water. Clays are generally formed by the chemical weathering of silicate-bearing rocks, or by carbonic acid. Some clay is formed by hydrothermal activity.

When wet, clay can be easily shaped. It becomes firm when dry, and hardens when subjected to high temperatures during firing. These properties make clay an ideal substance for durable pottery items with practical or decorative purposes. Clay can be found in various colors, ranging from a dull gray to tan to deep orange-red, depending on its soil content.

History of Clay-working in Africa

Traditionally, different regions of the world produce regionally distinctive pottery, using different types of clay, which is commonly mixed with other minerals. In West Africa, objects made from clay are still formed individually, by hand, using both primitive and individualized techniques.

After the clay has been kneaded—to homogenize the moisture content and remove entrapped air—it is then shaped, either by hand or with various tools and machines such as the potter's wheel. While the clay is still soft and moist, decorative patterns are applied by making impressions, using preformed stencils. Motifs can be incised into soft clay or carved out of the hardened clay after firing. The firing takes place in simple, charcoal-fired kilns, and afterward the pieces are allowed to dry in the air until hard. Sometimes a coating of clay slip is applied before firing. On new West African clay beads and spindle whorls, slip residue can still be observed, in the form of a white or light gray powdery substance that adheres to the surface of the object.

It is known that human groupings throughout the Sahara adopted the production of pottery as early as 9000 BCE. The style of decoration is strikingly similar across a vast region. The development of pottery is perceived to have been a milestone in human history. Because pottery items are durable, man-made artifacts, utilized by cultures around the world, they have proven to be a boon for archaeologists. Summing up Yoruba civilization, for instance, Frobenius was able to conclude that its technical summit was reached in the terracotta industry, and that the most important achievements in Yoruba art were not expressed in stone, but in fine clay baked in a furnace. Broken pottery found at archaeological sites, called sherds or shards, can help in identifying the resident culture and in dating the stratum. In fact, by its formation, style, decoration and relative chronology, pottery is essential for dating the remains of non-literate cultures and helpful in the dating of some historic cultures. Trace element analysis, mostly by neutron activation, allows the sources of clay to be accurately identified.

From the Western Sahara and Mauritania to the Red Sea coast, the most frequently applied techniques for decorating pottery items were the so-called rocker and alternately pivoting stamp techniques. The rocker technique consists in imparting a rocker movement to a double-pointed stick or to a short convex edged spatula with a central notch, along a horizontal line. The use of the plain, thin edge of a spatula or a bivalve shell resulted in a continuous line, like an incision, forming various kinds of zigzag patterns. A double-pronged object was applied and moved horizontally across the surface of the soft clay, pivoting alternately on one point and then on the other, resulting in a pattern of pairs of dotted lines. In all probability the craftsperson used motifs that were generally accepted by the community, and varied the patterns from one time to the next. The same may be assumed concerning the implements used. The tools were in all probability made or collected individually.

Some archaeologists believe that the Jomon in Japan first developed pottery around 10,500 BCE, and that it was used in Europe even earlier. It appears that pottery was independently

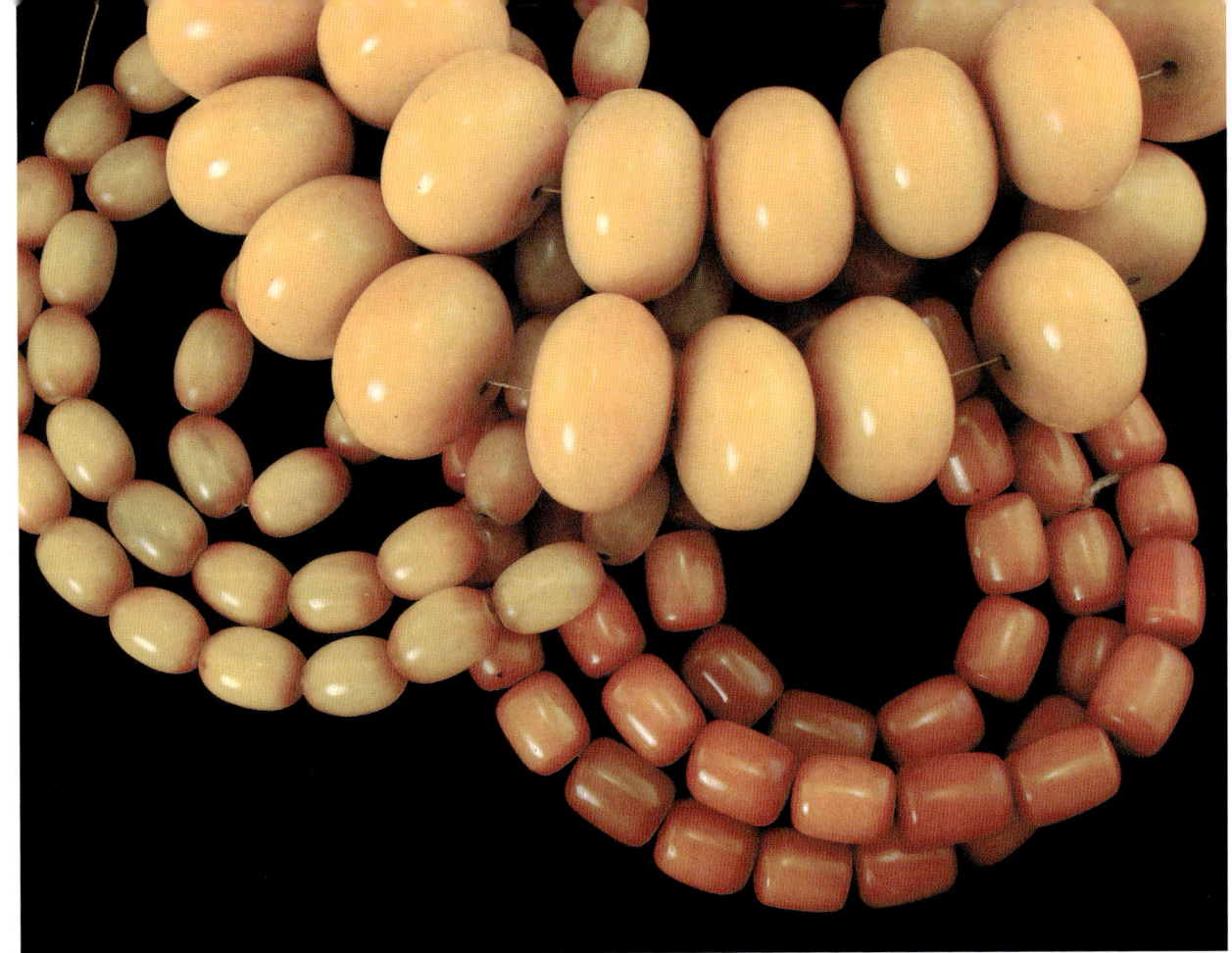

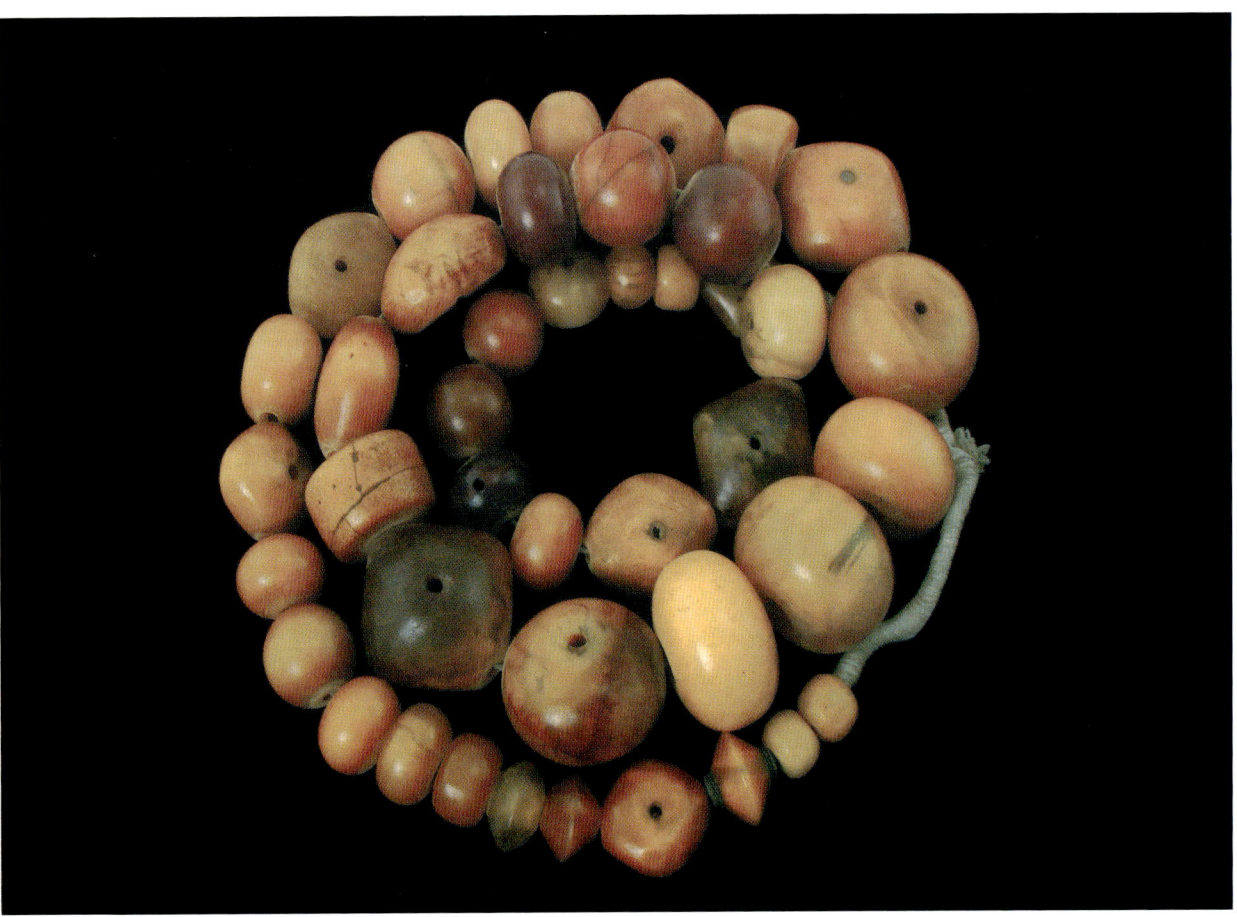

60 ⬧ Amber, Clay and Beads Made from Plant Materials

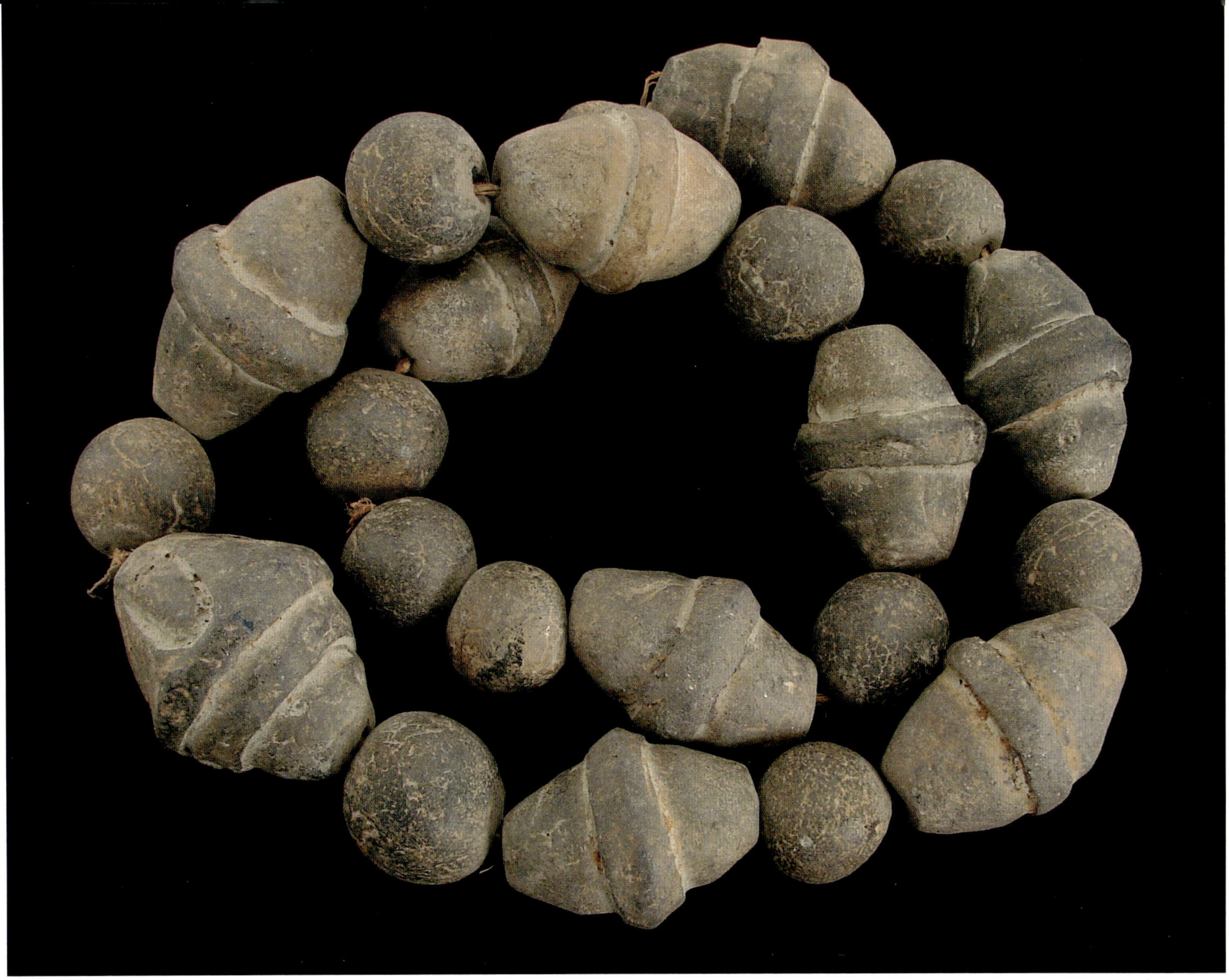

ABOVE This unusual strand of clay beads with raised equatorial bands is Bamileke in origin and was kept in the royal family until being presented as a gift to the Bennett-Luther Collection in Denver, Colorado.

RIGHT Spindle whorls in the styles depicted to the right are typical of Mali; a number of similar whorls were excavated in the old city of Jenné-Jeno. Spatulas or bivalve shells, made or collected individually, were used to impress the decorative patterns into the wet clay. The same techniques were used for decorating ceramic pots and other household utensils.

PREVIOUS PAGE Examples of the great variety of beads made from "African Amber" and other amber imitations.

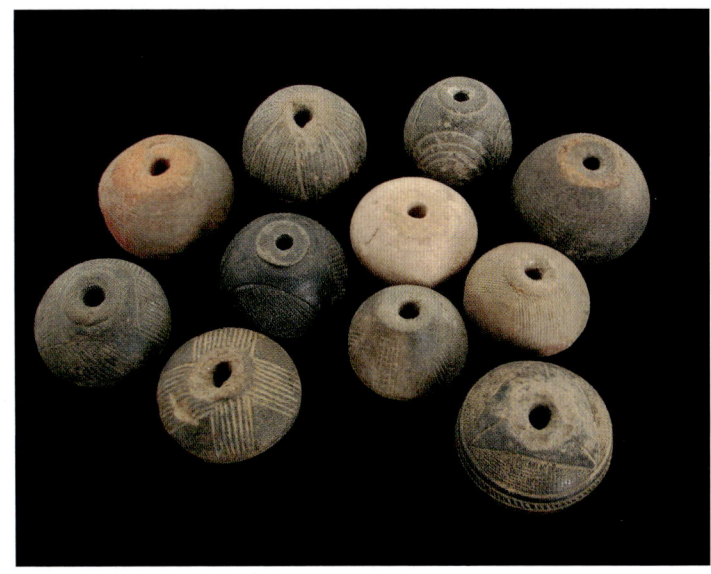

Amber, Clay and Beads Made from Plant Materials

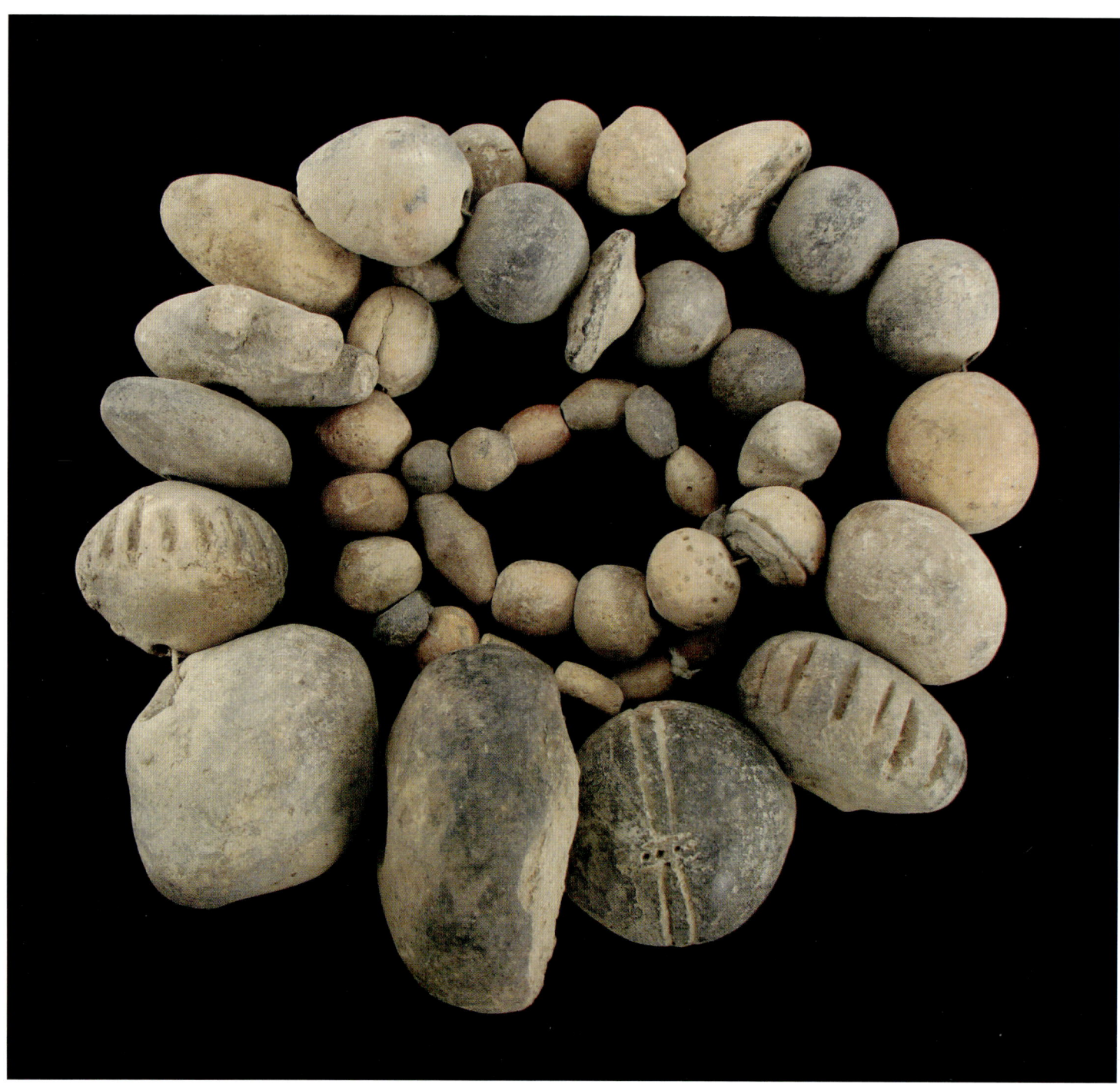

ABOVE *The old clay spindle whorls and beads depicted here are from the Sudan. The decorative patterns on spindle whorls often represent magical or mystical symbols that were well known, accepted and understood by the people who used them.*

Amber, Clay and Beads Made from Plant Materials

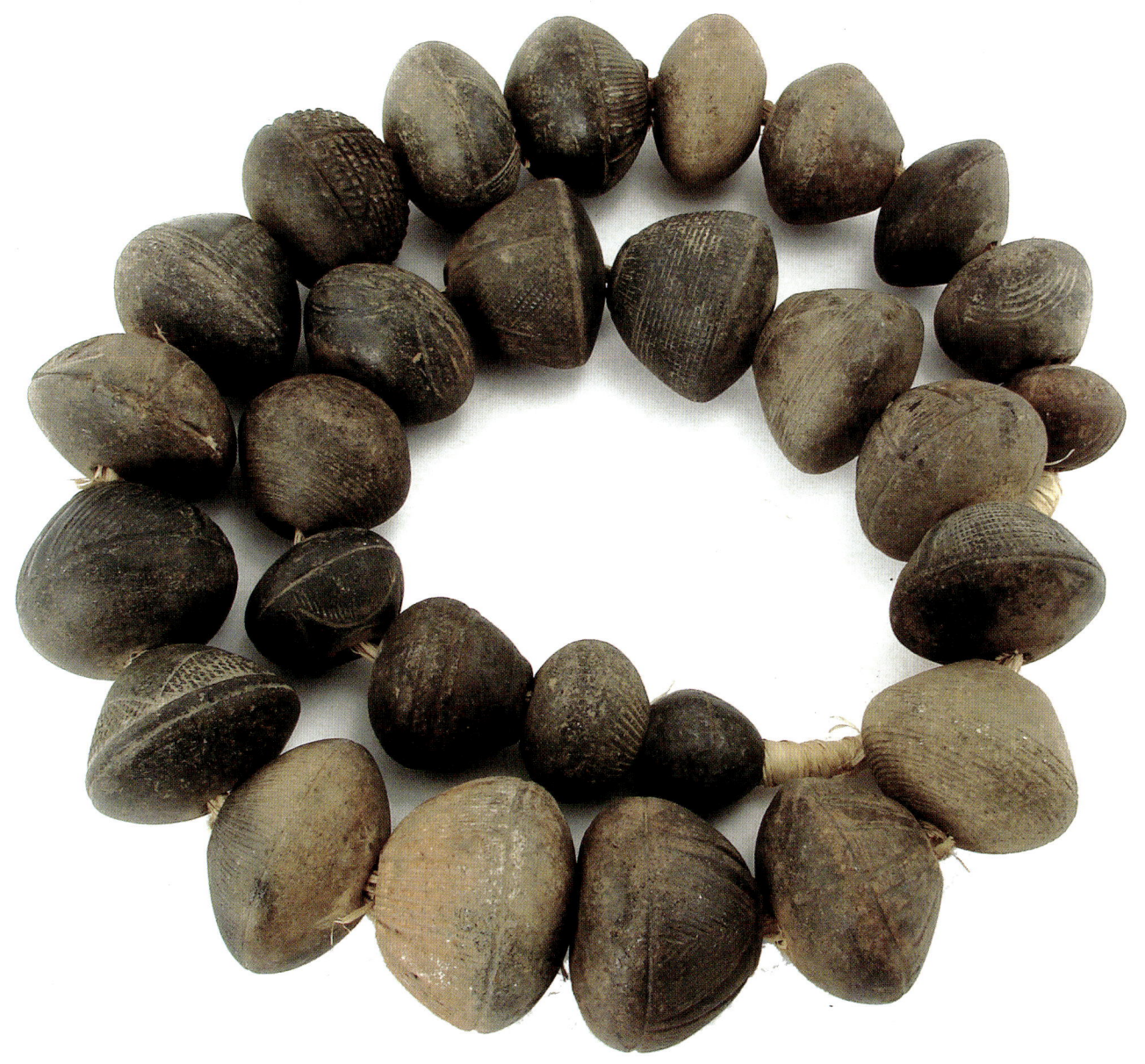

ABOVE *Obsolete clay spindle whorls can be seen threaded and suspended from house walls, commonly in the vicinity of doors and intended for protection against evil forces. Clay spindle whorls are occasionally used as beads, be it as adornments, charms or talismans, or incorporated into fetish necklaces.*

developed in North Africa during the 10th millennium and in South America during the 7th millennium BCE. The potter's wheel was invented in Mesopotamia sometime between 6000 and 2400 BCE.

Clay Artifacts of Djenne

A great number of clay artifacts, including spindle whorls and beads, were discovered in what is probably the most famous archaeological site in West Africa, located only a few kilometers from present-day Djenne. Djenne (Jenné) is a small town in Mali, situated in the Inland Niger Delta of West Africa, which is fed by the Niger and Bani rivers—a vast region of swamps and lakes, interspersed by grassland and scrub vegetation belts, with large areas being submerged under the waters of the Niger River for as many as six to nine months every year. The location became widely known during the 1970s, when S.K. and R.J. McIntosh, a husband and wife team of archaeologists, conducted licensed excavations at the settlement mounds of Djenne-Jeno (old Djenne), and the neighboring villages of Hambarketolo and Kaniana. The McIntoshes found stone tools, pottery, bone and metal objects, glass beads and fragments, clay spindle whorls, animal bones and human remains. The progress of their work was covered by the National Geographic Magazine, and their finds are described and documented in great detail in

Amber, Clay and Beads Made from Plant Materials

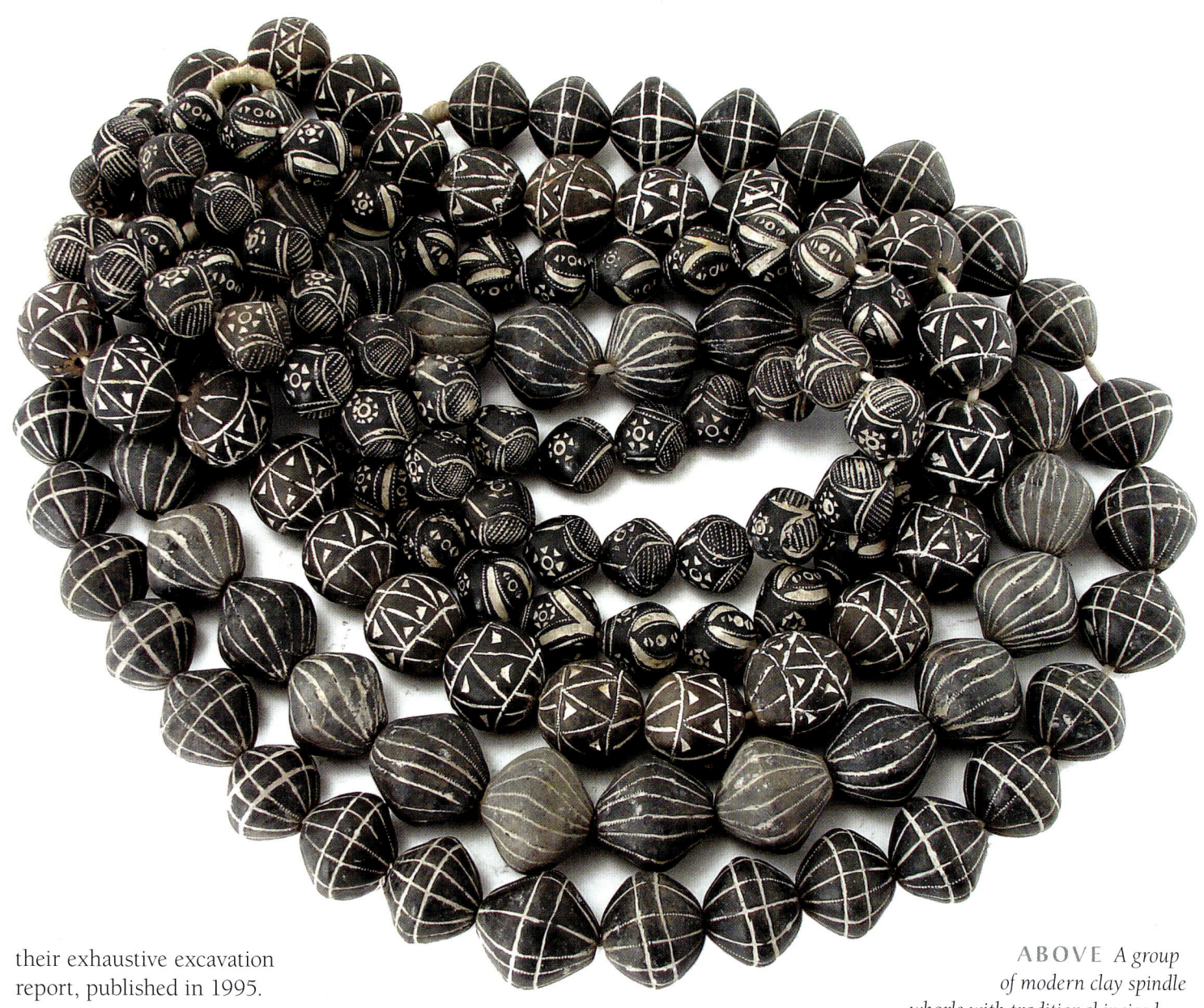

ABOVE *A group of modern clay spindle whorls with traditional incised decorations as they are produced in Mali today, mainly for sale at local tourist markets.*

their exhaustive excavation report, published in 1995.

The earliest excavated settlement in Africa, Djenne-Jeno, was dated to 250 BCE. It showed no northern influence. By 500 CE, the area had expanded rapidly to include large communities organized into complex societies engaging in both regional and long-distance trade with the southern savannah and the desert edge. Djenne-Jeno attained its maximum size by around 900 CE, with some twenty thousand inhabitants. The settlement was abandoned by 1400 CE. Old Djenne-Jeno, referred to by early 16th century sources as a prosperous trading town, is not to be confused with modern Djenne, which lies about three kilometers to the southwest of Djenne-Jeno. Oral traditions maintain that modern Djenne was founded during the 8th century CE on the nearby site of Zobora.

Sixty-four spindle whorls were recovered during the excavations of Djenne-Jeno. The greatest quantity was discovered in a single pit, together with a number of large pot sherds, which may have been used to blacken the whorls during firing. Spindle whorls were manufactured from a great variety of materials, and people generally used the materials most readily available to them—stone, clay and wood—especially in the earliest periods. In West Africa, the most widely used material for making spindle whorls was clay. The whorls were found in strata dated to the Islamic era (10th to 12th centuries CE). Many of the excavated black and buff-colored clay spindle whorls were decorated with incised or impressed bands, dashes, triangles, concentric and criss-crossing lines, and dots and circle motifs, the latter dating back as far as 3000 to 3200 BCE. The decorative patterns were applied by hand while the clay was still soft.

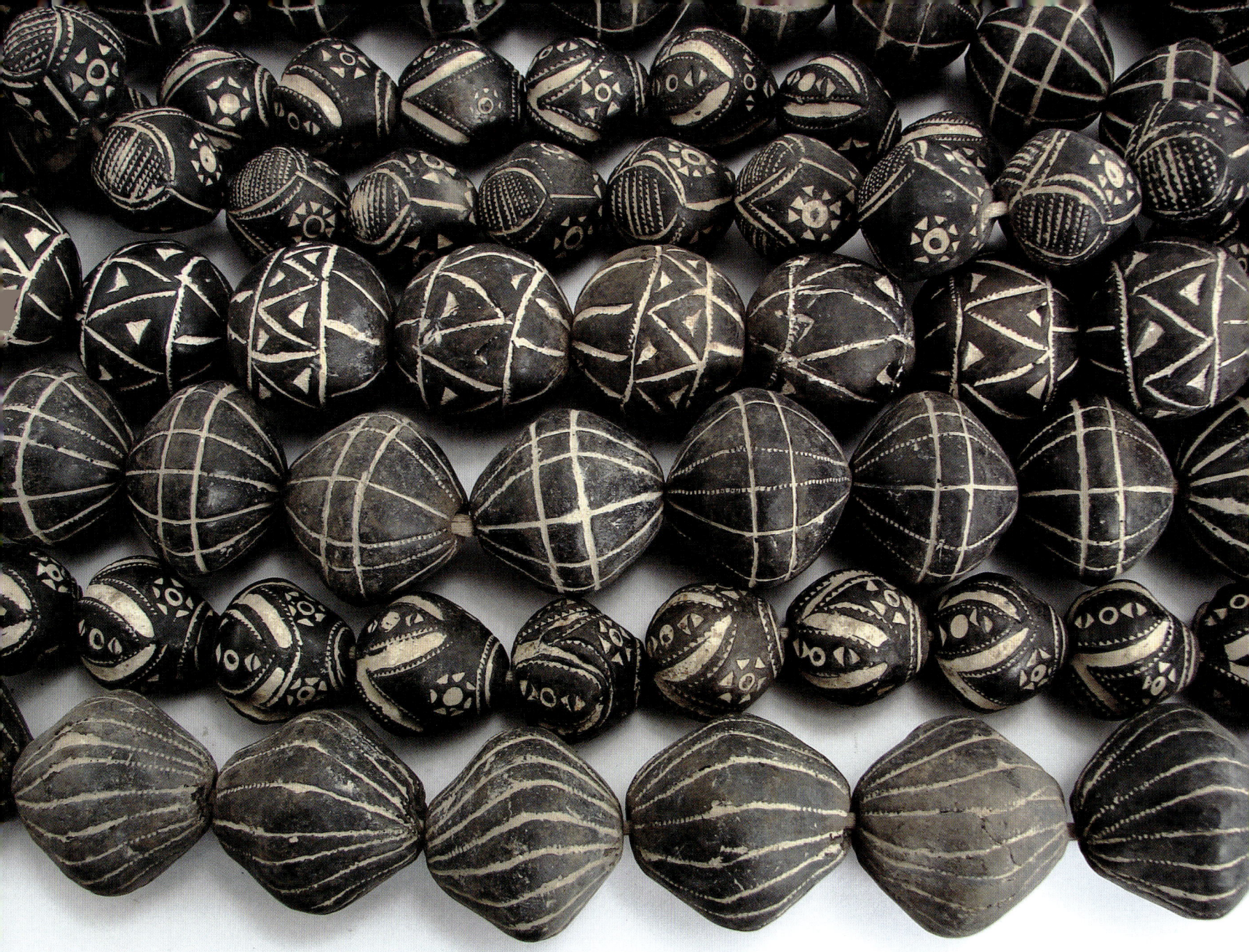

ABOVE *Modern spindle whorls from Mali, manufactured from dark gray or black clay. In order to highlight the decorative patterns, the grooves are commonly filled in with off-white kaolin paste or with light-colored clay.*

Amber, Clay and Beads Made from Plant Materials

On the great majority of whorls found at the Djenne-Jeno site, an application to the grooves of a white substance—a paste made from kaolin or of slurry containing lighter-colored clay—highlighted the decorative patterns after firing. In addition to decorated specimens, the archaeologists found a number of plain, undecorated whorls, and fired, undecorated black and buff colored spherical, tubular and lenticular clay beads. These came from small deposits in numerous locations throughout the site. [25] Very similar clay whorls were found during excavations of the ancient site of the trading town of Begho, located in the northwestern Brong-Ahafo region of Ghana.

Clay Spindle Whorls

Spindle whorls are small rounded or disk-shaped objects typically attached close to the end of a spike or stick, called a shaft in this context. The spindle shaft is commonly made of a thin, rounded length of wood. The spindle whorl serves the purpose of stabilizing and propelling the shaft during the process of twisting loose fibers into a thread. The assemblage, one of the first spinning tools invented by humans, is called a spindle. It is not known when or where spindles were first used, but India and the Near East are believed to be the most likely candidates. [26]

The great majority of spindle whorls have a plano-convex (one end that is flat or concave and one end that is domed) circular shape, but there are many variants, achieved by changes in proportion, circumference, perimeter and angles of the sides. It is rare to find a spindle whorl that is not symmetrically shaped in relation to the axis of its perforation. The perforations of spindle whorls vary greatly in size but are always accurately centered, and often tapered. In comparison with a bead of the same size, a spindle whorl will often have a proportionally larger perforation. [27]

In many cultures the craft of spinning is associated with mysticism and magic. The belief that spindle whorls have magical properties is shared by many cultures in addition to the West African countries, where strings of redundant whorls can be observed suspended from house walls, near the front door, for good luck, protection and to fend off evil spirits. It is customary for the Dogon people of Mali to incorporate spindle whorls into their fetish necklaces.

After modern textiles became readily available throughout West Africa, spinning as a means of producing homemade fabrics was no longer practiced on a large scale. Old spindle whorls are now being traded for other commodities, and whole strands of clay whorls find their way onto collectors' markets, where they are sometimes erroneously classified as beads.

Because of their great popularity as collectors' items, clay spindle whorls are still manufactured in West Africa, with the great majority of these being produced in Mali. The shapes and method used for making new spindle whorls closely adhere to traditional concepts. The traditional decorative patterns are stenciled by hand while the clay is still soft. Black ceramic colorant is commonly added to the clay, and the incised or stenciled patterns are filled in with a white paste for greater contrast, after firing.

Clay Beads

Before imported glass beads became available in any quantity, jewelry was made from other materials such as wood, nuts and seeds, stone, iron and clay. The founders of the Kanem kingdom—the so-called Sao civilization, situated to the east of Lake Chad—manufactured a large number of anthropomorphic and zoomorphic terracotta sculptures in the 12th and 13th centuries, in addition to clay beads. Ancient clay beads in a variety of shapes and often very large in size have also been documented from Sudan. Tiny clay beads are found in great quantities in the vicinity of Djenne. Based on results obtained from radiocarbon dating (a method of estimating the age of organic materials), it has been established that these primarily tan-colored, seed-bead-sized barrels and segmented tubes date from 1400 to 1500 CE. [28]

There are countless varieties and styles of contemporary African clay beads, often decorated with traditional motifs created by incising or stenciling patterns into the wet clay. The Baoule people, who are members of the Akan and are located in the central region of the Ivory Coast, make low-fired clay beads which they decorate with stripes, circles, dots and triangles in hues of tan and ochre. These decorative patterns are applied to the bead surfaces after firing, using water-based clay slurry that will rub or wash off easily. A more permanent decoration can be observed on clay beads of undetermined origins, found primarily in Burkina Faso (formerly the Republic of Upper Volta). Decorations on these beads resemble the woven patterns of African textiles, and they appear to have been transferred onto the surface by an as-yet-unidentified method, after the beads were fired.

Wood, Seeds, Nuts and Other Plant Materials

Wood

Wood is readily available in nature, and it is frequently used for making beads, pendants and other adornments, as well as statues, furniture, household utensils and other objects of everyday use. [29] In Africa, many beads are fashioned from the wood of local euclea species or from African mahogany (Khaya ivorensis), a group of species found in tropical West Africa from the Guinea Coast to Cameroon and extending eastward through the Congo basin to Uganda and parts of Sudan.

Euclea is a member of the Ebenaceae (ebony) family and includes twenty species of evergreen trees and shrubs, all native to Africa, the Comoro Islands and Arabia. Several other species are used both for timber—producing very hard, dark, heartwood similar to ebony—and for the manufacture of smaller objects such as pendants and beads. As a result of unsustainable harvesting, many species of ebony are now considered threatened. Ebony heartwood is one of the most intensely black woods known, which, combined with its high density, fine texture and ability to take a smooth polish, has made it very valuable as an ornamental wood. It has a long history of use, with carved pieces found in ancient Egyptian tombs. The word ebony derives from the ancient Egyptian term hbny.

The black beads used for making Islamic prayer bead strands and the tasseled necklaces worn by Mauritanian griots (professional singers and storytellers) are commonly decorated with inlays of plain or twisted silver wires arranged as circles, dots, triangular patterns or meandering lines that encircle the bead's equator. [30]

In Mauritania, there has been a revival of the tradition of manufacturing beads with inlaid wire decorations, which has resulted in the production of new shapes and styles, featuring wire inlay decorations in colorful combinations of copper, brass and silver.

Seeds, Seed Pods and Nuts

Thousands of different seeds, seed pods and nuts are being used for making beads all around the world. Large seeds can also be worn as pendants. At Kew, one of the world's leading botanic gardens, situated near London, England, the oldest examples of jewelry are four Graeco-Roman necklaces which are about 2,000 years old and comprised of seeds, fruit, leaves and flowers. The necklaces were discovered in ancient Egyptian tombs by the British archaeologist Sir Flinders Petrie. [31]

Sea Beans

Seeds are readily available and easily perforated or pierced when fresh or soaked in water. They are generally uniform in size, shape and coloration, and often colorful and hard-wearing. [32] Many of the robust seeds used as beads are known as "drift seeds" or "sea beans." These seeds are produced by trees and vines. They fall into waterways such as the Amazon River and float and drift, often traveling vast distances with the currents, until they wash up on a faraway beach. The sea heart (Entada gigas) is a very popular drift seed used in necklaces. Mucuna seeds (Mucuna holtonii), originating in Costa Rica, are another popular drift seed. They have a multi-layered appearance and are very durable.

Kekeore

The tiny donut-shaped tan-and-brown Kekeore seeds are derived from a local West African shrub and are used for food as well as for making jewelry. The small brown seeds of the Lead tree (Leucaena glauca) can be observed in combinations with other seeds as well as with seashells. In northern Transvaal areas of South Africa, this tree was mainly planted for firewood. It also prospers in West Africa.

Job's Tears

One of the most widely known and most commonly used seeds is produced by the so-called Job's tears plant (Coix lacrymajobi), a tall tropical plant of the Gramineae (grass) family, native to East Asia and Malaya. It can easily be cultivated in gardens as an annual and it prospers almost everywhere, from the United States to the New World tropics. The plant produces a fruit that is shaped like a teardrop, and its name is derived from the Biblical Job. It was one of the earliest domesticated plants, and some varieties are still harvested for the production of cereals or for medicinal purposes. The seeds are widely used as beads because they are perfect for stringing. When picked off the stem, the rounded end breaks off and leaves a hole. [33] The inside is very soft and easily pierced. Depending on the variety, the seeds' colors range from white to tan and gray. A Ghanaian sub-species produce white seeds.

Rosary Pea

Despite being very attractive, some seeds used for the manufacture of beads and jewelry are highly poisonous. One of the most well-known is Abrus precatorius, also

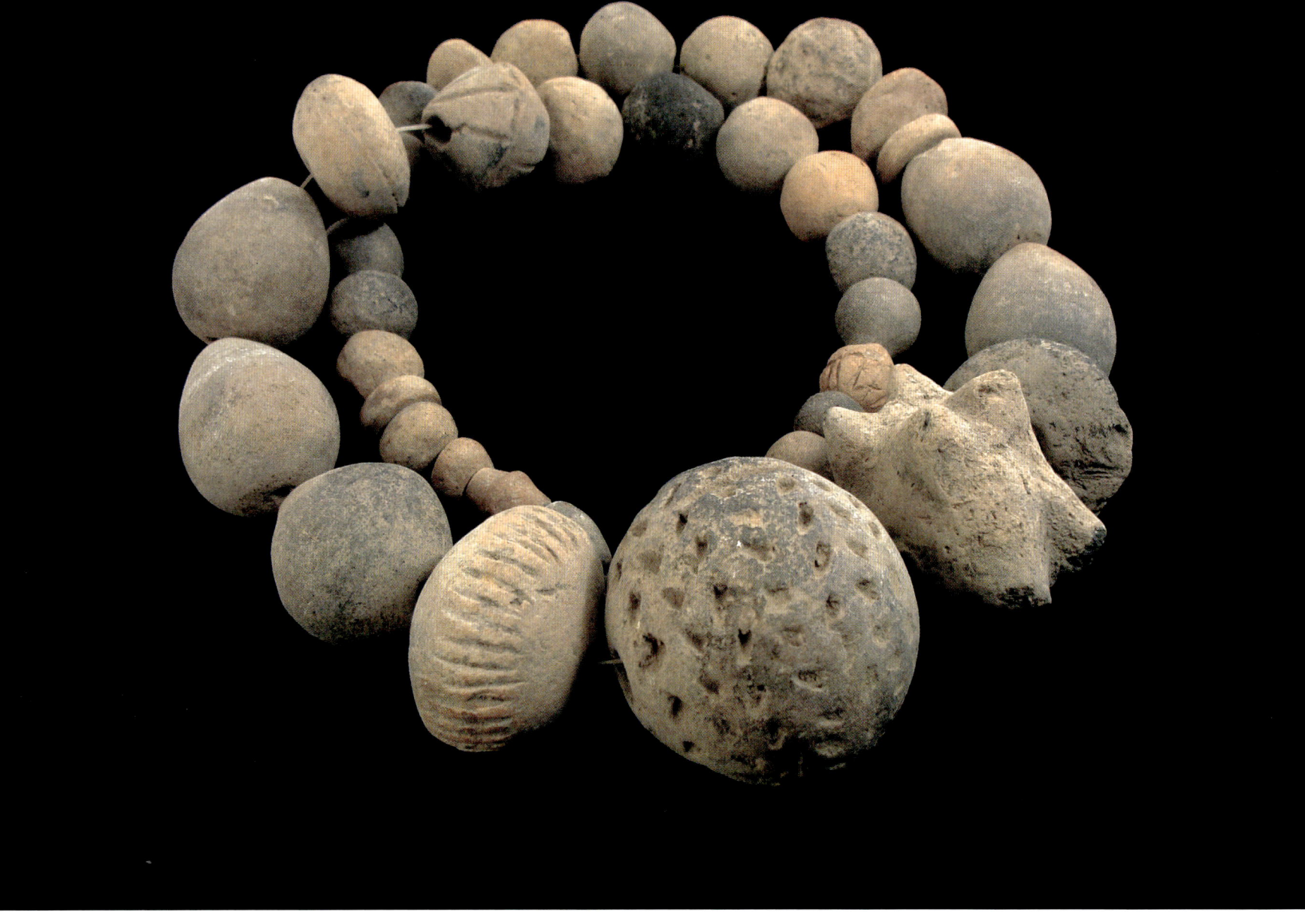

ABOVE *Old clay beads from the now-extinct Sao civilization of Chad and Sudan.*

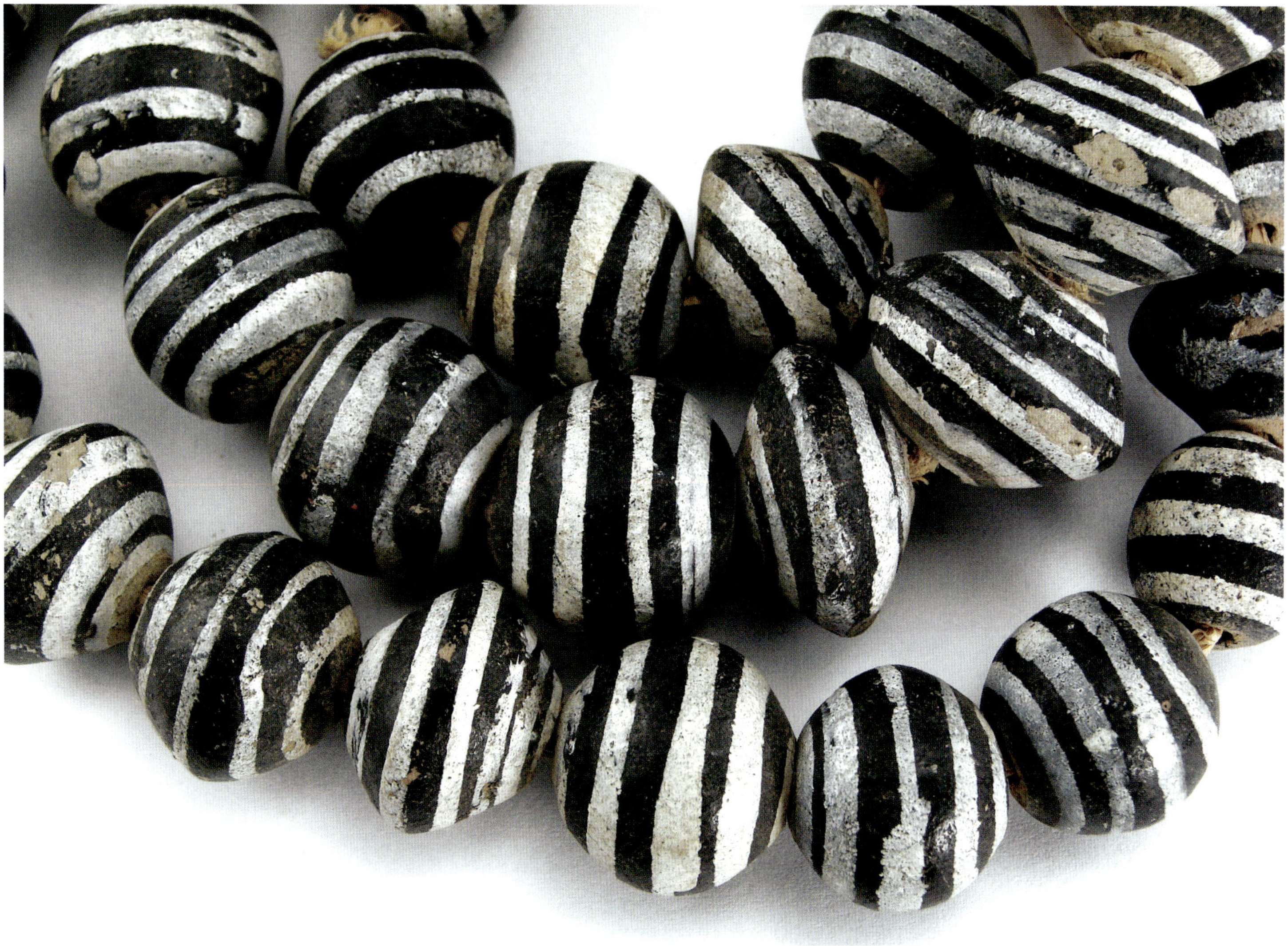

ABOVE Clay beads manufactured in the Sudan that have been decorated with patterns of spiraling bands (occasionally combined with dots) are made with water-soluble paints or slurries, possibly based on kaolin or clay.

RIGHT Contemporary clay beads decorated with what appear to be patterns applied by a transfer technique. These are being produced in Burkina Faso.

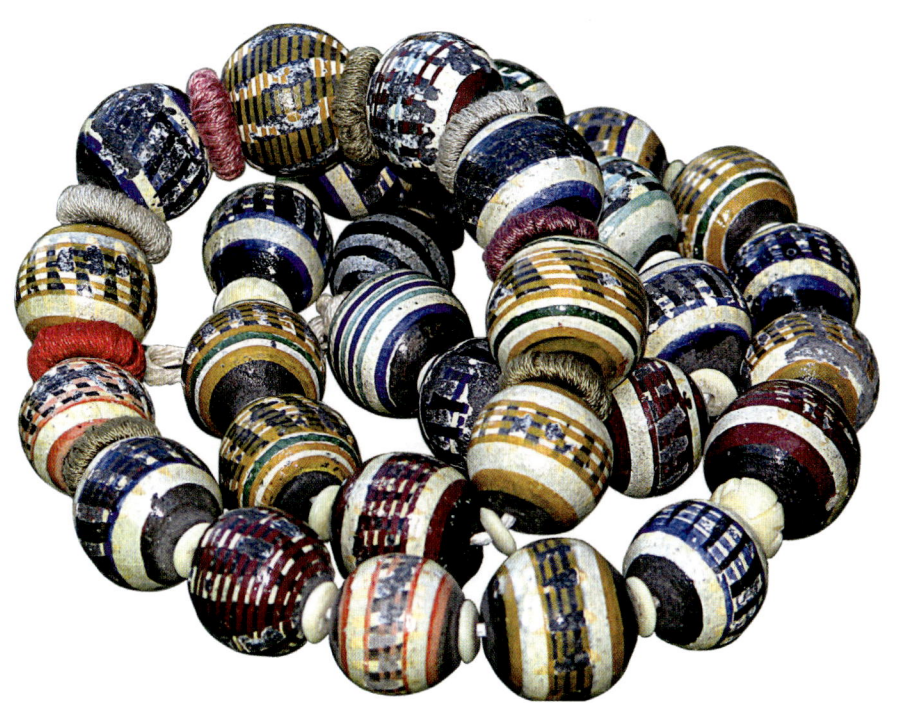

Amber, Clay and Beads Made from Plant Materials

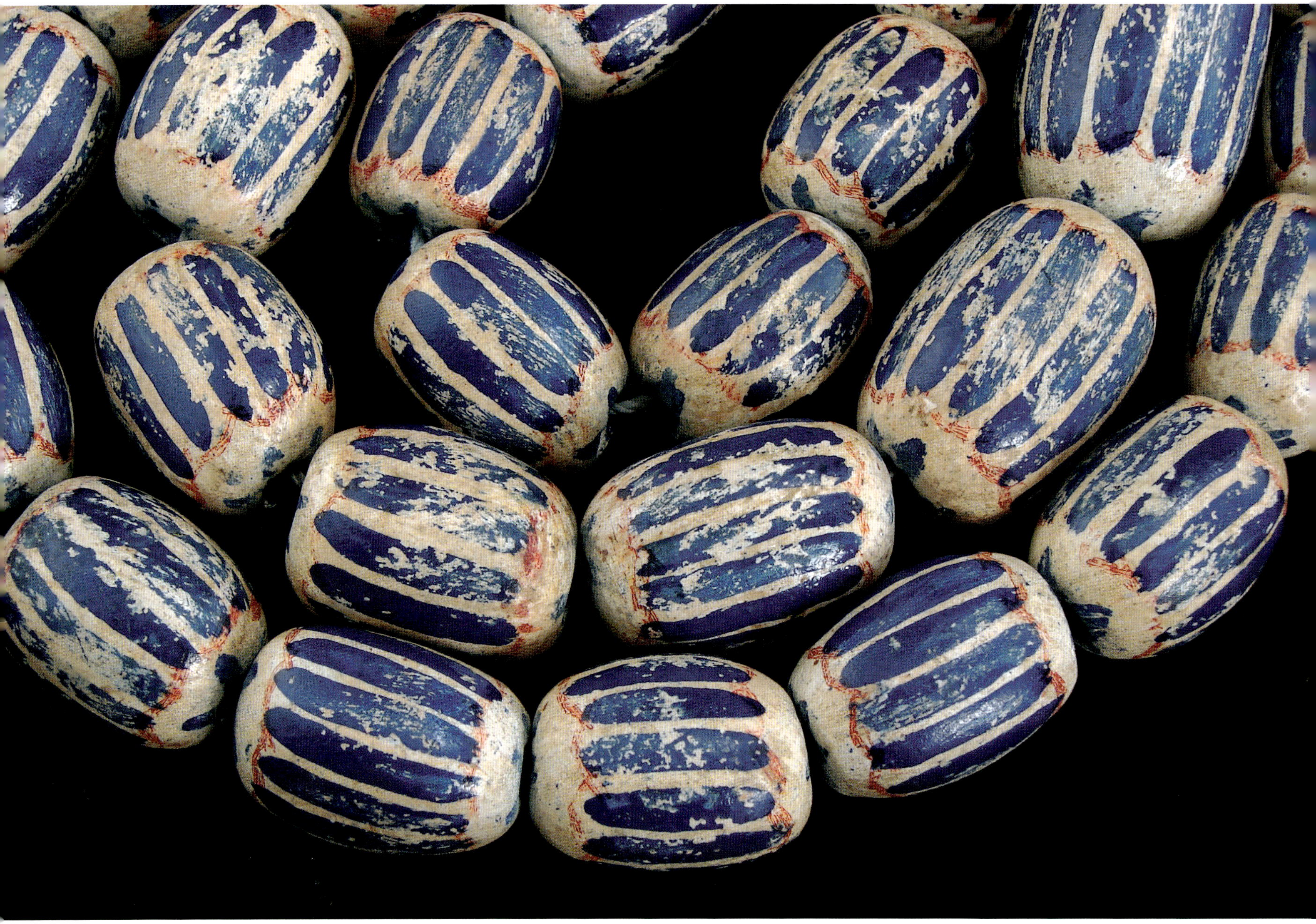

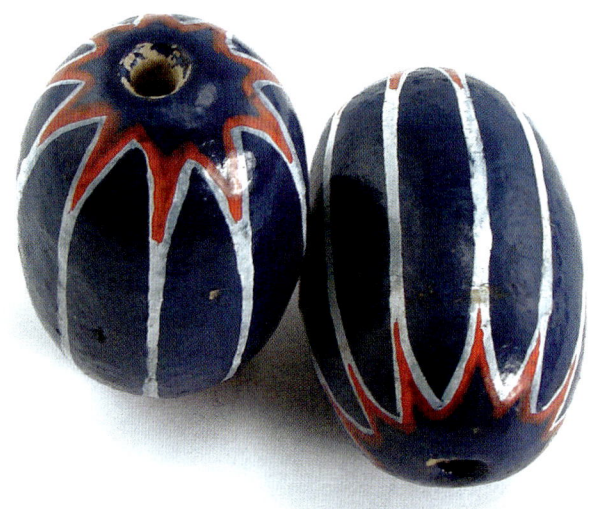

ABOVE AND LEFT *Several versions exist of painted clay imitations of Venetian chevron beads, such as the examples depicted above, which were manufactured in East Africa.*

70 ◆ Amber, Clay and Beads Made from Plant Materials

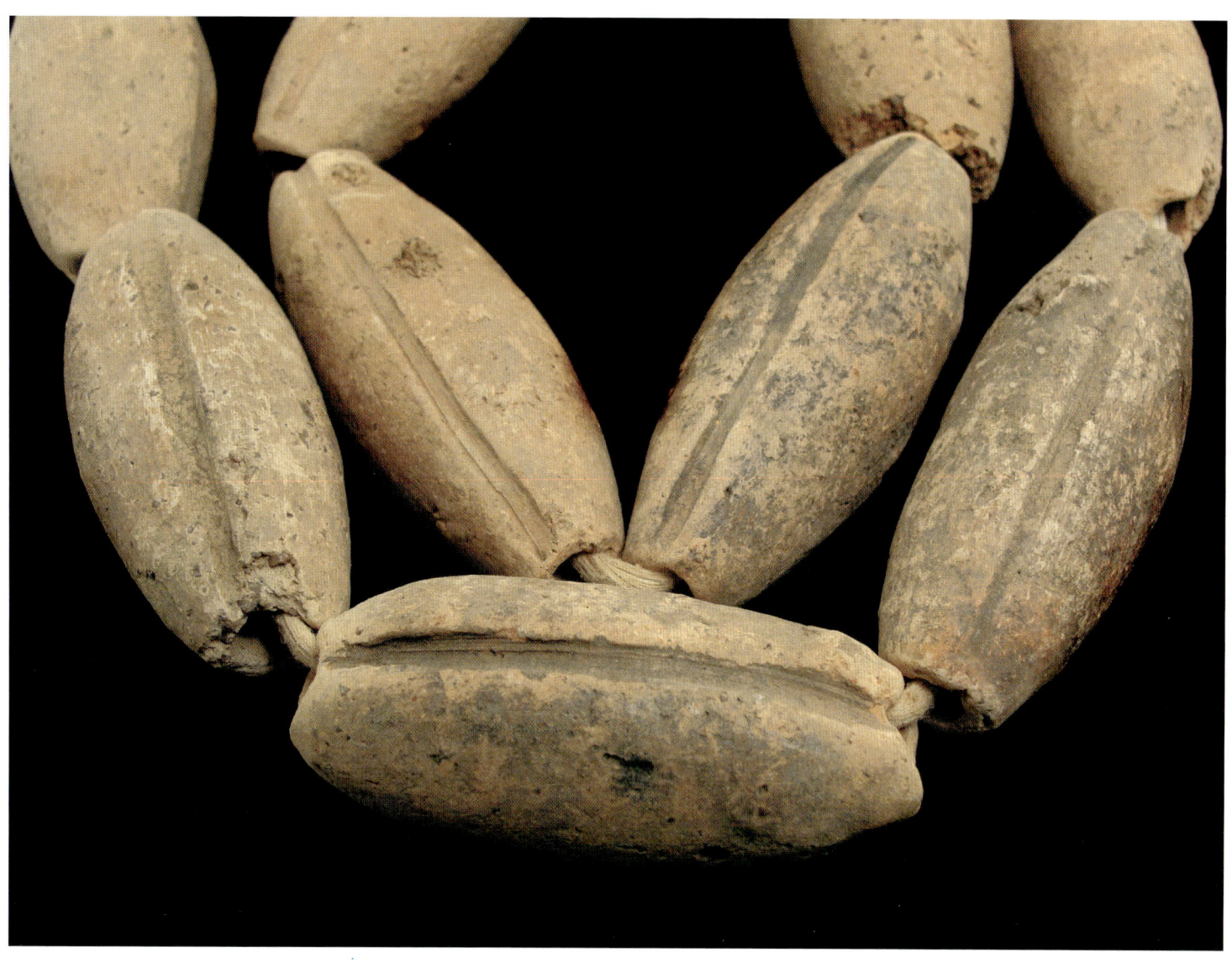

ABOVE *Ancient, perforated weights made of buff-colored clay, formerly used to weigh down fishing nets, are occasionally used as beads, charms or talismans.*

Amber, Clay and Beads Made from Plant Materials

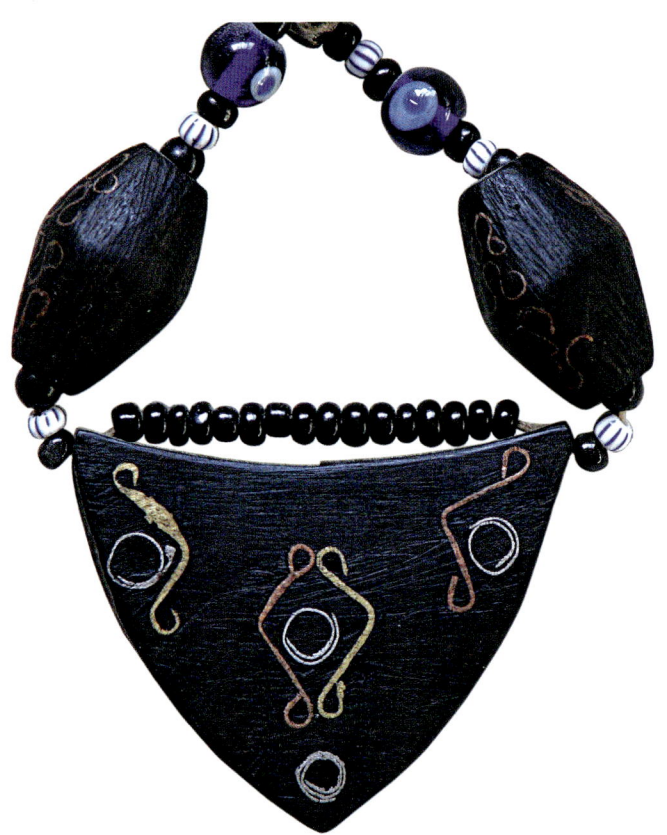

LEFT *Contemporary ebony wood pendant and beads from Mauritania, decorated with traditional inlaid motifs that are created by using copper, brass and silver wires.*

BELOW *Ebony wood beads are worn in separate strands or in combination with other beads. Mauritanian silversmiths traditionally decorate ebony wood beads, often with elaborate inlaid patterns created of twisted silver wire.*

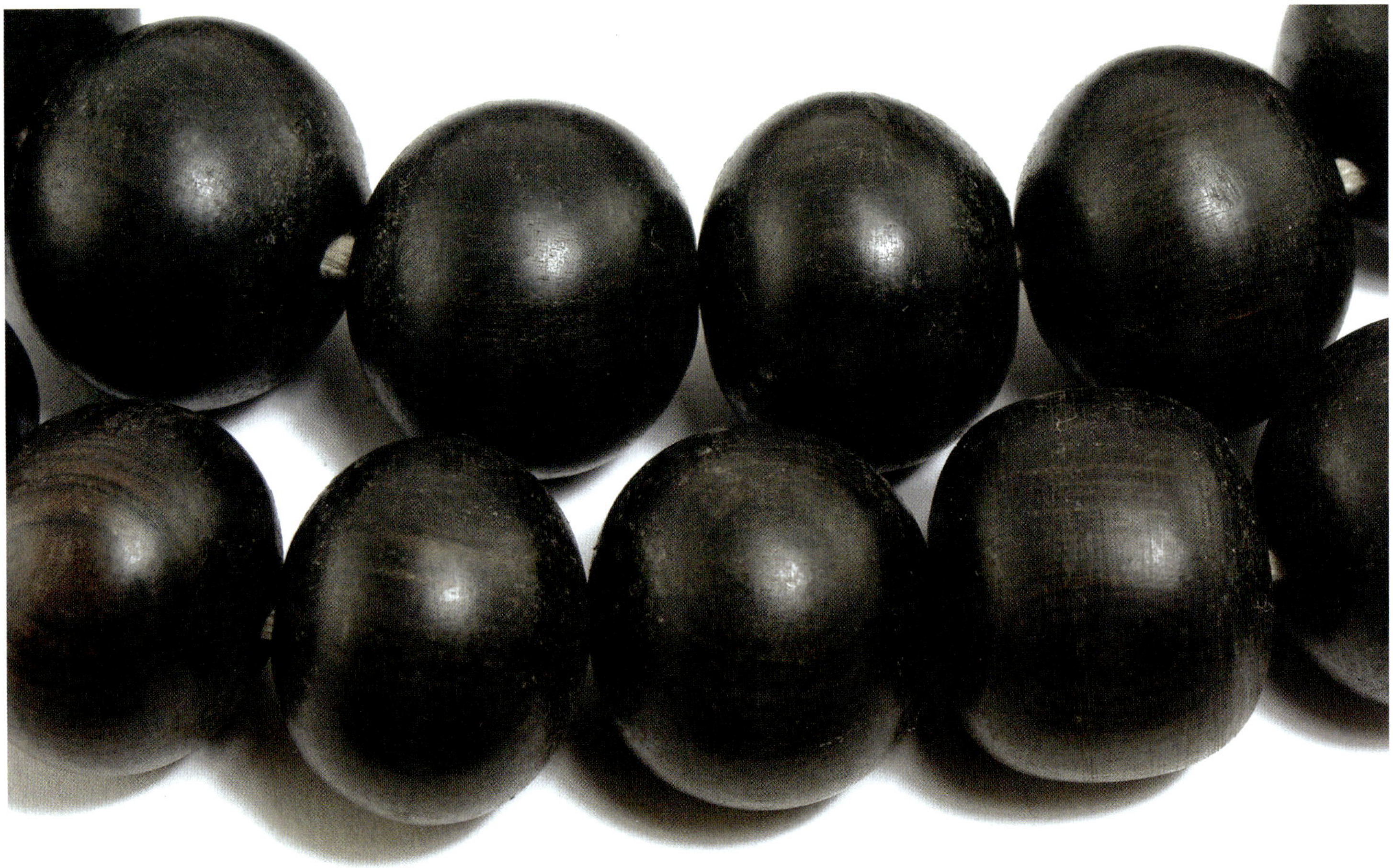

known as the rosary pea or crab eye. It is a small oval seed, bright scarlet in color, with a jet-black spot surrounding the area where it was attached to the tree. Once the seed coat is broken it is highly toxic and can cause severe gastroenteritis, leading to dehydration and shock. Ingestion of even very small amounts can be lethal.

Coconut Palm

Almost any part of a plant can be used to manufacture beads and jewelry. Leaves, stems, bark, roots and petals have all been used, although beads made of colorful and durable seeds, fruits and wood are the most common. In Ghana, young men fashion beads from bamboo and give them to girls they like, and if the girl likes the boy, she will wear his beads.

In West Africa, Guinean necklaces comprised of thin, ground, perforated disks manufactured from the shells of the coconut or palm nut are very popular. Coconuts are the fruit of the coconut palm (Cocos nucifera) and the thin disk-shaped beads made from them are commonly called coconut heishi, although the literal meaning of this term is "shell" and, as noted earlier, it refers specifically to pieces of shell which have been drilled and shaped into beads by grinding. More and more frequently, however, the term heishi (pronounced hee-shee) is used to refer to hand-made disk-shaped beads made of any natural material. [34]

Scented Paste Beads

Spices and aromatic products—such as flower petals, perfumes and incense—used in the preparation of scented pastes were an integral part of the merchandise transported on camels' backs from North Africa to sub-Saharan Africa. Special necklaces comprised entirely of scented paste beads, or combined with amulets, gold, silver, glass beads and cowry shells, can be observed in West African countries, worn in various combinations according to local traditions. Scented paste necklaces are believed to have aphrodisiac properties and to have the power of seduction and conjuration when enhanced by magic. Beads made of scented pastes, resins and woods, perfumes and spices are believed to have strong magical properties, and they are highly appreciated and sought after throughout North and sub-Saharan Africa.

Tunisia

The following information is based on research conducted by M.J. Opper during the 1990s. In Tunisia, scented geraniums are cultivated in large quantities to serve as one

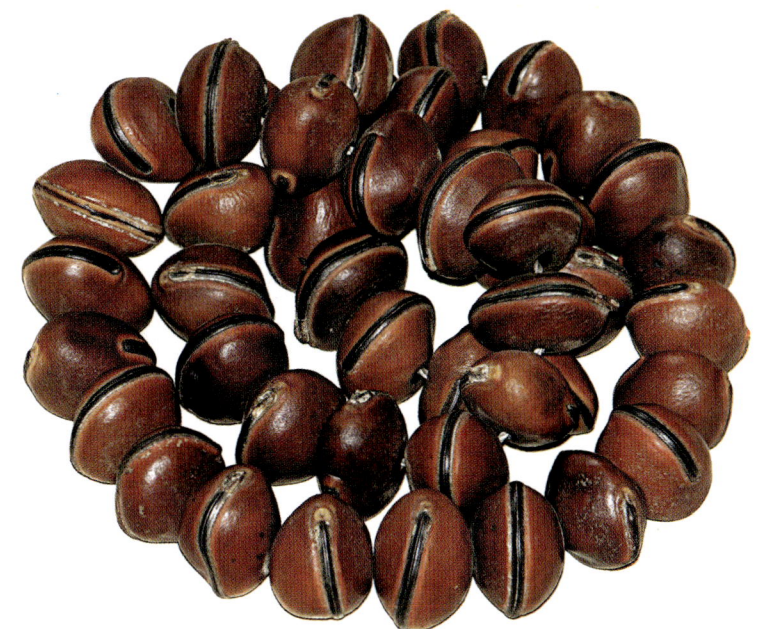

ABOVE *Sea beans are seeds from a variety of trees and vines that fall into waterways and drift with the currents, often over vast distances, before they wash up on a beach. These drift seeds can be found on beaches all over the globe and are often fashioned into beads.*

BELOW *Kekeore or coffee bean seeds are found in many West African countries; besides being used as food they are also threaded into necklaces and worn for adornment.*

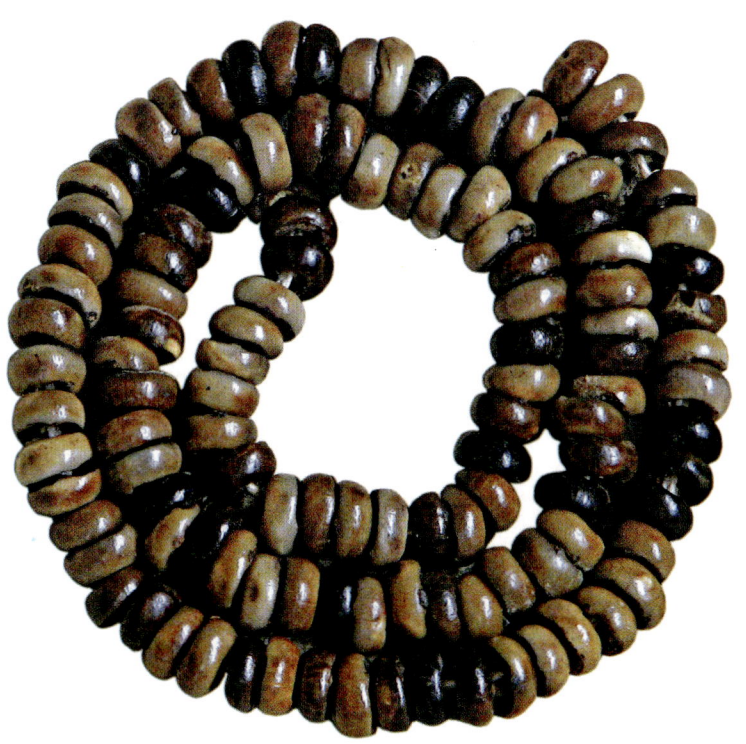

Amber, Clay and Beads Made from Plant Materials

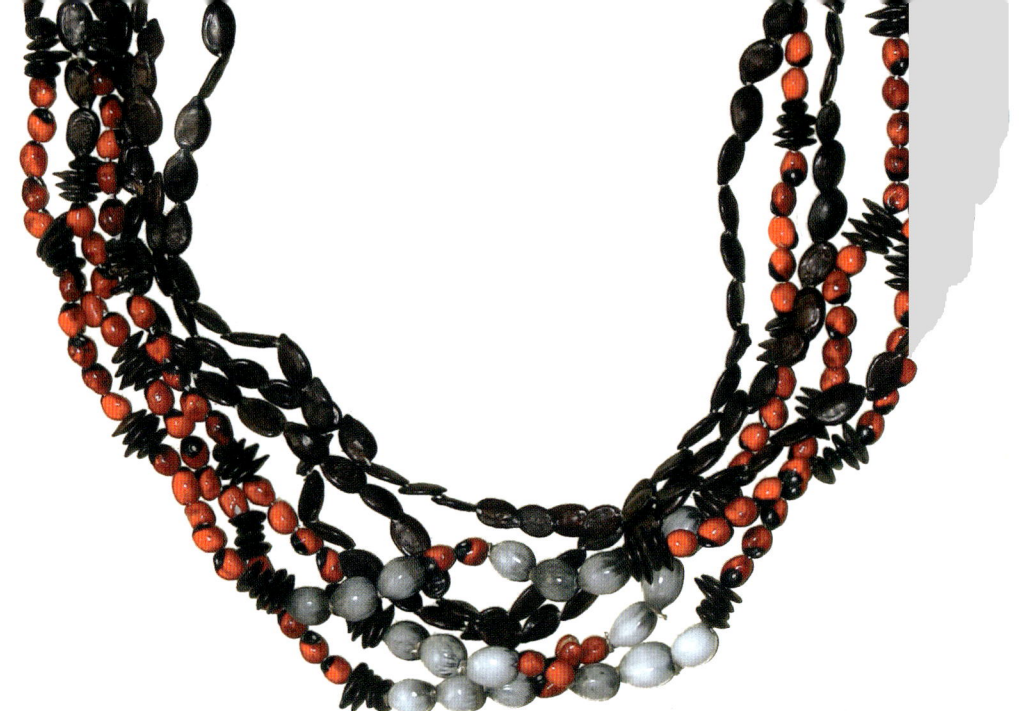

ABOVE *Contemporary necklace from Senegal comprised of a variety of seeds such as the shiny gray Job's tears (Coix lacrymajobi) and the small red and black, highly poisonous crab eye or rosary pea (Abrus precatorius), a perennial vine belonging to the pea family. The toxin contained in the raw seed is similar to snake poison and is used for treating snakebites. It is believed to be rendered harmless when boiled. In some cultures, powdered seeds boiled in milk were considered a tonic and aphrodisiac.*

of the ingredients of so-called amber paste from which beads and amulets are being manufactured. The necklaces made from these beads are called skhab. One of the many recipes for making scented paste includes pounded wood from the Aquilaria agallocha tree, called q'mari. A quantity of ground wood is mixed with ambergris and diluted in rose water. Pulverized fragments of amber paste are commonly also added for their magical properties. The paste is left to settle for several days in order to permit the wood to absorb the rose water. More rose water is then added, pounding is resumed, and the operation is repeated several times. The resulting paste is formed into the desired shape and left to dry. Once dry it is finished off with a rasp and a chisel.

In Tunis, the word "skhab" is used for a particular type of cross-belt that women wear from the shoulder to the hip. It is composed of a series of small light shields (peltas) similar to those once used by foot soldiers in ancient Greece. The beads are made of amber paste and shaped to resemble three-pointed crescents similar to Thracian and other buckles that are depicted in antique images of the Amazons. Amber paste is also often used for the manufacture of scented prayer bead strands, which are highly prized by Muslims. When used, these chaplets take on a velvety polish, which adds to the charm of the vapors they emit.

Benzoin derived from the Ficus benjamina tree, oil from unripened almonds and resin from the Mastic tree can also be used as ingredients, as well as cloves, which are sometimes combined with nutmeg and inexpensive commercial perfumes. Beads manufactured from these ingredients have a more rustic appearance and a stronger odor.

In southern Tunisia, the skhabs can be composed of one or several strands of cloves, sometimes embellished with pompons of dark red wool, cowry shells and coral and silver beads. Depending on regional tradition, scented paste beads

RIGHT *The designs and styles of scented paste necklaces differ from region to region, as do their ingredients. Shown to the right is an elaborate necklace from Mauritania, comprised of small seed bead-sized beads combined with large squares that are decorated with small glass beads of many different colors, with a piece of mirror glass at their centers to protect from the "evil eye." The necklace of red beads is also from Mauritania. These beads are often referred to as "Coral of Mauritania" because of their coral red color. The necklace of larger spherical brown beads interspersed with red and blue faceted Bohemian glass beads is of a type worn by women in Senegal. Nut grass corms emit a pleasant scent and are one of the natural ingredients used for making certain styles of scented paste beads.*

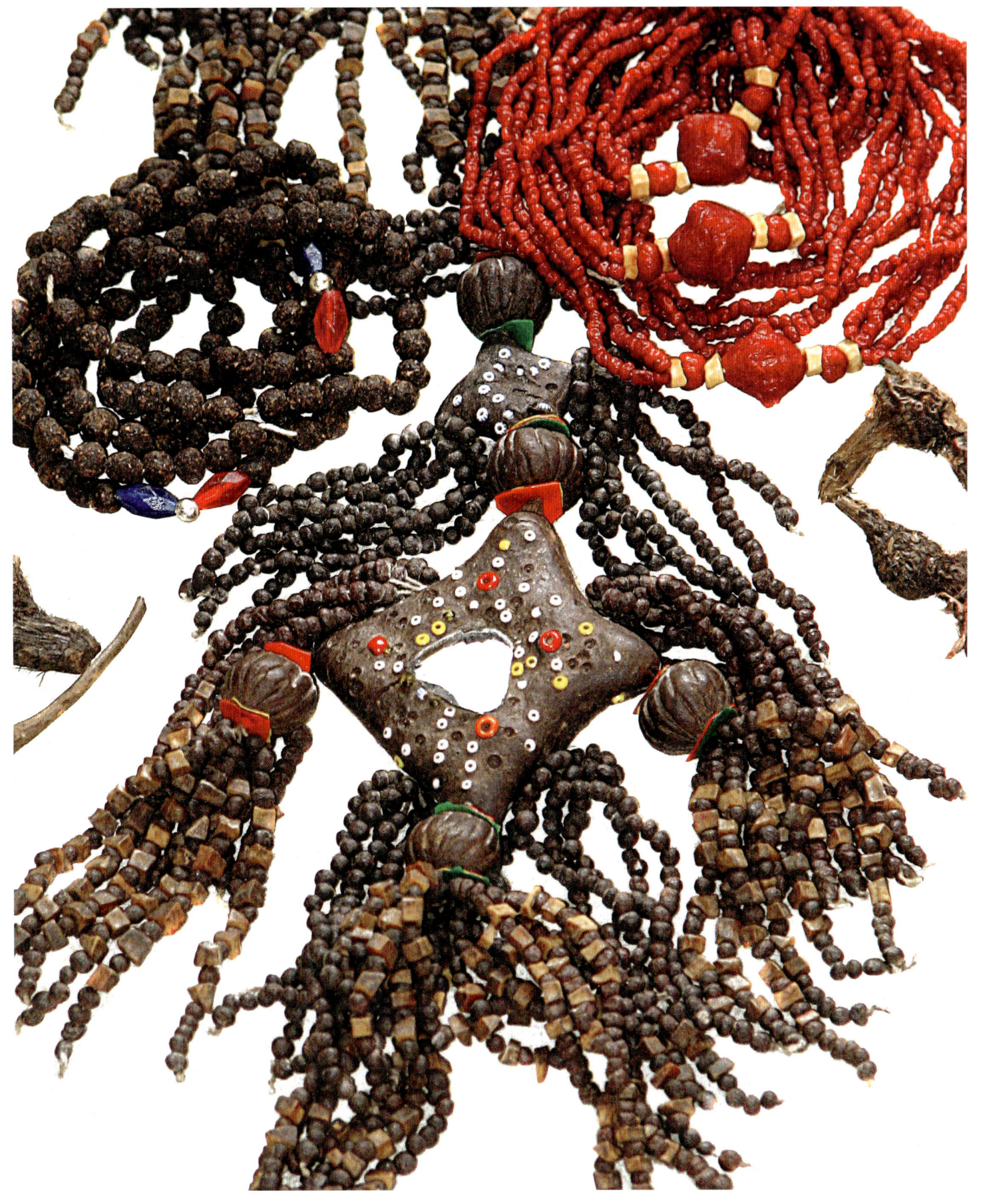

Amber, Clay and Beads Made from Plant Materials

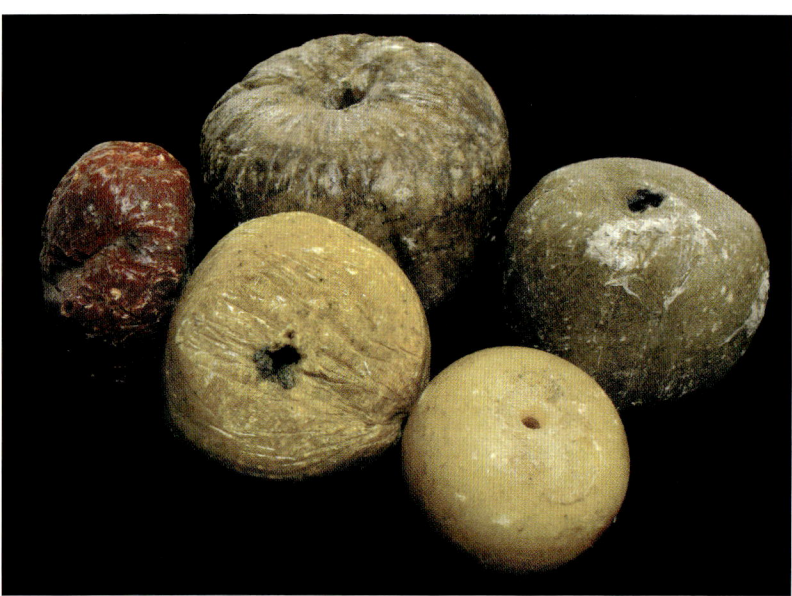

ABOVE *The beads depicted here are fashioned from beeswax. They come from Guinea-Bissau.*

can be inlaid with coral beads or pieces of coral, seeds, cowry shells and glass beads, or encased in silver amulet cases.

Algeria

Algerian skhabs are large, elaborate assemblages of multiple bead strands in which scented paste beads are combined with gold filigreed or silver ornaments and branch coral. The beads can be round, flat or square, heart-shaped or triangular. The composition of the scented paste used in their manufacture can include agalloch wood, rose petals, cloves, nutmeg, saffron, rose and orange essence and ambergris. The bead maker pounds the seeds and cloves and kneads the mixture with a small amount of saffron water. When the paste is fairly dry, it is divided into small pyramid-shaped pieces, which are pierced when almost hardened to allow a thread to pass through.

Wedding necklaces in southern Algeria are very delicate compositions, comprised of one or several strands of round and square beads, the scented beads alternating with coral, gold or gold-plated metal and occasionally with a "Hand of Fatima" pendant. A sequence of a specific number of scented beads is usually followed by one coral bead or by a number of round gold beads.

Morocco

Necklaces can be made specifically to cure medical conditions. Pastes for treating skin conditions contain a mixture of corrigiola, cloves, rose petals, myrtle leaves, benzoin, small seeds and some liquid perfume. In Morocco, necklaces composed of a combination of scented paste beads, glass beads, and spherical gold or silver beads, often combined with a pendant of silver or gold at their center, are believed to cure headaches. Women also wear clove necklaces for forty days after they have given birth.

In Morocco, Berber women wear necklaces comprised of scented beads that are capped with gold or silver and often have a large round gold or silver bead or a "Hand of Fatima" pendant at their center. In southern Morocco, beads made of agalloch wood are worn in combination with scented paste beads, or gold, silver or amazonite beads. Small spheres formed of amber paste are wrapped in pieces of colored fabric and sewn onto women's clothing.

Mauritania

Scented paste necklaces from Mauritania are commonly composed of multiple strands of small brownish-red paste beads interspersed with larger beads of the same substance. Round or star-shaped pieces cut from sheets of soft plastic, in green, yellow and red are often added. A unique method of using scented paste in Mauritania protects the already well-worn perforations of ancient and highly valued glass beads. It is evidenced by the presence of amber paste which has been used to fill in the perforation and then re-pierced. Further protection is often achieved by fastening metal caps to both bead ends.

Mali

In Mali, scented paste beads are made from the seeds of the Dentarium microcarpum tree (local names are dank, danha, doli and danh). The fruit cores are pounded and sifted to obtain a powder. Hot water is added and the mixture is boiled until it thickens. The resulting paste is shaped into small round beads that are perforated with a needle and set aside to dry. Glass beads can be added when assembling these beads, and the resulting necklaces are often erroneously described as myrrh necklaces by collectors. It is traditional for married women to wear multiple joined strands as waist belts beneath their skirts.

Senegal

In Senegal, butter and Indian perfume are often added as fragrances. Strands are worn around the waist, either separately or combined with strands of glass beads. Shark vertebrae are at times added to these assemblages for their protective properties.

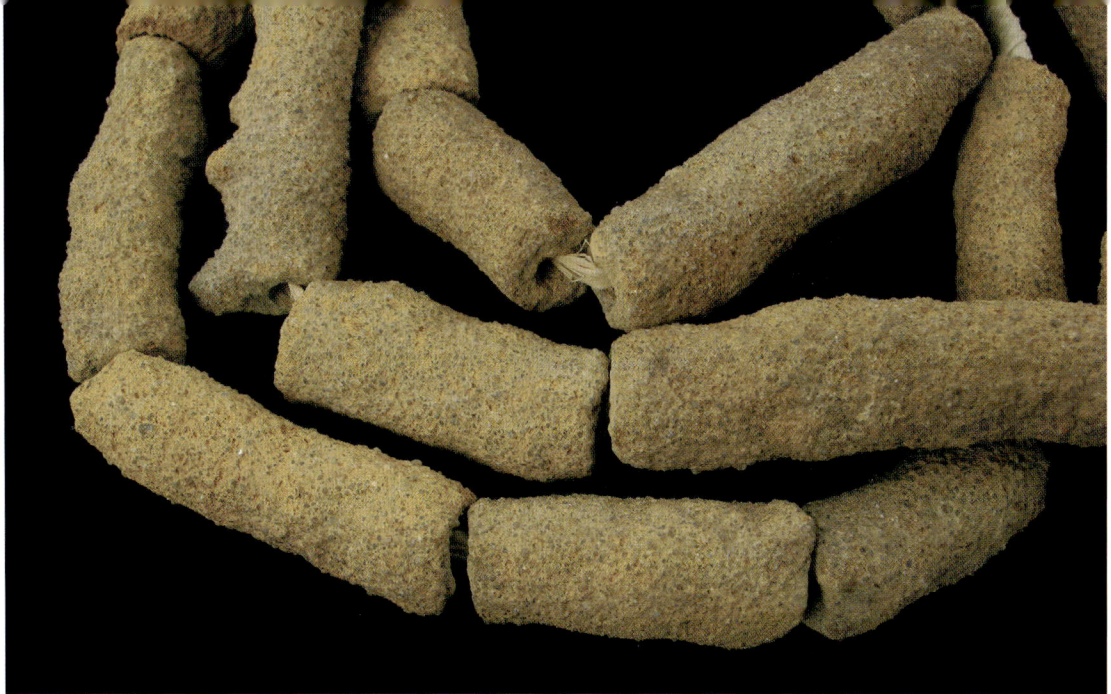

ABOVE *In the recent past, necklaces reportedly originating from Nigeria were comprised of what appear to be broken segments of termite galleries. It could not be established whether these beads were strung and worn as adornments, or whether they were assembled for the collectors' market simply because they are free to anyone who cares to pick them out of termite mounds, have a different look, and can be worn like beads. They have strong walls, consisting of coarse quartz sand and clay, materials which are gathered by the termites from the environment and compacted and shaped into tube-like walkways for protection against ants. The knobs observed on some of these segments were originally parts of bridges between galleries.*

Nut Grass Corms

Apart from being used to manufacture scented pastes to be shaped into beads, parts of certain plants are also used in their original forms, serving a similar purpose. The fragrant tubers or corms of nut grass (Cyperus rotundus L.), a herbaceous perennial and member of the sedge family, are crudely carved, perforated, strung and worn as necklaces or waist belts by Senegalese women. Nut grass tubers are reported to possess medicinal properties, and a concoction of the roots and tubers is considered an excellent antidote to all poisons. Herbal remedies including nut grass are used to treat high blood pressure, colic, cold, flu and fevers. In India, nut grass is used in commercial hair and skin care products and the oil extracted from this plant is used for making perfumes. [35]

Recycled Plastic Beads

Plastic beads are being manufactured by a small cooperative of Hausa women in Kumasi, Ghana, by recycling worn out plastic basins and other discarded plastic containers. [35a] In fact, there are a number of community projects—such as Life in Africa Foundation in Kampala and Gulu, Uganda—which manufacture beads from recycled scrap paper, magazine covers, cigarette and cereal packages, drink box containers, dated and misprinted company brochures, old poster ads and calendars. One of these initiatives, called BeadforLife, invests all profits in community development projects. Many of the bead makers involved are women from the Acholi tribe who were forced to leave their homes in northern Uganda. Beginning in December 2005, a project initiated by Voices for Global Change and called Paper to Pearls has sponsored beading cooperatives in five camps located in the Gulu District of the Northern Region. It also works with a group of widows and orphans in the town of Gulu. Thin strips of paper cut from discarded calendars or colorful magazines are rolled by hand and secured with glue. A coat of varnish is applied to achieve a glossy and durable surface before the beads are assembled to form necklaces. Paper beads come in a variety of shapes and cheerful colors. [35b]

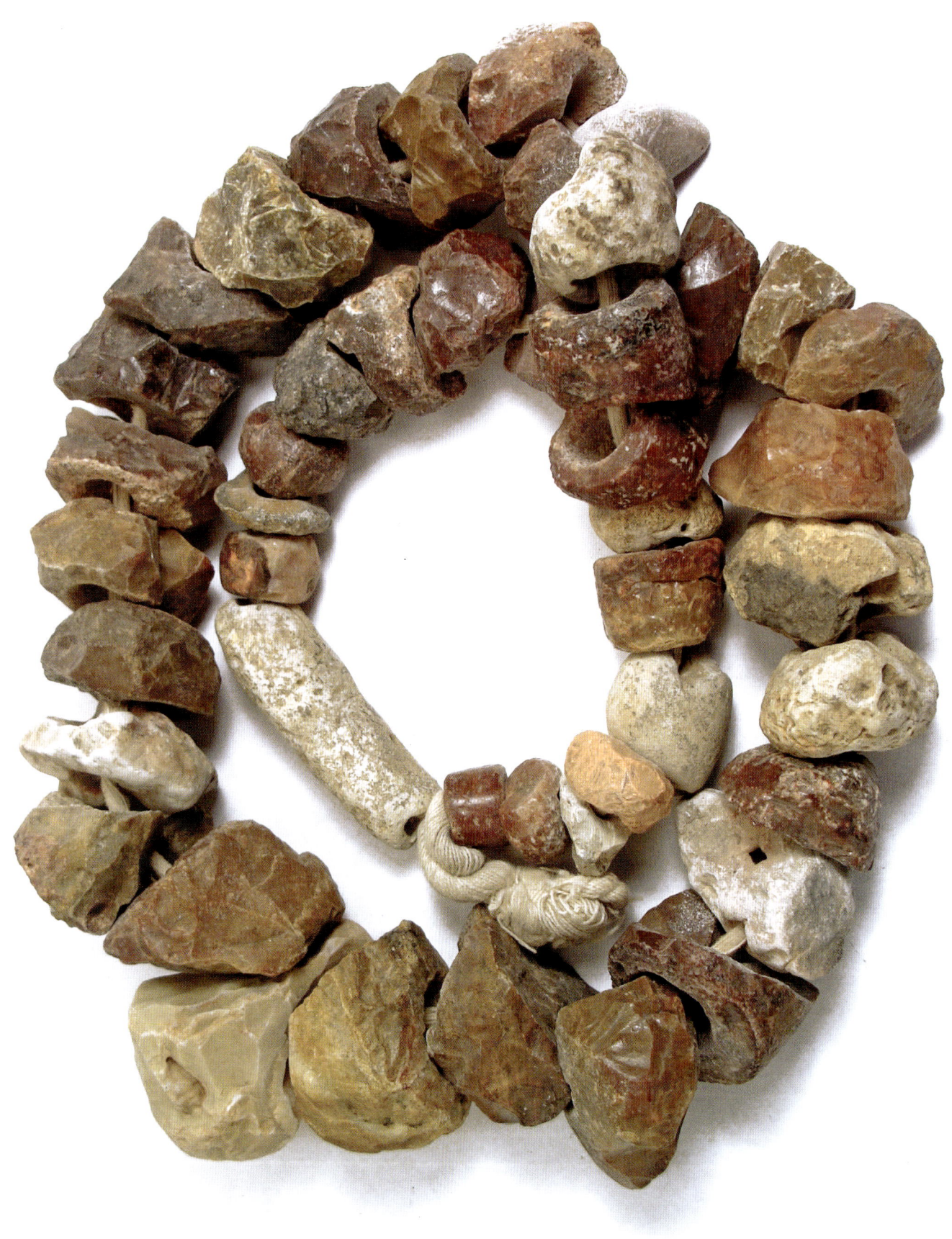

ABOVE *Large hand-tooled stone beads. Their exact age and region of origin are uncertain.*

Stone Beads

The First Stone Beads

As early as the Paleolithic period (about 40,000 years ago), humans began to express themselves by creating cave paintings, carving circles and lines on bones for decorative and magical purposes, and manufacturing objects for personal adornment—such as beads, which also served as status symbols, for ceremonial purposes, for burying with the dead and as offerings to the gods. Since it was readily available in the natural environment, stone was one of the earliest materials to be used for bead making. [36] In Africa, stone beads fashioned from amazonite and greenstone, quartz, granite, gneiss, jasper and bauxite have long been produced and widely traded, some of them for thousands of years. Many of the stone beads that are being excavated in the Niger Bend region of Mali and in the vicinities of the ancient cities of Djenne and Timbuktu reached Africa via the trans-Saharan trade routes and some came from regions as distant as India and China. [37]

The first stone beads were produced with simple stone tools, such as mallets, hammers and drill bits manufactured from a hard stone like chalcedony, which according to the Mohs hardness scale has a hardness of 6 to 7. (In 1812, the German mineralogist Friedrich Mohs devised a system for measuring the hardness of rocks by selecting common minerals and testing their resistance to scratching or abrasion. The Mohs scale ranges from 1 to 10, 10 denoting the hardest, the diamond, which can be used to scratch all other known minerals. Mohs established that talc is the softest mineral. It can be scratched by a fingernail (hardness of 2.5) or by a knife blade of an approximate hardness of 5.5. Feldspar can scratch a knife blade and window glass, and so forth.)

The bead makers chose pieces of homogeneous rocks that were free of flaws, cracks or inclusions. The pieces of rock were broken into smaller fragments and crudely shaped into the desired forms and sizes by chipping and pecking with stone hammers and mallets, commonly fashioned from chalcedony. Perforations in the beads were created by drilling, using chalcedony drill bits in hand-operated bow drills, or by punching or pecking, starting from both ends and working towards the center until the two openings met. This method of making a bead hole always results in tapered openings that are widest at the bead's ends and decrease in diameter towards the center, where often they do not align precisely, which may cause an obstruction when the beads are strung. The beads received their final shapes by being ground on a grinding stone, commonly made of sandstone, of a size that could easily be held in one hand.

Great numbers of ancient stone beads are found in the desert sands of Mali, where the archaeological sites in the region of the Niger River Valley are considered to represent a continuum of civilizations from the Neolithic period to the 18th century, and constitute virtually the only known source of information pertaining to the great civilizations that once existed there. For centuries, the upper inland Niger Delta of the Middle Niger between modern Mopti and Segou has been an important crossroads for trade. Historical sources also provide evidence of the central trading role of the community of Djenne (alternatively spelled Jenné). In fact, the mud architecture of Djenne, with its distinctive Sudanic style, is a legacy of early trade ties with North Africa. Insights gained from scientific excavations conducted during the 1970s and 1980s indicate that earlier assumptions concerning the development of long-distance trade only after the arrival of the Arabs in North Africa in the 7th and 8th centuries were incorrect. The archaeology of Djenne and of the surrounding area provides conclusive evidence for an earlier, independent and indigenous growth of trade.

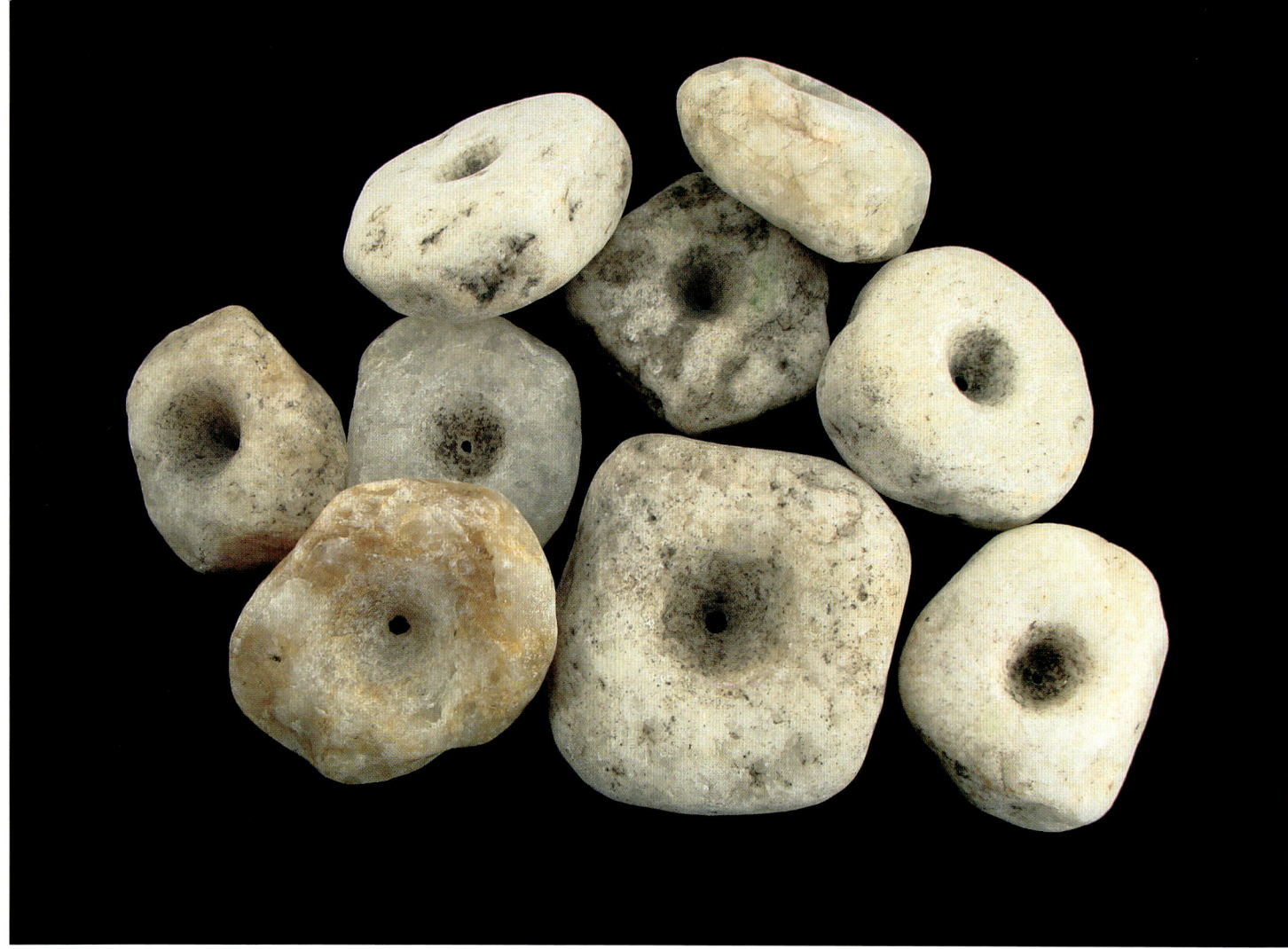

ABOVE *In ancient times stone beads like the specimens above were produced by using simple stone tools, such as mallets, hammers and drill bits made from hard stone. Bow drills were used to make the perforations.*

A total of 633 pieces weighing almost 140 kilograms, the great majority being sandstone, were recovered during the 1970s, during excavations conducted in old Djenne and in a number of ancient settlements in the vicinity. Besides basalt beads, they include Hombori "marble" (granitoid stone) beads, quartz pebbles with and without facets, several styles and varieties of quartz beads, pieces of hematite and a rectangular hematite pendant, fragments of a basalt ring, a carnelian bead believed to have been imported from India and a granite hand axe. Most of the other stone objects were classified as belonging in the category of household utensils or tools, such as pestles and stone hammers. Other artifacts were identified as ritual objects. [38] These included a number of different types of round stones which were consecrated with chicken or goat blood in order to bring rain, in a ceremony called toru which is still practiced today.

Granite and Gneiss

Although very similar in appearance, gneiss and granite are considered to be two different minerals. Most geologists define granite as an igneous rock that is composed of quartz and a variety of other minerals, such as feldspar, biotite, muscovite and hornblende. Overall appearance, colors, and properties depend on the proportion of the different minerals present. The colors of quartz range from transparent clear colorless to transparent or translucent milky white or smoky gray. Quartz has a hardness of 7. The color of alkali feldspar varies from a semi-translucent or opaque off-white, to tan, pink or brick red. Its hardness ranges from 6 to 6.5. Gneiss is defined as a roughly foliated or banded metamorphic rock consisting largely of granular minerals such as quartz. Due to its high quartz content, Gneiss has a hardness of 7. Its colors vary from opaque black and white

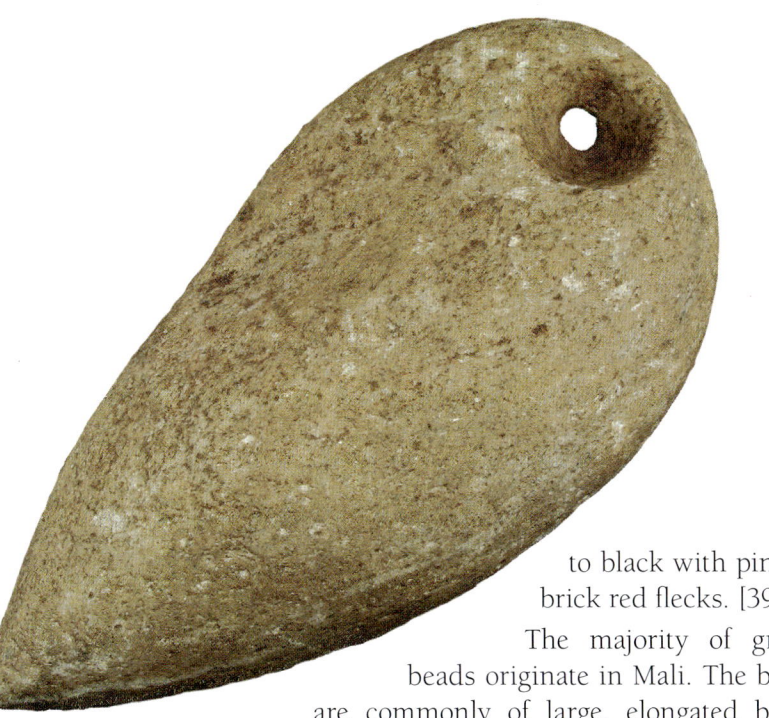

LEFT Arrowhead-shaped pendant with bow-drilled, hourglass-shaped perforation.

BELOW Ancient stone beads from Mali, with characteristic hourglass-shaped perforations.

to black with pink or brick red flecks. [39]

The majority of gneiss beads originate in Mali. The beads are commonly of large, elongated barrel shapes and show evidence of hand-drilling and finishing. The oldest specimens are believed to date back to the 13th to 16th centuries, but beads are still being produced with traditional methods. An examination of the bead perforation can help determine a bead's age since ancient beads commonly have large perforations that are smooth from wear at both ends whereas newly manufactured beads often have small crisp holes and also lack the well-polished appearance and patina of the older beads.

Although beads and pendants manufactured from granite are generally associated with the Dogon people of Mali, in fact both granite and gneiss were used interchangeably. Due to the source materials being so similar in appearance, it is often difficult to tell them apart. Granite beads are characterized by the presence of various hues of dark and light grays mixed with specks of off-white, pink or brick-red. Like gneiss beads, the granite beads found in West Africa are almost always of tubular shapes, with perforations that are hand-drilled from both ends, meeting at the center.

Dogon Ancestor Stones

The Dogon people, who originate in the Niger Bend area and live on the cliffs of the Bandiagara Plateau in the

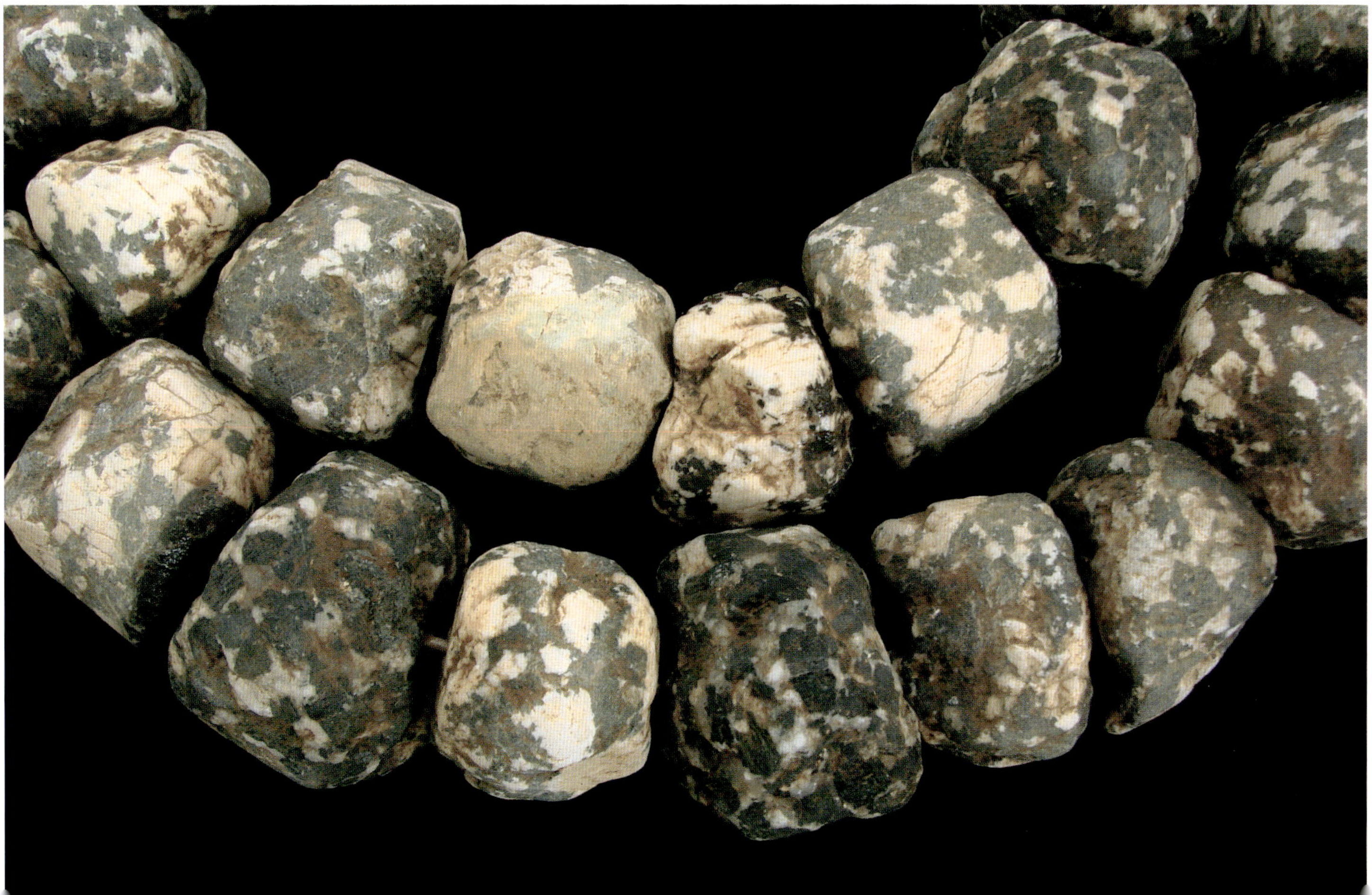

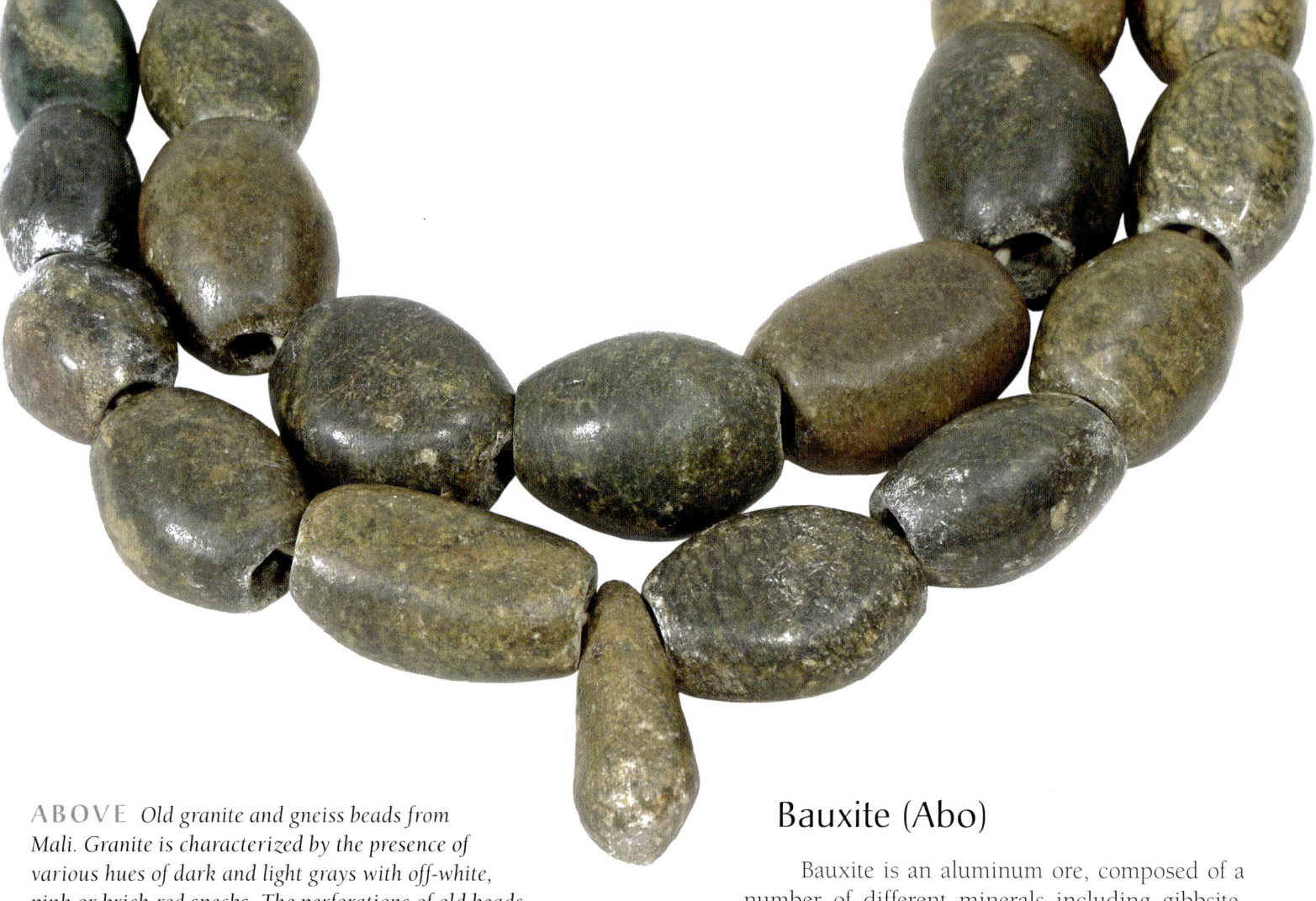

ABOVE *Old granite and gneiss beads from Mali. Granite is characterized by the presence of various hues of dark and light grays with off-white, pink or brick-red specks. The perforations of old beads were created by drilling from both ends, and are often not properly aligned where they meet.*

central region of Mali, use ceremonial and sacred stones, called douge, in their everyday life as well as in their rituals. The Dogon spiritual leader, called Hogon, and his assistants wear iron necklaces comprised of forged lengths of iron connected by chain links, with round, smooth and well polished stones of granite, gneiss or quartz. These stones are either encased in a cage-like device, wrapped in and connected to the necklace with a plain strip of forged iron, or perforated and threaded onto thin iron links that connect to the rest of the necklace. The sacred stones of the Dogon are attributed to the Tellum, a culture believed to have inhabited the area before the arrival of the Dogon. The Dogon retrieve these stones from the ancient graves found in the cliff faces of the Bandiagara Plateau.

Bauxite (Abo)

Bauxite is an aluminum ore, composed of a number of different minerals including gibbsite, boehmite and the clay mineral kaolinite. The primary sources of bauxite in Africa are large blanket deposits located in Guinea and Ghana. Bauxite is important to the Ghanaian economy, and the Akosombo Dam on the world's largest man-made lake—Lake Volta—was created in the 1960s for the purpose of providing electricity for smelting bauxite. [40]

In its raw state, bauxite is found in various shades of brown, ranging from dark red-brown to yellow-brown hues. Residents of Akyem Abompe, a small village in the mountainous region to the north of Accra and situated in the vicinity of Ghana's largest bauxite deposit, use a small portion of this attractive material, locally called abo, for bead making. The local artisans purchase raw chunks of bauxite from the miners. The material looks like unformed clay. Bead makers break it into smaller fragments and, using knives and other sharp instruments, painstakingly chip or knap the pieces to fashion the desired sizes and shapes. The perforations are drilled with bow and spindle drills, using a process that has been applied for thousands of years. After the frag-

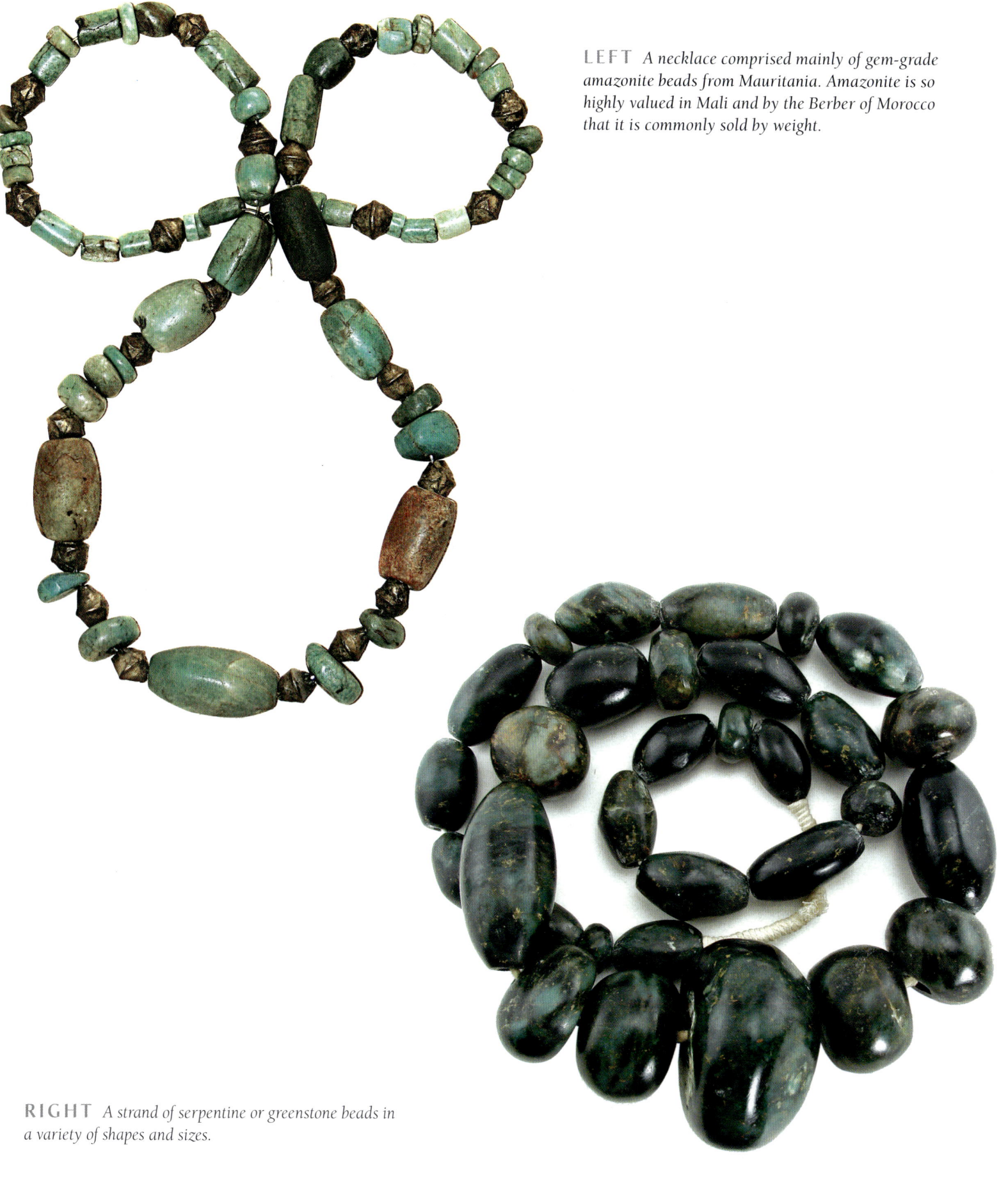

LEFT *A necklace comprised mainly of gem-grade amazonite beads from Mauritania. Amazonite is so highly valued in Mali and by the Berber of Morocco that it is commonly sold by weight.*

RIGHT *A strand of serpentine or greenstone beads in a variety of shapes and sizes.*

Stone Beads

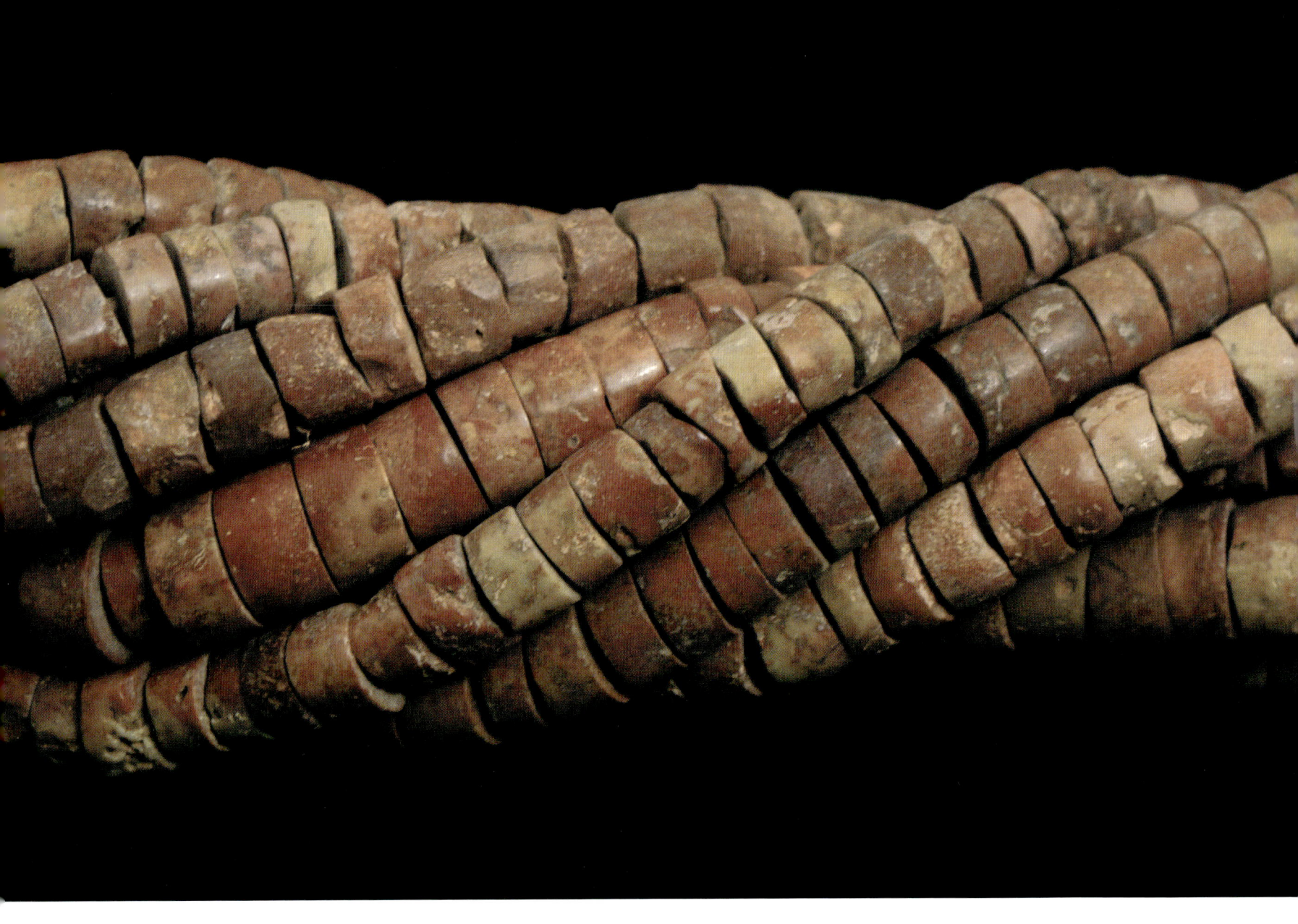

ABOVE *These smooth and evenly-sized bauxite beads—locally called abo, and manufactured by residents of Akyem Abompe, a small village north of Accra, Ghana—are produced using a variation of the heishi technique. The drilled fragments are threaded onto a wire and moved against a grinding stone until all beads are round, smooth and uniform in shape and size. After threading on raffia fiber, the finished beads are oiled in order to enhance their color.*

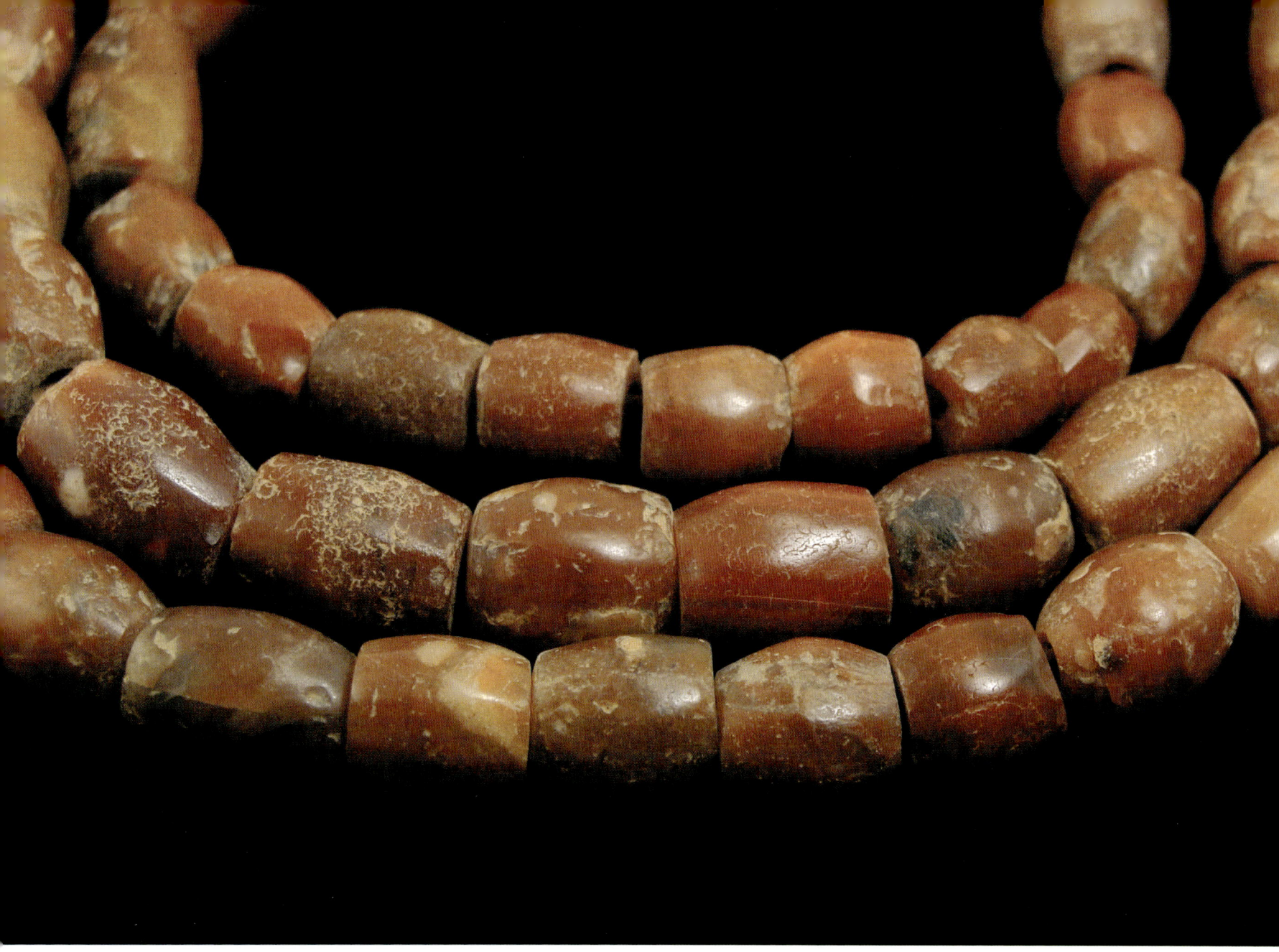

ABOVE *In the old kingdom of Benin, jasper beads—locally called lantana—were one of the bead types reserved for royalty and a small elite group of family and court members. The wearing of royal beads by ordinary citizens was punishable by death. Traditionally the perforations of Lantana beads are not drilled but pecked with a special tool, called esoro. The making of eighteen beads, the number required for a necklace, took up to a week.*

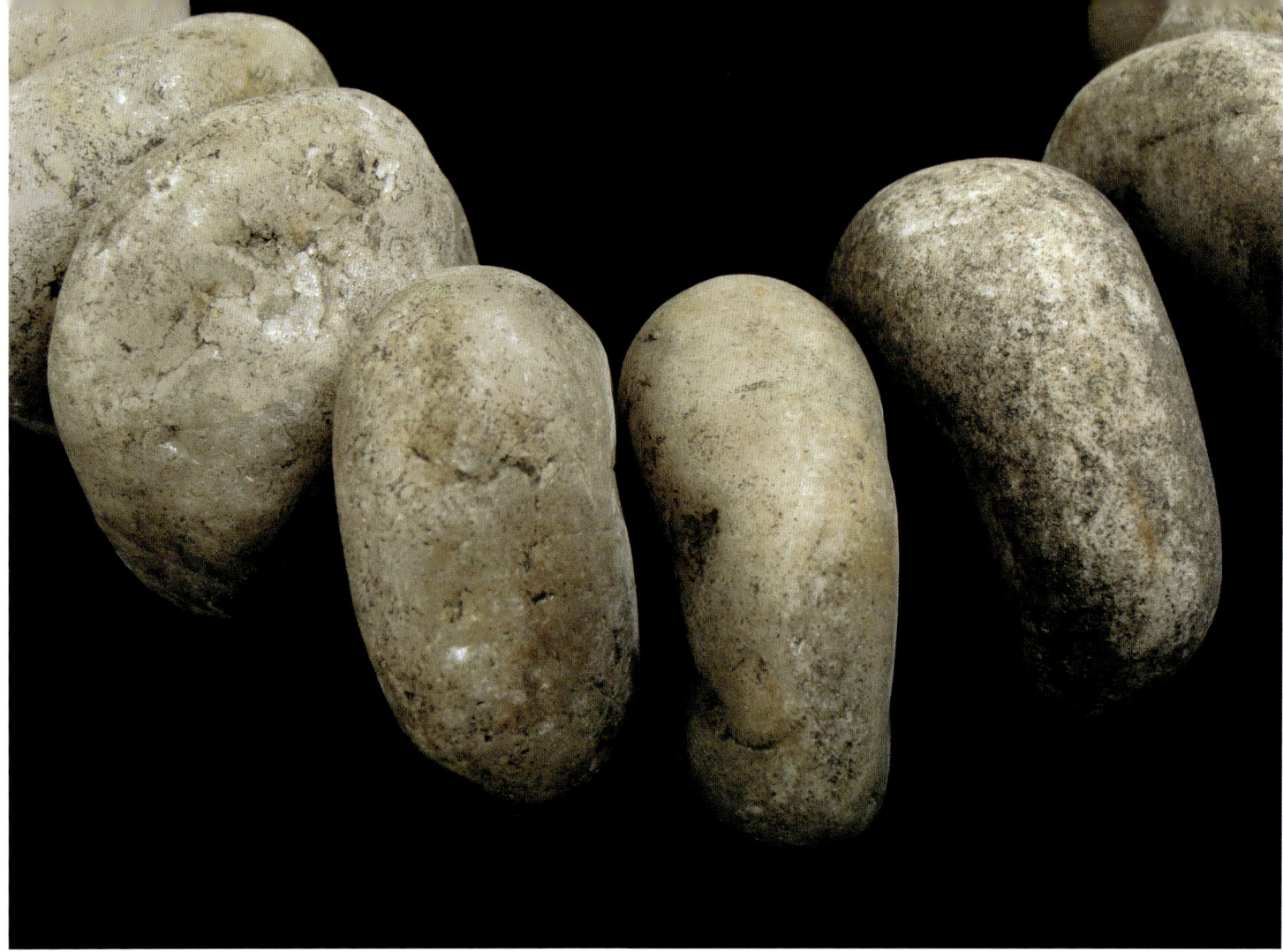

ments have been perforated they are threaded onto a length of wire. The still raw beads receive their final disk shape by being repeatedly moved against a grinding stone until all beads on the strand are round and uniform in shape and size. Once the outer surfaces are polished and smooth, the beads are threaded onto tough raffia fiber and oiled. The oiling deepens and enhances their beautiful earth-tone colors.

The Abo bead industry is believed to be a century old, or even older. Ghanaian bauxite beads were first introduced to the American and European collector markets in the late 1960s, along with "Trade Beads" and African powder glass beads. With their rich, dark, earthy brown-red color, bauxite beads soon attained great popularity amongst jewelry designers. They are often found in combination with other African-made beads, such as ostrich eggshell heishi and clamshell heishi, manufactured with the same finishing technique.

A typical strand of African bauxite beads is comprised of cylindrical or truncated barrel shapes, and, less commonly, of thick disks and small barrel shapes. Occasionally multi-strand waist belts are offered for sale on the collectors' market, but these are rather rare finds.

Jasper (Lantana)

Jasper is a dense microcrystalline quartz of typically deep red or brown-red hues with a hardness of 7 on the Mohs scale. [41] It is sometimes described as being similar to chert or chalcedony. The manufacture of red stone beads, locally called lantana, was a major industry in 19th century Ilorin, the present-day capital of Kwara state in northwestern Yorubaland (now part of Nigeria), and the great majority of these beads were made from jasper. A Hausa term, lantana means "Monday child," i.e. a child born on a Monday.

86 ◆ Stone Beads

LEFT *A strand of old quartz beads.*

RIGHT *This elegant serpentine pendant, representing Nyami Nyami, the Zambezi River god, was carved by the Shona people of Zimbabwe. Shona stone pieces like this one began to be produced after 1965, when Frank McEwan, an Englishman in what was then Southern Rhodesia, founded a school and encouraged his students, who had been painting, to move to stone.*

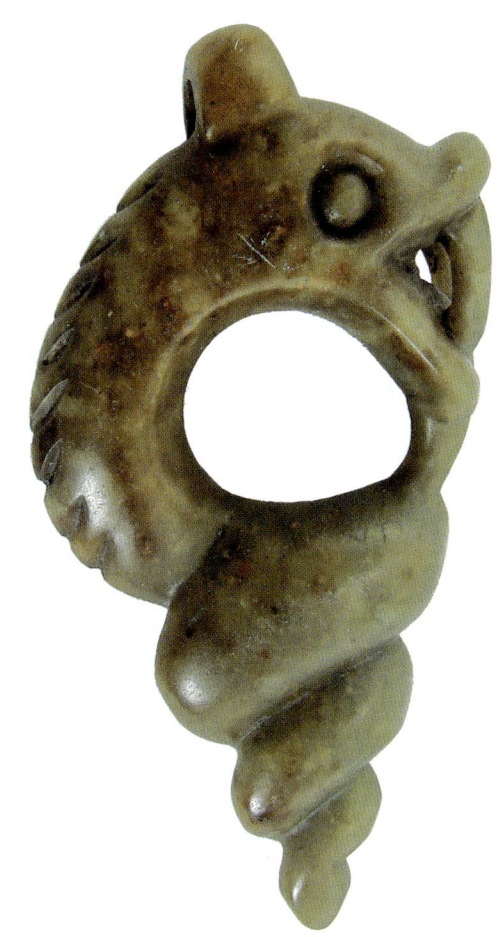

Jasper in the Kingdom of Benin

Quarried far to the north at locations close to the River Niger, now in the Niger Republic, jasper stone was brought downriver on boats and carried overland to Ilorin. In earlier times, similar red beads were manufactured in Old Oyo, the capital of the empire of Oyo, and from there they were traded to the kingdom of Benin and to neighboring chiefdoms, for use in regalia. The mutual importance of the trade to both Ilorin and Benin was reflected in an annual presentation of beads by the Emir of Ilorin to the Oba of Benin, who reciprocated with other products. This gift exchange is still remembered today.

In Benin, beads—especially red beads—were very important. Possession of royal beads was the privilege of kings and of a small elite group of family and court members. Certain red beads were deemed royal and were unaffordable to ordinary citizens. A subject wealthy enough to acquire such beads risked execution if caught wearing them. In a centuries-old annual ceremony called "The Honor of the Bead," which equaled the status of knighthood in Europe, the Oba (Divine Ruler) rode through the city on one of his richly-adorned horses in order to personally confer upon specially selected subjects the honor of wearing the royal beads. To appear before the Oba without wearing these beads thereafter was an offence punishable by death, and since this privilege was not hereditary, the beads had to be returned to the Oba on the death of the owner.

Originally, these royal beads were made from jasper, and occasionally also from carnelian and chalcedony. When Mediterranean coral was introduced by the Portuguese in the 16th century, local bead production slowed. It was revived during the 19th century, as Benin's trade with the Europeans declined, thus reducing the supply of imported coral. More than 600 male bead makers were counted in a tax assessment exercise in Ilorin, in 1912. The artisans made the jasper beads by chipping the stone into rough shapes. These were then pierced (pecked) with a sharply pointed metal tool, called esoro, which was at the same time twirled against the stone. It is said that progressively finer esoros were used as the work progressed. The final shapes were achieved by working the rough beads against a grinding stone. The beads were given their glossy finish by polishing on a smooth board. It took from four days to a week to make eighteen beads, the standard number required for a necklace. The finished beads have a highly polished appearance and are a deep reddish-brown in color. They were made in a wide variety of shapes and sizes from long cylinders to barrel shapes and disks. Jasper was made not only into beads but also fashioned into pendants and earplugs.

Bead making in Ilorin declined in the 1920s and 30s. Its demise is said to have been caused by a shift in fashion among women, due to the availability of cheaper imported substitutes, although imitations had been produced as early as the 17th century. The industry has now ceased, but some elders still remember the old techniques and retain the old bead-making equipment. Benin and Nigerian royalty still wear coral beads in their regalia, as well as the ancient beads made of jasper and agate. [42]

Amazonite

Amazonite is a gemstone variety of green microcline, a feldspar mineral; it has a hardness of 6 to 6.5 and is found in a wide variety of hues, ranging from teal and turquoise, to greens and blues, to almost white with only a splash of green or blue. While some beads have a dark turquoise or brown color, varieties displaying lighter shades of greens and blues are the most sought after and are often referred to as gem-grade amazonite. [43]

Amazonite used for bead making occurs in crystalline forms that extend into open spaces (referred to as vugs) in pegmatites or in metasomatized rocks. The great majority of ancient amazonite beads are found in Mali, Mauritania and Morocco, where they are highly esteemed and commonly sold by weight.

The two most common and most popular shapes of ancient amazonite beads are the elongated cylinders and ellipsoidal pendants, the oldest versions having been shaped by hand on grinding stones. The bead perforations were made with hand-operated bow drills using stone bits made of chalcedony. As with other perforations already described, the holes were started from both ends and usually do not line up exactly where they meet.

Amazonite beads were most likely worn for their perceived protective properties and healing qualities. Worn extensively as a "stone of courage" by the early Egyptians, amazonite is still used today for the same reason. In Egypt most available gemstones were used for making beads, pendants and amulets. Many precious and semi-precious stones were also used for the manufacture of seals and for creating colorful inlays. Turquoise was quarried in the Sinai whereas agate, amethyst, carnelian and other chalcedonies, jasper and rock crystal were found in the Nubian Desert. Other gemstones were imported from countries as far away as Afghanistan (lapis lazuli) and India (carnelian, onyx, ruby and sapphire). [43a]

Serpentine

Serpentine (also called greenstone) beads in shapes similar to amazonite beads can often be found combined with amazonite beads in traders' strands. Serpentine is a uniformly dark green or greenish yellow stone with a hardness varying from 2.5 to 5.5, depending on the variety. [44]

Quartz

The colors of quartz range from transparent colorless clear to transparent or translucent milky white, pink, or smoky gray. Quartz has a hardness of 7. The quartz beads originating from West Africa occur in two distinctive types. The ancient smoky quartz beads found in the desert sands of Mali are generally small and uniform in size. They have well-polished surfaces and their size typically does not exceed ten millimeters in diameter. Another common type consists of larger hand-cut and crudely-formed oblate or disk-shaped beads, the largest specimens measuring fifty millimeters or more in diameter. [45]

Pietersite

Sid Pieters first discovered this mineral in 1962 while he was prospecting farmland. He registered his find in the mineral records of Great Britain, where it was given the name Pietersite. In recent years, a small number of oblate and short barrel-shaped beads made from Pietersite have been produced in Swakopmund, Namibia, which at present is the world's only remaining mine. Another location where this rare mineral was once found is in Hunan, China. The site is believed to have been flooded and hence has been non-operational for many years. Pietersite is formed from a crocidolite type of asbestos or a variety of Riebeckite and is widely used in jewelry due to its toughness, its high hardness of 7, and its attractive range of marbled hues.

Metal Beads

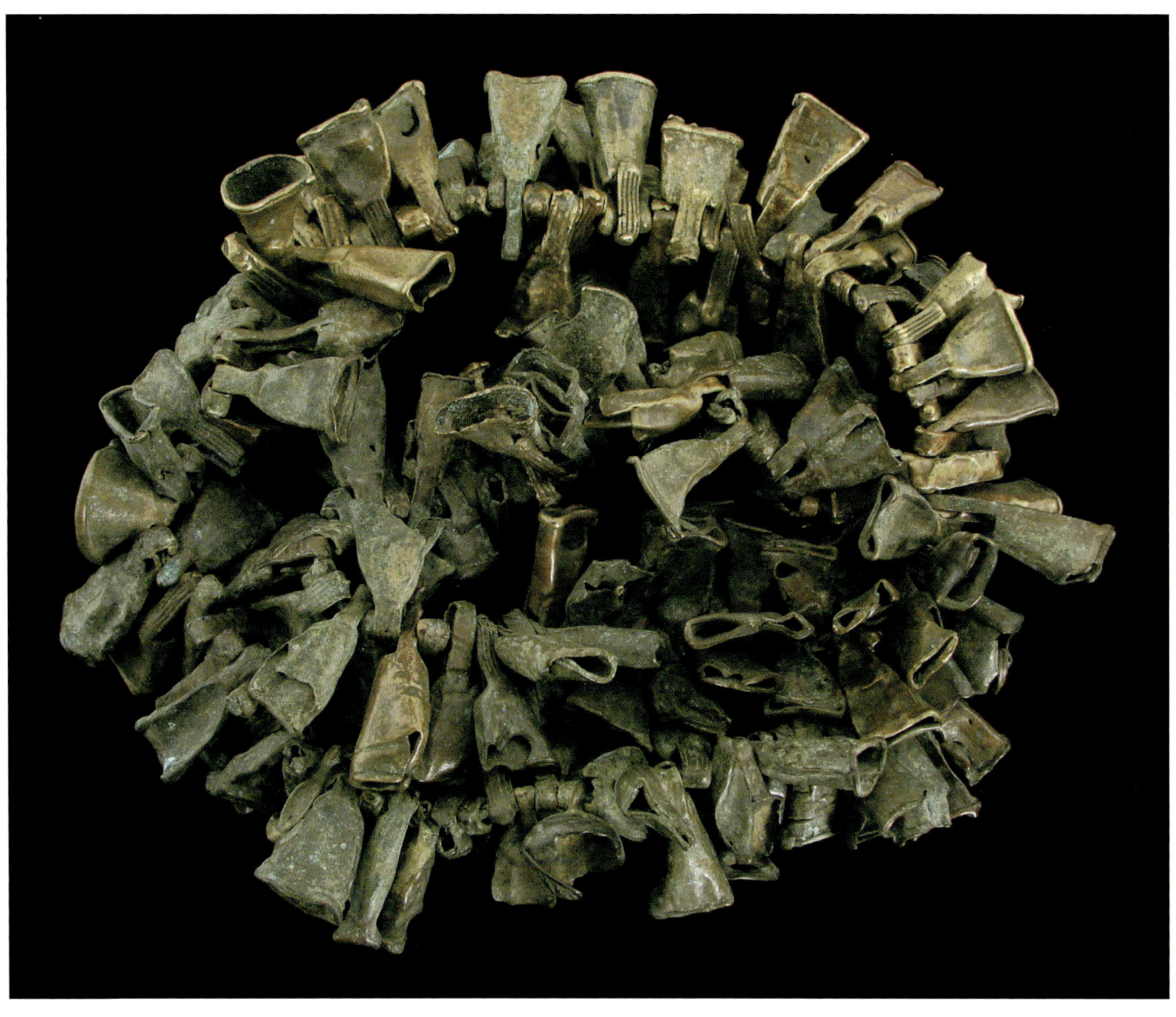

ABOVE *Besides representing power and authority, beads fashioned from iron or other metals, such as the irregular bell-shaped pendants depicted here, were worn as metaphors for courage, strength and great cunning. Necklaces of forged iron beads also indicated that in addition to magical powers and the ability to control the forces of nature, their wearer possessed the means required to commission the making of such valued objects.*

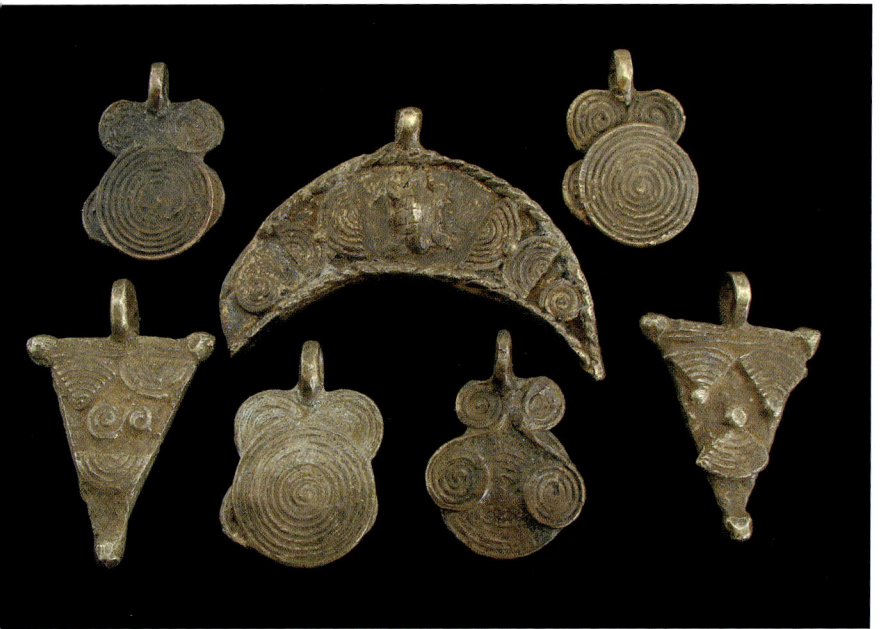

LEFT *Metalworkers of the Akan people of Ghana produced pendants decorated with the same elaborate designs that can be observed on their gold jewelry.*

History of Metalworking

One of the major forces which shaped pre-colonial African societies was the impact of ironworking, established with the arrival of the Phoenicians around 814 BCE. African peoples had been using gold and copper in Nubia and Egypt since 4000 BCE, and there is evidence of early trading of gold in exchange for copper from West Africa across the Sahara to Libya. However, these metals were not hard enough for the production of weapons and tools. When Egypt became a part of the Assyrian empire in 662 BCE, the craft of ironworking spread south to the Sudan. There it became an important part of the economy, resulting in economic and military advantages for those who practiced it. Later, around 200 CE, the area came into contact with the trading kingdom of Axum (present day Ethiopia, founded in the 5th century BCE), which had gained its power by controlling trade between the Red Sea and the Nile Valley. Ironworking spread across the savannah to the Nok culture (covering a region about 500 kilometers long and 170 kilometers wide on the Bauchi plateau, extending from northern and central Nigeria to the areas around Katsina and Sokoto in northwest Nigeria), and from there eastwards and southwards. By the beginning of the 13th century, locally produced iron was traded from the South African port of Sofala to India and possibly further. Kings, priest and diviners all along the West Atlantic coast were wearing necklaces forged from iron as symbols of power, authority, courage, strength and cunning. Iron and its forging were understood to be the result of the manipulation of magical forces. The technical skills involved were highly-guarded secrets, and necklaces of iron not only indicated that their wearer possessed magical powers and the ability to control the forces of nature, but also that he was a person of substance and authority, who had the means to commission a blacksmith to make such an object.

African Blacksmiths

In African society, the mystical and mysterious powers of transformation are associated with status and authority. Blacksmiths, with their ability to create and shape pieces of metal through the metamorphosis of heating iron ore and forging it into new shapes, became respected and feared for the powers they possessed. The blacksmith provided his village with knives, hoes, horse trappings and weapons, as well as objects of ritual adornment, such as pendants and amulets. The caste of blacksmiths was complex and significant. Since the introduction of firearms, blacksmiths have also acquired the skills needed for the manufacture and repair of guns. Due to their importance, blacksmiths were associated with divine kingship and with spirituality. Ancient kings often used the anvil as a symbol of royalty. Ogun, the deity of war and iron, was believed to live in the blacksmith's forge. Many West Africans to this day will not dare to look a blacksmith directly in the eye, fearing instant death because of his magical powers.

Blacksmiths commonly act as mentors to male adolescents in their village, providing spiritual guidance about the path to adulthood. They also perform the rite of circumcision. Often, they act as diviners and healers, and contribute to their communities with their unsurpassed knowledge of the bush and of herbal healing. Many African societies have their own special caste of metalworkers, such as blacksmiths, silversmiths and other craftsmen who work in metal. [46]

Mande

Among the Mande—who are credited with the founding of the largest ancient West African empires and are closely related to both the Fulani and the Wolof (as well as the

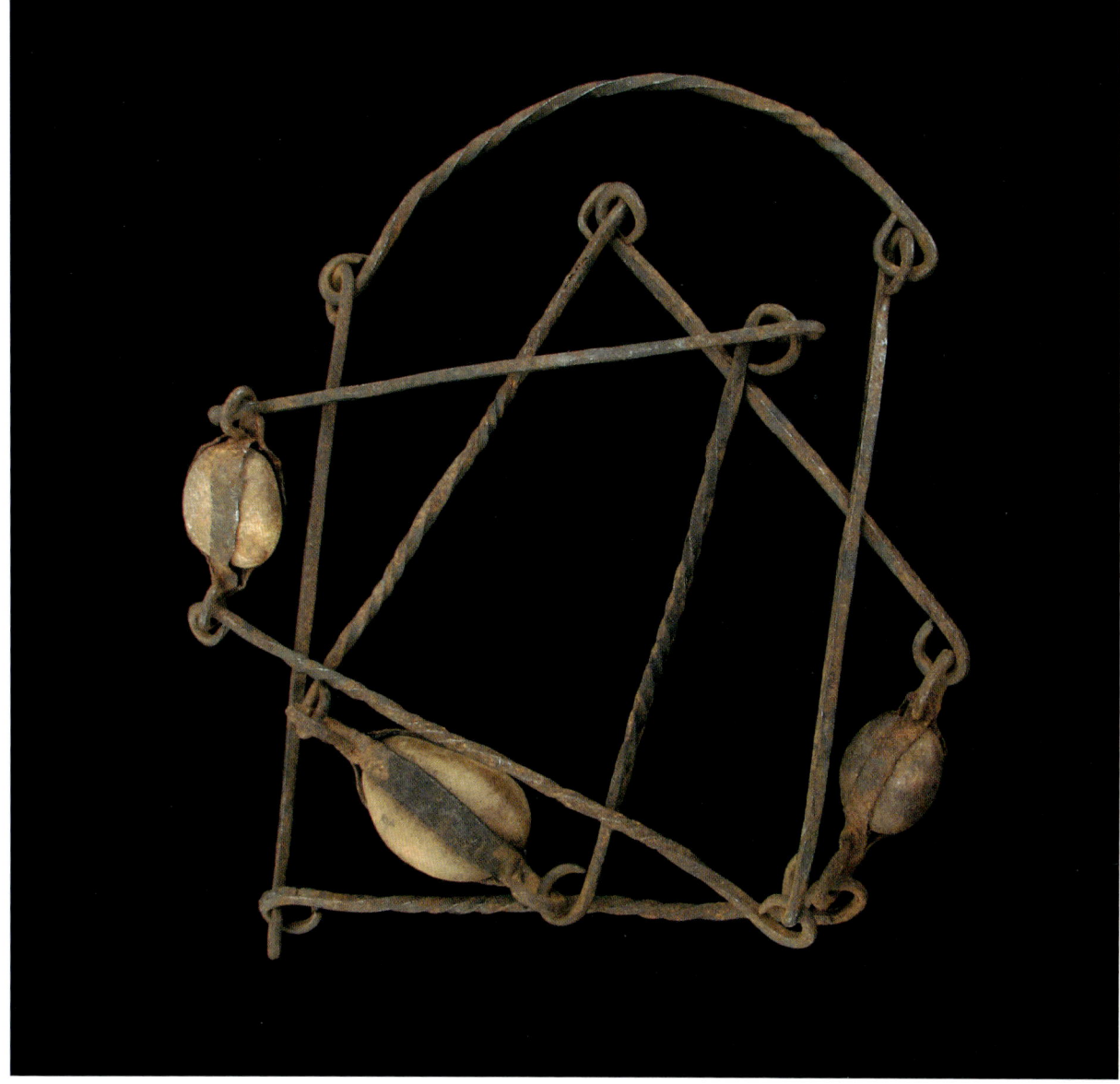

ABOVE *The necklaces produced by Dogon blacksmiths are worn by spiritual leaders, called Hogon. When designed for everyday wear, they are made from rather plain segments of chain-linked strips of iron, with perhaps a stone pendant attached. More elaborate necklaces are comprised of twisted and hammered lengths of forged iron, interspersed with segments which hold smooth, rounded, sacred stones, held in a cage-like structures typically made with four hammered elements.*

Songhai in terms of culture and race)—blacksmiths belong to a caste of artisans called nyamakalaw which also includes leather workers, weavers and poets. By tradition, their wives are usually potters. Blacksmiths are believed to possess the inherent ability to control a wild and powerful spirit called nyama. Nyama is thought to control the universe and to exist in all rocks, trees, people and animals that inhabit the earth. Since a blacksmith is believed to control this powerful force, he is also deemed to be able to control all energies present and hence all decisions taken in a village. Blacksmiths inherit large amounts of nyama from their ancestors. Nyama is viewed as neither good nor evil and it is believed that the direction it takes depends on its bearer. For this reason, a blacksmith must learn how to handle the power he possesses. A young son of a blacksmith will spend many hours at his father's forge, observing his work and performing small tasks, such as operating the bellows and carving wood, before he is ready to begin his apprenticeship. Only male children of blacksmiths can inherit the magical powers necessary to become blacksmiths. Intermarriage between artisan castes is not prohibited, but the sons of smiths commonly marry women from other blacksmith families.

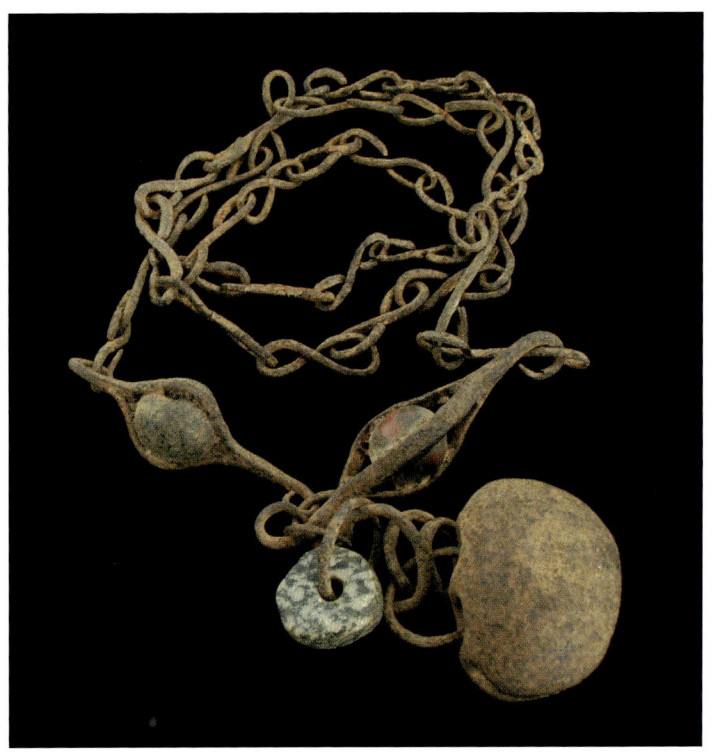
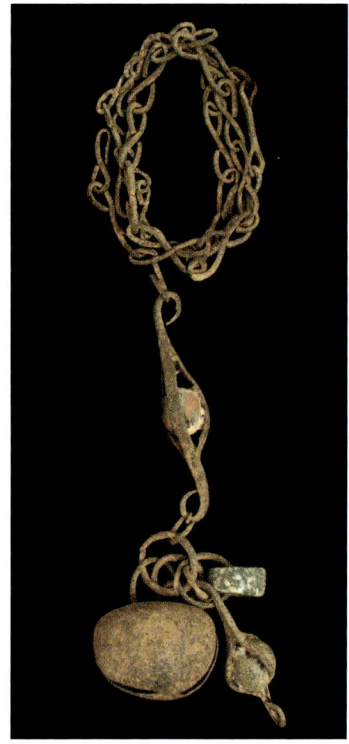

LEFT *The Hogon is assisted by a number of guardians, usually the oldest men in a village, who help with the preparation of fetishes intended to be used in rituals. The guardians also wear forged iron necklaces, often with a number of sacred stones, called ancestor stones, held in place by cage-like forged iron elements. [50]*

Bamana

The Bamana, descendants of the Manding Empire, are divided into castes based on occupation and prohibit marriage outside the group.

Wolof

Among the Wolof of Senegal, the concept of castes is also founded on occupational groups: the jeff-lekk is comprised of artisans who are subdivided into leatherworkers, woodworkers, weavers and blacksmiths, who also make jewelry.

Hutu

In Rwanda, only members of the Hutu ethnic group were allowed to be blacksmiths.

Dogon

Blacksmiths of the Dogon people of Mali were the only persons permitted to create objects for use in Dogon rituals. Brass and iron figures manufactured by Dogon blacksmiths are identified with Dogon creation myths in which the blacksmith was one of the first primordial beings, known as Nommo, created by Ama, a major Dogon deity. The identity between the Nommo and the blacksmith effects a bond that gives the blacksmith special powers, including the important ability to call down rain.

Iron

Dogon

Largely by their own choice, the Dogon people, who originate in the Niger Bend area, live isolated from the outside world between the forest regions and the savannah grasslands, on the cliff face of the Bandiagara Plateau in the central plateau region of Mali. The principal Dogon area is dissected by the Bandiagara Escarpment, a sandstone cliff of up to five hundred meters high and about 150 kilometers wide. The origins of the Dogon are shrouded in myth, but archaeological excavations in the Dogon area have revealed evidence of settlements from previous cultures such as the Toloy (3rd to 2nd century BCE) and the Tellum (11th to 15th century CE). With a population count of about 300,000 and inhabiting seven hundred-odd villages, the Dogon are best known today for their animist beliefs and mythology, their mask dances, the wooden sculptures produced by their

RIGHT *The forged iron necklaces of the Dogon give evidence of the highly skilled and artistic workmanship of their blacksmiths. Some of these necklaces, comprised of plain, hammered or twisted segments of chain-linked iron are adorned with bells, iron pendants, looped rings, dangles and fetishes.*

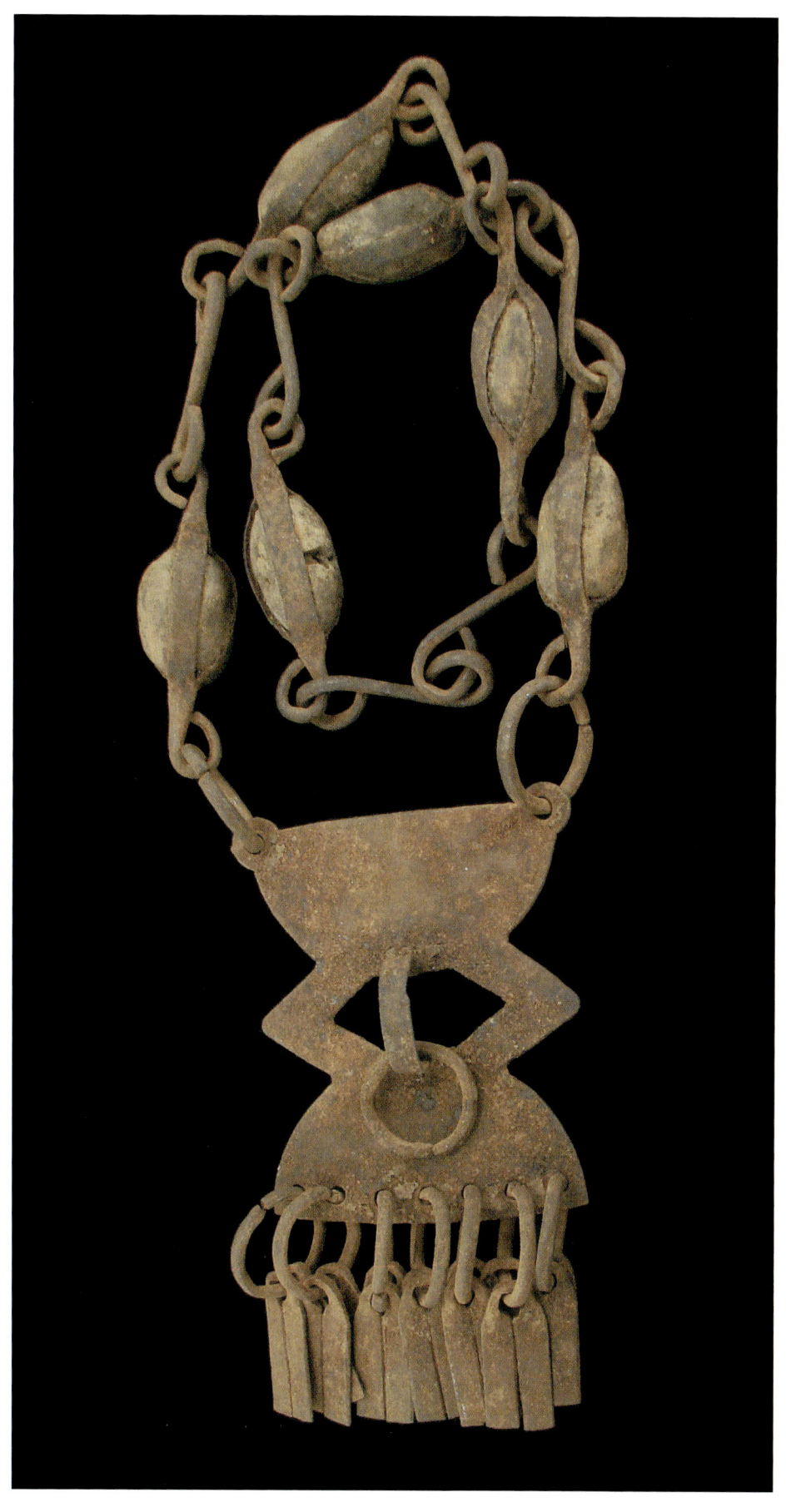

Metal Beads

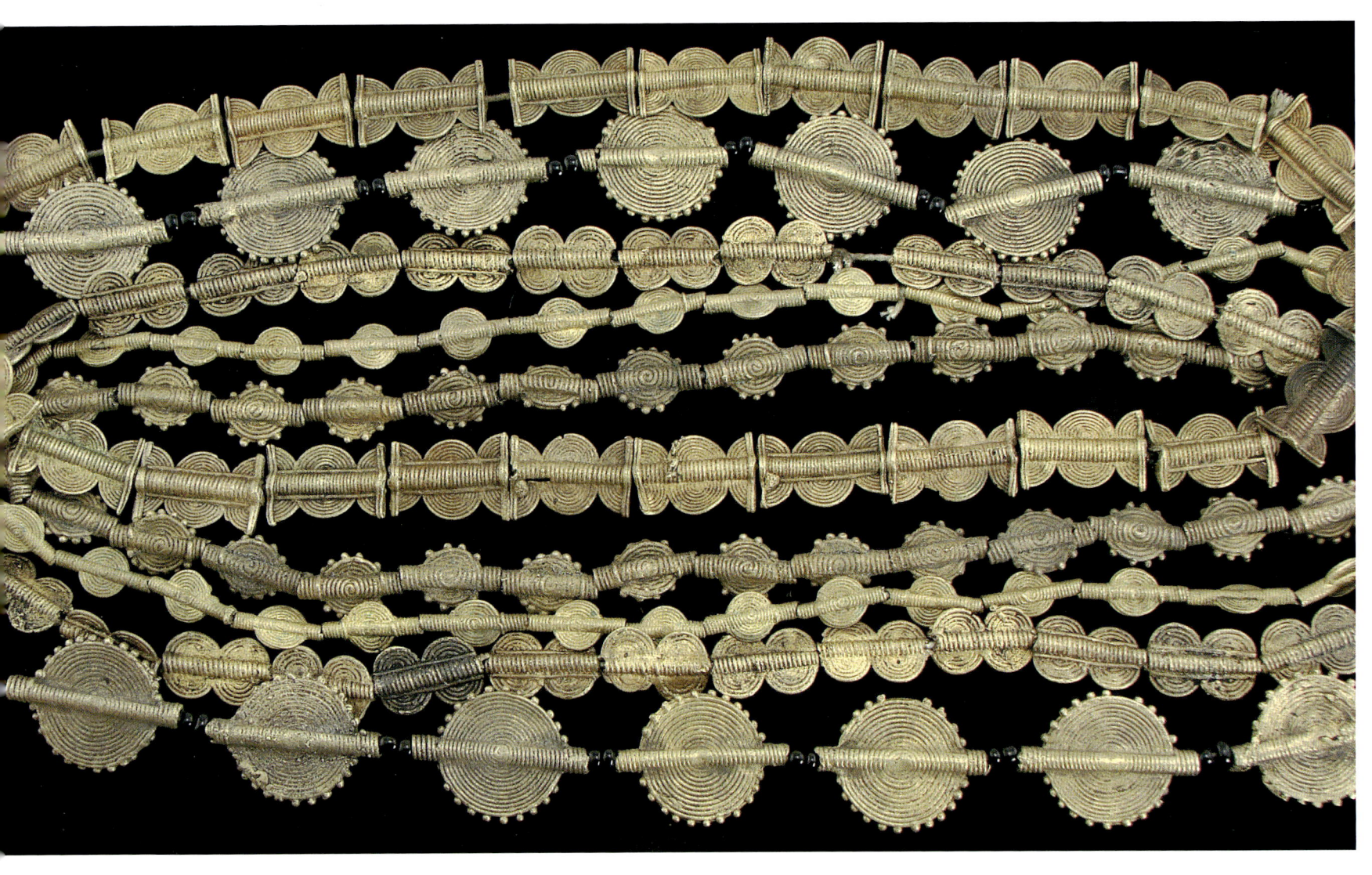

ABOVE *Akan metalworkers have a long tradition of metal casting and are masters of the lost wax casting technique, a technique that is still in use today. A wide variety of pendants and other jewelry objects continues to be produced, featuring traditional designs, such as so-called sun disks, twin crocodile and knife pendants, and Sankofa birds.*

RIGHT *19th century Ashanti gold beads, from the collection of Sarakata Sylla.*

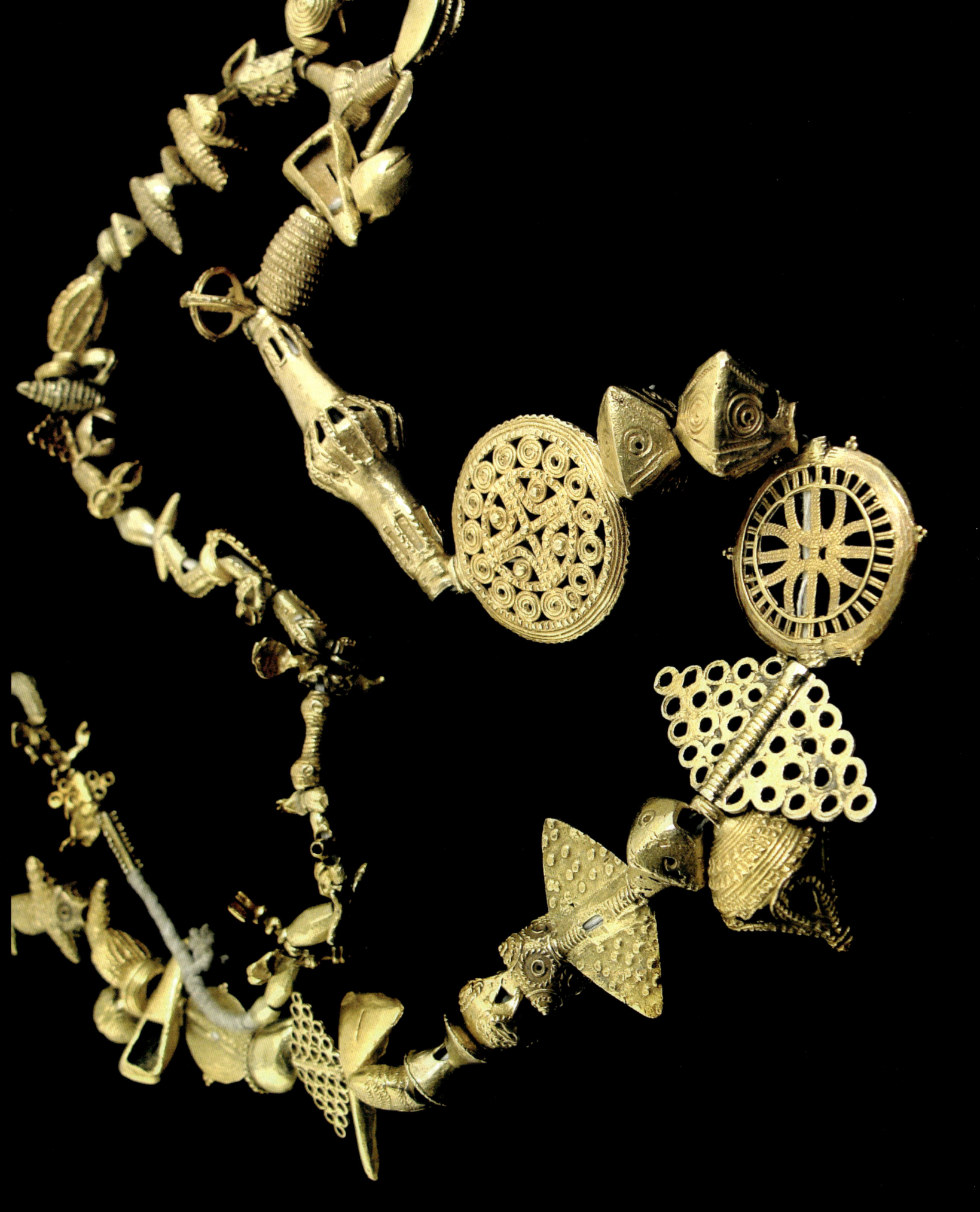

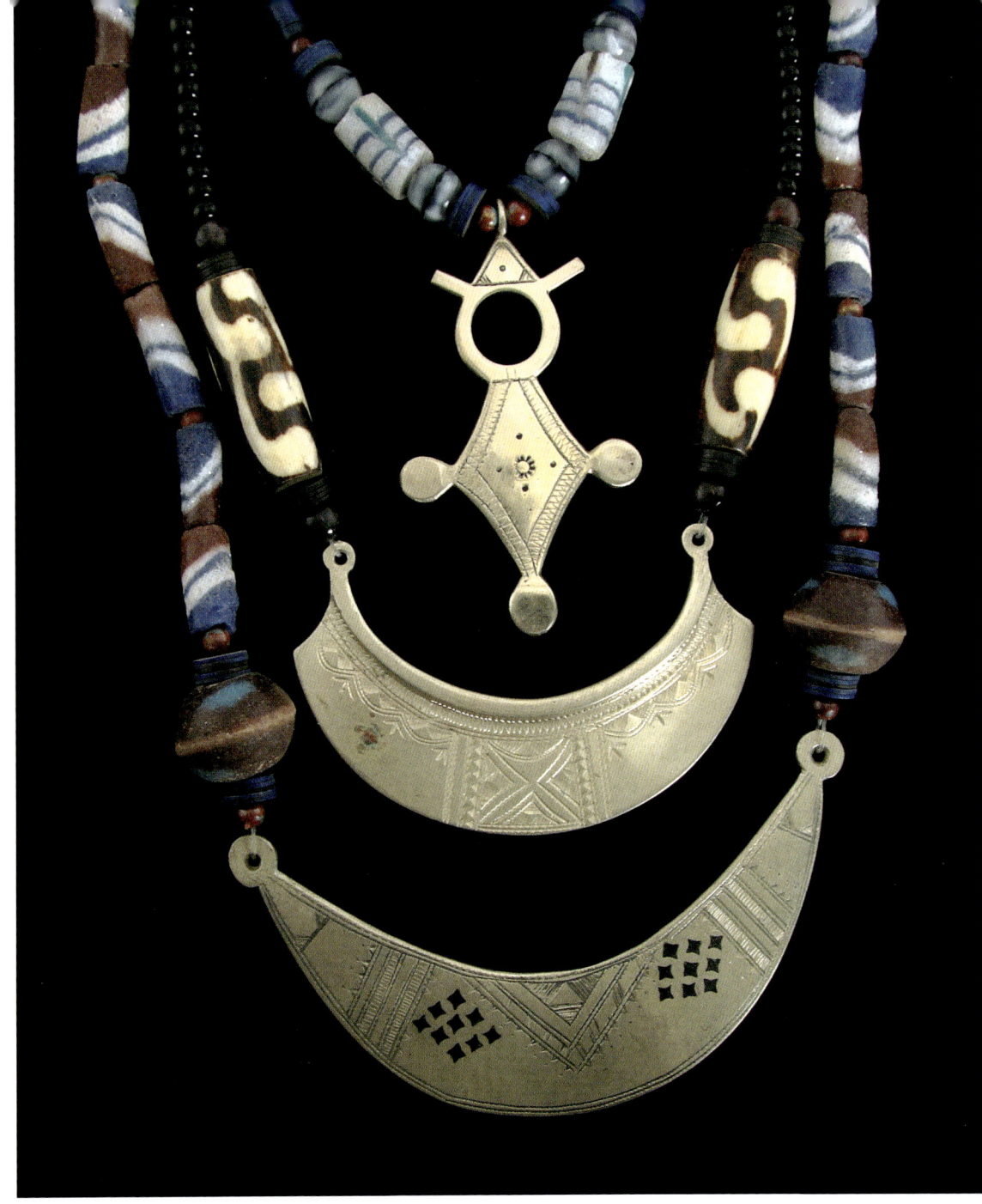

talented woodcarvers, and their unique architecture. [47] Dogon art, revolving around religious values, ideals and freedoms, serves both everyday and ritualistic functions. However, the past century has seen significant changes in the social organization, material culture and beliefs of the Dogon, partly because Dogon country is one of Mali's major tourist attractions. Due to the influx of tourism, Dogon art has become widely recognized and much sought after on the global collectors' market.

The carvers, and even more so the blacksmiths, were important figures in Dogon society. Only the blacksmiths were permitted to manufacture objects intended to be used in rituals. In our time, the work of Dogon blacksmiths has been reduced to forging mainly scrap metal recuperated from old railway lines or from car wrecks. The long process of iron ore reduction, a process that demands perfect knowledge of firing and temperatures, is gradually being forgotten. One of the last smeltings conducted by Dogon blacksmiths occurred in 1995. The procedure was captured in the film "Inagina" (the House of Iron). The last house of iron's eleven blacksmiths, who still held the secret knowledge of their ancestors, agreed to perform this smelting. Be-

LEFT *The preferred metal for Tuareg artisans is silver because gold is considered to be impure and unlucky. Tuareg silversmiths belong to a guild of blacksmiths and related metalworkers. The manufacture of traditional styles and designs continues to this day, as can be observed on contemporary pieces such as the pendants depicted here.*

fore constructing the mineshaft and making the charcoal, they gathered to invoke the spirits. Earth and slag were used for the construction of a furnace which they called Inagina. Sixty-nine kilograms of iron were produced for use in forging traditional tools, weapons and items of jewelry. [48] The rich patina often observed on pieces of recent manufacture is derived from submersion of the piece in urine or cattle dung, a common practice of "ageing."

The forged iron necklaces, which are produced by Dogon blacksmiths and worn by their spiritual leaders, give evidence of highly skilled and artistic workmanship. The Dogon spiritual leaders, called Hogon, are elected by consensus of the oldest men of the village, and the election is followed by a six-month initiation period. It is the Hogon's privilege to wear a red bonnet and forged iron bracelets and necklaces, fashioned from elaborately twisted and hammered lengths of forged iron connected by chain links. The more complex and elaborate assemblages were worn for ceremonial purposes only. Necklaces intended for everyday wear were comprised of rather plain segments of chain-linked iron strips, at times adorned with a stone pendant, or with more artistically fashioned cage-like shapes which hold sacred stones, typically within four hammered elements. Some of these necklaces are adorned with bells, flattened iron pendants of symbolic shapes, and fetishes. A Hogon is commonly assisted by a number of guardians, usually the oldest men in the village, who help with the preparation of fetishes for use in rituals. These guardians also wear forged iron necklaces, often with pieces of metal, iron bells, looped rings or pendants attached. [49]

Yoruba

The Yoruba is another society renowned for its smiths' craftsmanship in fashioning adornments made from iron. The heavy iron beads manufactured by Yoruba metal workers are typically plain and have spherical shapes, measuring from ten up to thirty millimeters in diameter.

Gold

Although the ancient empire of Ghana, situated in the upper western part of West Africa, was rich in gold, the region lacked adequate supplies of salt, a necessity for the survival of the empire's population. Since the desert regions of present day Morocco and Algeria contained huge salt resources, trade routes developed, which made it possible to transport gold from the Ghana Empire to the north, where it was traded for salt. The northern end of the route began in Sidjilmassa, a city on the Moroccan-Algerian border, and passed through the salt-rich village of Taghaza. From there it went across the Sahara and on to the gold region of ancient Ghana, known as Wangara, believed to have been located in the vicinity of the Bambuk and Bure regions, near the Senegal River. In order to keep gold prices high, the king maintained tight control over the kingdom's gold production. Only the king was allowed to possess gold nuggets. His subjects could own only gold dust. The main producers and users of gold artifacts and jewelry were the Ashanti, whose skilled craftspeople, casters and smiths were treated with the greatest respect. [51]

Ashanti

The Ashanti are members of a group of related societies which have Akan as their common language. Akan is spoken in many dialects by groups of people living in the south-central forest zone and coastal areas of Ghana and in southeastern Ivory Coast. The Ashanti and Fante are probably the best-known Akan groups in Ghana. Historical accounts and Akan traditions suggest that they migrated from the north as early as the 13th century. [52]

The Ashanti Kingdom, or Ashanti Confederacy, was a powerful nation in West Africa from the late 1500s to 1902. Today, the central part of its territory is one of ten administrative regions in Ghana. At its height, it encompassed what is today southern and central Ghana and the eastern part of the Ivory Coast. The Ashanti (also spelled Asante) people are a major ethnic group who speak a dialect of Akan. They are said to have migrated from the vicinity of the northwestern Niger River after the fall of the Ghana Empire. Ashanti wealth was based on the region's substantial gold deposits, which were used to create intricate works of art and for trade. [53]

The Ashanti gold mine is located at Obuasi, situated south of Kumasi. It has been producing since 1897. Situated on one of the world's major gold deposits and said to be one of the ten largest gold mines in the world, it was originally state owned, but is now privately owned and listed on the New York Stock Exchange. In 2004 it merged with Anglo-Gold to create the world's second-largest gold producer, the AngloGold Ashanti Company. AngloGold is based in South Africa and majority-owned by the Anglo American group.

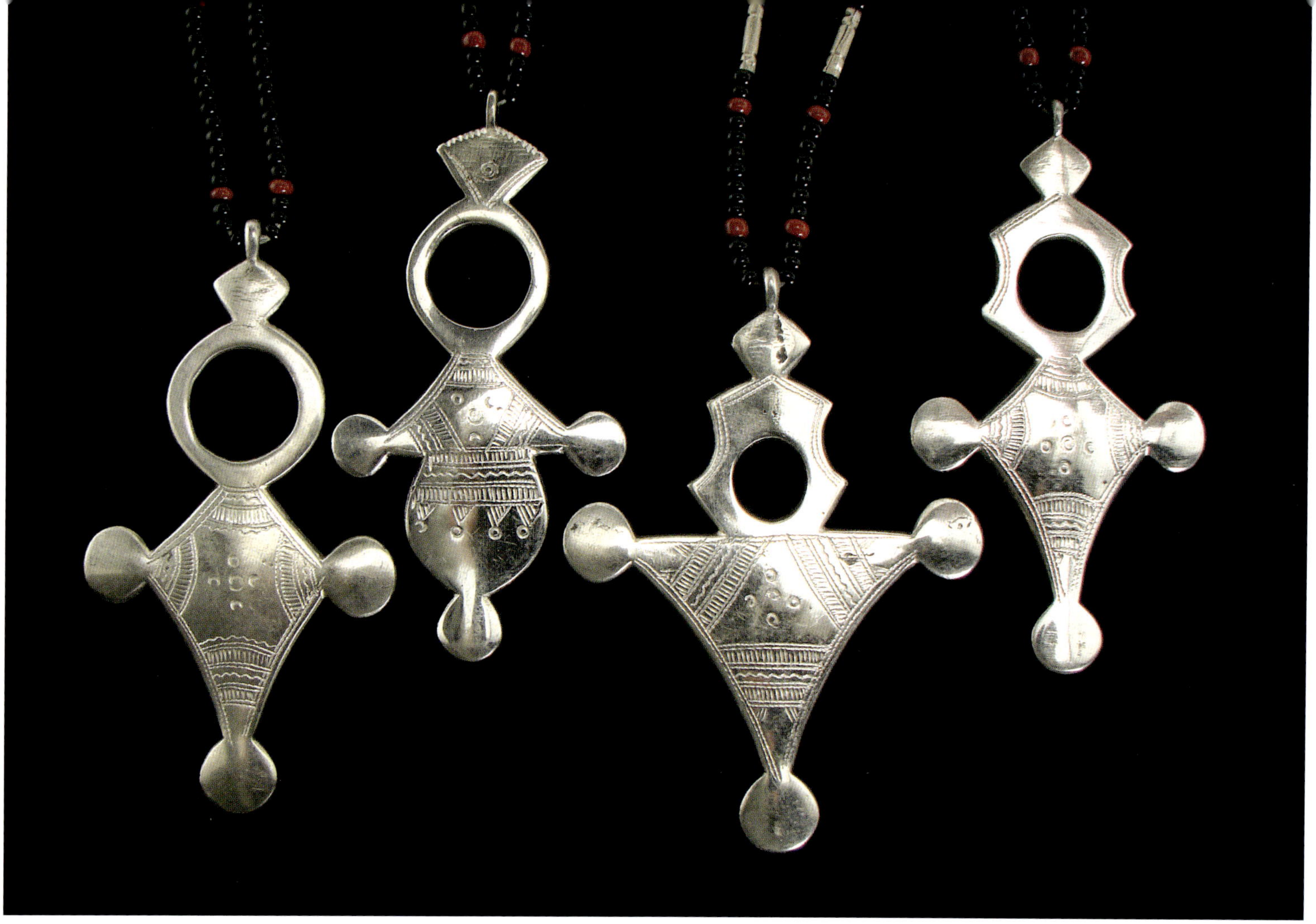

ABOVE *Tuareg or Agadez cross pendants symbolize the four corners of the earth, and they also represent different towns and oases situated between Agadez in Niger and the Ahaggar highlands in the north. Passed on from father to son, and originally worn only by men, these crosses are now also worn by Tuareg women.*

RIGHT *Tcherot are pendants of square or rectangular shape assembled by combining several structural layers, each decorated with intricate decorative patterns, usually consisting of raised diamond shapes within squares. Tcherot are manufactured from a variety of materials such as silver, copper, brass and leather, and typically contain small objects with amuletic properties and carefully folded magical formulas, as well as verses from the Quran, all designed to protect and strengthen the wearer or to ensure her fertility. A Tuareg girl receives her first Tcherot and Khomissar from her mother at the age of seventeen.*

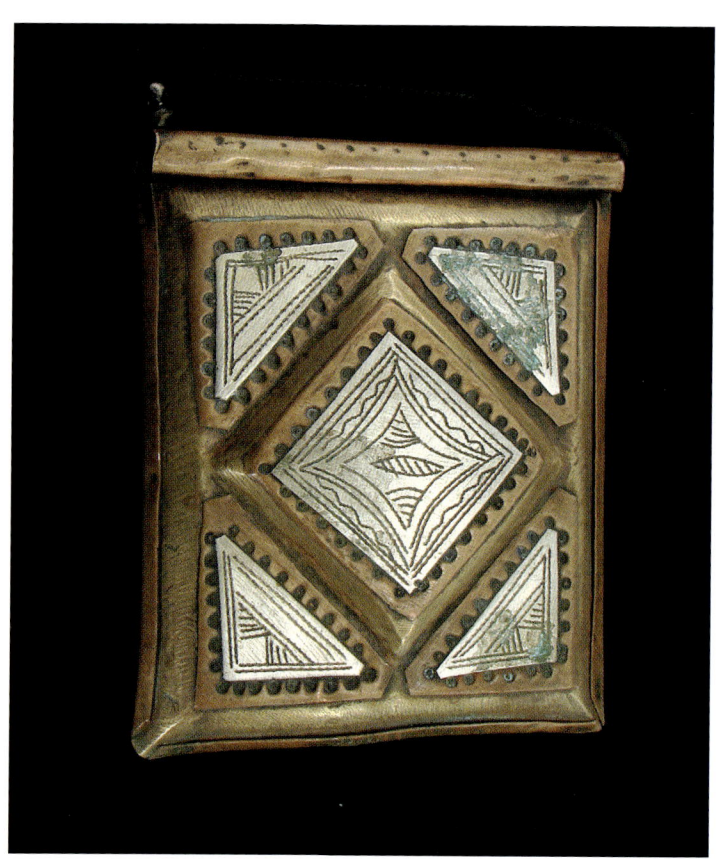

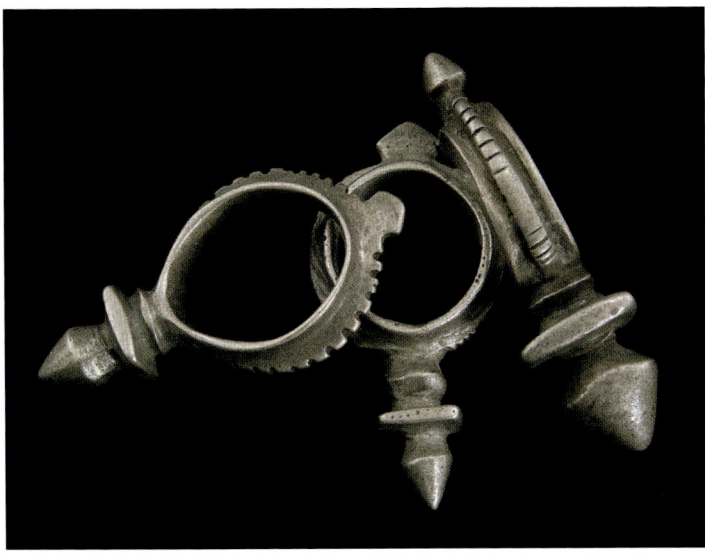
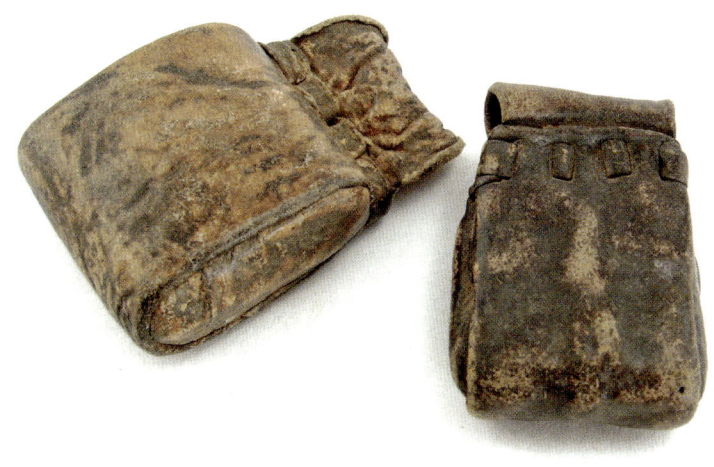

ABOVE AND RIGHT *In some Tuareg tribes, it is customary for men also to wear Tcherot around the neck, but more typically Tuareg men wear a number of Tcherot affixed either to their headdress or to their shirts, often combined with leather kitabe amulets and ingall pendants, traditionally made from carnelian, a stone which the Tuareg believe protects its wearer from blood disorders and heals wounds. Ingalls were originally finger rings worn by men.*

Closely identified with the Ashanti is the legend of the Golden Stool (Sika 'dwa), which tells of the birth of the Ashanti kingdom. In the 17th century in order to win their independence from Denkyira, another powerful Akan state, the Ashanti held a meeting of all the clan heads of the Ashanti settlements. In this meeting Okomfo Anokye, the fetish priest or sage, commanded down from the heavens the Golden Stool, which is said to have floated straight into the lap of Osei Tutu I, the first Asantehene (Ashanti king). The stool was declared to be the symbol of the new Ashanti union (Asanteman) and allegiance was sworn to the Golden Stool and to Osei Tutu as the Asantehene.

The ruler of the Ashanti, the Asantehene, is still crowned on the sacred Golden Stool, the Sika 'dwa, which came to symbolize his power. The Ashanti hold that the Golden Stool contains the "Sunsum" spirit or soul of the Ashanti people. Just as man cannot live without a soul, so the Ashanti would cease to exist if the Golden Stool were to be taken from them. The Golden Stool is not only sacred, but is deemed to be the central symbol of the Ashanti Confederacy, a symbol of nationhood, a symbol that binds and unifies all Ashanti. In 1900 an attempt by the British Gold Coast governor-general, Frederick Hodgson, to capture the Golden Stool led to an uprising which took several months to put down.

Akan

Religion and rituals exercise a major influence on the design and usage of Akan jewelry. Each piece is worn for a particular reason, rather than for personal use and adornment. Ideographic and pictographic symbols, each associated with a specific proverb, are used extensively on pottery, textiles and woodcarvings, and in metal casting. The Akan have a long tradition of metal casting, using brass, copper, gold, silver and iron. They differentiate between the blacksmiths and the artisans. The former were the makers of swords, knives, agricultural tools and traps, door hinges and locks. The latter manufactured the gold weights, spoons, jewelry boxes and other containers, jewelry (agudee) such as necklaces (ayannee), wrist bands (nsaknnee), anklets (aberemp nnaasee) and rings (mpatea) made of wrought or repoussé gold, combined with beads and interspersed with gold nuggets.

An example of Akan symbolism expressed in their jewelry is the depiction of twin crocodiles joined at the stomach which is said to represent the Akan belief in democracy. Another example is the handcrafted blade (ekan) or knife, which symbolizes state authority, power and legitimacy, and is associated with the proverb, "A cut from the household knife can be very painful," i.e. a familiar object can be a source of pain. A very popular symbol is the Sankofa, a bird facing backwards and touching its back, or picking up the egg of wisdom with its beak. This pictogram is associated with the saying, "It is alright to make a fresh start in life as long as you learn from your mistakes," the idea being that the bird, although advancing forward, periodically makes a point to turn and examine its past, thus ensuring a better future. A variety of Akan symbols can also be observed on gold weights, amulets, cast metal beads and pendants. [54]

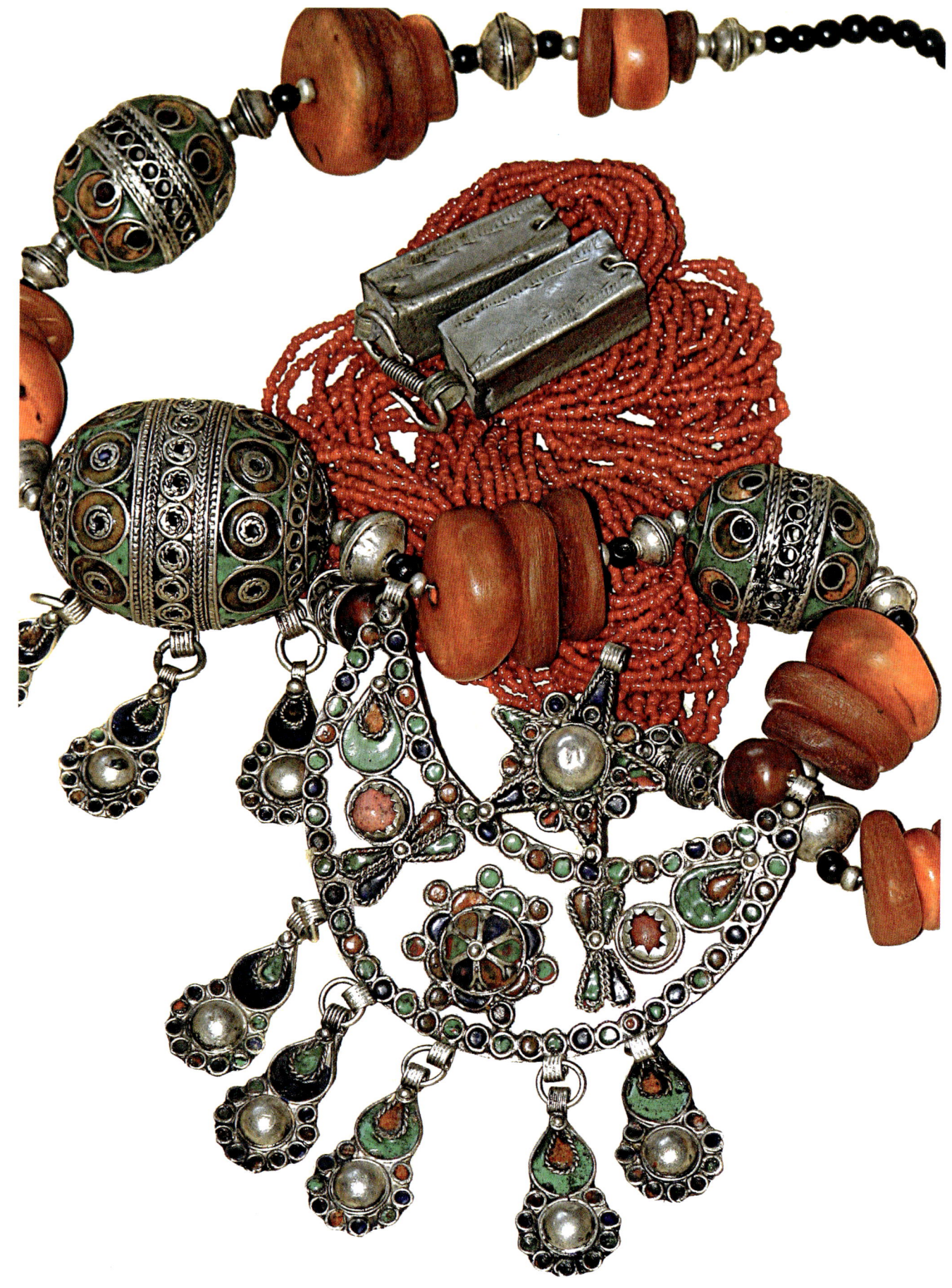

100   ◆   Metal Beads

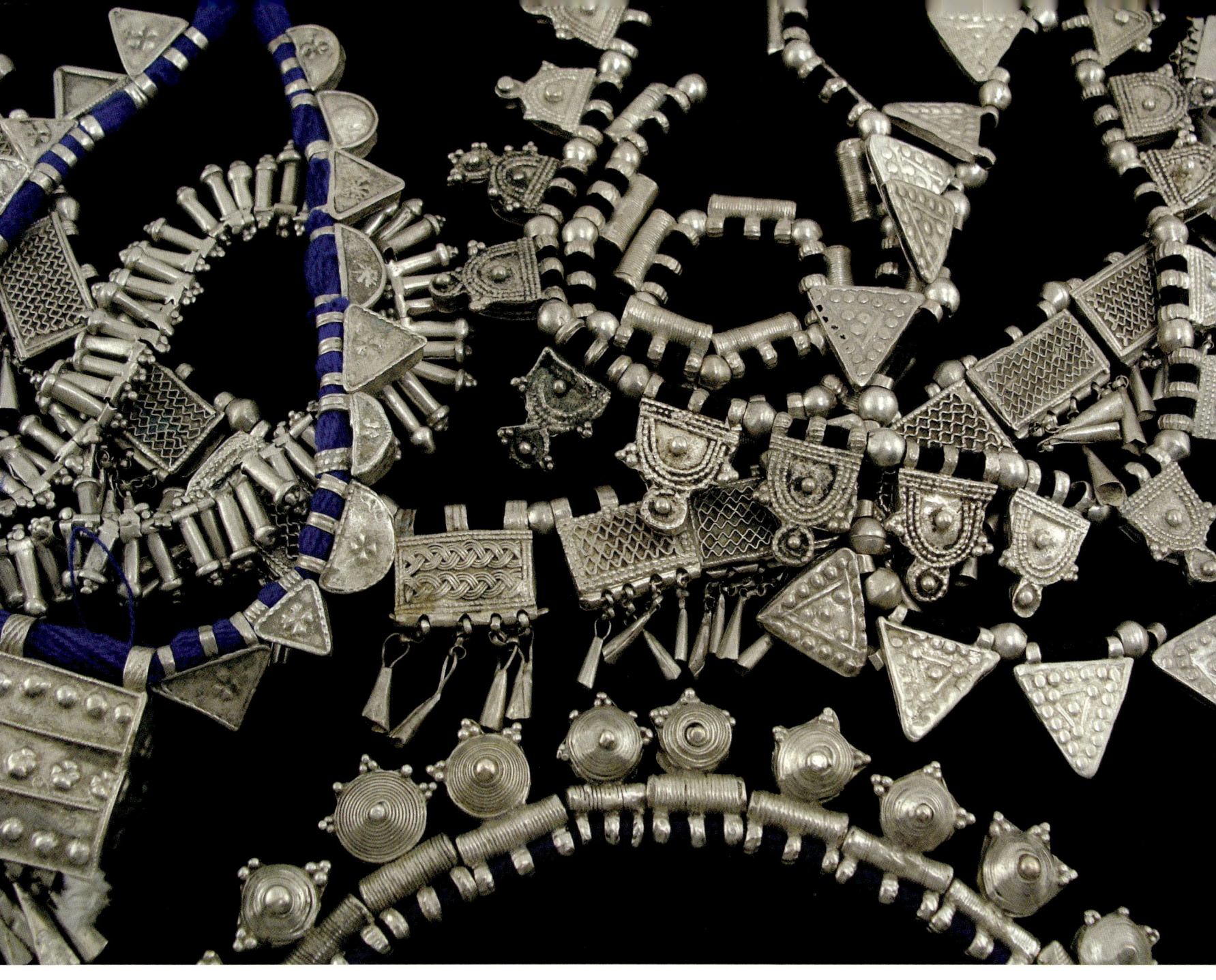

LEFT Traditional Berber jewelry is made from silver, copper, glass, agate and reclaimed metals. The most widely known and sought after Moroccan beads and ornaments are typically large in size and elaborately executed in silver or white metal, featuring intricate decorative patterns in plain and twisted wire. Enameling is often used to further enhance these designs, a technique that was introduced by Jewish silversmiths who shared their knowledge before leaving the country during the 1960s.

ABOVE Telsum prayer boxes are typically triangular or crescent-shaped, but a variety of other styles exist, as can be seen here.

Metal Beads   ◆   101

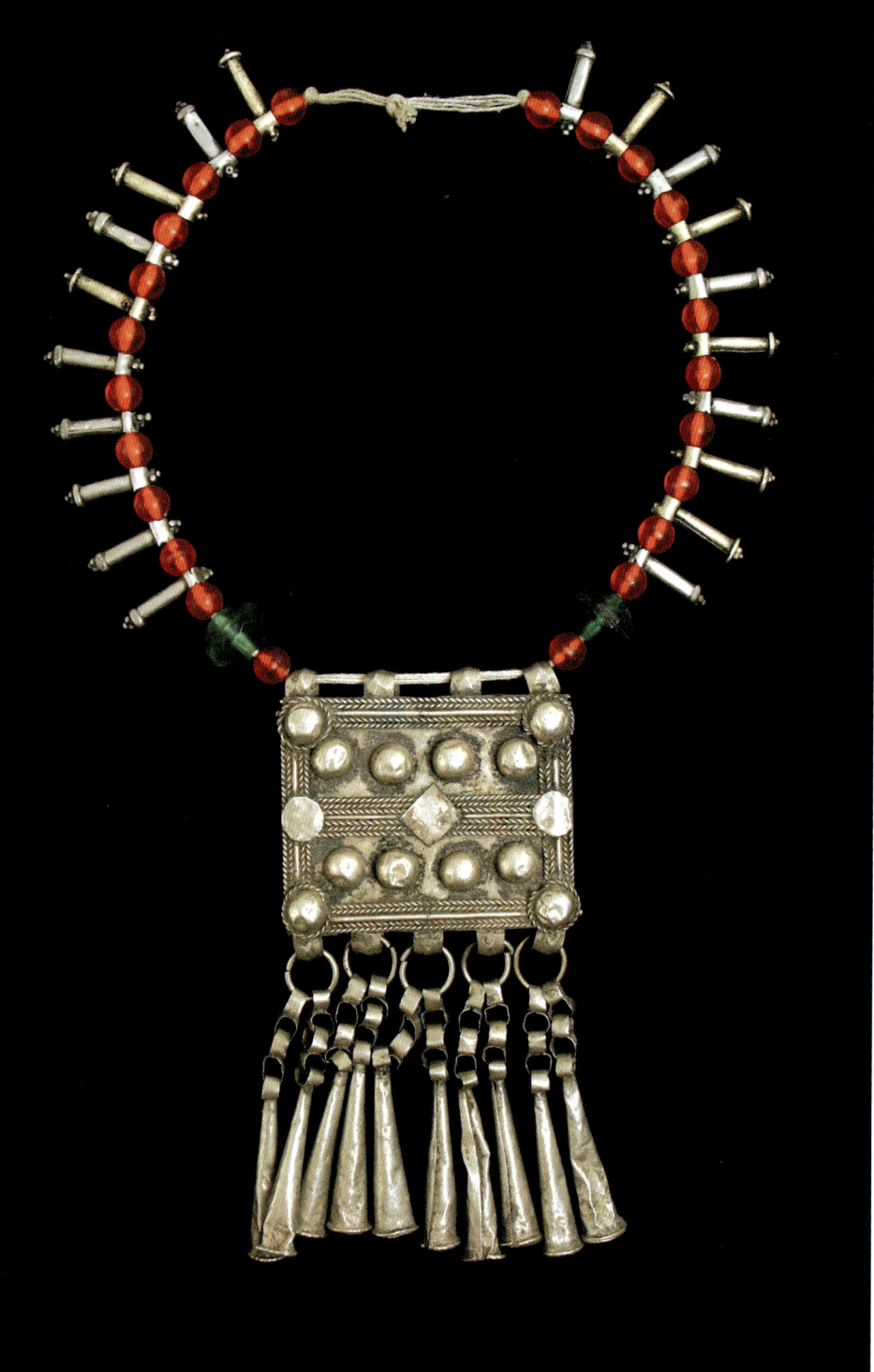

LEFT *Necklace comprised of red glass beads combined with phallic fertility pendants, with a mergaf as the centerpiece.*

Silver

Tuareg

The great majority of silver beads and pendants produced in West Africa originate in Algeria, Morocco and Ethiopia, where they are still manufactured, mainly by Berber and Tuareg metalworkers. The Tuareg, also known as "blue men," are by tradition nomadic, originating mostly in the Ahaggar (or Hoggar) highlands in southeastern Algeria. They speak a Berber language called Tamachaq. In their role as traders, the Tuareg connected African cities on the southern edge of the Sahara to trade centers on the Mediterranean coast. They also used the trans-Saharan trade routes to reach western and central Africa. Bringing their religion with them, they settled in parts of present-day Mali, Niger and Burkina Faso. Characteristically, Tuareg men cover their

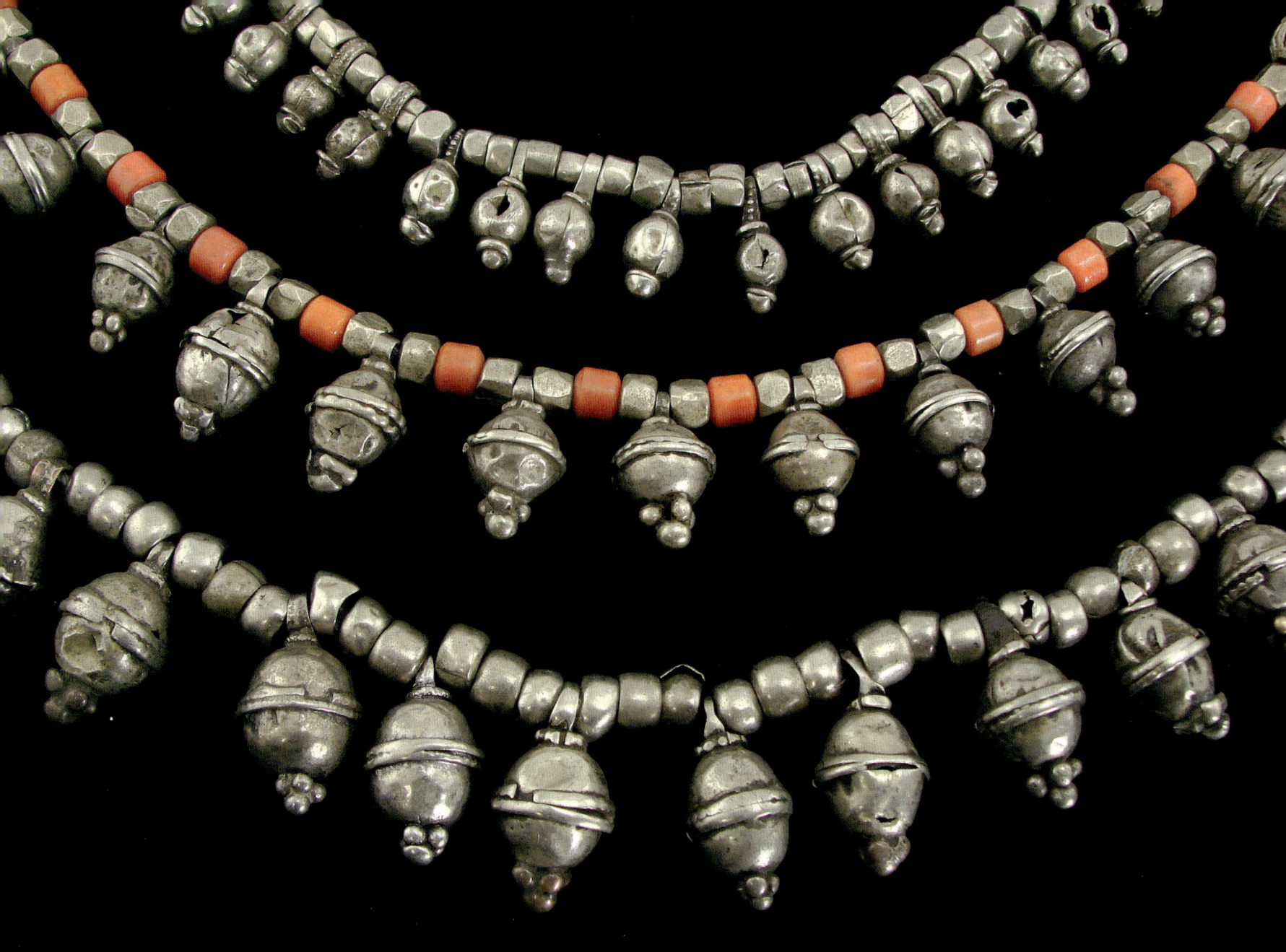

ABOVE *Rounded, breast-shaped beads, decorated with a raised dot to form a nipple-like protrusion, represent another style of fertility pendant.*

faces, and their skin often becomes stained a dark blue due to the indigo dyes used in their face-covering headdresses, called tagelmoust. Tuareg women do not cover their faces, and they have a great deal of influence over matters of marriage, finance and social affairs. It is women, rather than men, who inherit from parents and families. [55]

The Tuareg are accomplished and skilful leatherworkers and silversmiths whose traditional designs are repeated in their jewelry, leatherwork and embroidery. The austerity of desert life is evident in their characteristic combinations of animist motifs and Islamic symbolism. Tuareg silversmiths belong to a special caste of blacksmiths and craftsmen, called belas. Their preferred metal is silver, since gold is considered an impure and unlucky substance. The Tuareg or Agadez cross pendants are believed to represent the Muslim belief that the four points of the cross will disperse evil to the four corners of the earth. The distinctive crosses—formerly used as units of account when buying cattle, cloth or food—represent different towns and oases between Agadez in Niger and the Ahaggar highlands in Algeria to the north, and the craftsmen who created them typically engraved their signature on the reverse side, either in Tamachaq or in Arabic.

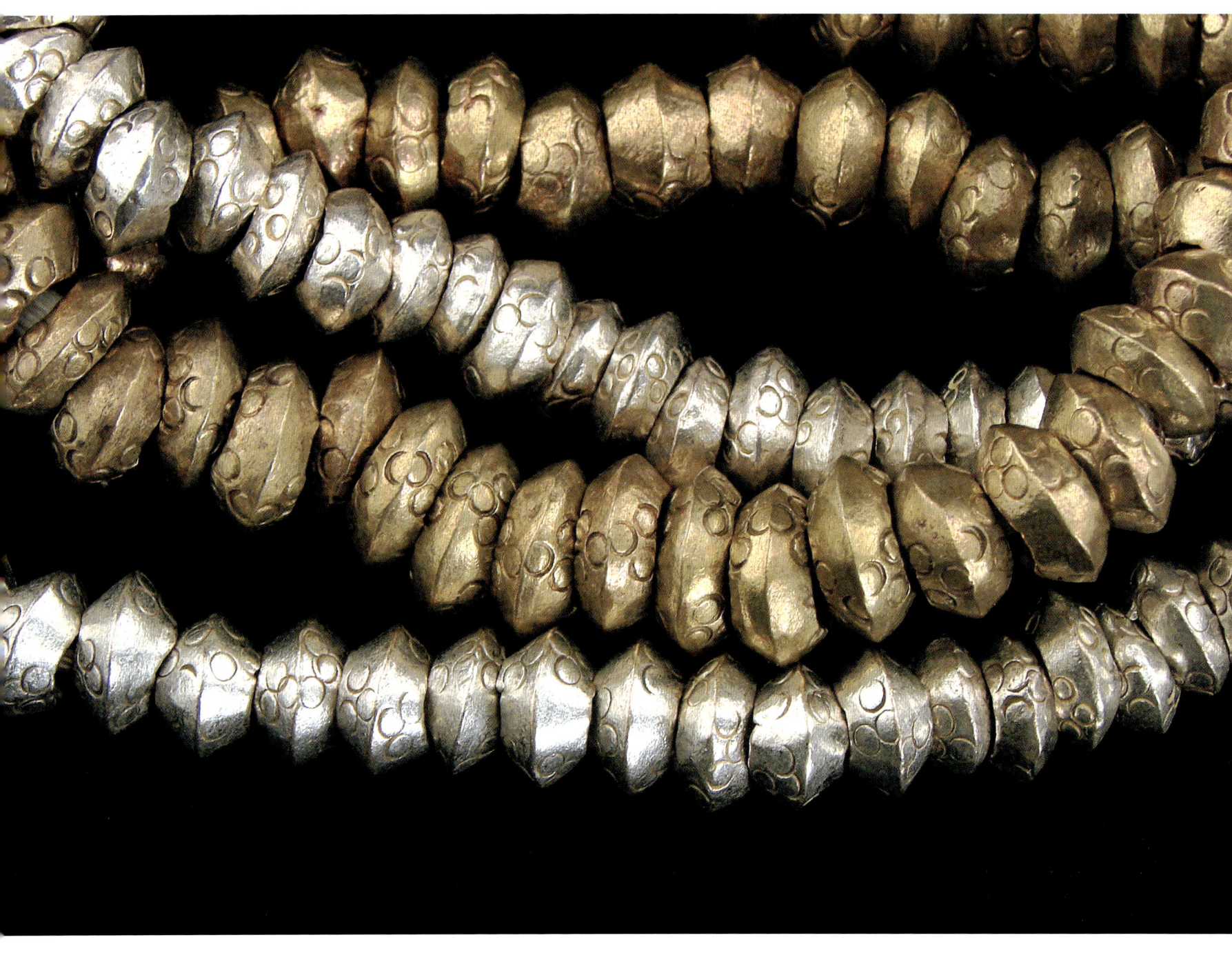

ABOVE *The contemporary white metal beads shown above are decorated with stamped-in circle-dot motifs.*

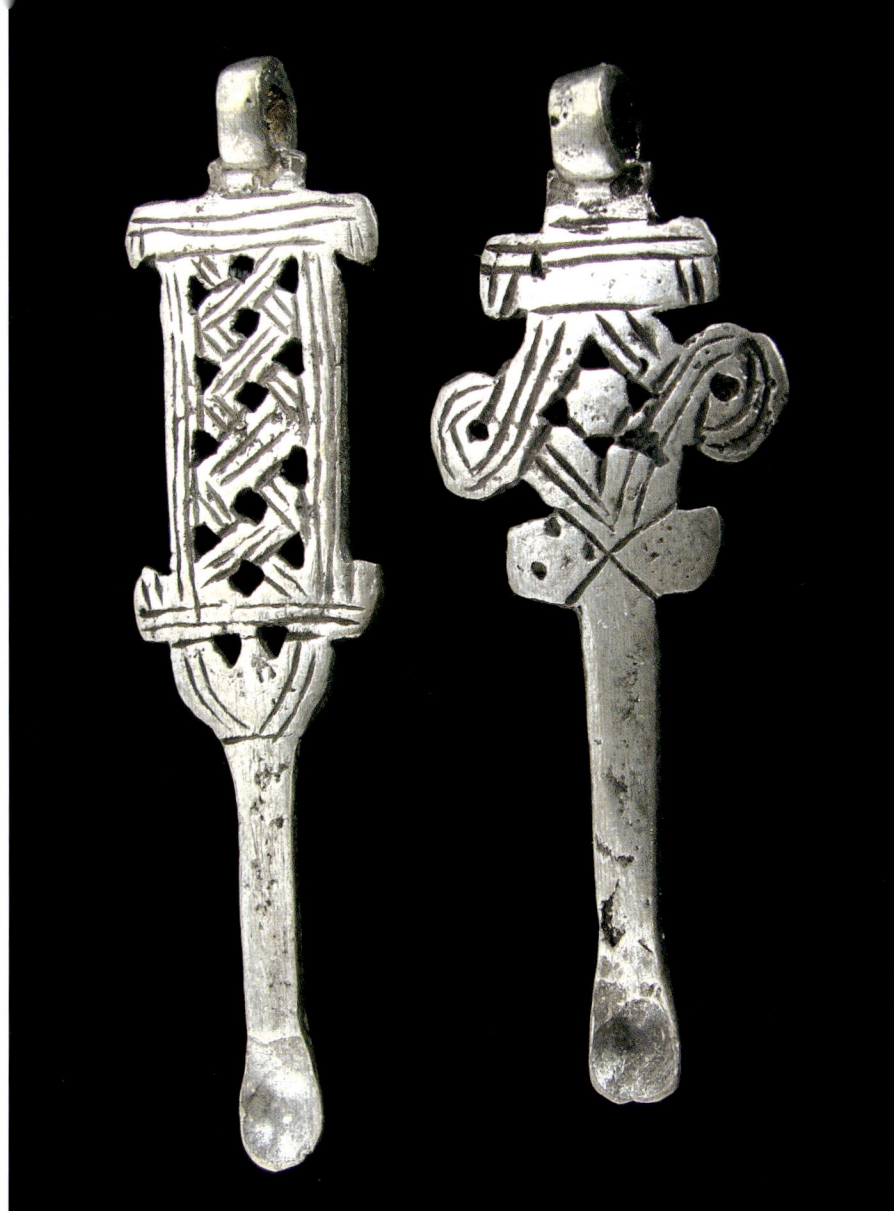

LEFT *Objects of everyday use, such as the ear cleaners depicted here, were often made from silver and decorated with incised designs. They were worn as pendants, within easy reach when needed.*

BELOW LEFT *Strands of Islamic prayer beads like these are manufactured by Ethiopian silversmiths and are called musbaha.*

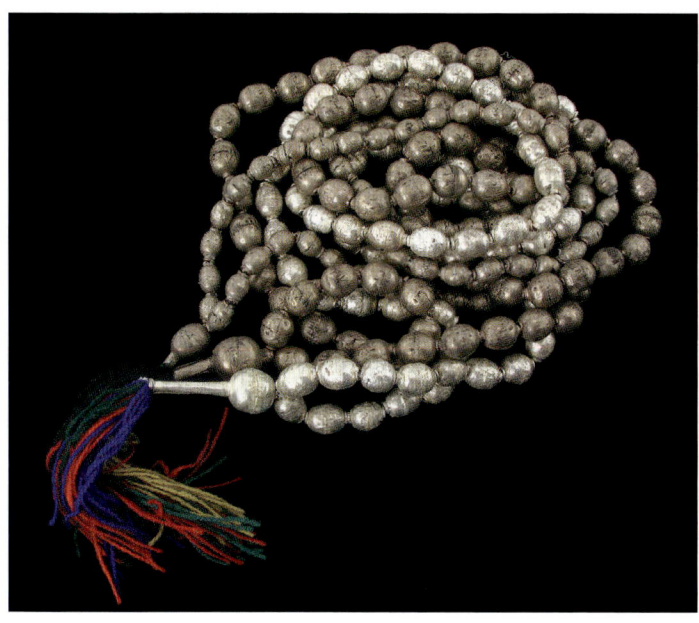

Whereas Agadez cross pendants used to be worn by men only—passed down from father to son with the words, "I give you the four corners of the world because one cannot know where one will die"—these crosses are now worn as neck ornaments by Tuareg women as well. [56]

For additional protection, Tuareg women also wear Tcherot [57] and Khomissar [58] pendants. The Khomissar is commonly fashioned from a square or rectangular piece of leather on which are attached five flat, diamond-shaped fragments of shell, two in the top row and three below. Diamond shapes are believed to offer protection from the "evil eye." According to Berber tradition, the eye is the mirror of the soul, and a hateful or jealous glance can harm both humans and animals. Motifs expressing stylized eyes, such as diamonds that resemble an eye, are believed to deflect evil spirits and thoughts and hence are worn for their protective properties. The Khomissar represents the Hand of Fatima

Metal Beads 105

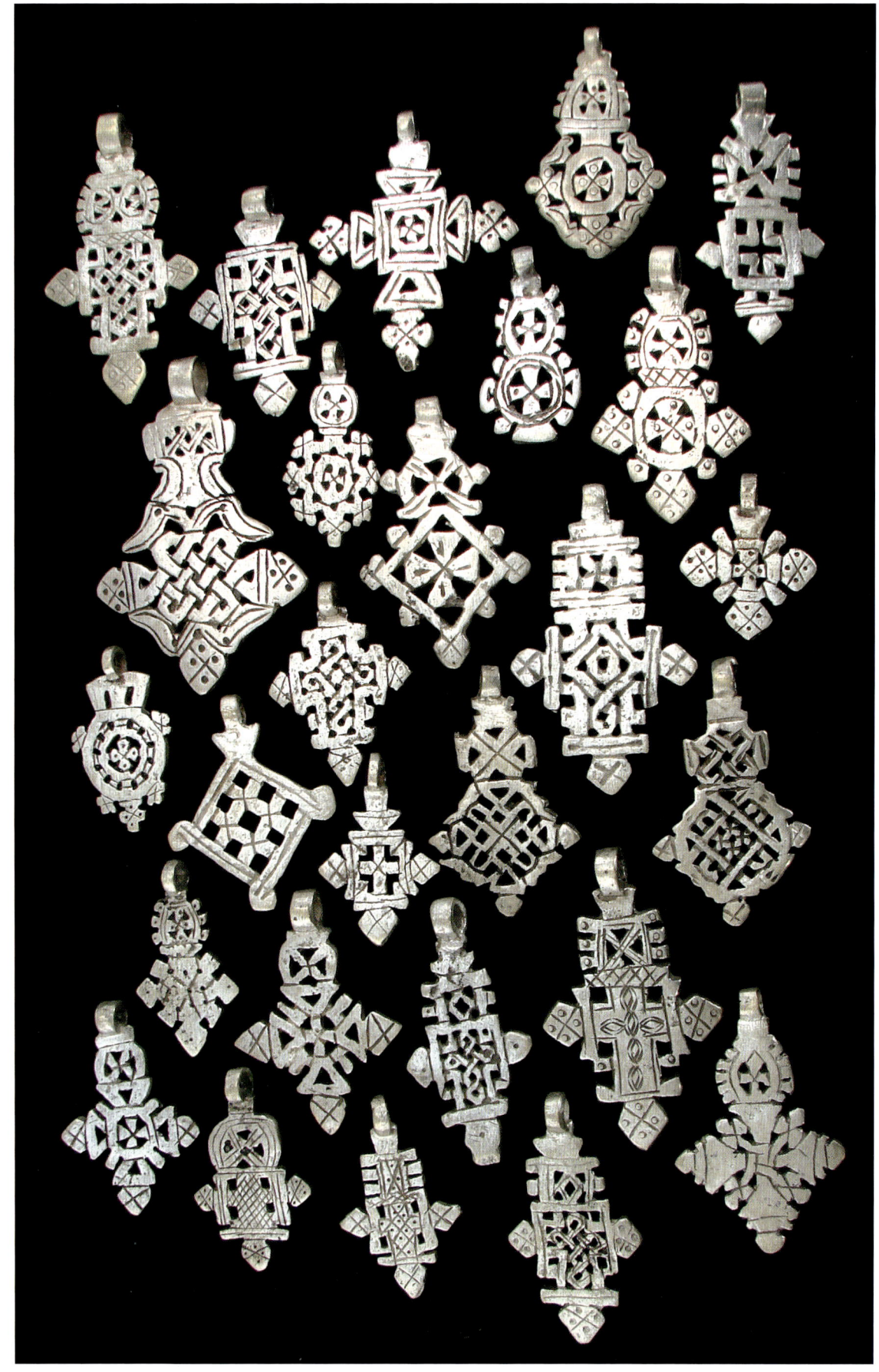

LEFT *A group of cross-shaped pendants called Coptic crosses, worn since the inception of Christianity in Ethiopia in the 4th century CE. They continue to be made today. While Ethiopian Christians were long isolated from the Christian world, they have been able to maintain their independence and their culture, as well as their faith.*

RIGHT ABOVE AND BELOW *Silver Coptic crosses are being made in a number of styles ranging from plain to very elaborate. Some are hinged and reveal a painted motif when opened.*

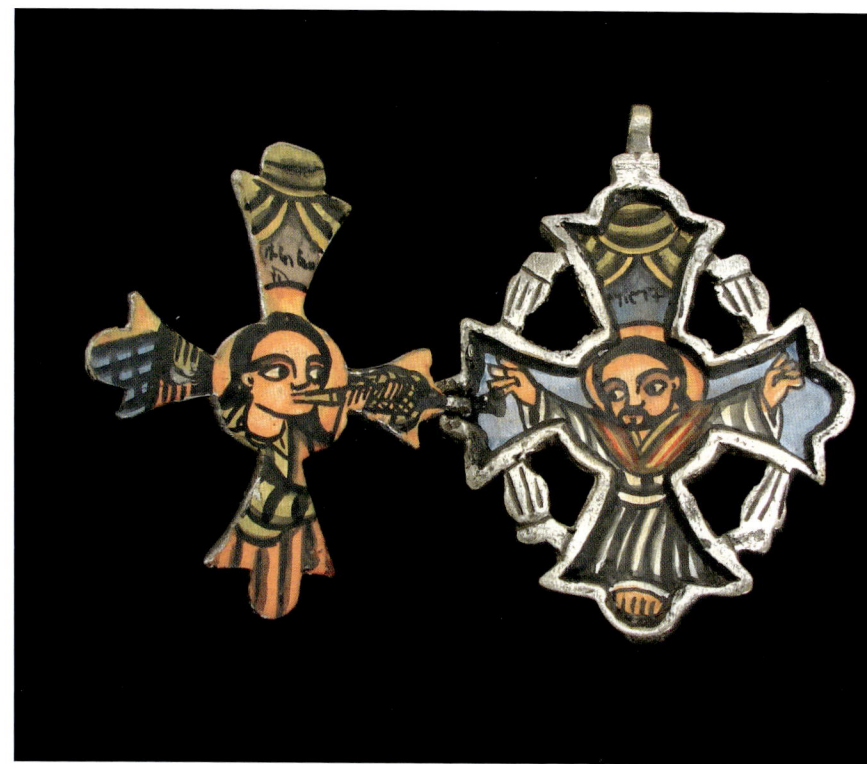

(also called khamsa, derived from the Arabic word for five, i.e. the five fingers on a hand) and is traditionally passed down by a mother to her daughter as she approaches adulthood. [59]

Over the past thirty years, Tuareg jewelry has gained popularity in high-end boutiques in America and Europe, especially in Paris and New York. Hermes of Paris, for instance, has added to its range of fashion products purse locks and belt buckles designed and manufactured by Tuareg artisans. While maintaining traditional Tuareg designs, the decorative patterns found on new pieces and especially on the silver crosses of Agadez appear to be more elaborately executed.

Berber

The Berbers are the earliest known inhabitants of northern Africa, having lived there long before the arrival of the Arabs. Their culture dates back more than 4,000 years. A Berber alphabet has existed for around 2,500 years, but the language—collectively called shilha in Arabic—is not officially recognized in Morocco, whereas French, the old colonial language, is. From the 11th to the 13th centuries, the Berber dynasties, known as the Almoravids and the Almohads, controlled large parts of Spain and northwest Africa. Two Berber states, Mauritania and Numidia, existed in classical times.

Substantial Berber populations are found in Morocco—where forty percent of the population acknowledges a Berber identity, and even more have Berber ancestry—as well as in Algeria, Tunisia, Libya and Egypt. In Algeria, ethnic Berbers form a minority of around seventeen percent but maintain a strongly separate identity and speak their own language, called Tamazight or Amazigh, which is related to Zenete, a language spoken by many Saharan Berbers. The

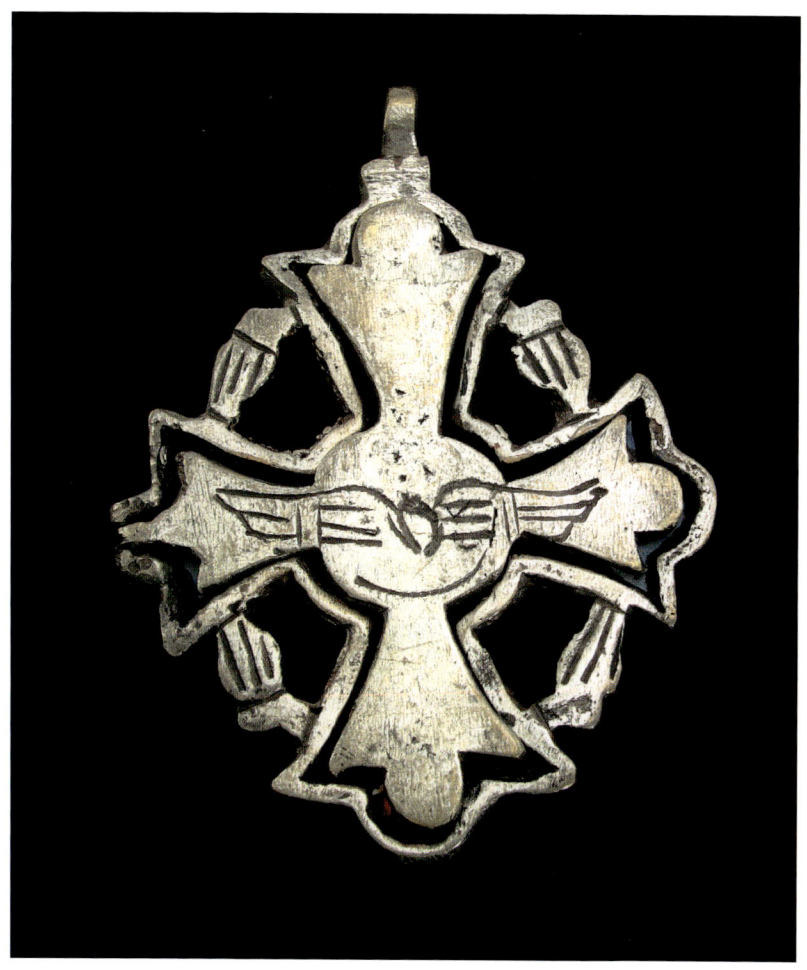

Metal Beads ◆ 107

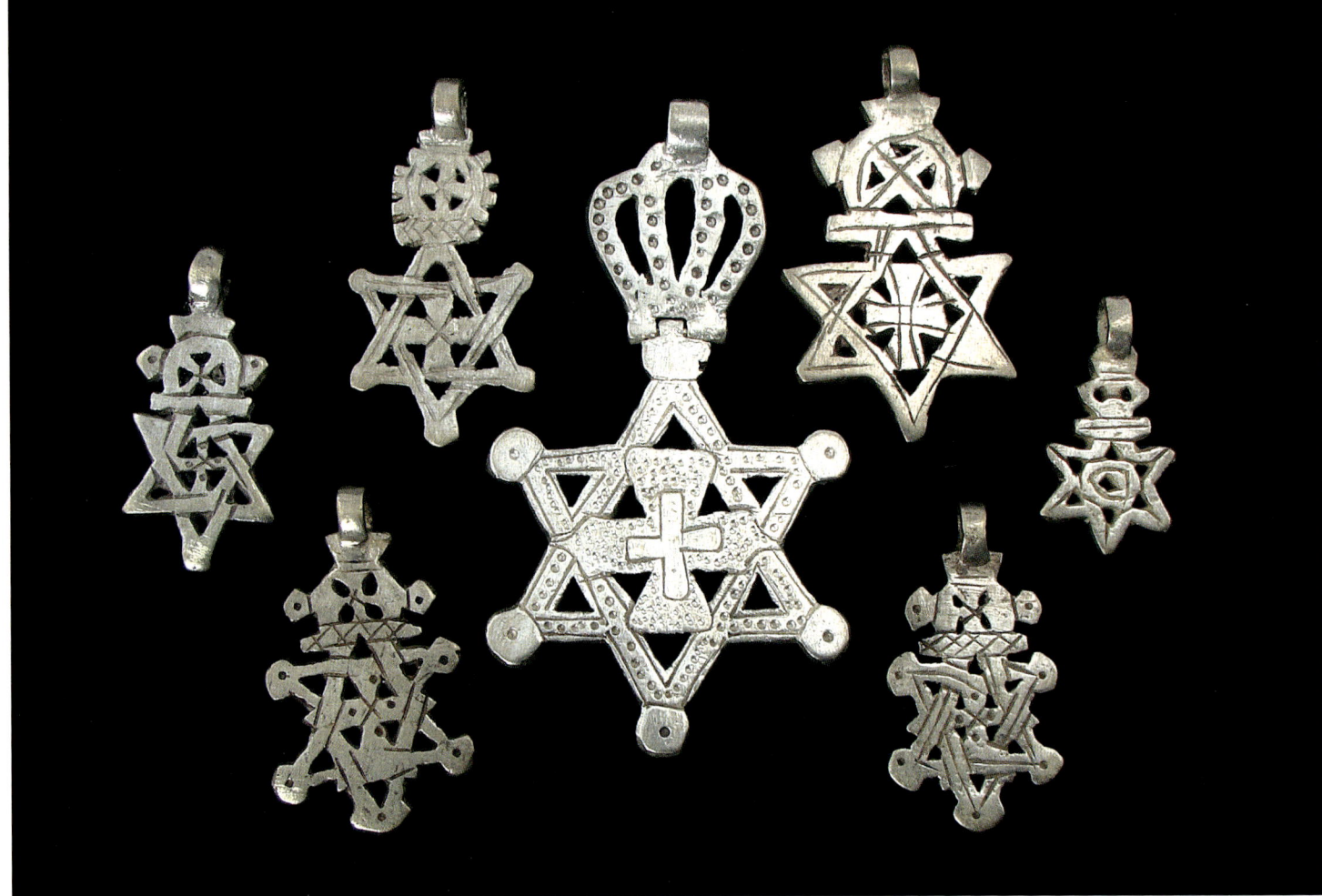

ABOVE *The Falasha (Ethiopian Jews) manufactured these Star of David pendants.*

RIGHT *Massive ring-shaped beads made from brass, with incised decorative designs in various styles. Some of these beads have long appendages.*

north Algerian Berbers, the Kabylie, who live in the Kabylie Mountains, and the Chaouia, from the Aures Mountains, call themselves and their culture Amazigh (plural Imazighen), meaning free or pure. Berbers are identified primarily by language, but also by their traditional customs and culture. Many Berbers are pastoralists, cultivating crops and raising livestock, while others continue to maintain nomadic or semi-nomadic lifestyles as traveling herders and traders. Thousands still populate the Sahara, navigating its wastes from oasis to oasis and town to town, using ancient knowledge passed down through the generations. [60]

Silver beads featuring enameling are nowadays produced primarily by members of one Berber family in the vicinity of Tiznit, a town in southern Morocco. The members of this family produce silver enameled beads and pendants of various shapes, ranging from cross-shaped pendants (Croix du Sud), square and rectangular amulet boxes, and Khamsa (Hand of Fatima) pendants, to spherical beads and large ovoid pendants that are often adorned with drop-shaped dangles. These large enameled "eggs" are called tagmout when worn as pendants, as is the tradition amongst the Ida ou Semlal from the Anti-Atlas Occidental highlands. More often these large ornaments, with two fibulas forming the center pieces, are an integral part of large pectorals, called tizerzai—possibly the largest, heaviest and most impressive ornaments in Morocco. They are commonly used as ceremonial or bridal jewelry. While most Moroccan beads are produced from silver it should be borne in mind that the silver content is often less than seventy-five percent real silver, never higher, and that the hallmarking of silver is, for this reason, illegal according to Moroccan law. [61]

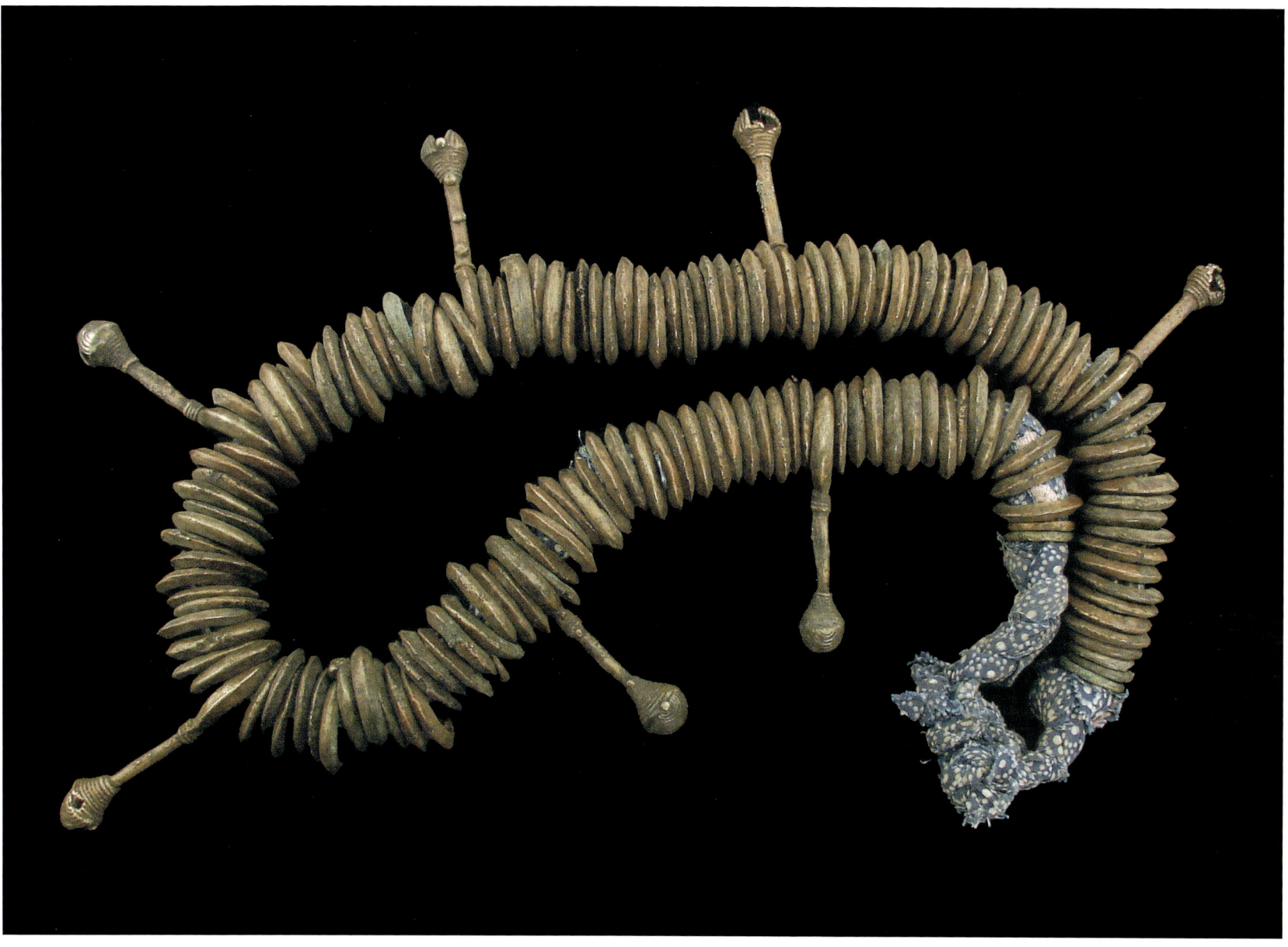

Silver in Ethiopia

Oromo

Besides the Tuareg and the Berber, another group of highly skilled metalworkers in Africa are the Oromo of the Ethiopian highlands. According to ancient traditions, the Oromo originate in Boorana in southern Ethiopia, where they lived until the beginning of their migrations, in about 1530. By 1896, they were by force made subjects of the Abyssinian king Menelik II, and by 1904 fixed borders had been established for a self-contained territory created on both sides of the Ethiopian-Kenyan border. At present, Oromo peoples inhabit central and southern Ethiopia and part of northeastern Kenya. While most still practice their Oromo religion, traditional practices are often combined with Islamic and Christian religious customs. [62]

Maria Theresa Thaler

Only negligible amounts of indigenous silver are found in Ethiopia. For this reason, most silver beads and adornments are derived from imported silver, mainly in the form of the Austrian Maria Theresa thaler, a silver coin minted during the reign of Maria Theresa, Archduchess of Austria and Queen of Hungary and Bohemia (1740-1780). Extensively traded and accepted as currency in many African countries, the Maria Theresa thaler is one of the most widely

Metal Beads

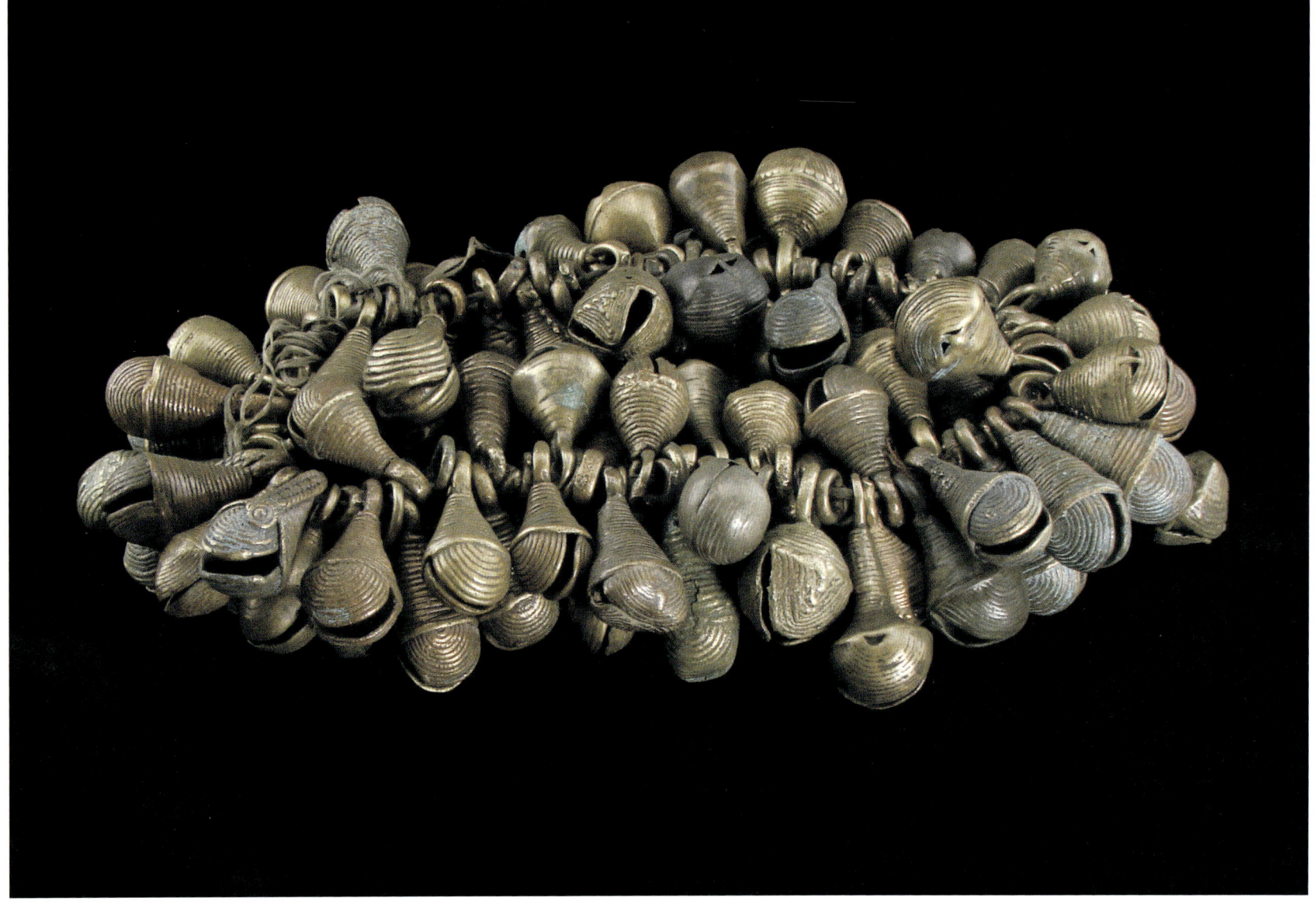

ABOVE *Besides beads and pendants, the Yoruba also produced brass and bronze bells in great quantities, in designs ranging from plain to very elaborate, and in sizes from pea-sized to as large as a golf ball. Brass bells can be found on large strands by themselves or in combinations with other brass beads, as parts of a ritual piece, a dance costume or an anklet or wristband.*

circulated coins in the world. [63] It spread from the Horn of Africa to the coast of East Africa and to the West African Gold Coast, where it replaced older units of account, such as iron and copper bars and brass rings. During the 1850s, the thaler represented one of the accepted currencies in Kano (capital city of Hausaland, present-day Nigeria), the value of one thaler being equivalent to 2,500 kurdis (cowries). By the early 1900s, the Maria Theresa thaler had become the official currency of Ethiopia.

Telsum

Triangular or crescent-shaped prayer boxes, called telsum, are worn for their protective properties. The triangular specimens in particular are believed to fend off evil spirits and the "evil eye," whereas crescent-shaped amuletic boxes are worn as protection against the spells of the crescent moon. Square, rectangular and irregularly shaped pendants are also manufactured, serving similar purposes. Some of these telsum are elaborately decorated and feature granulated designs created with melted silver. Often they are gold washed or gilded. Telsum prayer boxes are traditionally worn as necklaces, strung on purple yarn or strips of cloth. Older specimens were made from silver derived from the Maria Theresa thaler; modern versions are typically made from an amalgam of nickel and alloy.

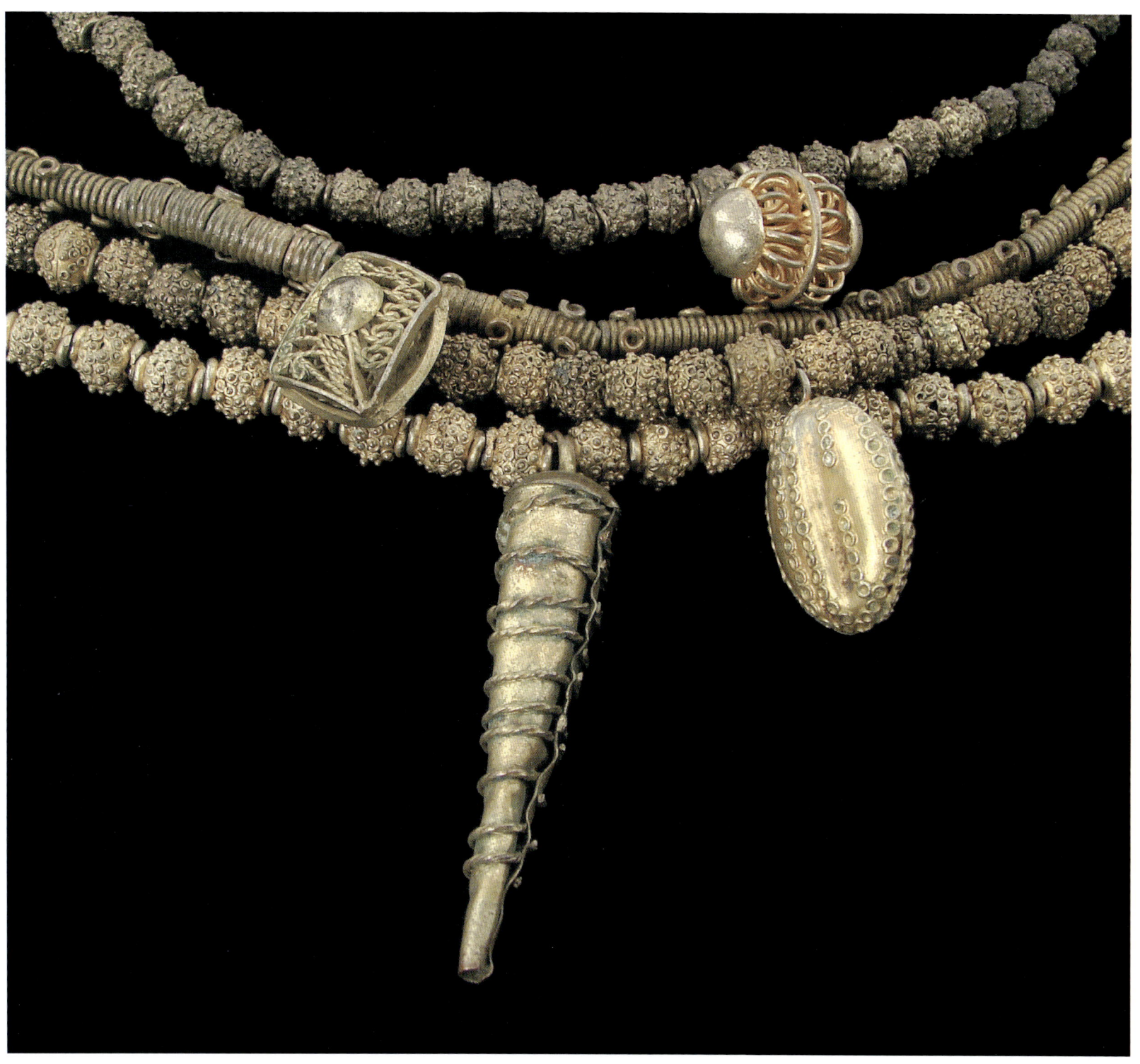

ABOVE *Yoruba metalsmiths are talented and skillful artisans who produced, and continue to produce, a great number of different bead styles, such as the variants depicted here, some gold-washed in order to create additional pleasing effects.*

Metal Beads

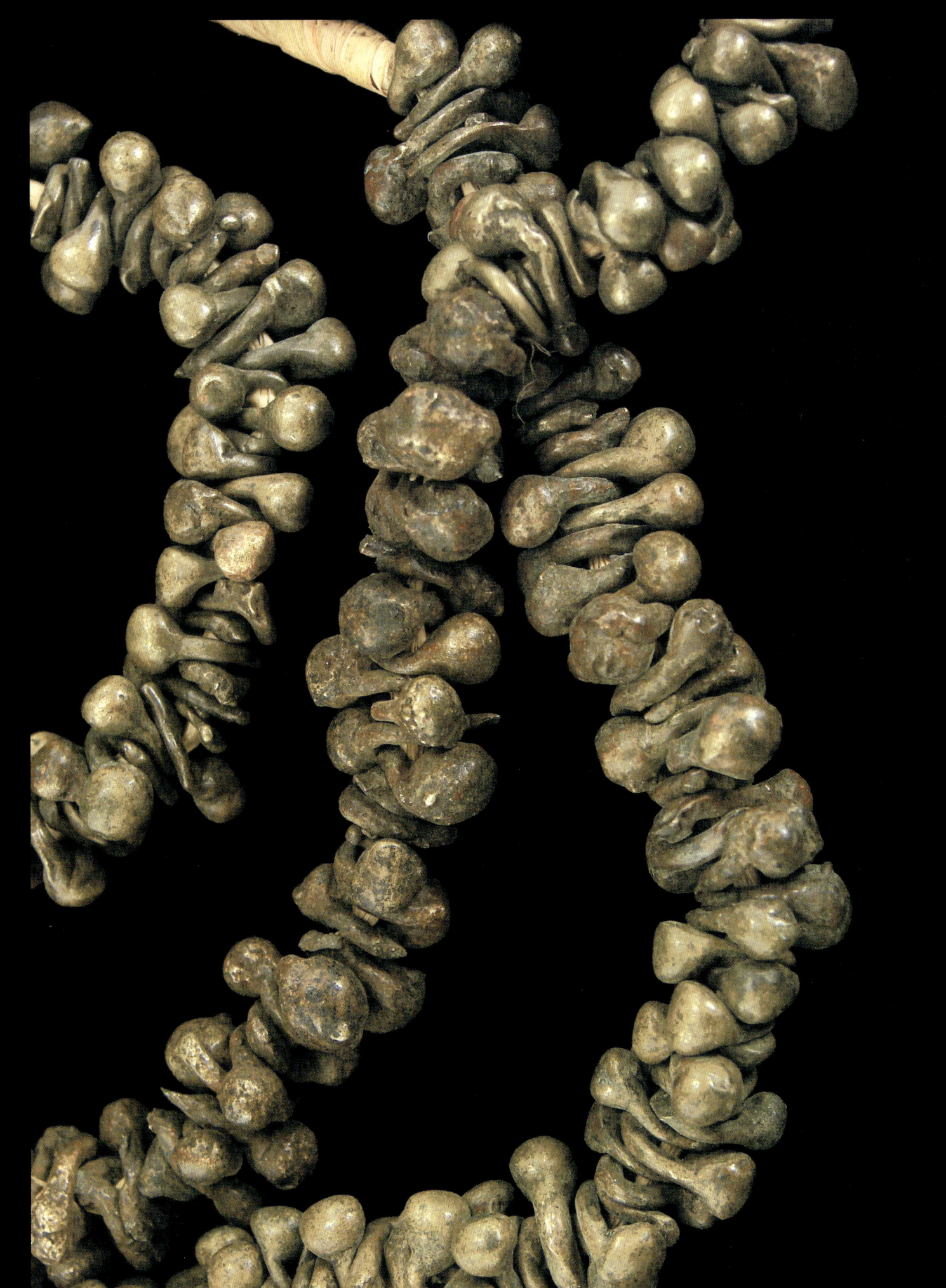

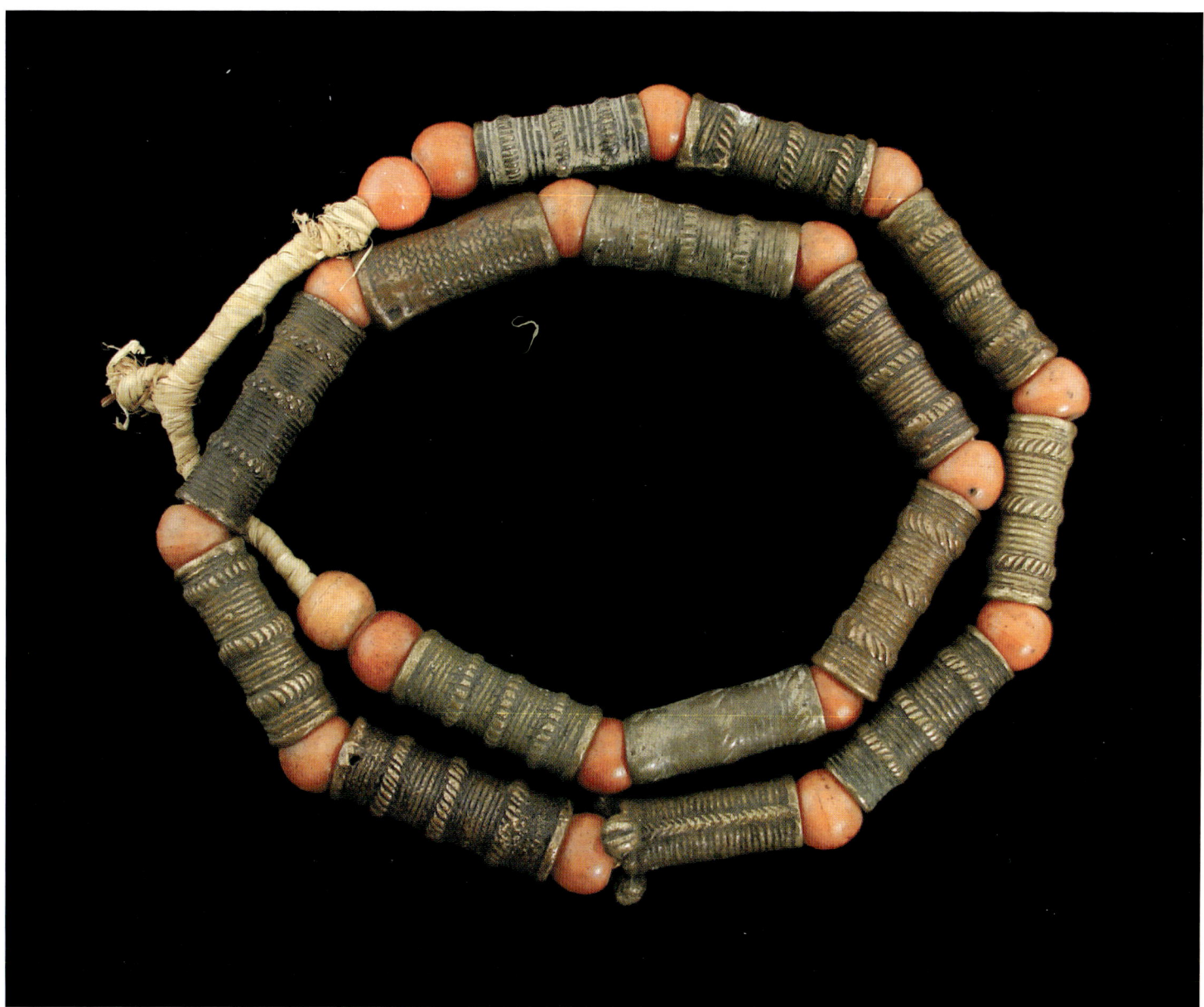

LEFT *Necklace of small fertility pendants known as "Igbo bugs."*

ABOVE *Metal workers of the Tiv, a minority group originating in Cameroon, manufacture large, often elaborately decorated brass beads cast with the lost wax technique. Women of the Wodaabe, an offshoot of the Fulani which has adhered to the traditional nomadic lifestyle, wear these beads as hair ornaments.*

Mergaf

Mergaf pendants represent another type of protective amulets. Mergaf were manufactured in a variety of shapes, sizes and materials, such as silver, amalgams of silver with other white metals, and nickel alloys. Sometimes elaborately and sometimes sparsely decorated, the pendants can be rectangular, spherical or tube-shaped and are typically adorned with dangles or small bells of conical shape. They typically measure from twenty to forty millimeters in diameter but can be as long as eight centimeters. Most of the tubular amulet boxes have a hinged lid on one end that can be opened. They often contain small objects believed to possess amuletic properties, special herbs, or a piece of paper with verses from the Quran. Square mergaf are usually flat in profile and often decorated with eight or more raised dots and a series of conical bell dangles. This particular style is some-

Metal Beads   113

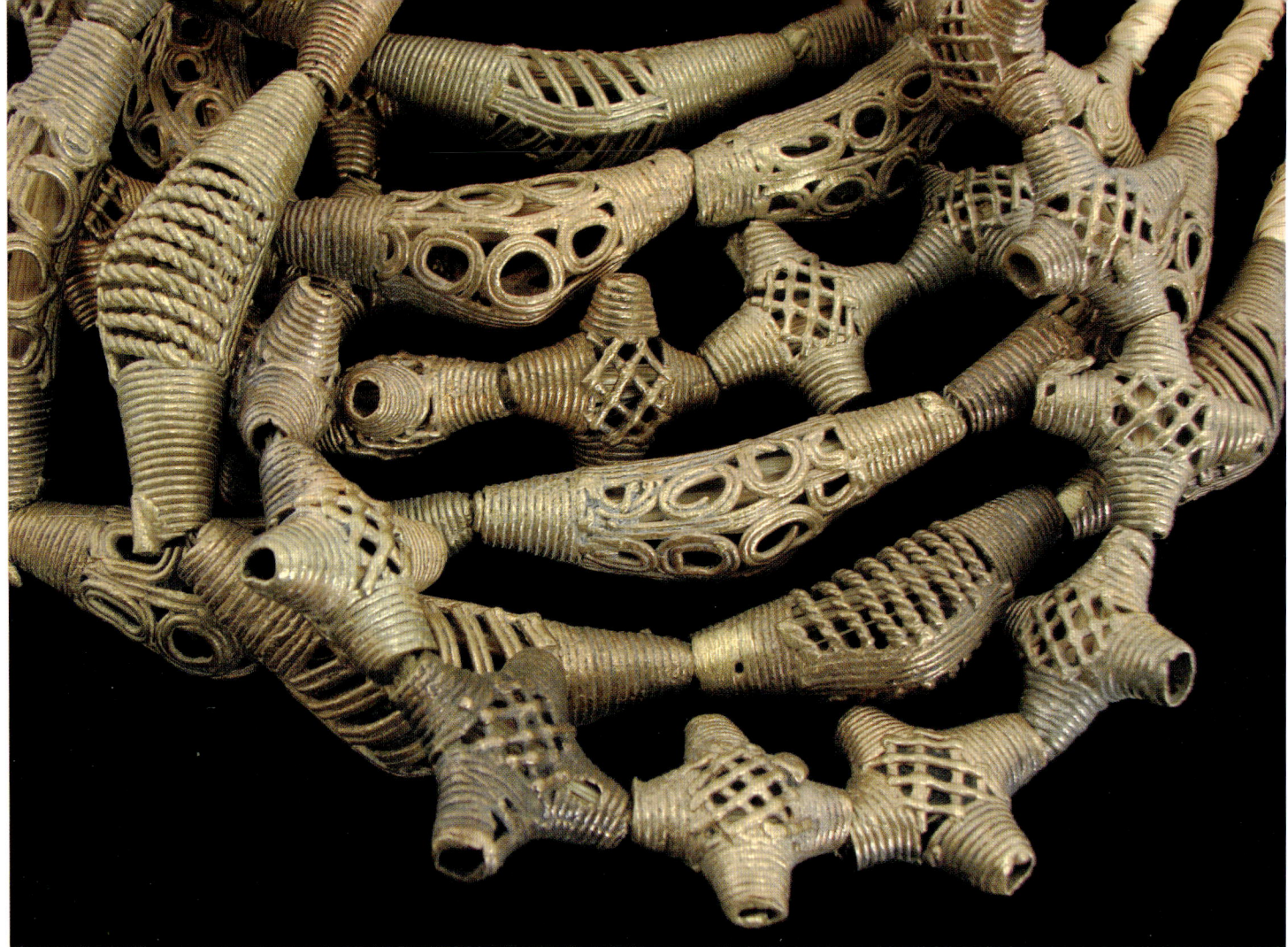

ABOVE *Contemporary styles of brass beads produced in Ampabame Krofrom, the only brass casting village in Ghana today. Featuring traditional shapes and decorative designs, they evidence a long tradition of metal working.*

times referred to as an "engagement pendant" and was worn on necklaces, often in combination with a number of small phallic pendants flanking it on each side. Considered to be symbols and enhancers of fertility, these phallic pendants typically measured about fifteen millimeters in length and were made of silver or an amalgam of silver and alloy. They were also worn separately on necklaces.

Pendants and Amulets

Besides prayer boxes and amuletic pendants, Ethiopian silversmiths have produced a great variety of small silver and white metal beads in a number of shapes and sizes. Commonly these spherical, biconical or barrel-shaped beads are not larger than ten millimeters in diameter, although larger beads measuring up to twenty-six millimeters in diameter were manufactured using thin strips of silver or white metals, which were shaped into biconical forms and soldered together at their seams. A number of these large beads have granulated surfaces or are decorated with raised dots, stripes, bands and ribs. [64]

Musbaha

Ethiopian silversmiths also manufacture beads that are assembled to form Islamic prayer bead strands, called musbaha. The musbaha are commonly comprised of small hollow and lightweight beads, measuring approximately ten millimeters or less, and made from nickel alloy or so-called white metal with a copper wash finish and a yarn tassel attached to the elongated Imam or baluster bead.

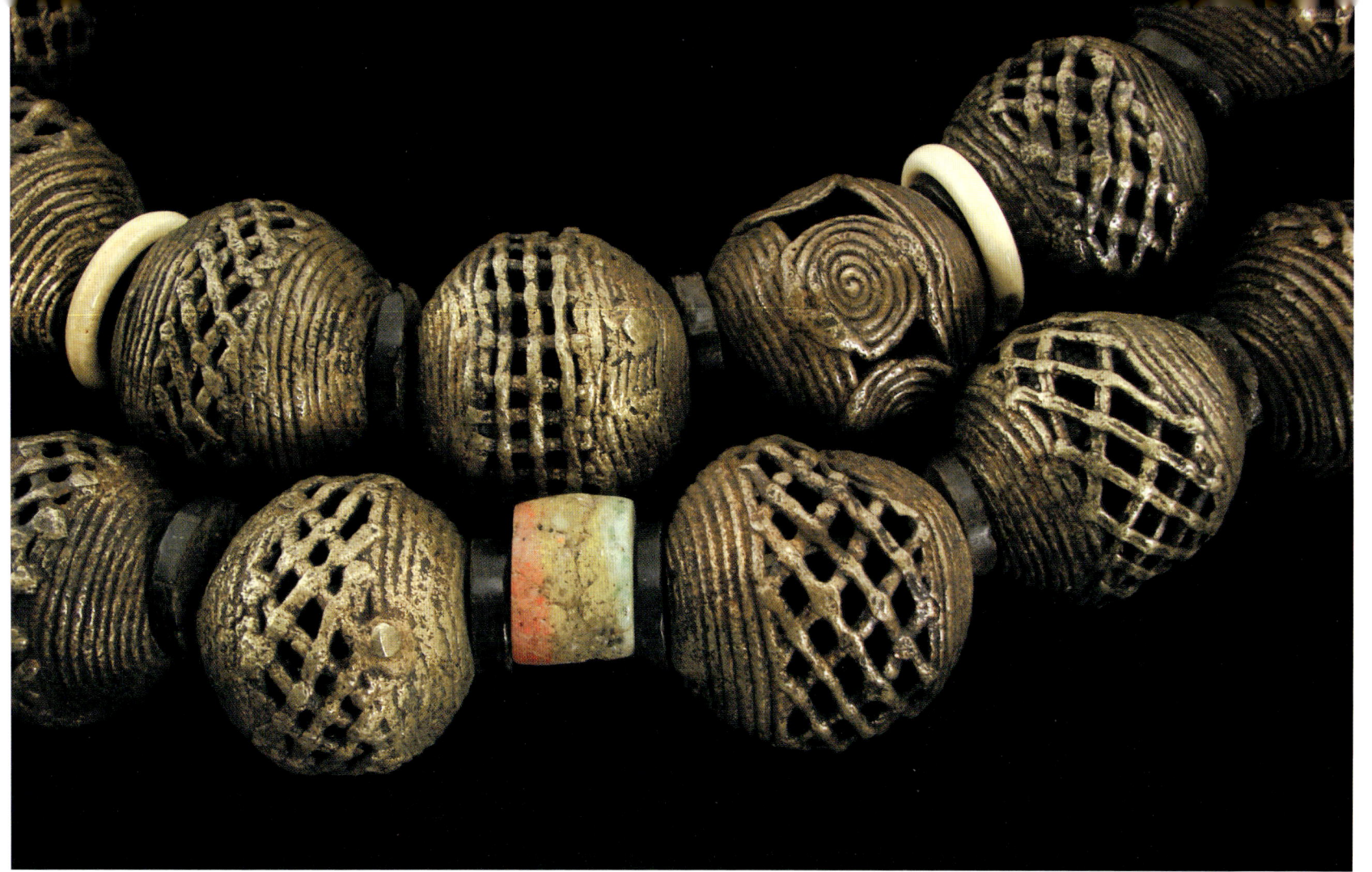

ABOVE *A strand of large, contemporary cast brass beads, produced by Ghanaian metalworkers.*

Coptic Crosses

Probably the best-known products of Ethiopian manufacture are the elaborately designed Coptic crosses, which have been manufactured and worn since the arrival of Christianity in Ethiopia in the 4th century CE. Although Ethiopian Christians were cut off from the Christian world by the Muslim conquests, they managed to maintain their independence, their culture, their identity and their faith. Coptic crosses were made in a wide variety of styles and sizes, ranging from small pieces, measuring twenty-eight millimeters, to large specimens of up to ten centimeters in length; their style was influenced by many cultures both inside and outside of Africa. One of the most famous and commonly used symbols was the Ankh, associated with life after death and representing stability and strength. It was perceived as a powerful amulet, which could invoke God's protection over the bearer. To Christians it represented the halo of Christ. Other designs that were used show Greek, Roman or Celtic influence, and some decorative patterns are reminiscent of European medals and crowns. Ethiopian Coptic crosses may be hinged or plain. They were manufactured by using the lost wax technique, or cut from silver Maria Theresa thalers or silver plates. Coptic crosses of a more recent production are made from a nickel alloy or other white metal amalgams. [65]

Falasha

So-called Star of David pendants were made and worn by the Falasha, also called 'black Jews'—a small minority of Ethiopians who retained the Jewish faith that spread

Metal Beads   115

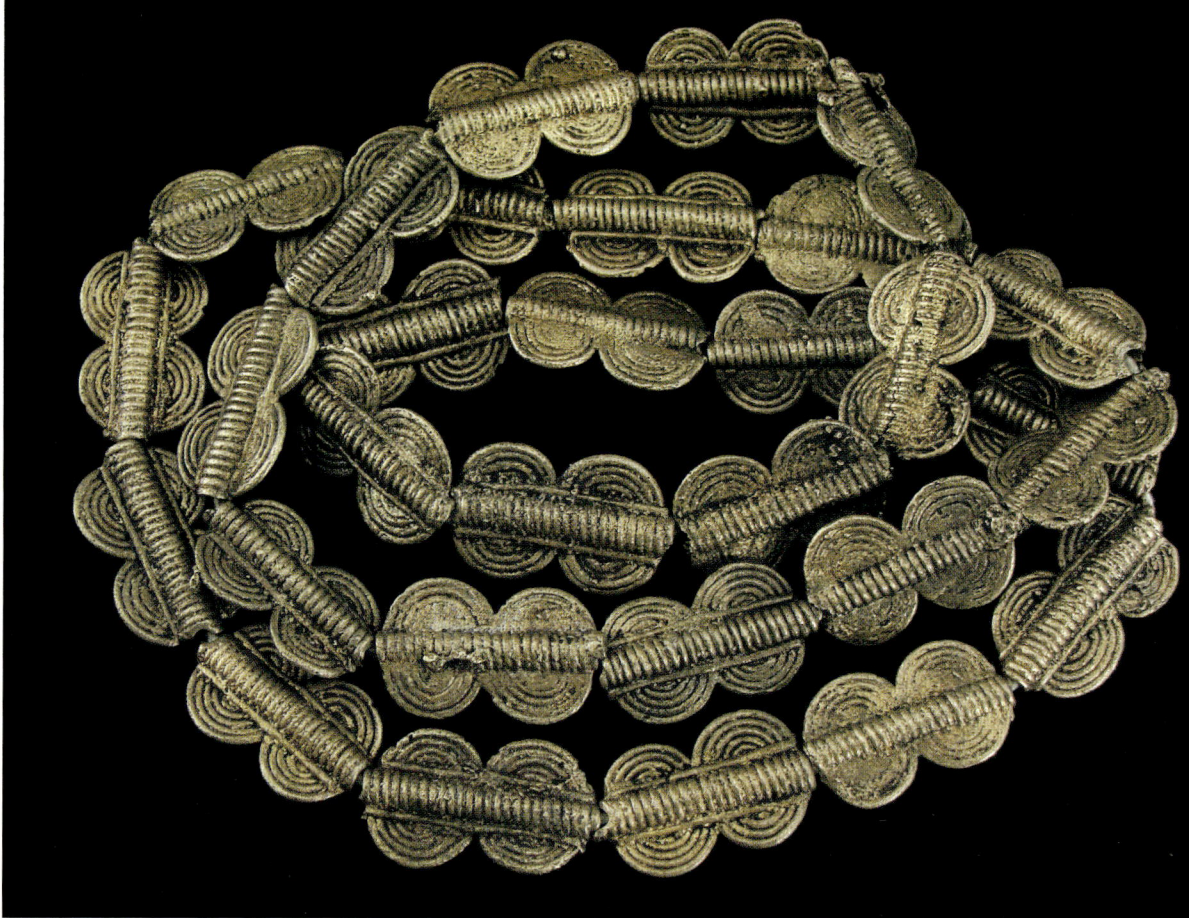

RIGHT AND BELOW
Contemporary Baoule beads often copy traditional designs. They come in many different shapes and sizes, ranging from round disks and rectangular tabulars to flat triangles, with decorative patterns often consisting of concentric raised circles or of stylized animals in the form of spiders, crocodiles, lizards or birds. Baoule artisans also produce distinctive face pendants, sometimes described as "maskettes" because they resemble traditional ceremonial facemasks, which were originally made to represent an enemy killed in battle. Such facemasks were believed to give power to their wearer. Finely cast and modeled in high relief, these face pendants can be as large as ten centimeters.

to Ethiopia from South Arabia before the introduction of Christianity.

Brass

Brass in Nigeria

In Nigeria, African artisans were using the lost wax casting technique to manufacture ornaments and other objects as early as the 11th century CE, two centuries before the arrival of the first Portuguese explorers in 1484. The materials most commonly used by Nigerian smiths were bronze and brass, although beads were also made from iron. Where gold was available, on the Gold Coast (Ghana), Ivory Coast, and in Senegal, elaborate beads and ornaments of gold were being produced as well. Nigerian cast brass statues and sculptures have been well researched and documented, including the famous heads of Ife dating from the 13th century. However, there is not much information pertaining to the manufacture of metal beads and jewelry. The great majority of old beads originating from Nigeria which have become available on the international bead markets date from the late 1800s and early 1900s. Then during the influx of "African Trade Beads" in the 1960s, many brass and bronze beads

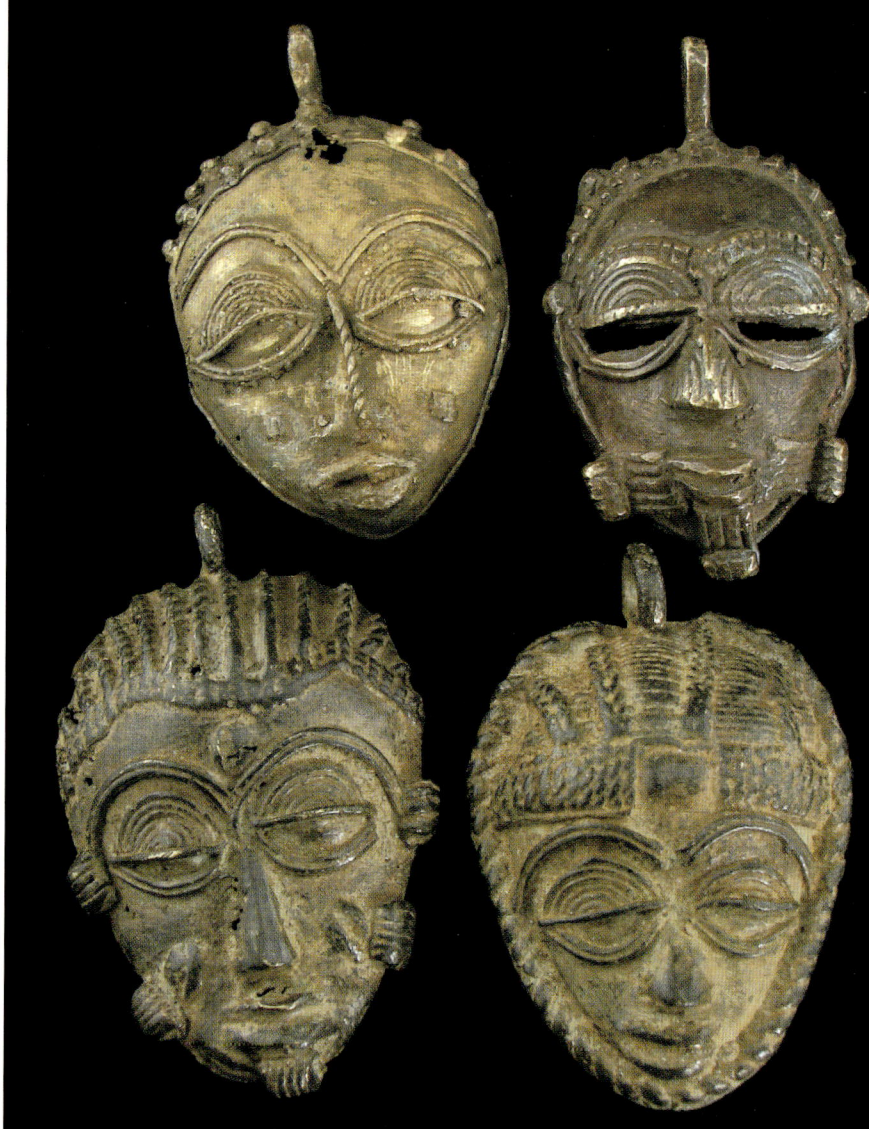

116 ◆ Metal Beads

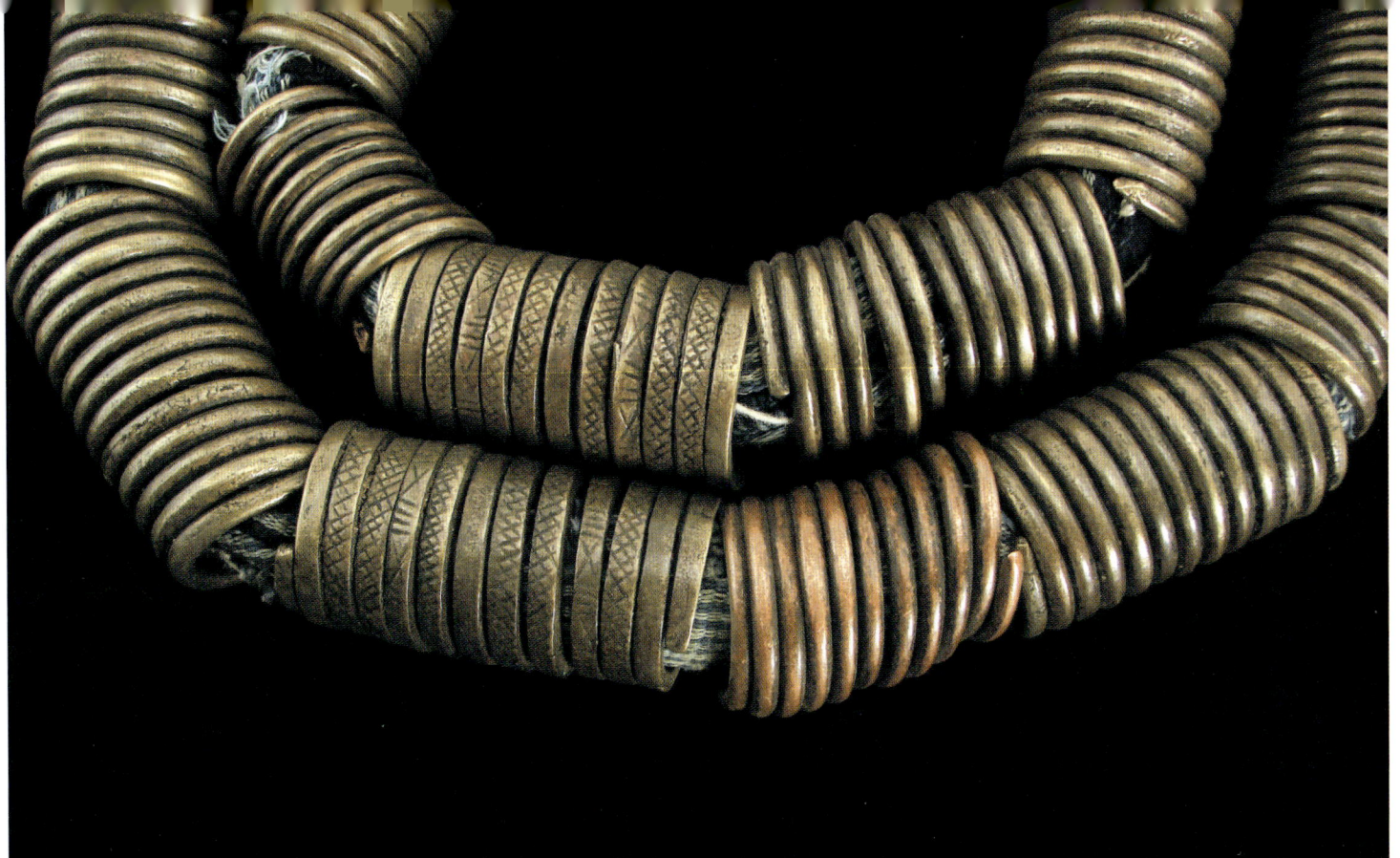

ABOVE *Disk or ring-shaped beads were worn in West Africa for centuries. They were made in a variety of types and styles and from a number of different metals. Some are very small and disk-shaped while others are large enough to be worn as finger rings or pendants. One specific style features a single attachment fifty millimeters in length fashioned from a brass rod, with a small bell attached at one end, representing a stylized phallus. The smallest types of disk-shaped brass beads are believed to originate in Ethiopia and Kenya and measure about three millimeters in diameter. They are typically worn in a fashion similar to heishi, which they visually resemble.*

were brought from Africa to the United States of America and Europe. Still, it was not until the 1990s that many of the older and often larger beads became available outside of Africa. [66]

The land that is present-day Nigeria was once one of the oldest and largest empires in Africa. Located on the Gulf of Guinea and bordered by Chad, Niger, Benin and Cameroon, Nigeria is rich in cultural history and home to more than 250 different ethnic groups, of which the Hausa-Fulani, Igbo, Iljaw and Yoruba are the most dominant. Both the Yoruba and the Fulani are renowned metal workers, as are the Tiv, a minority group. [67]

Yoruba

The Yoruba—the word was originally the Hausa name for the Oyo kingdom—live in southwestern Nigeria, in the neighboring Republic of Benin (not to be confused with the City of Benin), and in Togo. They are probably the best known and the most prolific makers of metal beads, pendants, bells and fetishes in West Africa. Using the lost wax method, they have produced brass beads measuring up to 95 by 150 millimeters. Commonly their beads are of large flattened biconical shapes, and decorative patterns consist of protrusions placed around the beads' equator. Ring or tire-shaped beads with large perforations, detailed outer surfaces similar to latticework, and crisscross designs or arrow-like patterns were often also worn as finger rings or pendants. [68]

Certain bead types made by Yoruba metal workers are manufactured from hammered sheets of bronze and brass which have been cut into strips. The strips are formed into biconical beads of various sizes, lengths and widths. Similar but lighter beads dating to the early 1900s were produced from a variety of metals, most often in spherical shapes smaller than ten millimeters in diameter, although biconical and ovoid shapes can also be found. Typically, the surface

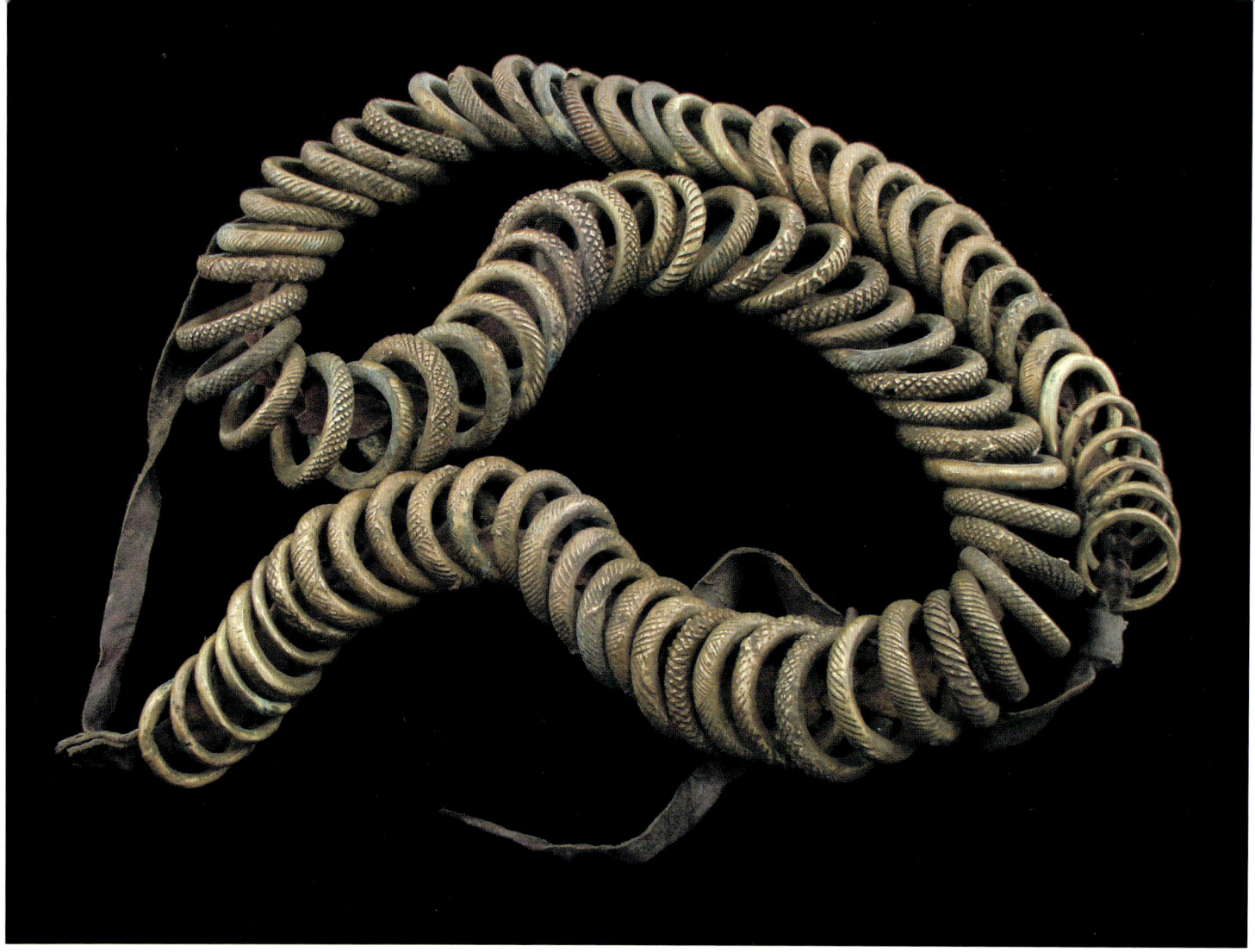

ABOVE *During the 17th and 18th centuries, cast brass, bronze and copper rings were one of the accepted currencies in Africa, from Cape Verde and The Gambia all along the Gold Coast, including Sierra Leone, Liberia and Ghana, to the kingdom of Benin (present-day Dahomey) and Nigeria. Typically measuring about twenty-eight millimeters in diameter with designs ranging from plain to crisscrossed incisions or grooves, these rings were fastened together in lots of ten, and braided onto strips of leather. Forty rings (four strings) were equivalent to the value of one iron bar; the price for one butt of water was two rings.*

of these beads is decorated with minute circles fashioned from metal wire. Often they are gold-washed, which gives them a shiny appearance. When used in necklaces, they are frequently combined with a number of odd-shaped pendants executed in filigree work that may resemble bells or lanterns.

Fulani

The Fulani, who in past centuries have migrated and spread out over a vast area, can today be found from Senegal and Guinea to Nigeria, Cameroon and Chad. After having established a number of kingdoms between Senegal and Cameroon, they conquered the Hausa in 1810. Like the Yoruba, the Fulani are known for their manufacture of bells and unusually shaped pendants. Heavily ribbed pendants, shaped like flattened bananas, have a bail or loop at each end, and can measure up to fourteen centimeters. They represent female fertility and are worn by Fulani women, as are the small, anvil shaped pendants often described as "Igbo Bugs." Brass bells of Fulani manufacture can be differentiated from Yoruba-made bells by their smaller sizes and openings, and by their different decorative patterns, which usually consist of circular, rounded grooves on each side.

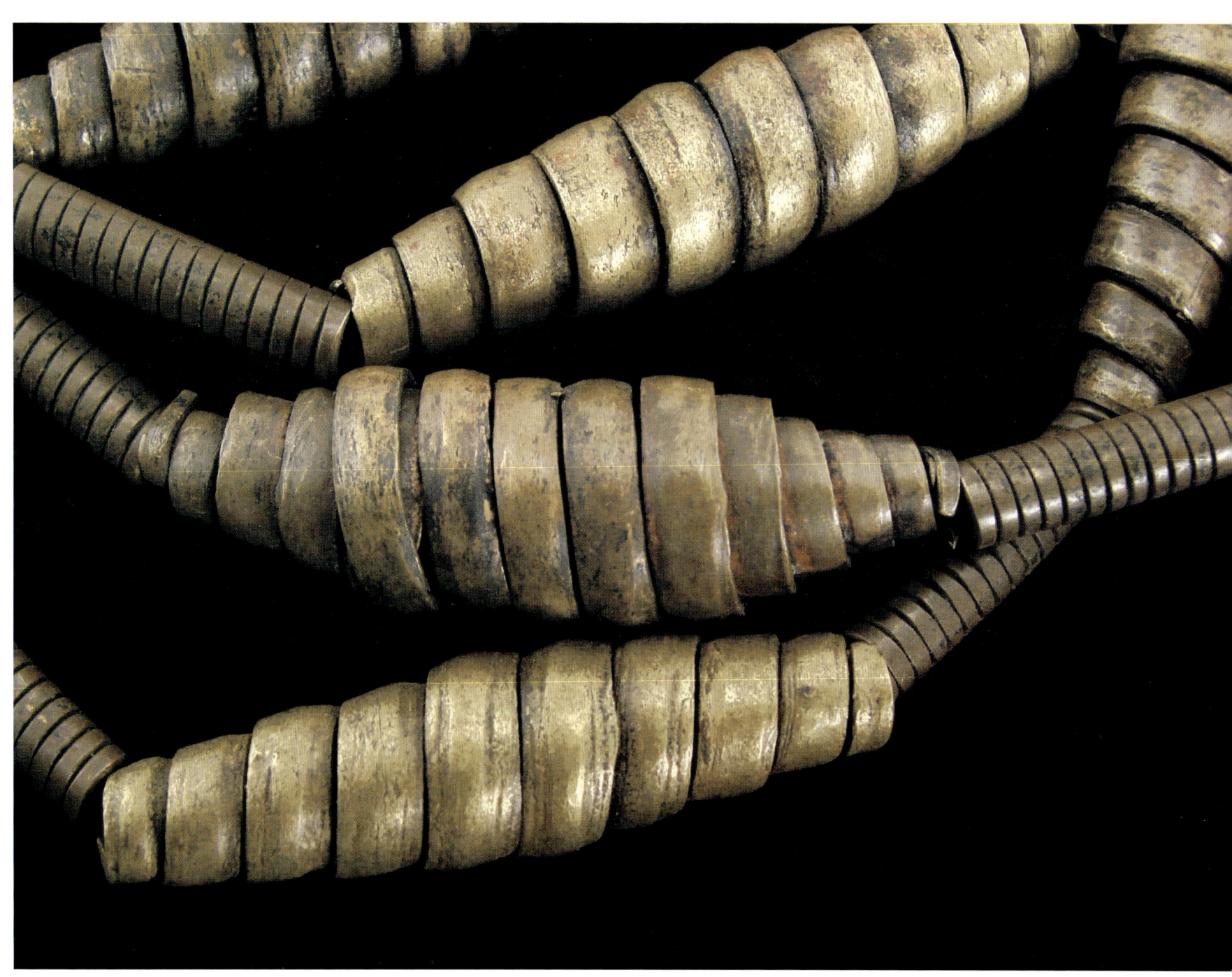

ABOVE *These beautiful wound copper alloy beads probably originated in Nigeria.*

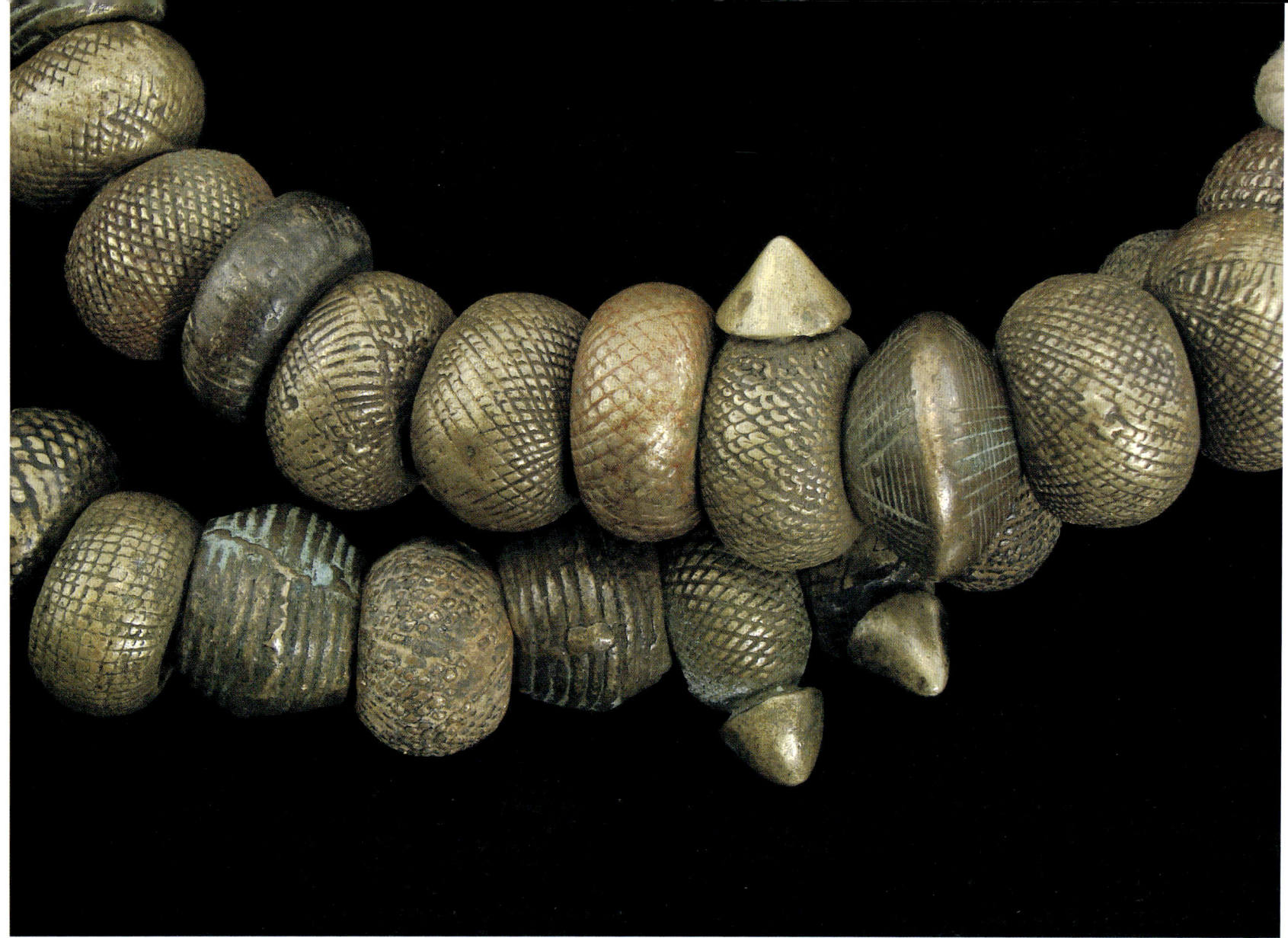

ABOVE *Thick textured and studded rings like those shown here are another example of the variety of copper alloy beads produced by African metalworkers.*

Tiv

Distinctive beads of brass and bronze are being produced by the Tiv, an ethnic minority group whose members speak their own language and live in Benue State, on both sides of the Benue River in Nigeria. Originating in Cameroon, the Tiv settled in the Benue region during the 17th century. Their elaborately decorated brass beads are shaped like stylized elongated pyramids, measuring up to six centimeters in length, with one half being considerably smaller than the other. The decorative patterns typically consist of ribbed and braided designs. Tubular beads, measuring fifteen millimeters in diameter, and of varying lengths, represent another design unique to the Tiv. Cast individually, no two beads are the same. Almost always extensively decorated with ribbed and banded designs, raised circles, and dots and twisted ribbons, their original use is not documented. It is believed that these beads were used as hair ornaments, and it has been established that they are used in this fashion by women of the Wodaabe, a group of Fulani who still maintain the traditional lifestyle of their nomadic ancestors. Both bead types date from the late 1800s.

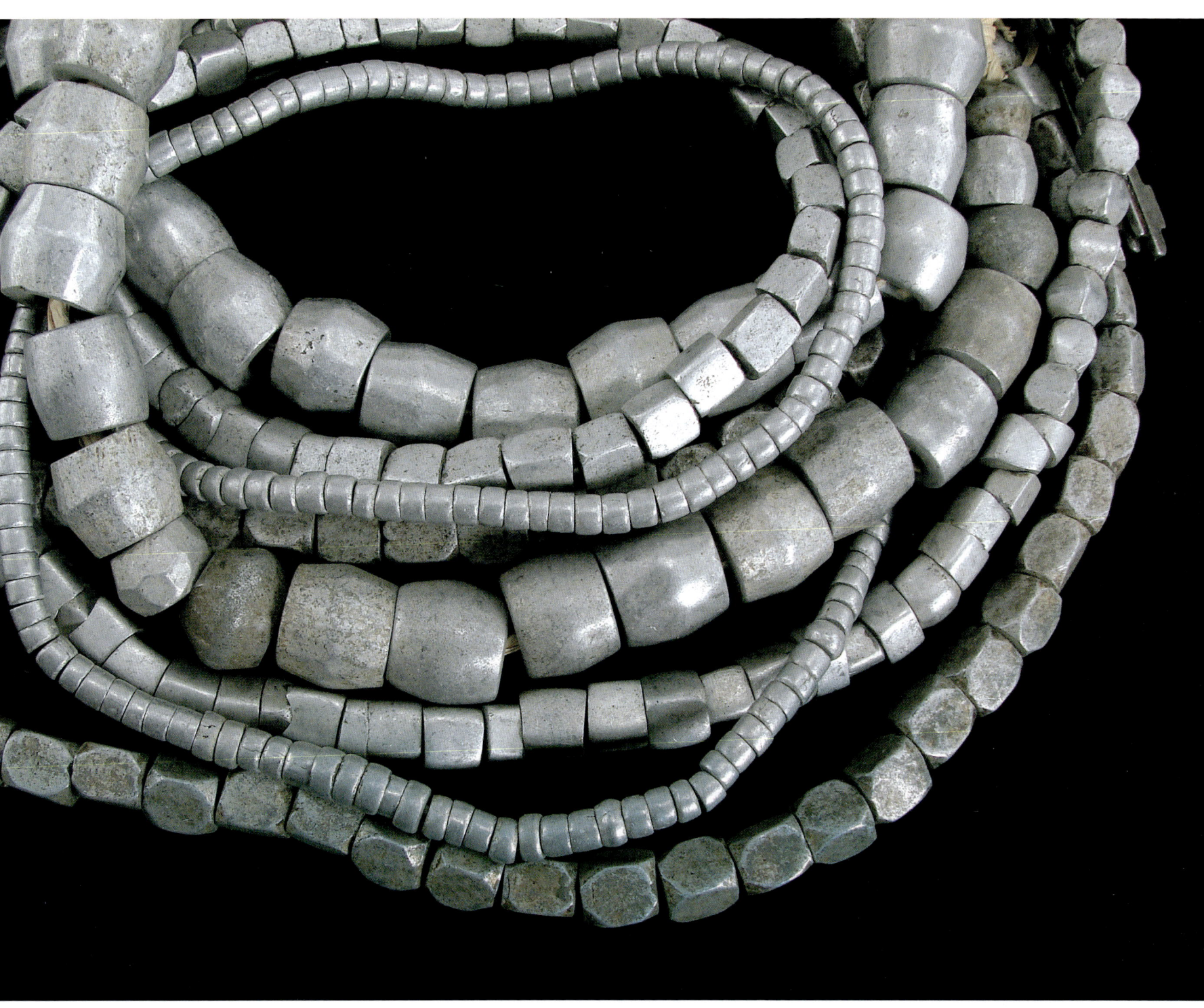

ABOVE *Aluminum beads manufactured from recycled household utensils. Created in a variety of styles, shapes and sizes, they are typically worn by Gabbra and Erbore women of Ethiopia.*

Metal Beads

What Is Lost Wax Casting?

The lost wax casting process is an ancient practice that is still in widespread use today. It requires the use of material that can burn, melt, or evaporate to leave a mold cavity. The completed object made with this technique is usually bronze or brass. With local variations, the basic steps involved in casting small bronze sculptures are as follows.

The artist creates an original piece of work using clay or a similar material. Then a mold is made of the piece. Most molds consist of two (occasionally more) parts and are made from clay or plaster. Melted wax is poured into the mold to cover all inner surfaces and to fill all hollow spaces. After cooling and hardening, the mold is removed and the newly created wax copy is carefully smoothed to remove any mold marks. It is then placed into a cup-like container where it is held in position using a treelike structure also fashioned from wax. The technical term for this process is spruing. The wax spruing will provide the paths through which the molten metal (usually bronze) will flow. The wax copy is then repeatedly dipped into a mixture of powdered clay and sand together with the structure that holds it in place. After each dipping it is set aside and allowed to dry. When the crust is sufficiently thick and sturdy, the wax copy and the spruing contained within its protective shell of fine sand and clay are placed into a kiln and fired. Because of the heat the wax inside will melt and flow out via the paths provided by the spruing. The remaining ceramic shell is now empty. After any cracks have been mended and all flow paths have been cleared and made fully functional, the ceramic shell is reheated. When sufficiently hot so as not to shatter due to a difference in temperature with the molten bronze, it is placed into a container filled with sand. Molten bronze is then poured in through the shell's feeder tubes. After cooling, the ceramic shell is broken with a hammer and the cast metal copy of the original artwork contained inside is removed. The finishing process involves cutting off the spruing, smoothing and polishing rough surfaces, and sometimes applying chemicals resulting in a patina that resembles ancient bronze. [69]

Brass in Ghana

Ghana, once called the Gold Coast, is another West African country with a long tradition of metalworking. Excavations of the site of Begho (also called Bighu or Bitu) have revealed that trading in gold, salt, ivory, leather, cloth, copper alloys and kola nuts was occurring as early as 1100 CE. Begho was an ancient town located in the transitional zone between forest and savannah in the northwestern Brong-Ahafo region and was frequented by caravans from the north until its abandonment during the 18th century. The use of accurate systems of weights and measures and the style of certain features of Begho architecture give evidence of contacts with the Muslim Mande, as do spindle whorls nearly identical to those found at Djenne.

Ashanti

Iron smelting in Ghana dates back to the 12th century. The technology of brass casting—and the production of brass vessels—was imported from the Islamic world. Famous for their cast gold weights and gold jewelry, Ashanti artisans in Ghana still practice their craft, manufacturing a wide range of brass beads and pendants in the old traditions and designs, and often copying old beads fashioned from gold. Ampabame Krofrom, the only brass casting village in Ghana today, is located near Kumasi, which also boasts the largest market in West Africa. Just like the originals, modern Ghanaian brass beads are produced in a great variety of shapes, sizes and designs. However, unlike the old beads, which were created primarily for ceremonial use, today's output is aimed mainly at the collectors' market.

Ghanaian brass beads can have spherical, ovoid, tabular or biconical shapes, with decorative patterns ranging from plain to elaborate, often representing traditional symbolic designs. The largest of these beads are very heavy and have the size of a man's fist. The work is very detailed and no two beads are exactly alike because the wax mold is destroyed in the process of making each bead.

Brass in Ivory Coast

Baoule

Like the Ashanti from Ghana, the Baoule (or Baule) of Ivory Coast are renowned for their cast gold, brass, bronze and copper artifacts and jewelry. They work in the same techniques as the Ashanti and often use motifs reminiscent of Ashanti symbolism. The Baoule speak a dialect of Akan and live in the savannah of the central region of Ivory Coast.

Other Brass

The origins of many of the styles and types of brass, bronze, copper and other metal beads that are produced in Africa have not been documented. One of the most interesting metal bead types is represented by large coiled beads, which are reported to have been manufactured in Ghana. These beads are made from brass, copper or white metal, which is hammered into long flat strips about six millimeters wide and then wound around a wooden rod to form

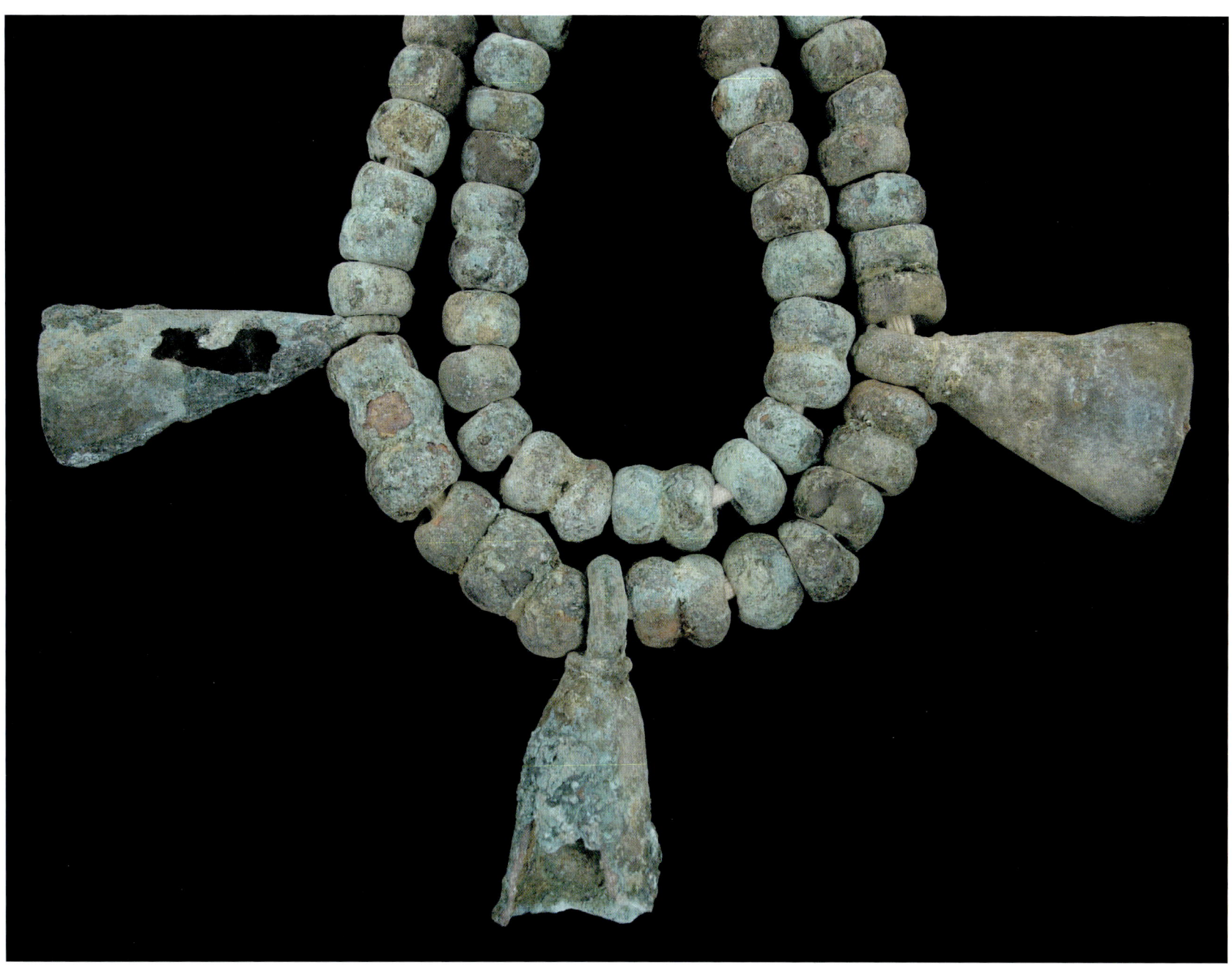

ABOVE *This metal necklace with bell-shaped pendants was excavated in Mali and may date back to the 19th century or earlier. It is another example of the long tradition of metalworking in sub-Saharan Africa.*

tube-shaped spiraling coils of metal wire. Some of the wire coils can be heavily decorated with stamped or punched designs. The beads are large, measuring up to three centimeters in diameter and ten centimeters in length. They were worn by royalty and also used as protective amulets against knife or bullet wounds. Other styles of cast brass beads were made to replicate lion's teeth and claws, and were worn for their amuletic properties.

Copper

Copper was not readily available in West Africa before the arrival of European traders. It had to be obtained from Libya in exchange for West African gold, which was transported in camel caravans across the trans-Saharan trade routes. The Portuguese, followed by French, Dutch and English merchants, introduced various metals, including copper, which they used in trade for African gold, hides, ivory and slaves. Soon most trade goods came to be valued in terms of metal bars made from copper and iron, and these rapidly became established as units of account and accepted standard currencies in many regions. The bars measured about fifty centimeters in length—this being the standard size used throughout West Africa—and eighty iron bars weighed one ton. The value of one iron bar at the end of the 17th century was equivalent to four copper bars or to four strings of brass rings with ten rings in each.

During the time that copper and bronze were rare materials, objects manufactured from them were commonly associated with mystical properties and magical powers and were used for ceremonial purposes. Some of the trade goods brought to Nigeria by the Portuguese included copper armlets made locally at Laonda de S. Paola in Angola. [70] The copper used in the production of modern beads is imported from Romania.

Aluminum

Typically, aluminum beads are produced from recycled household utensils which have been melted down after becoming obsolete due to wear and tear. They often replace the traditional beads made from iron, which are heavier and more difficult to manufacture. The Gabbra people, who live on both sides of the Ethiopian-Kenyan border, and their neighbors the Erbore, wear whole strands of recycled aluminum beads, separately or in combination with old European beads. Aluminum beads are produced in a variety of shapes and sizes and each bead is individually hand-made. The great majority of aluminum beads are spherical or biconical, or occasionally square, and small in size, measuring not more than ten millimeters in diameter. Large biconical beads measuring up to twenty-five millimeters can occasionally be found. Typically the beads have a dull and slightly rough surface. [71]

The export of aluminum beads, mainly from Ethiopia, is a recent development, furthered by Hausa and Soninke bead traders during the past two decades. The exact origins of these beads are not known, but it is believed that they are being produced by the Gabbra in the Omo valley. Some of the first African metal beads to become available in larger quantities on the American and European collectors' markets are the small brass biconical beads measuring about ten millimeters in diameter, said to originate in Cameroon.

Glass Beads

History of Glass Beads

In many parts of the Muslim world glass is believed to hold magical powers. It is thought to protect against bad spirits and most importantly, to deflect envy, the main danger of the "evil eye." As we have seen, symbols representing eyes are widely used, both in ornamentation and on everyday objects, in order to counteract evil powers. Glass colors and in some instances specific color combinations and sequences are often associated with deities. Decorative patterns have symbolic meanings, such as the triangular shape of a bead or pendant, which symbolizes an eye. Glass beads are identified with wealth, status and power, and they play important roles in West African cultures and societies where the manufacture of glass beads for personal use and ritual adornment has a long tradition. Indigenous glass bead industries have been documented in Nigeria, Ghana, Mauritania and medieval Egypt.

Glass-working in Egypt was at its most prolific around 1400 BCE, and many production sites have been dated to the 12th century BCE. A wide range of artifacts was produced, mainly in shades of blue but also green-blue and brownish yellow. Possibly the blue hues were preferred because they were similar to turquoise, a highly esteemed gemstone of opaque blue color with green overtones which is found in Egypt and has been widely used for its decorative and perceived magical properties. So-called spot beads, often decorated with protruding eye or dot patterns, are known from the 18th dynasty, which spanned 255 years (1550-1295 BCE) and represents one of the most impressive periods in Egyptian history. Several of the more famous Egyptian rulers—Queen Hatshepsut, Akhenaten, Tutankhamon and Tuthmosis III—belong to it. Small plain beads are documented from Gurob for the same period.

The invention of mosaic glass is attributed to Egypt's glass workers and became common during the 1st century BCE. Stone moulds used for shaping drawn biconical beads were found among the debris of a Coptic period workshop at Kom el-Dikra, Alexandria. Fused rod beads, mosaic and eye beads have been documented also from excavations in Europe, but the most numerous finds have been made in Egypt. In fact most are believed to have been manufactured in the glassworks at Fustat (old Cairo) during the 9th and 10th centuries CE, before its destruction in 1168. Eye or dot decorations were created either by applying a trail of glass of a different color onto the bead surface or by adding several layers (strata) of contrasting colors, making each layer smaller in diameter than the previous. Beads decorated by the latter method are called stratified eye beads. Mosaic eye decorations were made by applying thin slices of a multi-colored cane onto a bead surface. The Fustat glassworks also produced segmented beads.

In Mauritania, Fustat fused rod beads—a term coined by the late Peter Francis—are known as Morfia (also spelled Morphia) and are among the most highly valued beads on the international collectors' market. In Mauritania they are passed down within the family, from generation to generation. In Arabian countries fragments of Morfia beads are traditionally part of a girl's dowry, and when fragments are not available, perfect beads are broken just for this purpose. Most fused rod beads are made from eight sections of different colored canes (some have only six) that were twisted during drawing and then arranged around a rod or mandrel, adjacent to each other in alternate directions before fusing. The result was a longitudinal non-continuous zigzag pattern. [71a] The cane colors typically alternate between red, yellow, green, blue, white and black, and the color sequences are similar to those observed on Kiffa beads. Some

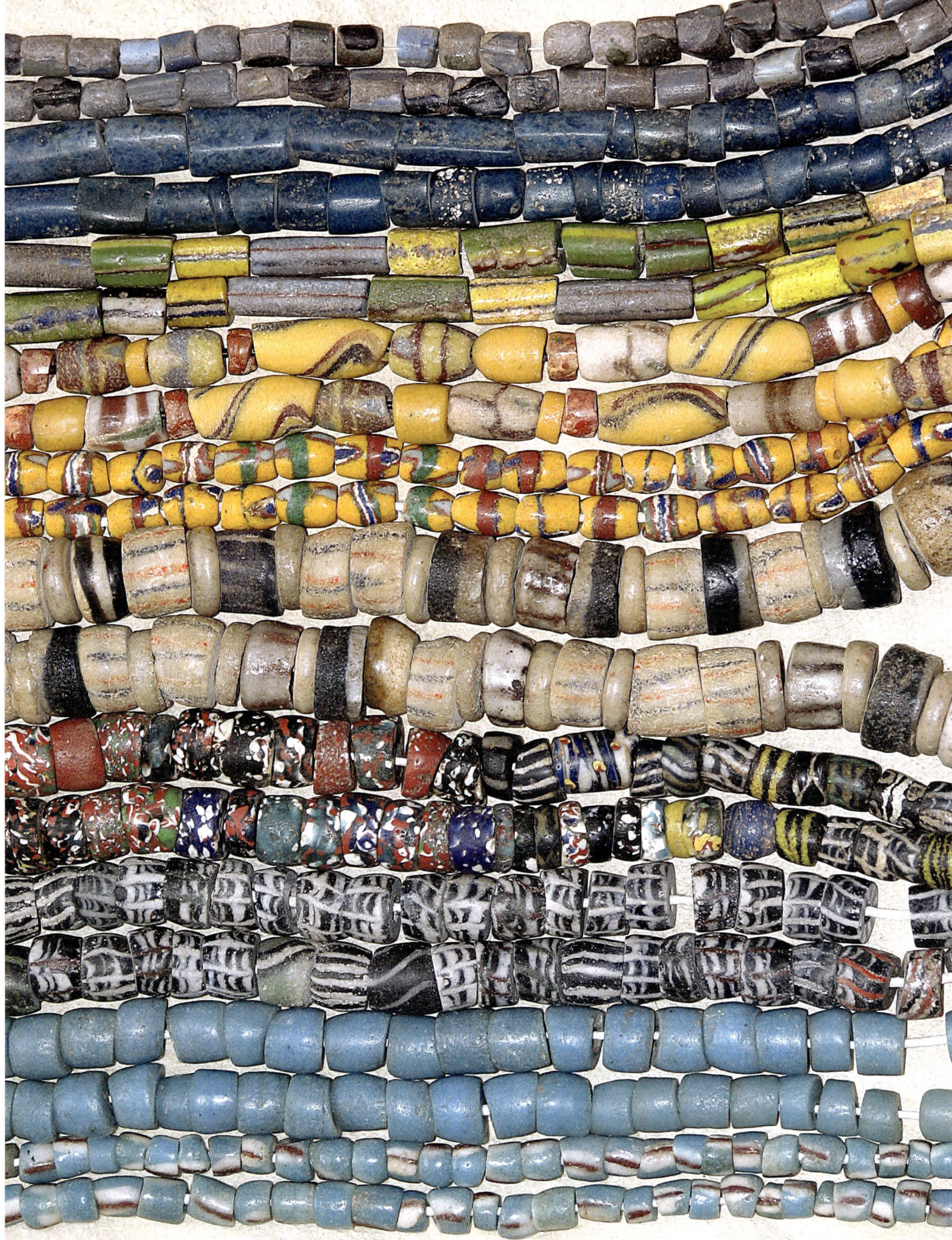

LEFT *Depicted at left are a variety of powder glass beads made during the 1960s: the four strands at the bottom of the photo are Awuazi, Kwau and Miti Metee, made by Krobo bead makers; the next four strands show striped Powa and layered, twisted Zagba and Adjagba styles, as well as horizontally molded Meteyi in three color variants, made during the first half of the 20th century. The blue beads on the two strands at right were manufactured by the Yoruba and are called Keta Awuazi and Tehe Koli, respectively, the latter having been made from fragments of Koli beads held together by powder glass.*

specimens are decorated with rows of eyes alternating with the zigzag pattern.

The first European to document African-made glass beads was a Portuguese merchant called Pacheo Pereiro. In 1506 he noted that slaves, cotton cloth, leopard skins, palm oil and blue beads with red lines, which the locals called "coris", were traded for gold on the Gold Coast (Ghana). Jean Barbot, a commercial agent from France, mentions the production of powder glass beads on the Gold Coast in the late 17th century. [72] In West Africa, glass beads were manufactured by the Yoruba, the Ashanti and the Krobo people, the latter probably being the most well known, the most highly skilled, and indubitably the most prolific bead makers in Africa today.

Drawn and Lapidary Beads

Kori Stones

In historic times, Yorubaland consisted of groups of independent city-states, each ruled by its own king and centered on its own royal court. The Yoruba system of divine kingship extends back to the beginnings of the great Ife Kingdom that was founded during the 11th century or earlier. Kings who could trace their descent back to the founder of the Kingdom of Ife were considered divine. They alone could legitimately wear beaded veiled crowns, the supreme symbols of divine authority. For centuries Ife was a powerful empire. It lost its pre-eminence to the Oyo Empire around the 15th century, but its capital city continued to be the primary religious center for all of Yorubaland. According to legend, the first glass beads were made by Olokun, a female deity and member of the Yoruba founding family. The "kori" stones, interpreted by archaeologists to be an intermediate step in the process of bead making, were objects of veneration and worship, known locally as aje ileke and aje Olokun ("wealth of beads" and "wealth of Olokun"), and kept in special shrines. [73]

During the 1970s, the British archaeologist F. Willett excavated glass-lined crucibles in the vicinity of the town of Ife in southern Nigeria and concluded that they indicated a past practice of glass melting. The so-called kori stones (aje ileke) that were later found in both Oyo and Ife, with glass and fragments of drawn glass beads still adhering to their surface, offered immediate proof of this practice. Glass samples and bead fragments derived from the aje ileke were first examined and compared with intact whole beads that had been found in the same area during the 1970s. The majority of these beads are opaque blue, green or black; some are decorated with red or purple stripes, and some are dichroic. The beads have a corded, knotty texture and micaceous luster, and are of tubular shape, often slightly tapered, which is an indication that the drawn glass canes from which they were made were of a short length. The bead perforations are generally small. [74]

It has been documented that during the early 1500s, the Portuguese traded coral, glass beads and cowries for "accory" (also spelled "akori"). Some authors believe these "akori" to have been locally produced beads which were manufactured from glass made in the "kori" stones, while others speculate that they had Middle Eastern or European origins and reached Yorubaland from the north. Akori were highly esteemed and played an important role in rituals and traditions all along the coast. Local Yoruba bead making may have commenced only after the original supplies were depleted, but the beads that were produced, called segi and fashioned from scrap glasses, could not withstand the fire test and were for this reason not as highly valued on the Gold Coast as the originals. [75]

Kori Beads

As has been noted, the first European to document Kori beads was the Portuguese merchant Pacheo Pereira (1506). Pereira noted that in Rio dos Forcados (Benin), brass and copper arm rings were being traded for slaves, cotton cloth, leopard skins, palm oil and "certain blue beads with red lines, which the locals call coris" [76] Three decades later, a ship's pilot whose name is now lost, observed that these beads would not melt in fire. Interestingly, the Krobos still use the fire test as a method to differentiate between the various types of their "koli" beads. In one of the earliest accounts of European trade with the Gold Coast (Ghana), Cape Verde (Senegal), Benin (Dahomey), Nigeria and Cape Lopez (Gabon),which was published less than ten years after the Dutch began trading in this region, Peter de Marees describes little bluish-green and black stones from which akori (acory) beads are ground, "which are much coveted among

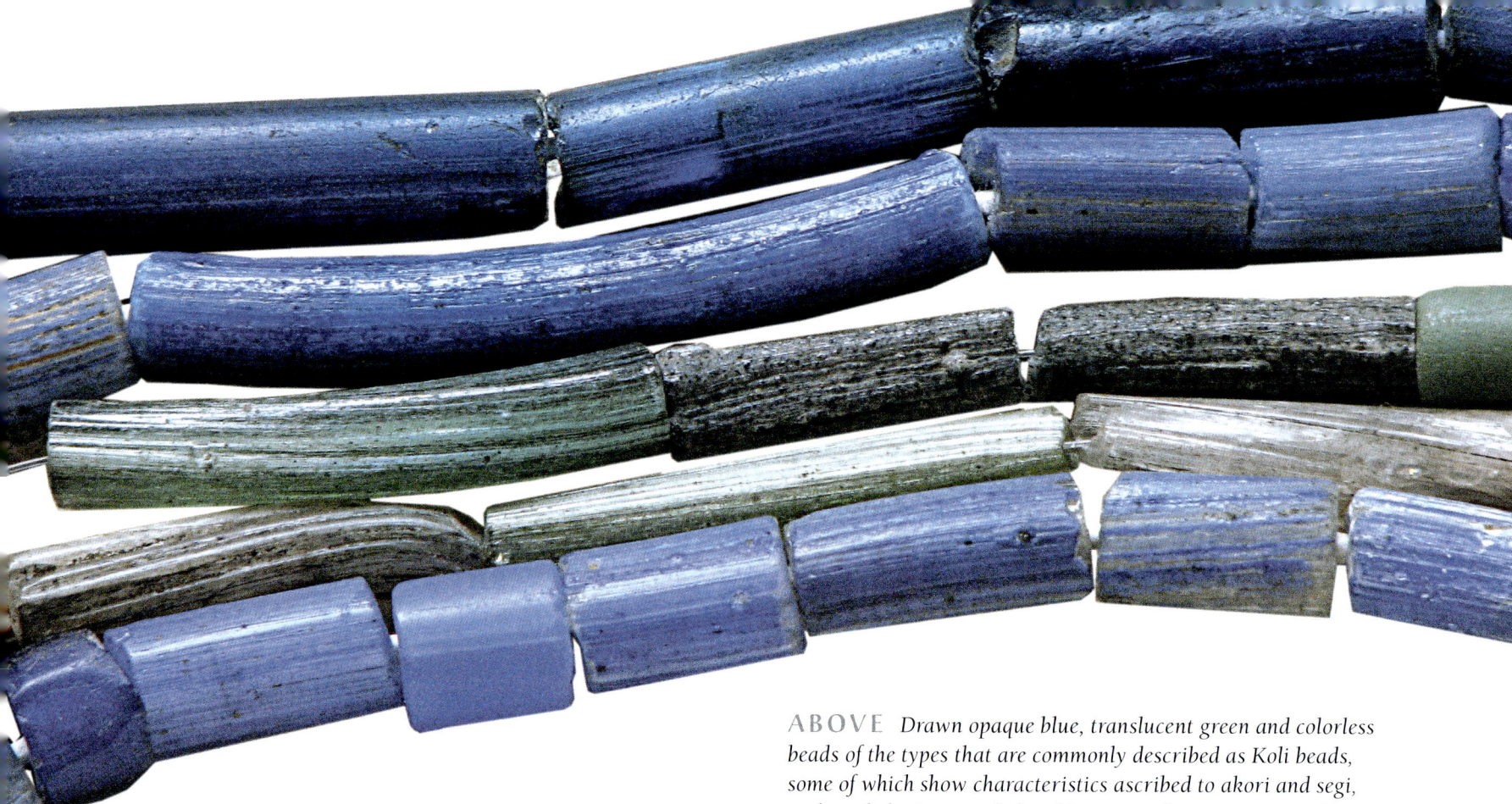

ABOVE *Drawn opaque blue, translucent green and colorless beads of the types that are commonly described as Koli beads, some of which show characteristics ascribed to akori and segi, such as dichroism, corded and knotty surfaces, micaceous luster and small perforations. Kori beads were traded extensively by the Portuguese, who acquired the beads from the Yoruba and traded them for gold on the Gold Coast (present-day Ghana). Numerous imitations have been produced ever since, but only the highly valued true kori do not melt in fire—a test still practiced by the Krobo. The drawn, tube-shaped translucent beads of European origins are boiled in order to make them opaque, so that they resemble the highly esteemed originals, at least in some respects.*

other blacks, particularly on the Gold Coast of Guinea, where they are much esteemed and valued." [77]

Others reporting on these beads deemed them to be made from blue coral. The fact that the term "coral" was also applied to glass beads in general contributed to the confusion. But because of the acid content of West African soil in general, usually too high to allow the preservation of coral or shell over any length of time, coral can be ruled out as a potential source material. L.F. Römer, a Danish national employed in West Africa from 1739-1749 by the Danish West India and Guinea Company, believed the beads to have been made from porcelain. He describes them as "longish pipe-corals (i.e. beads) with a hole through them, as thick as a man's little finger, and as long as the joint of a finger, with beautiful colors all the way through." Römer noted that the beads were of several different colors, such as red, green and blue, white and yellow, some with stripe decoration. He reported on how the inhabitants of Benin would find these beads in the ground, and that natives believed that members of the royal family had been buried in such places. [78] By that time, however, a number of akori imitations had already been produced and circulated, and Römer's description may well refer to some of them. All variants were used in rituals, including burials. The original koris were highly valued on the Gold Coast, and the Portuguese merchants who traded other goods for Yoruba beads made high profits by trading them for gold to the Akan. A Portuguese agent at Elmina is reported to have received tens of thousands of koris between 1532 to 1535.

Based on recent microscopic and chemical analyses of crucible fragments and glass beads found in Olokun Grove, Ile-Ife, Nigeria, and of various glasses found in Orun Oba Ado, Ita Yemoo in 1972, it has been established that a glass making industry unique to West Africa, and possibly unique to southern Nigeria and to the Yoruba culture, did indeed exist. Test results suggest that a significant proportion of the early Ile-Ife glass has a very unusual composition

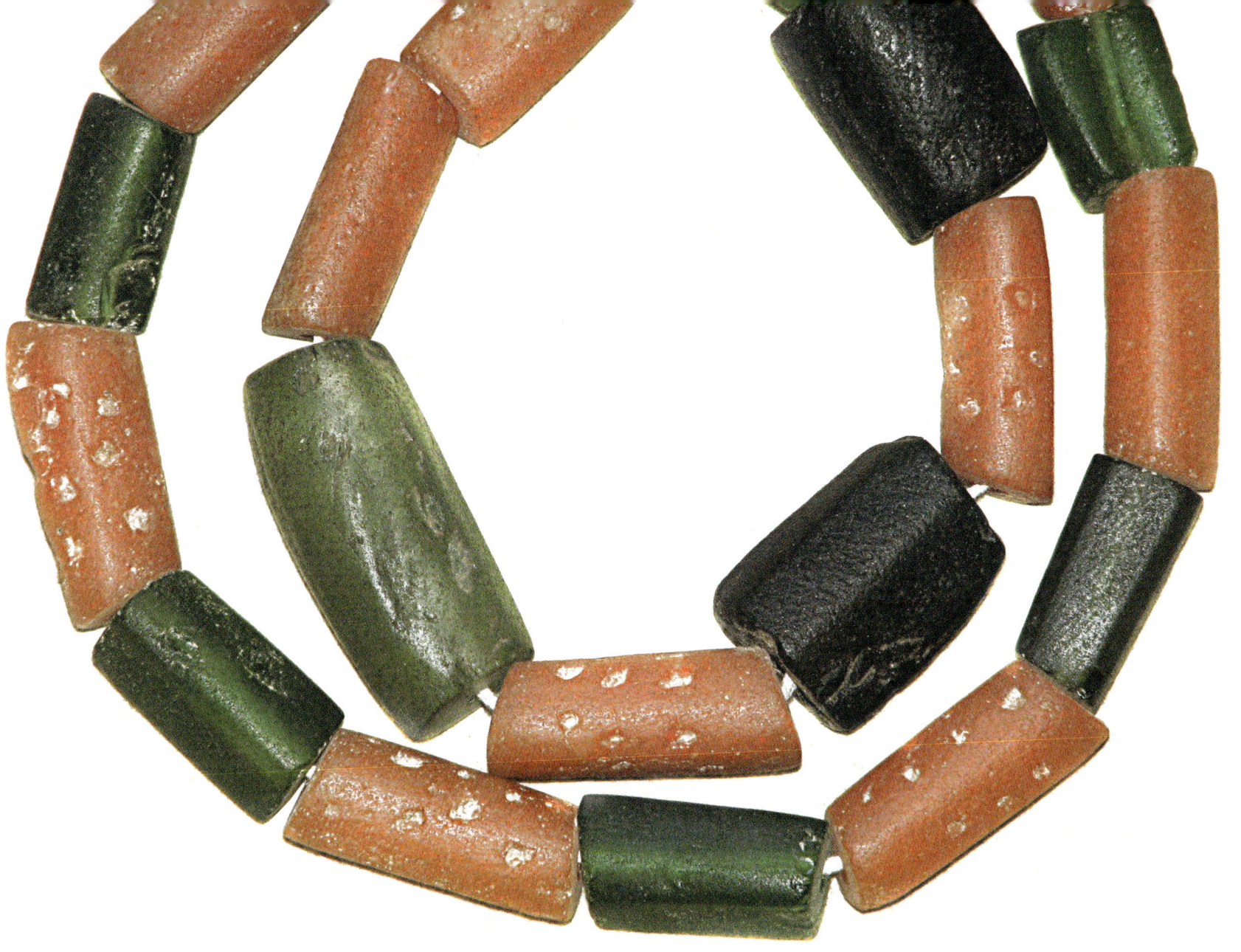

ABOVE *Necklace comprised of dark green beads, lapidary worked from bottle glasses, that represent the dark colors of the Olokun cult, combined with imitation coral powder glass beads, called Iyun, representing one of the hot colors.*

of high lime and high alumina that is found in neither European nor in Middle Eastern glasses. Glass beads high in lime and alumina have also been documented from Igbo-Ukwu, which is situated three hundred kilometers southeast of Ife. [79] Similar glass beads, with closely related early radiocarbon dates, have been found in Gao, Mali; Kissi, Burkina Faso; Koumbi Saleh, Mauritania; Onikroga and Ilesha, Nigeria; and in Elmina, Ghana, indicating that high lime, high alumina glass may have been traded widely at an early date. Because of the predominance of indigenous high lime, high alumina glass at the earliest sites in Ile-Ife and other locations in southern Nigeria, combined with archaeological evidence for the presence of technical ceramics required for glass working, and a strong oral tradition

Glass Beads 129

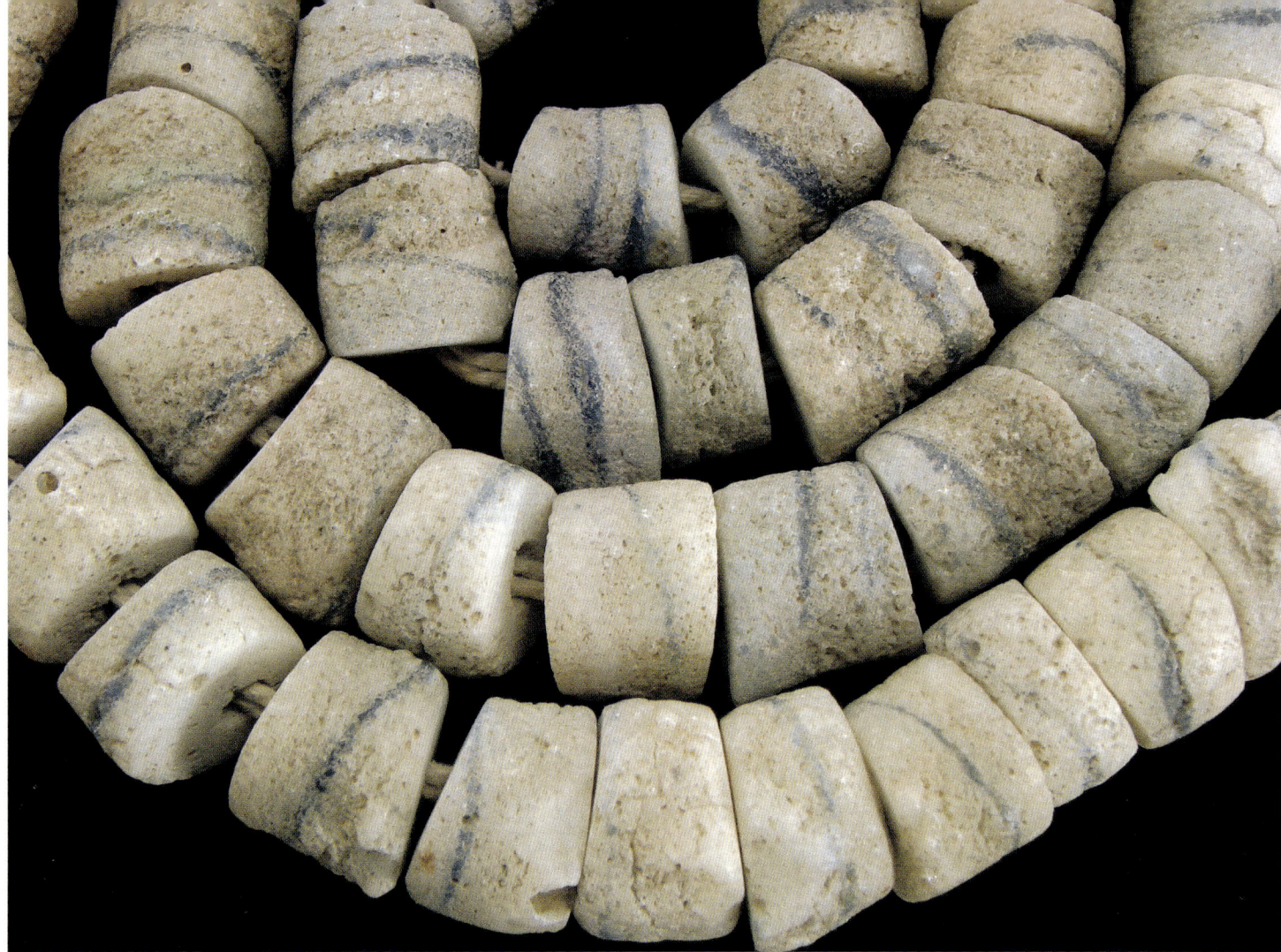

ABOVE *Layered powder glass beads made during the 1960s by Ashanti bead makers.*

for ancient glass working in this area, it is believed that local glass production in southern Nigeria commenced during the early centuries of the 2nd century CE, or even earlier. Results gained from radiocarbon testing of artifacts found in the same strata indicate a time frame ranging between 800 and 1200 CE. Much other Ife glass has also been found to be of quite an unusual composition and may have been made locally as well.

Kori Bead Imitations

"Kori" bead imitations are manufactured by the Krobo, the Yoruba, and other African bead dealers, all using drawn, tube-shaped translucent blue beads of European origins that are boiled in pots filled with water and organic matter until the beads are opaque. Ingredients and exact compositions of these concoctions are closely guarded secrets but the formulas appear to consist mainly of herbs and roots. The resulting opaque blue beads are commonly called Koli beads. [80]

Lapidary Worked Glass Beads

Apart from manufacturing drawn glass beads, the Yoruba are also noted for having produced lapidary worked and powder glass beads. Yoruba lapidary beads are found in a variety of bottle-glass colors, both antique and contemporary. The presence of other colors suggests that glasses other than those derived from bottle glass—some being dichroic when viewed in transmitted light—have occasionally also been used. Some of these lapidary bead types are centuries old, as is indicated by traditions among groups such as the Krobo, from southeastern Ghana but said to have originated in Nigeria, who not only value them highly but also believe them to possess magical properties and to have mysterious origins. [81]

The lapidary industry produced what the Yoruba call Segi beads. These are beads that were made of blue and green glasses, colors that represent the dark colors of the Olokun cult. The powder glass industry produced both the

130   Glass Beads

dark or cold colors and the light or hot colors; the latter, including red and yellow, are called Iyun. Similar to their Ghanaian counterparts, the Yoruba bead makers used a variety of techniques. It is said that the production of powder glass beads began after the lapidary technique had been introduced, and when supplies of materials suitable for making lapidary beads were exhausted. Among the Krobo, similar beads, especially when they are dichroic, are called Abaklé Koli. According to tradition, Kloweke, their female deity, carried beads of this type. The beads have a long tradition in both the Yoruba and the Krobo culture. However, the industry that produced them over the duration of several centuries appears to now be defunct. [82]

Powder Glass Beads

History

The earliest powder glass beads on record were discovered during archaeological excavations at Mapungubwe, in present-day Zimbabwe, and dated to 970 to 1000 CE. A study based on later excavations revealed that some of these beads were made by filling clay molds with crushed glass beads. Termed "Garden Roller Beads" because of their distinct shapes, they are the earliest known powder glass beads from Africa, and the only type from eastern and southern Africa. [83]

Powder Glass Beads in Ghana

The main area of present-day powder glass bead manufacture is West Africa, with industries in Mauritania, Nigeria and, most importantly, Ghana. The origins of bead making in Ghana are unknown. Today it is the Ashanti and Krobo craftsmen and women who produce the great majority of powder glass beads. According to tradition, the Krobo have been making beads "for a long time" and it has been documented that Krobo beads were being made as early as the 1920s. Despite the scarcity of archaeological evidence, it is believed that powder glass bead making in Ghana dates even further back. Jean Barbot, a Frenchman who served as a commercial agent on French slave-trading voyages to West Africa in 1678-1679 and 1681-1682, mentions the production of powder glass beads on the Gold Coast (present-day Ghana) in the same context as gold dust, which was one of the currencies for purchasing slaves: "The third sort of false gold, grown pretty common among the Blacks, is a composition which they make of a certain powder of coral glass which they cast." [84] The Krobo people are probably the most famous and skilled, and certainly the most prolific bead makers in Africa today. Beads still play a very important role in their society, be it in rituals of birth, coming of age, marriage or death. [85]

Dipo Ceremony

The coming of age is an important occasion for many African cultures, including the Krobo people in Ghana, for whom the Dipo ceremony is one of the most important events of the year. The Dipo is held every spring and symbolizes a girl's coming of age and her eligibility for marriage.

The ceremony begins by parading the girls in total nudity in front of the entire village. One by one, each girl is shown how to crush corn. On the following day, the girls are taken to the river for a ritual bath and in the afternoon of the same day each girl shares a traditional meal with her

BELOW *The majority of large-sized Krobo powder glass beads, commonly biconical or bi-pyramidal in shape, are produced using special molds. On close observation it becomes obvious that the beads are assembled from two matching cone-shaped halves, which are fused together at their wider ends. This bead style is called Ologo.*

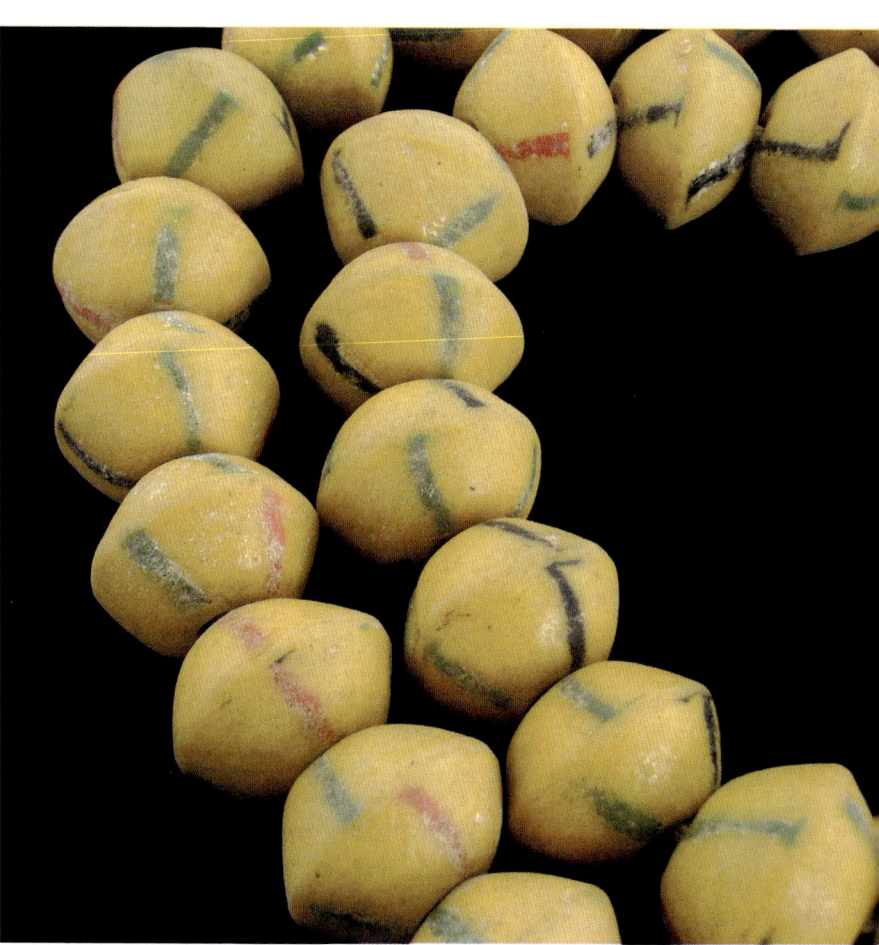

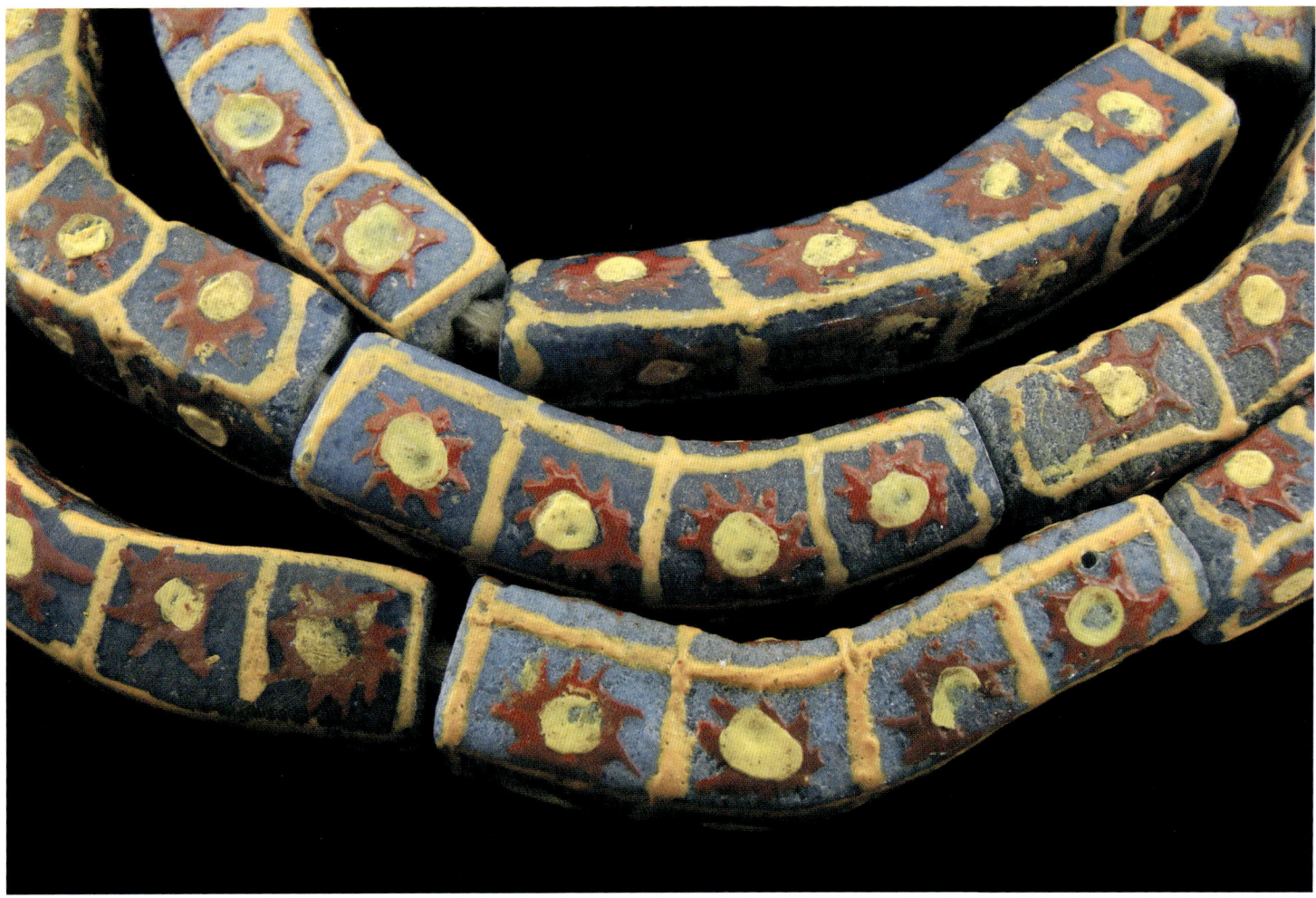

family. Over the entire five days of the ritual, however, she is not allowed to eat corn or rice, and she is forbidden to look into a mirror, to giggle or to exhibit any behavior deemed silly. On the third day, clay marks are painted onto the girl's body and she must tell a priestess about her virginity, knowing that a clay pot that is placed upon her chest will break or explode should she tell a lie. In the evening each girl is led to a sacred stone on which she is seated three times. From now on she will be treated as a woman and is not allowed to speak for the remainder of the ceremony. A brother or the son of a neighbor will carry her back to the village on his back. On the following day, the girls gather to receive instructions from the fetish priests, who tell them that they are now women and must act accordingly. The last day is a day of rejoicing. The girls gather at the village common, wearing the best cloth their families can afford, and the beads, which have been passed down from many generations, symbols of the families' wealth.

ABOVE *Elbow-shaped Krobo powder glass beads which have been decorated in the Mue Ne Angma style, a special technique of applying glass slurry decorations onto the surface of plain beads that was developed during the 1990s. Literally translated, "mue ne angma" means "a bead that has been written on." Mue Ne Angma are made in a great variety of sizes, and in shapes ranging from spherical to cylindrical and elbow-shaped. Designs may be a simple circle, dot or "eye" decoration, or an intricate pattern copied from designs on African textiles or on Venetian-made glass beads of the early 1900s. One of the earliest examples was made by Ransford Tetteh of Teranja Bead Works*

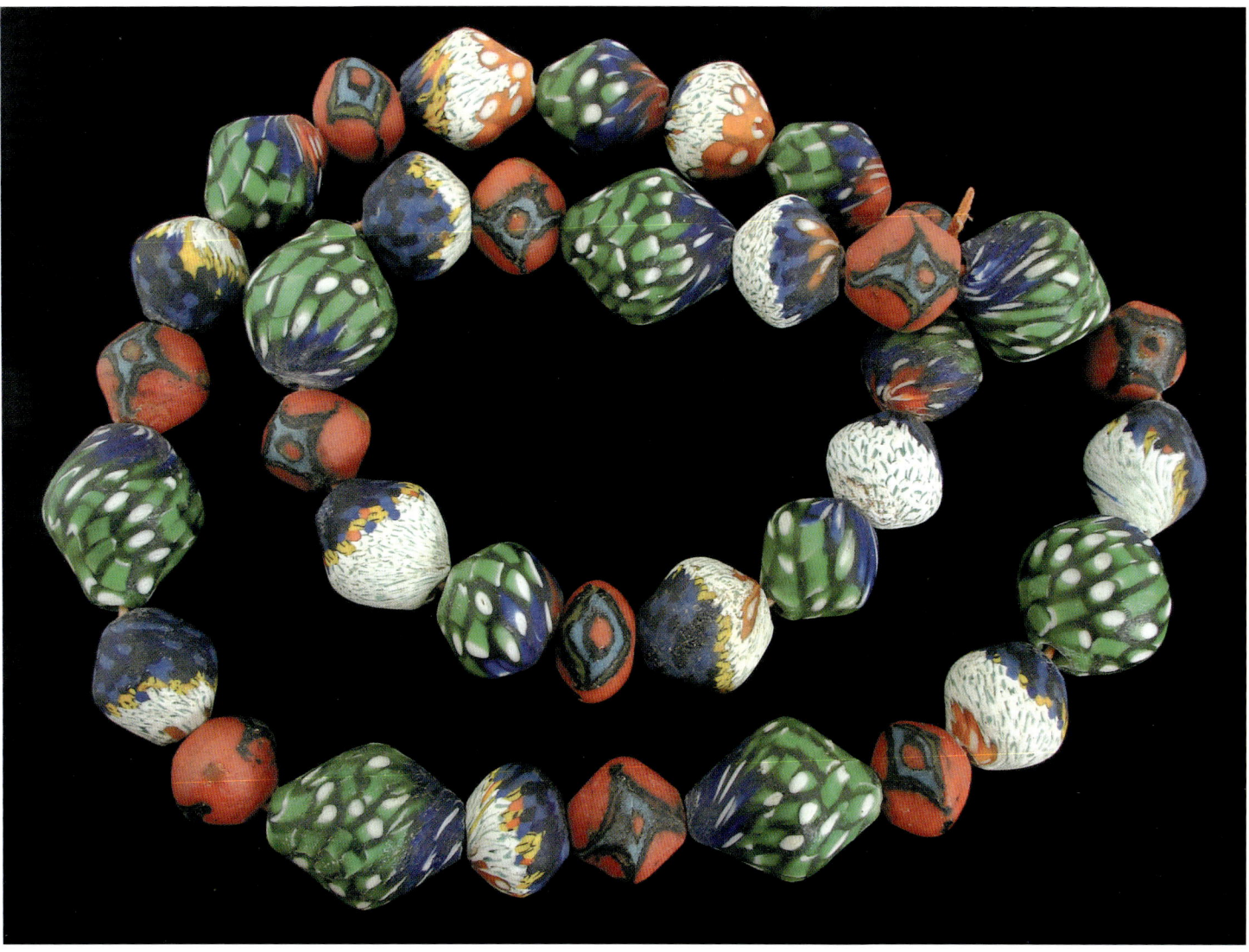

ABOVE *Large contemporary Krobo powder glass beads in biconical shapes, such as the beads depicted here, were manufactured by Cedi Glass Works in Odumase-Krobo. They are commonly made to resemble old Bodom beads.*

How Powder Glass Beads Are Made

Powder glass beads are made from finely ground glass, derived mainly from broken and unusable bottles and other scrap glasses. Damaged glass beads and even undamaged ones such as seed beads, usually obtained from Hausa traders, are also used as source material. The bottle glass is broken into shards and fragments which are then ground into a fine powder in metal mortars. Pestles are frequently fashioned from worn-out drive shafts. The quality of the future beads depends greatly on the fineness of the glass powder used in making them and several siftings are required before the finest glass "powder" particles are achieved. Another important factor is that different types of glass have different properties. Colorless clear glass gives the greatest control over color and over the use of colorants. Glass from Coca Cola bottles is preferred over that from Fanta bottles, because the latter has a very high melting point. Old medicine bottles, cold cream jars, and a great variety of other types of glasses, including plates, ashtrays and windowpanes, can be used. Special glasses may even be bought new, just for the purpose. [86]

Modern ceramic colorants (called "dyes" by the bead makers), as well as pulverized monochrome beads, or shards of colored glasses, may be added to the glass bead powder in order to create a greater variety of styles, designs, decorative patterns and colors. In addition, glass bead fragments of varying sizes, which have traditionally been used for the manufacture and decoration of specific types of beads, are being used in new combinations.

Krobo powder glass beads are produced with vertical molds made from locally dug clay. The molds have a number of depressions, designed to hold one bead each, and each of these depressions has a small central depression called fuwa, which holds a perforator such as a leaf stem or midrib of a cassava leaf. Cassava stems are readily available because cassava is a major food crop in the area. [87] The molds can be used repeatedly and come in various sizes.

Before a mold is filled with glass, it is soaked in a kaolin suspension to prevent the fired beads from sticking to the mold. A short length of cassava leaf stem is placed in the fuwa and the mold is filled with finely ground dry glass powder that can be built up in layers to form sequences and patterns of different shapes and colors. The cassava stem will burn away during firing and leave the bead perforation. This method is called the vertical-mold dry-core powder glass technique, as opposed to the wet-core powder glass technique employed elsewhere.

Firing takes place in a clay kiln consisting of a lower chamber for firewood and an upper chamber that can be floored with iron sheeting, or constructed from leaf springs or other suitable materials. The dome above the upper chamber is made of clay and built on a frame of branches. The firing can take many hours, including several hours for the kiln to reach optimum temperature. While the kiln is heating up, the bead-filled molds are set on it to warm. The molds are fired at a relatively low temperature for the first fifteen minutes, followed by a constant heat of 850-1,000° C for the next thirty minutes. During this phase the glass powder begins to fuse, or rather, to sinter. Sintering is a partial fusion or coalescing under heat without reaching the point of liquefaction of the glass. It gives the beads a characteristic grainy surface. If the temperature is too low, the glass will not fuse properly. Overheating or extended firing can cause the glass to flow, which can lead to collapsed perforations and revitrification, causing a fire-polished appearance on the surfaces. Once a kiln has been lit, it is used for a number of firings, and one kiln can serve many bead makers. After the cooling, the beads are tipped out, washed, and smoothed and polished individually, either by hand using sand and water, or on a grinding stone or grinding wheel.

Most of the larger-sized Krobo powder glass beads, commonly biconical or bi-pyramidal in shape, are made in special molds. On close observation it becomes obvious that these beads are made by combining two matching cone-shaped beads, which are fused together at their wider ends, at low temperatures during a second firing. The great majority of these two-part beads have a colored equator where the two halves have been joined. It appears that the ceramic colorants serve as a form of "glue." Although mismatched halves are common, the bead perforations always line up. This suggests that the beads are being pierced with a pointed tool subsequent to the joining together of the two halves. [88]

Krobo Powder Glass Beads

The Krobo people form the largest of seven Dangme ethnic groups in southeastern Ghana. According to oral tradition, the Krobo originated in eastern Nigeria, but most of the documented sources point to Sameh in Dahomey (Benin) as the probable source of origin. Kroboland encompasses approximately 750 square kilometers and is located in the southeast of Ghana.

Powa

During the 1920s, Krobo bead makers produced powder glass beads in a number of different styles. Powa (the term means "status") were made in vertical molds from a combination of glasses from old bottles and old beads, which were sometimes used to add colors. Powa beads are one of the earliest bead types made by the Krobo, going back to the 1920s and possibly earlier. The commonly blue, black and rust-colored stripes were created by running a pin down the side of a filled mold. The resulting grooves were filled in with glass powder in the colors of the stripes. The glass used for making these beads came from old imported beads and glass bottles, and the coloration was achieved by using soot, rust and red shale. After firing, the beads were pressed into yams and rubbed against a grinding stone in order to finish the ends, then strung on a wire to grind the edges as a group, resulting in a perfectly nested and graduated matched strand. Many powa have cores, and their decorations often show flecks of various colors, said to originate from the use of Venetian lamp work beads.

Miti Metee

The term Miti Metee translates as "mixed quality" and encompasses a range of beads which were often combined in

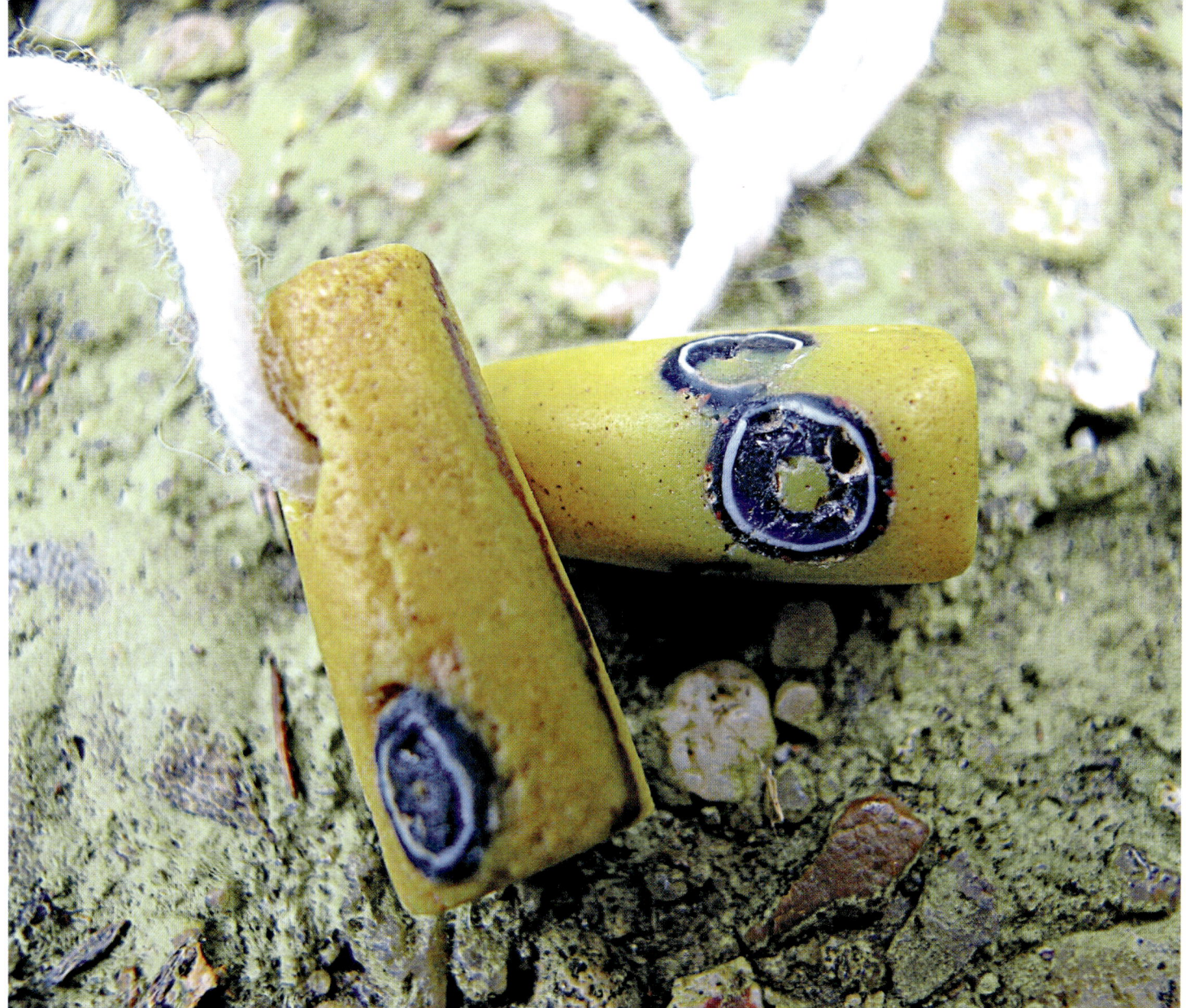

ABOVE *Pendants made in two halves which were joined together in a second short firing process. Fragments of old Venetian-made glass beads have been embedded for decorative purposes.*

NEXT TWO PAGES *First made during the early 1990s, translucent and semi-translucent beads with pierced perforations called Gige are being produced in a range of sizes and colors. Flower and star-shaped pendants are manufactured using the same technique.*

strands, such as Hengme, beads that are decorated with preformed "eyes," and Kashin Zomo, a Hausa term not used by Krobos, meaning "excrement of rabbit." Kashin Zomo beads are made by fusing small fragments of European beads. Other styles are called Obuoso and Kwau. The latter style, also called Kente, is characterized by a decorative pattern of both vertical and horizontal lines, which appear combed, on a dark background. The pattern is similar to the traditional woven Kente cloth that is popular among Akan and other local groups. The horizontal layers were set first and the action of adding the vertical stripes gave the combed effect. The Kwau (or Kwahu) people form one of the Akan groups located to the west of Kroboland. They are said to have favored the Kente types of beads, as well as related black beads, and to have traded them for food. Zagba is the name for beads that are decorated with stripes. When twisted in the mold so that the stripes form spirals these beads are called Azagba (Adjagba). [89]

Gige

Present-day bead making involves the manufacture of three distinct styles, which are produced in a number

Glass Beads 135

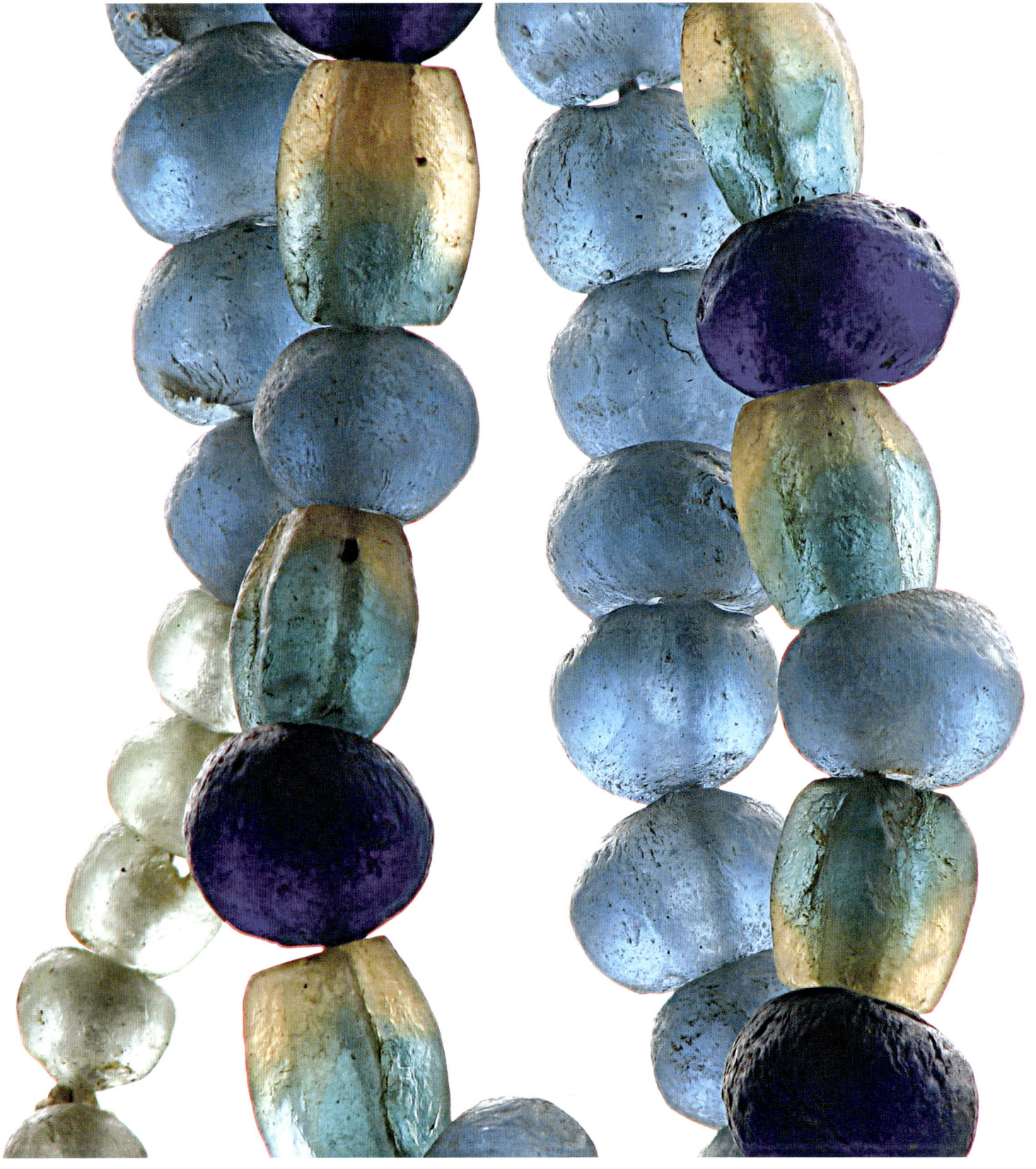

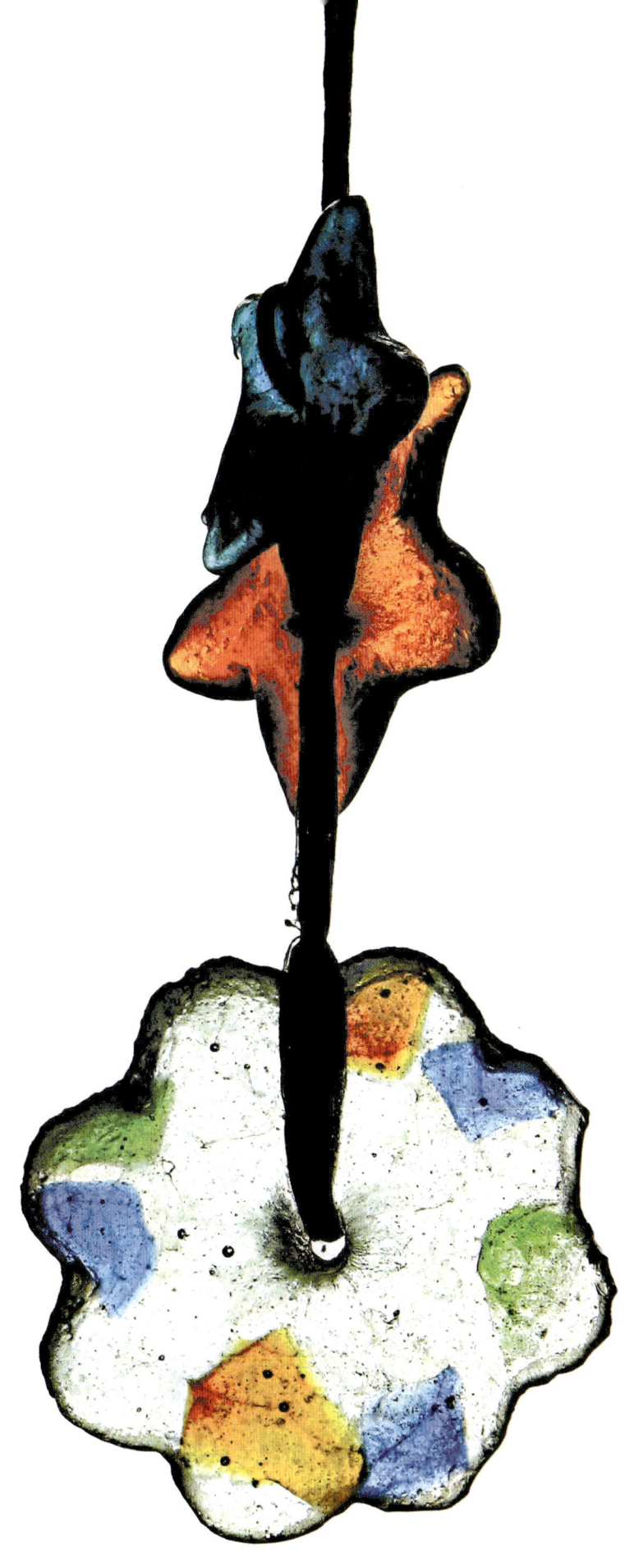

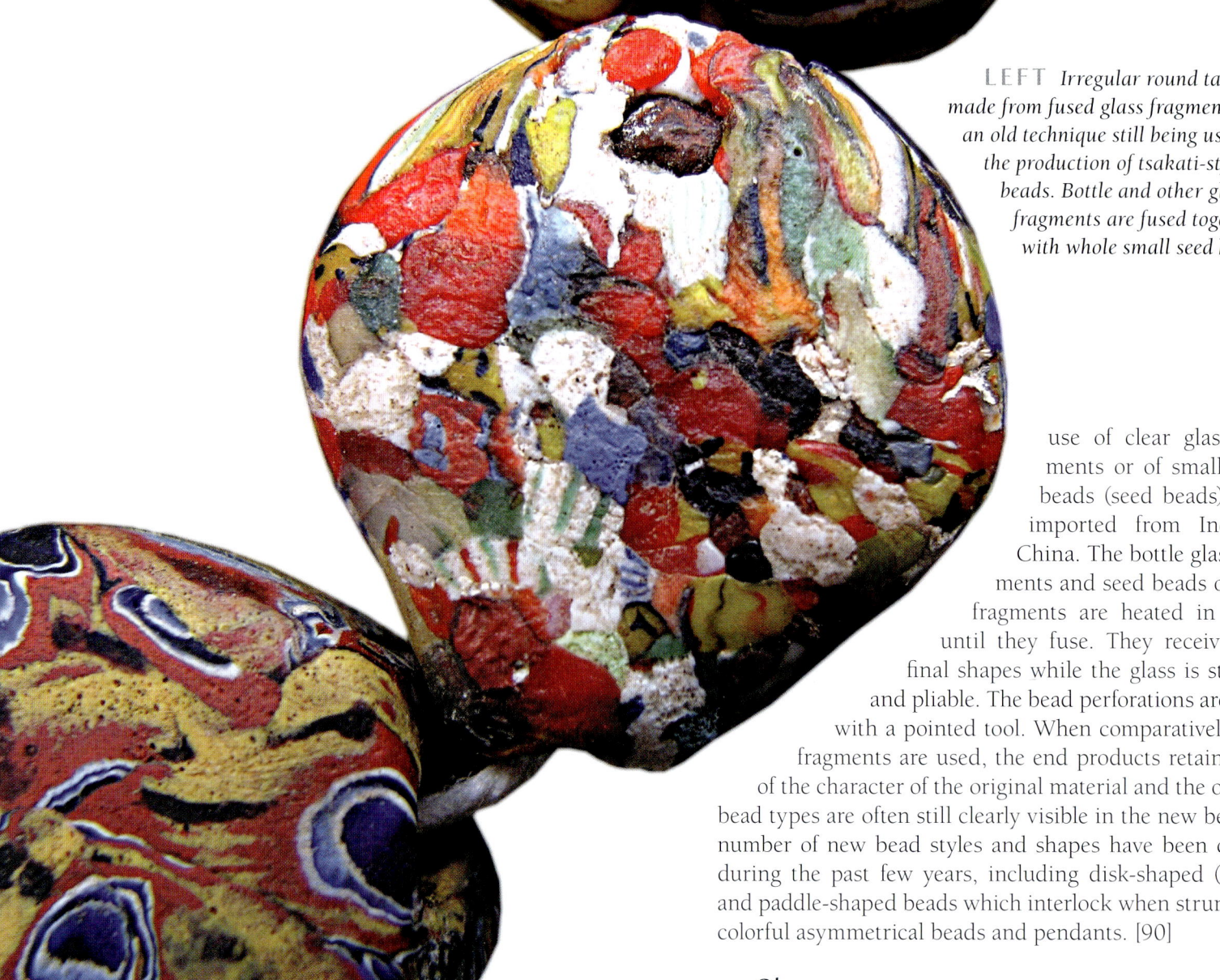

LEFT *Irregular round tabulars made from fused glass fragments— an old technique still being used in the production of tsakati-style beads. Bottle and other glass fragments are fused together with whole small seed beads.*

use of clear glass fragments or of small intact beads (seed beads), often imported from India or China. The bottle glass fragments and seed beads or bead fragments are heated in molds until they fuse. They receive their final shapes while the glass is still soft and pliable. The bead perforations are made with a pointed tool. When comparatively large fragments are used, the end products retain much of the character of the original material and the original bead types are often still clearly visible in the new beads. A number of new bead styles and shapes have been created during the past few years, including disk-shaped (Okata) and paddle-shaped beads which interlock when strung, and colorful asymmetrical beads and pendants. [90]

Ologo

Ologo (round) is the Krobo term for the biconical beads that are often made to resemble or imitate the so-called Venetian "King" beads, both in shape and decorative patterns. During the early 1990s, Krobo bead makers began with the manufacture of these biconical or bi-pyramidal bead types by joining together two cone-shaped halves which had been fired individually. A ceramic colorant was used as "glue" and is often visible as a band of a different color around the beads' equators. The patterns on both halves usually do not line up exactly, although the perforations always do. As previously noted, this suggests that they are being manipulated with a pointed tool subsequent to being joined. Ransford Tetteh (ca. 1955-1993), the founder of Teranja Bead Works (Odumase-Krobo), was one of the last classical bead makers. He was responsible for the revival of old techniques and was opposed to mass production. One of the most inventive of the Krobo bead makers, he was known

of variations. Translucent and semi-translucent spherical beads called Gige were first made during the early 1990s by fusing fairly large fragments of glass from discarded bottles and other glass objects. The beads are fired in multiple molds and receive their final shapes by turning them in their molds while the glass is still viscous. A pointed tool is used for piercing the bead perforations. Semi-translucent beads of various shapes that are made with the same technique and materials include grooved bicones, star-shaped pendants and a number of irregular shapes.

Tsakati and Okata

The manufacture of fused glass fragment beads is an old technique, which was used in the past to make Kashin Zomo and tsakati-style beads. Contemporary versions include the for having produced a wide variety of two-part Ologo beads as well as a number of other new styles including beads that showed the influence of American bead makers.

Terrazzo

During the early 1990s, Ransford Tetteh experimented with making powder glass beads that contained small flecks of color derived not from different colored glasses but from enamel pot scrapings. He produced a limited edition of these beads, which he made by using bottle glass, ceramic colorants, and flakes originating from imported Chinese enamelware pots. He called this style Terrazzo, from the floor type of the same name. Tetteh also made powder glass beads with millefiori-style decorative patterns, using pre-formed elements to create the eye motifs, his trademark being the cross-shaped "pupils." [91]

Mue Ne Angma

The group of beads with by far the most varied decorative patterns and designs is called Mue Ne Angma, a term that translates as "beads that have been written," because the decorative patterns are being "written" onto the beads. This technique, often described as being similar to enameling, is reminiscent of the method of applying designs onto wet-core powder glass beads made in Mauritania. A pointed wooden toothpick-like tool is used to apply decorative patterns onto the beads' surface with slurry composed of finely crushed bottle glass mixed with a ceramic colorant, a binder and a small amount of water. A great variety of designs can be observed on Angma beads, depicting simple circles, dots or eyes, or more intricate patterns that can often be traced to traditional African textiles. Many of the designs copy decorative styles that were characteristic of early 1900s Venetian millefiori and other Venetian-made glass beads. Some bead makers place their beads on wooden sticks during the process of decorating. After a certain number of beads have been made, they are put into the kiln and refired at low temperatures until the "written" decorations have fused. The first of these written beads date from the early 1990s. One of the earliest examples of this type, made of bottle glass and ceramic colorants, is thought to have been produced by Krobo bead maker Ransford Tetteh of Teranja Bead Works. [92]

Cedi

Possibly the most well-known contemporary, internationally acknowledged Krobo bead maker is Nomoda Ebenezer Djaba, or Cedi, as he is called. He is based in Odumase-Krobo, where he became involved in bead making as a child in the family business, working with his grandfather.

The business now employs nineteen bead makers and its products are valued by collectors worldwide.

Art Seymour

The first and, to-date, only non-African to have made African beads using an indigenous African technique is chevron pioneer Art Seymour from the United States. He has recently produced a limited range of powder glass chevron beads.

Bodom Beads

The highly valued Bodom bead has received considerable attention among collectors. Some authors have proposed that since all Bodoms, when ground or chipped, reveal a dark core, the beads are likely to have been manufactured by the wet-core powder glass technique, which was in use some one thousand years ago in what is now Mauritania. However, it is possible that instead of using saliva as a binder to hold the bead's core together (as is done with Kiffa beads), the beadmaker may have moistened the large Bodom beads with some other organic material such as gum arabic, honey or date juice, which would turn dark during firing. Others have suggested that the bead makers used cheaper glass for the cores and that this practice might explain the dark bead core color.

Despite the lack of sufficient information, some researchers suggest that Bodom beads are probably very old. Others believe that some of the materials used to make these beads did not exist before the early 1800s, and that certain other types could not have been produced before the early 1900s because of the bright yellow of the glass used for their manufacture, which was not available before that time. The technique used to apply the decorative patterns is, to date, not fully understood. Several theories exist as to whether certain decorations were pre-fabricated in special molds and then placed into the larger bead mold, together with the bead to be decorated, or whether decorations were added directly onto the bead surface, in a process similar to applying trailed decorations. [93]

The African historian Daaku Kwame Yeboah interviewed the Adanse (who claim to be the original Ashanti) in 1969. He reported that informants in sixteen villages acknowledged the importance of Bodom, and informants in twelve of the villages said that the beads came from the north. Similar information has been reported by the Ashanti of Asokore-Koona, who said that Bodom came from north of Djenne, located in the Interior Niger Delta. Given the antiquity of wet-core powder glass bead making in the ancient overlapping kingdoms of Ghana and Mali, and considering

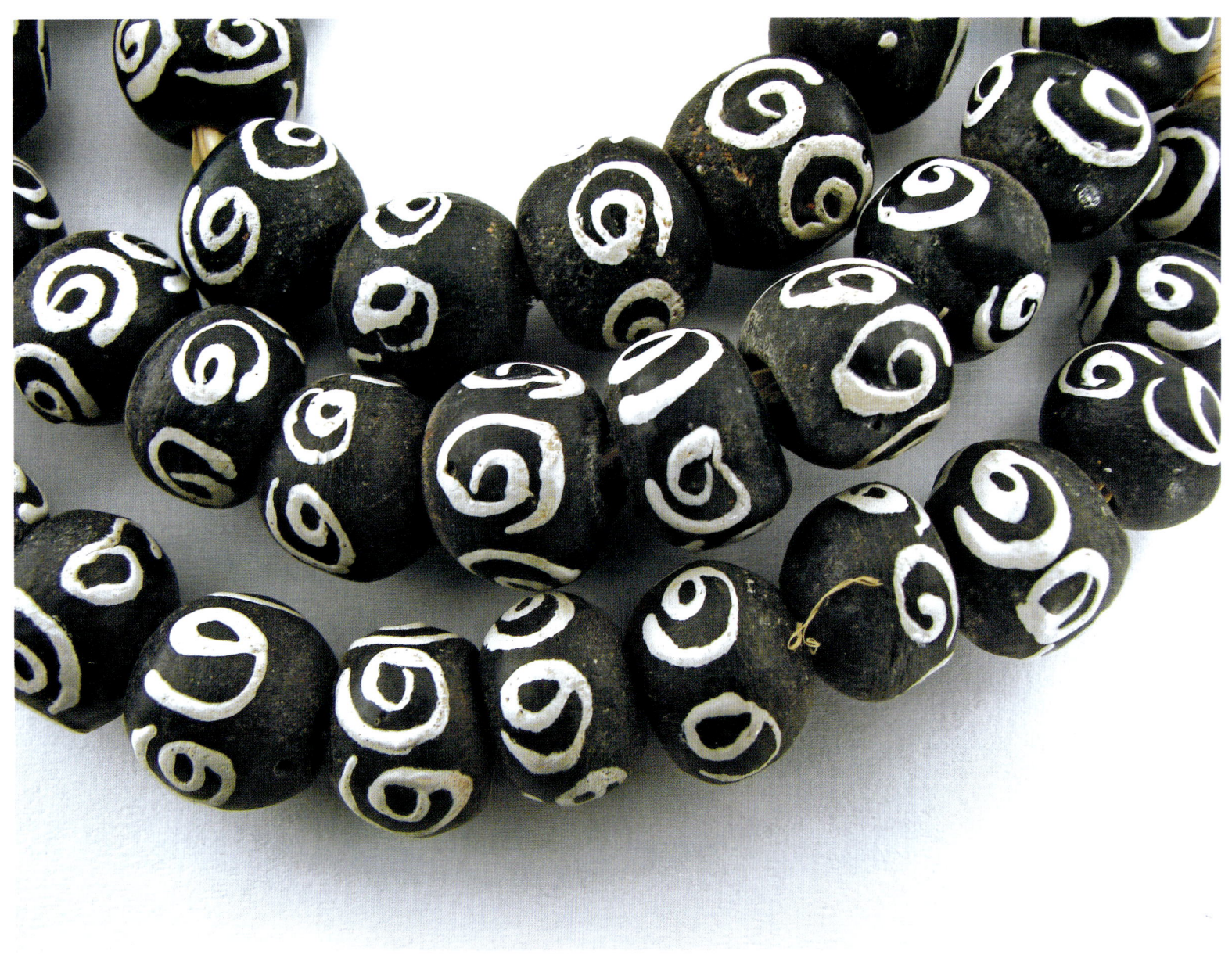

ABOVE AND NEXT PAGE *Contemporary styles of Krobo powder glass beads decorated in the Mue Ne Angma style, which imitates Venetian lamp work beads from the early 20th century.*

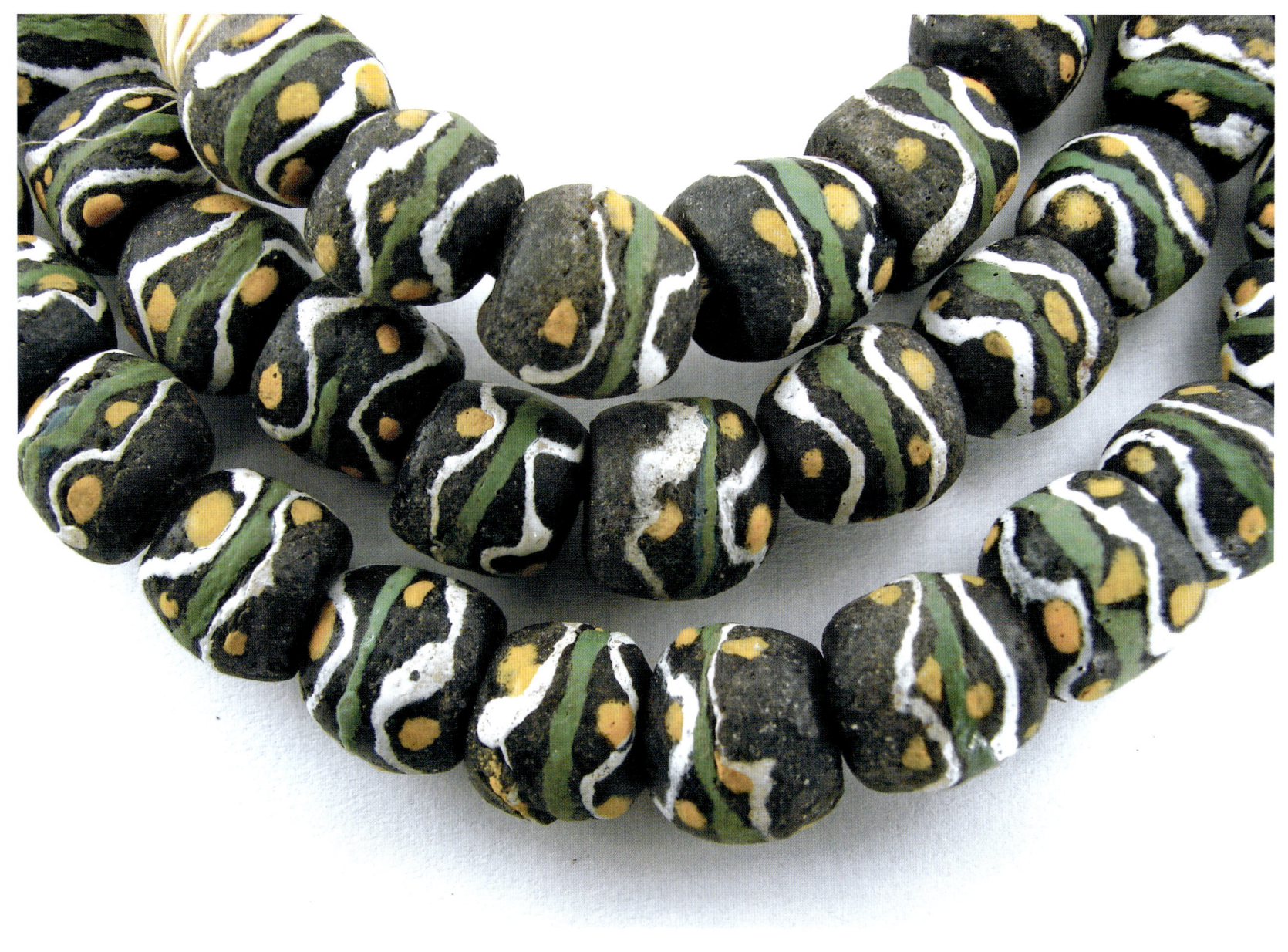

Glass Beads

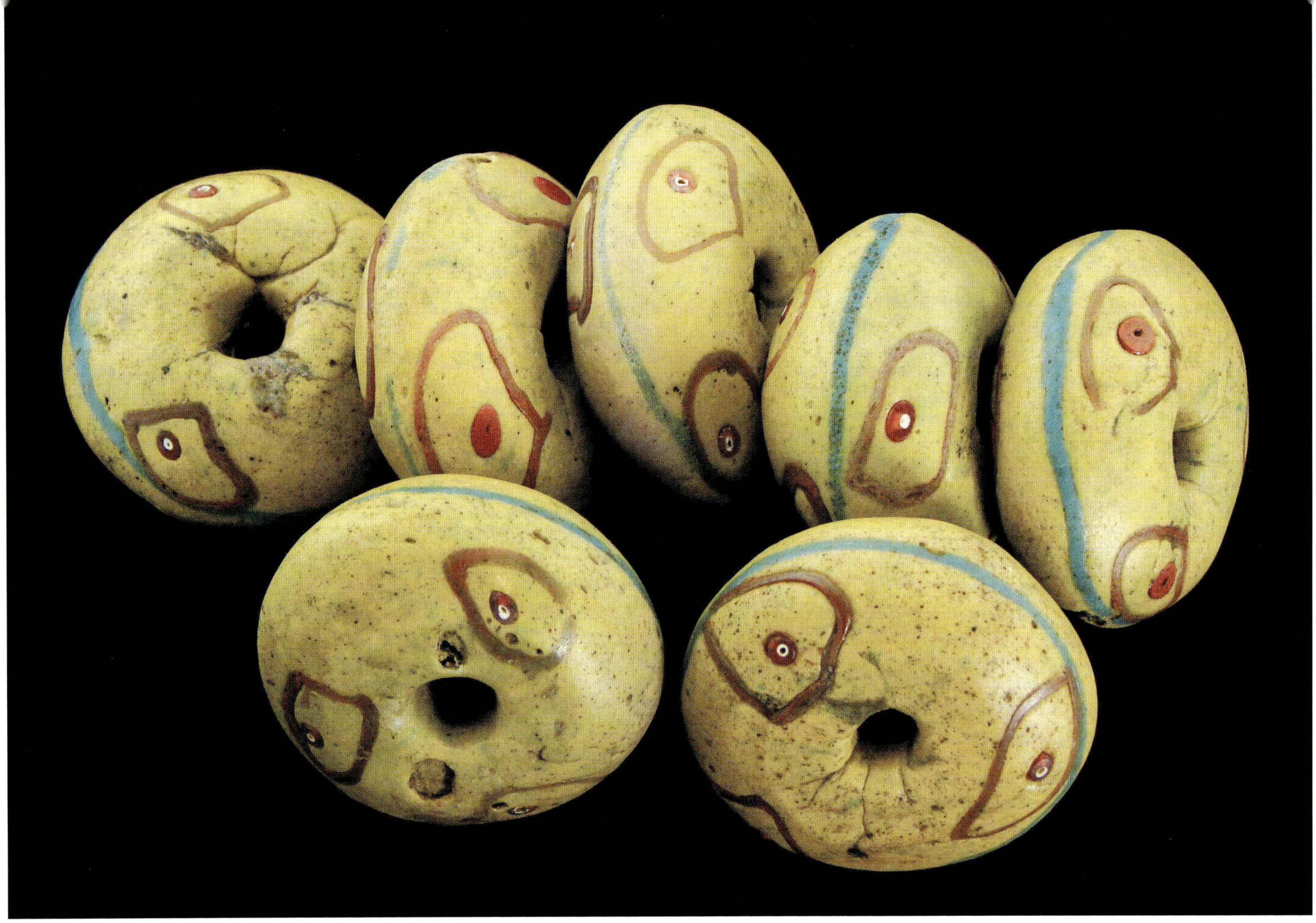

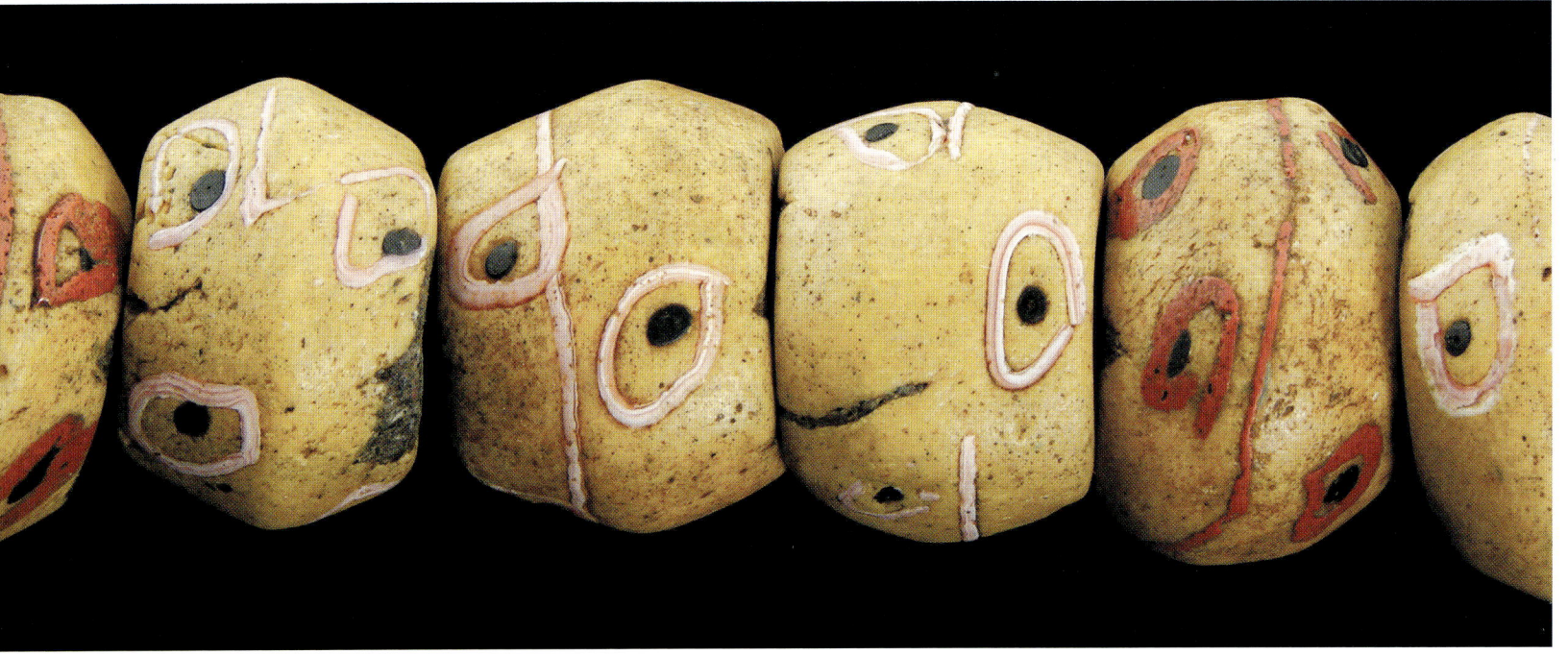

142 ◆ Glass Beads

LEFT AND TOP RIGHT *Two of the most highly valued beads in West Africa are the Bodom and the Akoso. Imbued with magical and medicinal powers, Bodom beads are passed down within families and are commonly used in funeral ceremonies. According to legend, Bodoms are born of the earth, and if buried again will reproduce themselves.*

BELOW LEFT AND RIGHT *Old Bodom beads have dark cores, giving rise to the suggestion that the beads were made in the wet-core powder glass technique. Another explanation may be that bead makers used cheaper glass for the cores.*

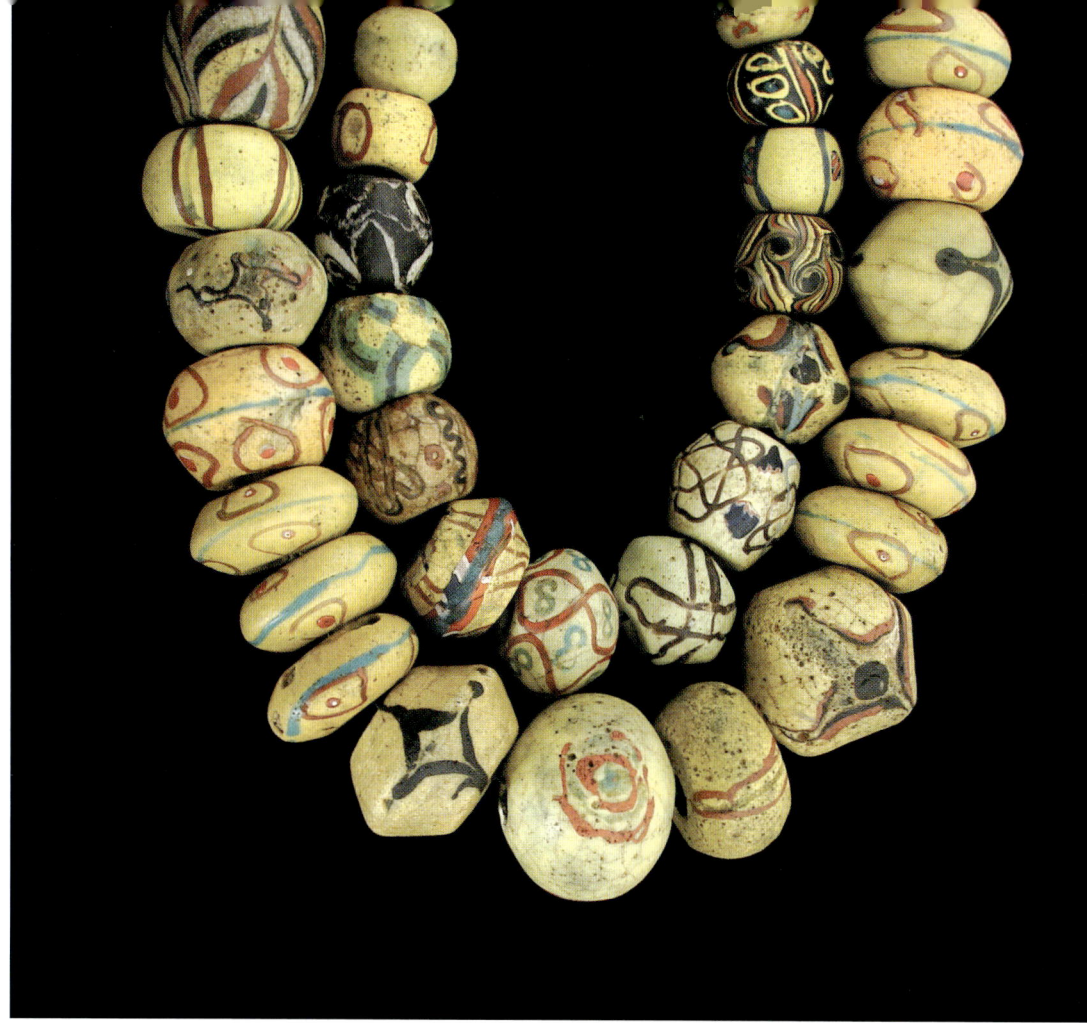

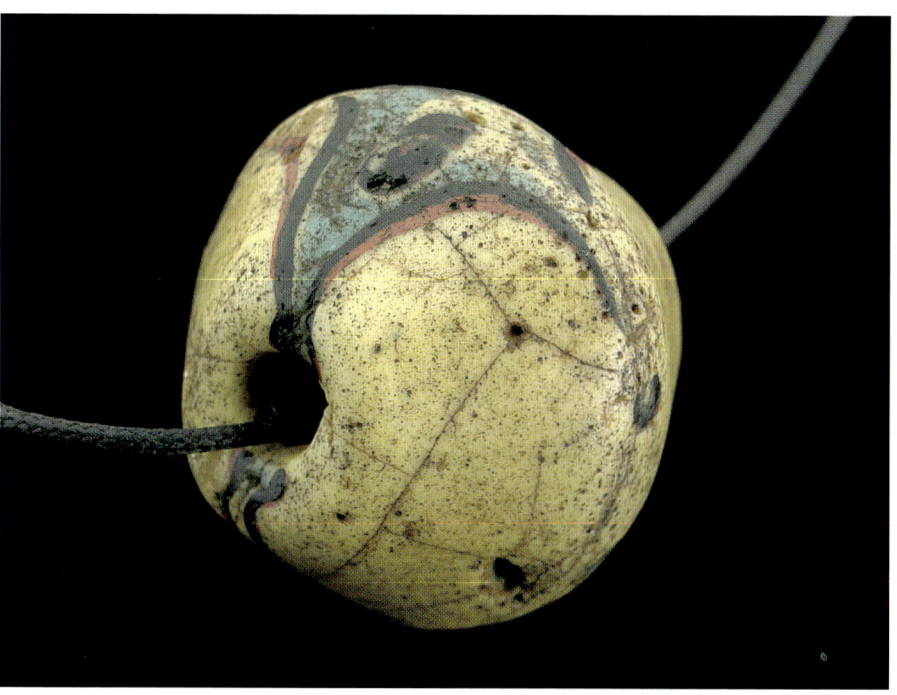

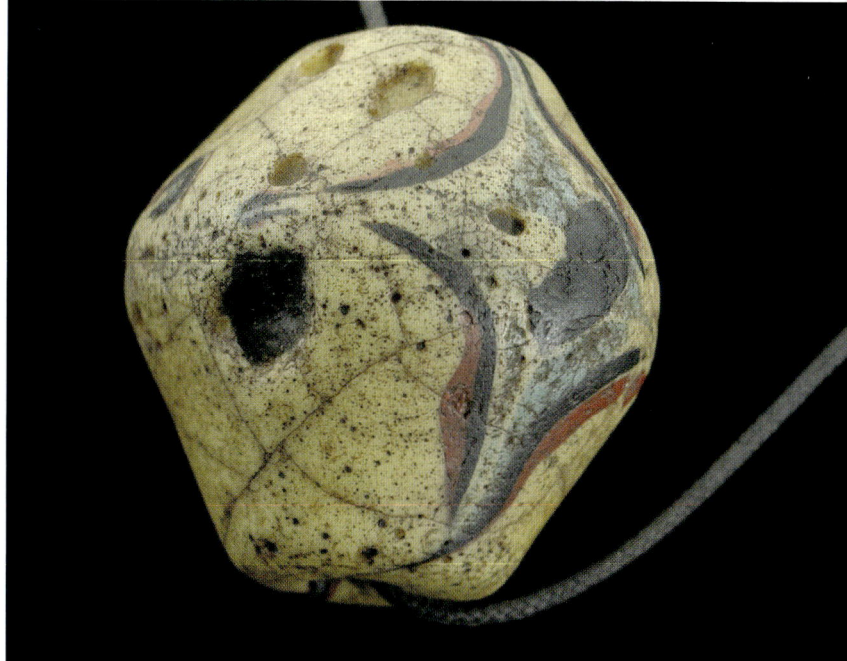

Glass Beads ◆ 143

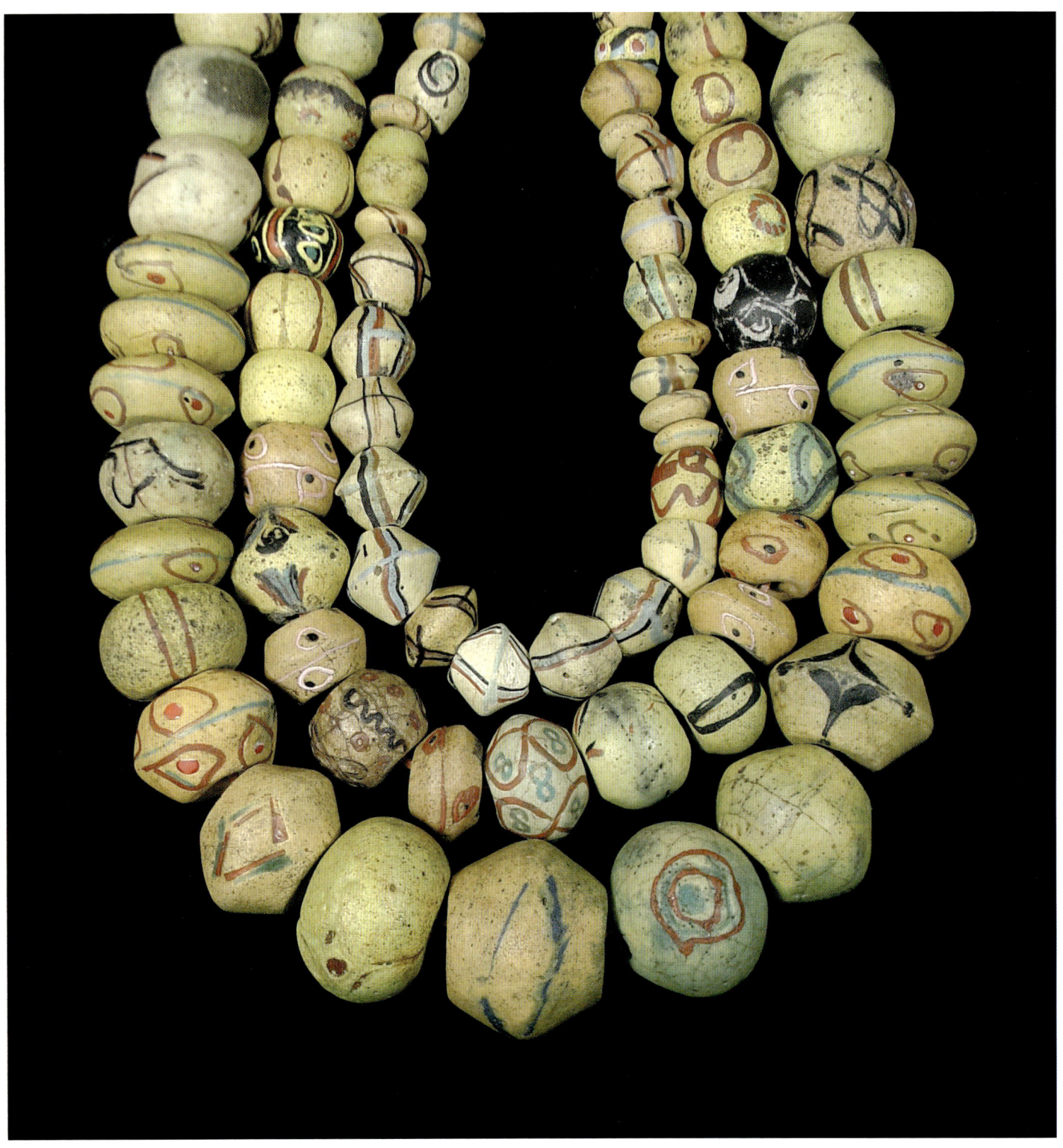

ABOVE *Bodom beads were manufactured in a variety of characteristic shapes and decorative styles such as those depicted above.*

144   ◇   Glass Beads

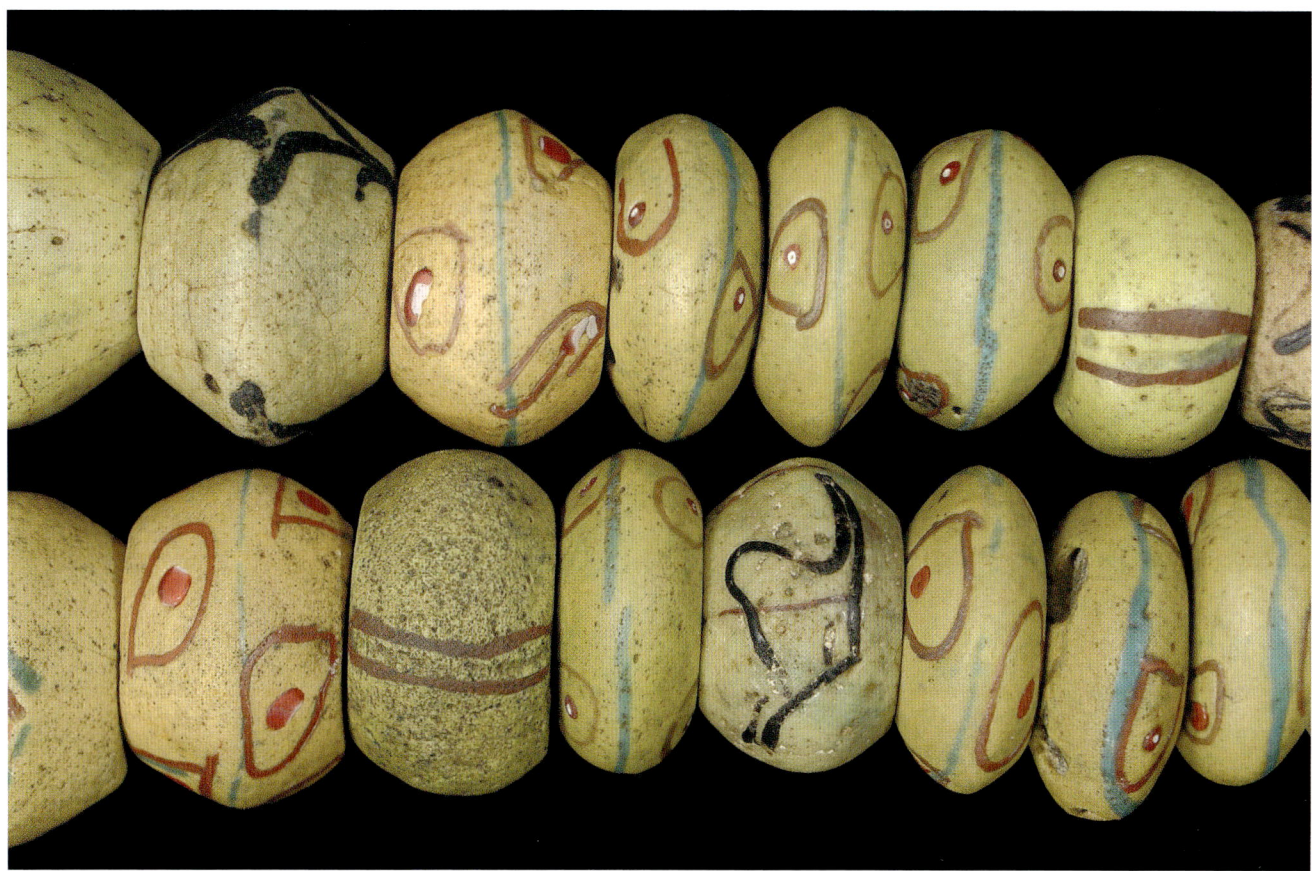

ABOVE *The bead style depicted here is only one of various characteristic styles and designs observed on traditional Bodom beads, which often consist of equatorial bands and "eye" motifs.*

the testimony of the Ashanti, an origin in or near one of the great cities of these two kingdoms appears plausible.

While the Krobo call some of their beads "Bodom" (literally translated this expression means "a bead that barks," i.e. a bead that stands out or draws attention), and use this word to describe the largest bead in a strand, the term as such is new to them and it appears to have been introduced in the early 1970s. The traditional Krobo term for the largest bead, commonly not placed at the center of a strand but next to where the strand is tied together at back, is kpo.

New Bodom

Krobo bead makers are producing contemporary powder glass beads that resemble old, traditional Bodom. Like the originals, the new beads are large in size and are decorated with the traditional red, blue and black "eye" motifs and crosshatched patterns. The technique applied in making these beads, however, differs from the traditional method. Old Bodom are described as having been manufactured in the wet-core technique, using a binder. The new beads are made in the dry-core technique. Also, the decorative patterns observed on traditional Bodom were applied to the bead's surface after firing. The decorative patterns on the new versions are created in the mold by layering dry, crushed, colored glass in such a way that the desired patterns are visible on the beads' surfaces before the beads are fired. Another difference is that the old Bodom were made in one piece. On close observation it can be discerned that the new beads are made from two cone-shaped halves that are joined together, the method of manufacture being the same as that for making the modern Ologo powder glass beads.

Akoso Beads

Like the old African powder glass Bodom beads, the origins of Akoso beads are shrouded in myths and mysteries. They are also equally collectible. Of the several spellings, "Akoso" is the most widely accepted version among collectors and researchers, and for this reason it is usually given preference over Akuso or Akosu. The origin of the word is

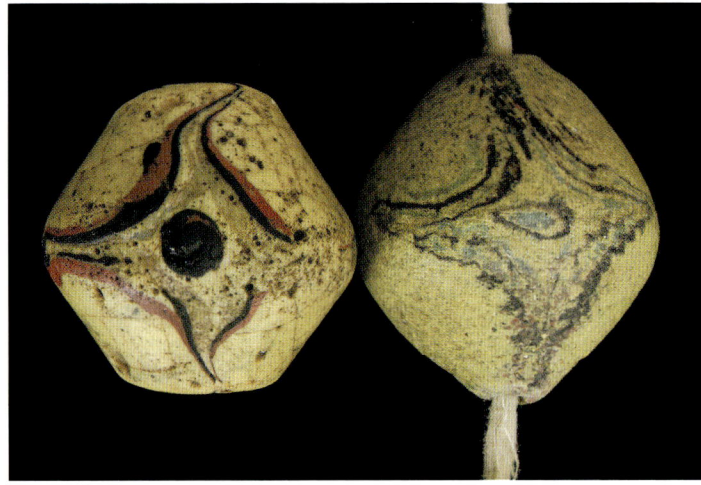

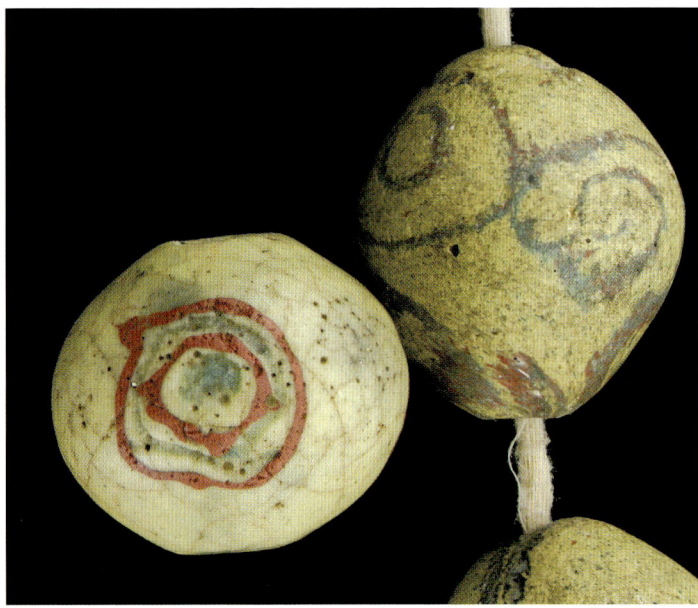

ABOVE *Comparisons between old (top) and new (bottom) Bodom. New Bodom are manufactured in the dry-core technique and their decorative patterns are created in the mold by layering dry, crushed, colored glass to form the desired pattern. Also, old Bodom were made in one piece, whereas it can be discerned that many of the new beads are made from two cone-shaped halves that have been joined together.*

unknown, although it has been suggested that it may derive from the Akosombo Dam, the hydroelectric complex situated on the four hundred kilometer long Lake Volta, built by Ghana's first President, Dr. Kwame Nkrumah, in the 1960s.

According to local tradition, Akoso beads were owned by the Kings of the Ewe. The Ewe people, located in Ghana, Togo and Benin (their original homeland being Oyo in western Nigeria—a region where a long tradition of local glass bead making has been documented), are believed to be the first makers of the highly treasured Akoso beads. The Ashanti people of Ghana, members of the Akan, have also been suggested as potential originators. There is no common consensus regarding the age of Akoso beads; most authors propose a time frame ranging from the late 1800s to the early 1900s, while some others think the beads date from the 1950s.

Although many of the Akoso-type beads are referred to as "Bodom," they are technically very different. Akoso beads are made with the dry-core powder glass technique, unlike traditional Bodom beads, which were manufactured using the wet-core method. All Bodom beads have cores. A number of smaller Akoso-type beads have no discernible cores, although larger Akoso commonly have gray cores which, due to surface wear, are often exposed at the ends and around the equators. The glass used for the manufacture of Akoso beads, which is similar to that of Bodom, is believed to come from Venetian biconical "King" beads made during the late 1800s and early 1900s. Another theory is that the source materials for making Akoso (and possibly Bodom) beads were derived from yellow and teal blue Hebron (Kano) beads.

Akoso beads are typically of cylindrical or elongated biconical shape. In size they range from small cylinders of eight by ten millimeters, to large and elaborately decorated bicones that can measure up to thirty by forty millimeters. Small cylindrical specimens with minimal decorations are the most common and readily available types. These usually have a plain yellow ochre base color with or without decorative patterns. A great number of smaller Akoso beads are decorated with overlay beads, such as the so-called red whiteheart and greenheart beads of Venetian manufacture. Venetian greenheart beads have been dated to the mid 1700s to the late 1800s and are characterized by a translucent green core and a brick-colored outer layer. It is this outer layer of the greenheart bead which was used for creating decorative patterns. Almost always the translucent green bead core is encircled by green, blue or red glass, creating an eye-like appearance.

From the late 1800s to the early 1900s, Venetian bead makers produced similar beads by applying trailed patterns, such as the "eyes" and loops that can be observed on small Akoso-type beads. Occasionally the question arises whether Venetian bead makers copied African bead makers, or vice versa. The truth may never be established, but in all probability bead makers of one culture were inspired by beads

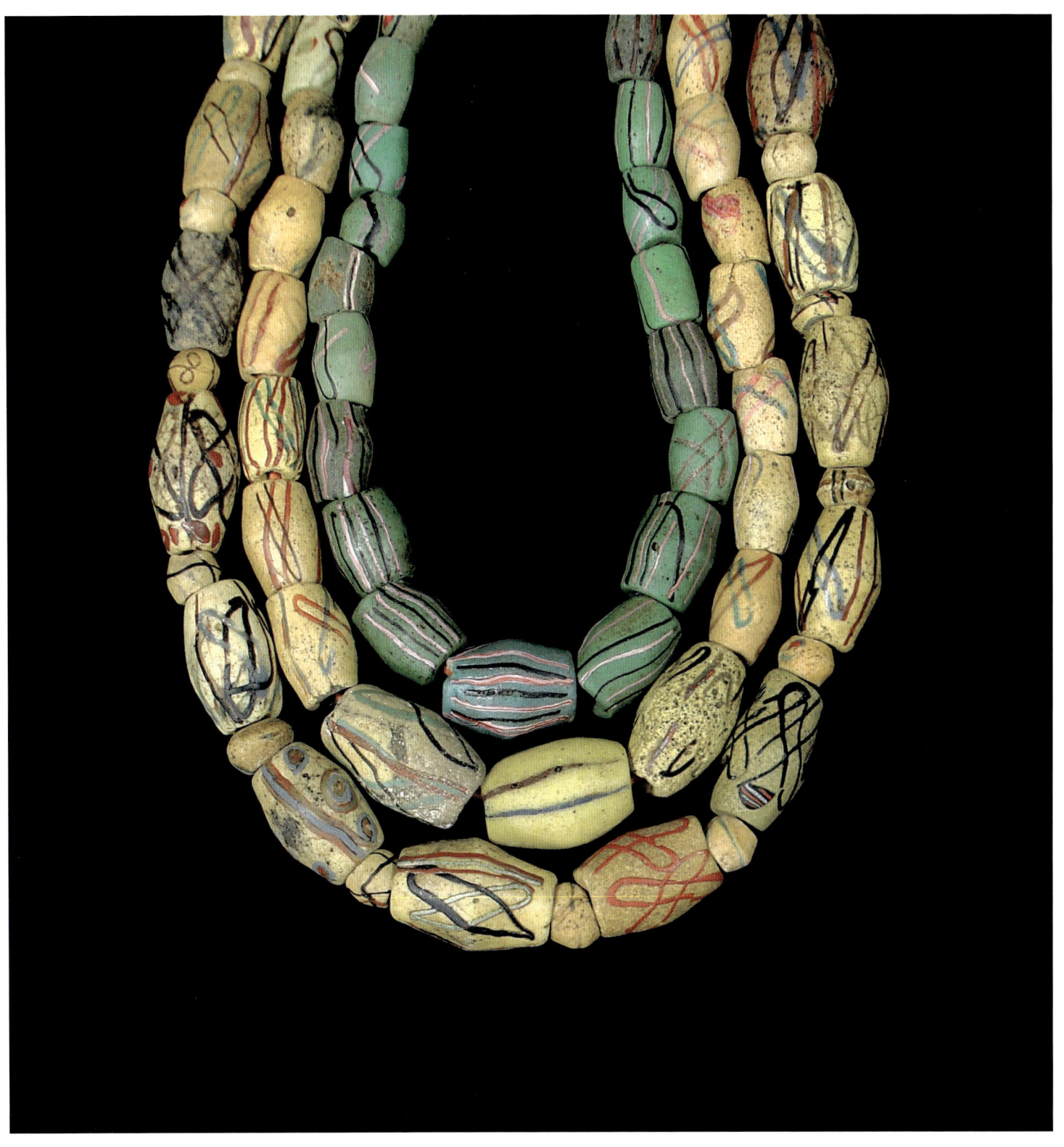

ABOVE *Old Akoso beads in characteristic shapes, styles and decorative patterns.*

Glass Beads

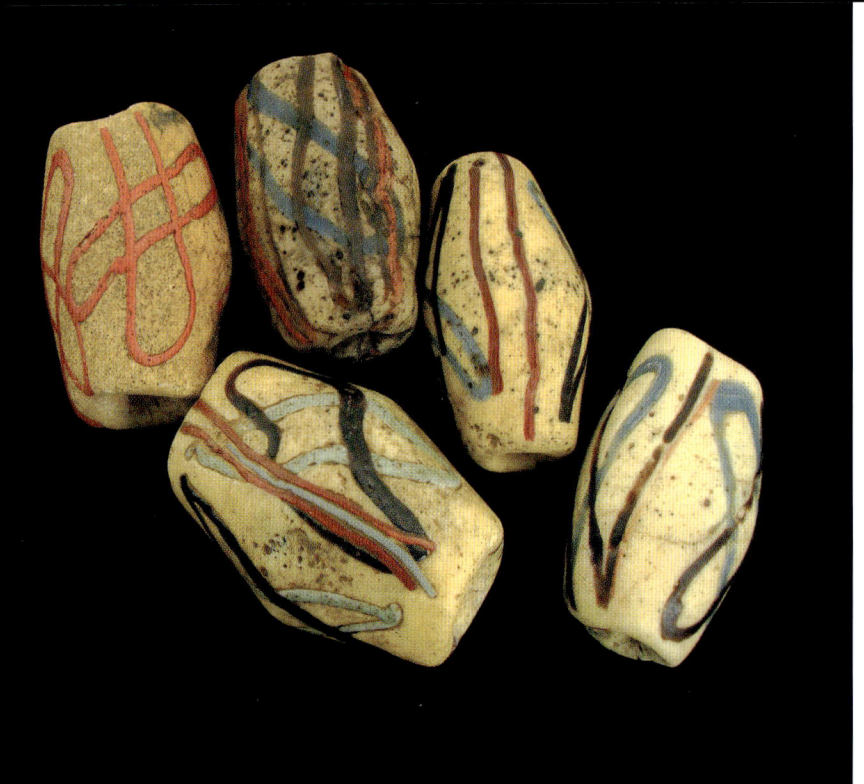
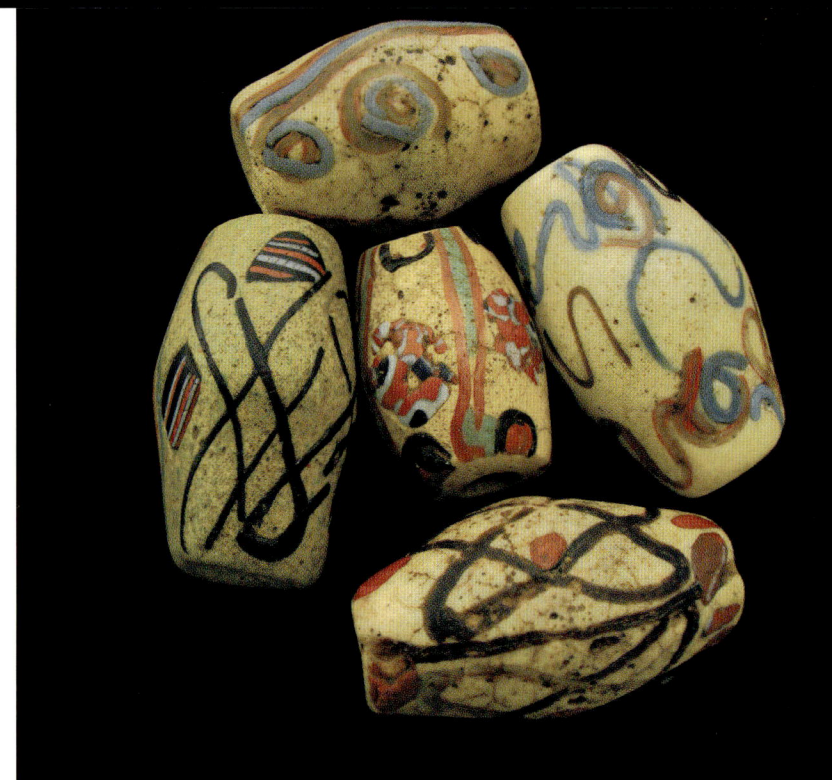

ABOVE LEFT AND RIGHT *Akoso beads are typically made in cylindrical or elongated biconical shapes in a range of sizes. The small beads have a plain yellow base color and are often decorated with red whiteheart or greenheart beads of Venetian manufacture. The glass used for the production of Akoso beads is believed to come from Venetian glass beads, mainly from so-called "King" beads that were manufactured from the late 1800s to early 1900s.*

that were manufactured by another, and occasionally copied what appealed to them.

The most sought after style of Akoso beads is represented by the group of large bicones, which were produced in various colors, including yellow ochre, brown, tan, whitish-green, teal-blue, blue and, very rarely, black. The prevalent decorative patterns observed on larger beads consist of crosshatched loops. These loops were created by applying different colors, often in several layers, with the predominant colors being brick red, black and a translucent light blue. Some authors suggest that the crisscrossed loop designs were prefabricated in separate molds and added to the bead surface before firing. Others believe that these elaborate designs were applied after firing in a process similar to making trailed decorations.

In addition to the characteristic loop designs, other decorative patterns can be observed, consisting of stripes and circles executed in a number of different colors. These decorations, reminiscent of the classic "eye" design, were applied on their own or in combinations of several different patterns. Often fragments of Venetian seven-layer chevron beads were embedded into Akoso bead surfaces. Equatorial bands are rare.

Not much has been published concerning these intriguing beads. The late Peter Francis, Jr., who devoted his life to bead research, suggested that the presence of gold flakes in the cores of Bodom and on the surface of Akoso beads might be markers of genuine old beads. This information, however, has not been verified. The origins of the Akoso beads of West Africa remain a mystery waiting to be fully understood.

New Akoso

For a number of years, Krobo bead makers have been manufacturing new Akoso-type powder glass beads in the vertical-mold dry-core technique. The characteristic decorative patterns consisting of crosshatched lines are applied by the writing method, i.e. the patterns are "written" onto plain powder glass beads with a pointed tool or with wooden sticks resembling toothpicks. After decorating, the beads are fired a second time to fuse the glass.

Ashanti Powder Glass Beads

The Ashanti (Asante) are located in northern Ghana and speak a dialect of Akan. Prior to European colonization, the Ashanti Confederacy was a major state in West Africa, and Ashanti wealth was based on the region's substantial deposits of gold, which led to the development of metalworking.

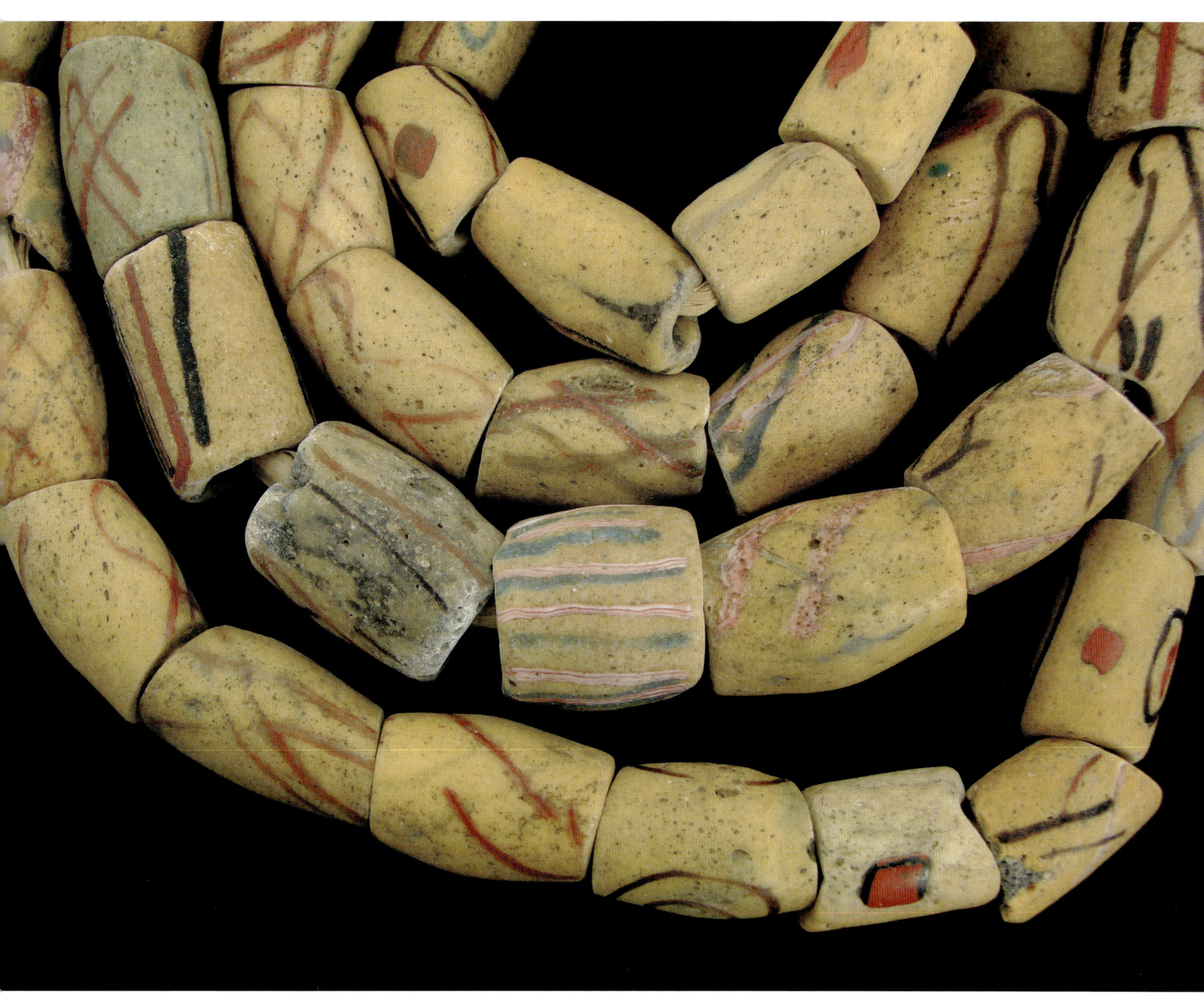

ABOVE *Most Akoso beads have a yellow ochre base color, as depicted above.*

Glass Beads   149

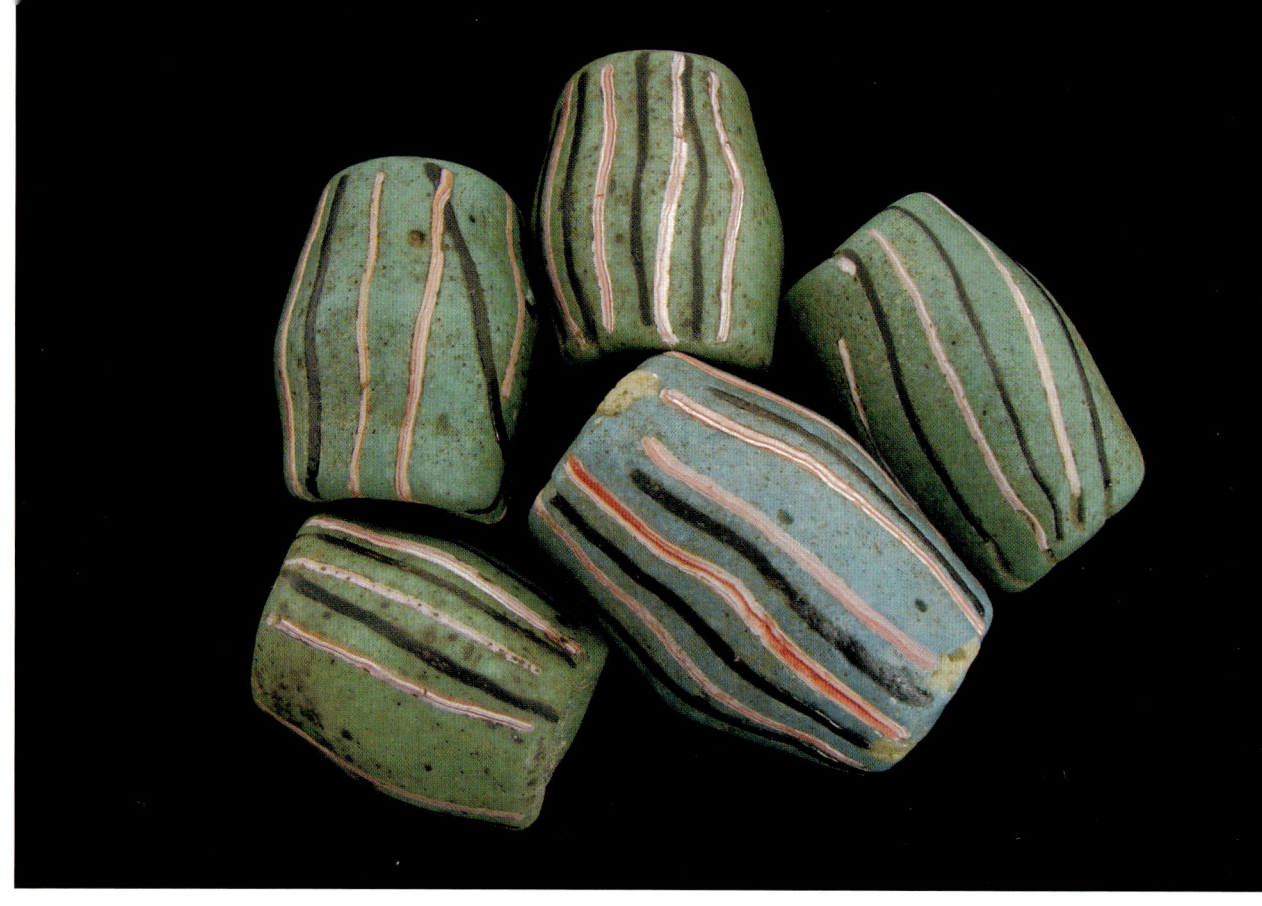

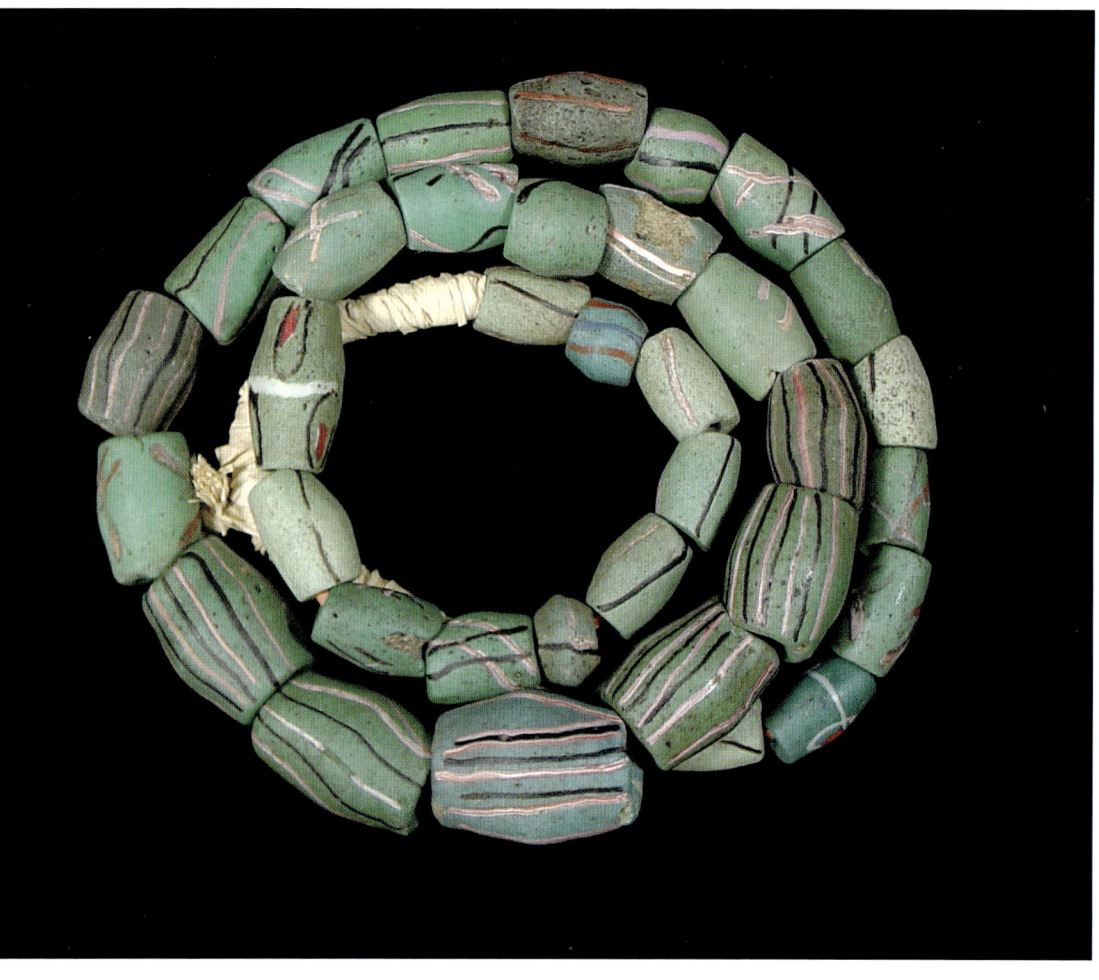

ABOVE AND LEFT *The green or teal-blue variant, usually found only in larger, elongated, biconical beads, is the rarest of all Akoso color versions. These beads were not usually decorated with the classic Akoso crisscrossed loop design but rather with a series of stripes, although specimens with cross-hatched loop patterns have been documented. The stripes are commonly black or pink or a combination of both colors, the pink being attributed to Venetian overlay (the so-called red whiteheart beads), which have an opaque white center and a translucent rose red outer layer, resulting in pink glass when melted.*

Ashanti bead makers have been proposed as one of the possible candidates to have produced the traditional old Bodom beads. They are known to have made a number of powder glass bead types, some of which can be distinguished from Krobo-made powder glass beads in that they were made in horizontal molds, whereas Krobo bead makers commonly used vertical molds. One of these bead types is called Meteyi. Mold marks and seams along their sides give evidence of the method of their manufacture in horizontal molds. They are often ellipsoidal rather than round in cross section, and they commonly have a rough surface on the side adjacent to the bottom of the mold used during firing. Meteyi beads were made in various colors, the most common being yellow, and all are decorated with stripes in combinations of blue, yellow, white or red. The manufacture of Meteyi beads ceased during the 1940s.

The Ashanti also made a number of styles of layered powder glass beads from bottle glasses, using natural, and later ceramic colorants. The older versions (up to the late 1970s) are easily recognizable in that they are well fused and finished, and have smooth and polished, glossy surfaces. In later years materials changed and there was a noticeable decline in craftsmanship. [94]

Yoruba Powder Glass Beads

Another West African people renowned for their long tradition of making glass beads are the Yoruba from Nigeria, who made drawn, lapidary and powder glass beads. Some powder glass beads of Yoruba manufacture differ technically from typical Ghanaian powder glass beads in that they are made without the use of molds and in a wet-core technique where finely crushed glass is moistened with water and shaped by hand. Yoruba powder glass beads are frequently confused with Ghanaian beads because of the latter's contemporary dominance in powder glass bead making, in contrast to the virtual extinction of the industry in Yorubaland. It is generally accepted that the Yoruba made powder glass beads, but which beads these are, as distinct from Ghanaian powder glass, remains problematic. The Nigerian scholar O. Euba, based at the Center for Cultural Studies of the University of Lagos, believes that the Krobo introduced powder glass techniques to the Yoruba, which suggests that powder glass technology among the Yoruba is a relatively recent development. The Krobo, however, cannot reliably attribute their own industry to much earlier than the 1900s and they say that they learned the technique from the Ewe. [95]

There appear to be at least two generations of Yoruba powder glass beads; the more recent group being comprised of beads made from coarse powder derived from bottles and other scrap glasses. They show little evidence of finishing. Beads from an earlier production phase appear to have been made of finely crushed old glass beads. On comparing the two types, one finds a marked difference in glass density, with the older beads being noticeably heavier, and their texture being much finer. The older beads also often show indications of lapidary finishing.

Keta Awuazi

The most favored colors for beads in many parts of Nigeria are red, blue and white. Bright sky blue beads, called Keta Awuazi by the Yoruba, appear to have been made in horizontal molds. Mold marks are often evident along their sides in the form of raised seams. The name of these beads is believed to originate in the town of Keta in eastern Ghana, near the Togo border. It is possible that the Yoruba made Keta Awuazi beads, but this information has not been verified. Until the 1940s, Krobo bead makers manufactured similar beads, which they call Awuazi, using fragments of cold cream jars to achieve the blue coloration. These beads were made in vertical molds and they are usually smaller in size than the mysterious Keta Awuazi. [96]

Niusisi Koli

Another bead type, the so-called Niusisi Koli, can be attributed to the Yoruba powder glass industry with more certainty. The beads are green and can be slightly translucent. They appear to have been made from wine bottles, with the decorations possibly derived from European beads. Most specimens are ellipsoidal in cross section and their sides are flat and rough in texture, which is characteristic of a moldless horizontal manufacturing technique. Production ceased during the 1940s and unlike the Ghanaian industries, which in the past couple of decades have undergone a renaissance, the Yoruba practice is now virtually extinct.

Tehe Koli

An unusual bead type, in which glass fragments were combined with elements made of powder glass, can be found in both Kroboland and Yorubaland. The beads are called Tehe (stone) Koli by the Krobo and they are composed of mainly blue, and to a lesser extent green, fragments of what appear to be Kori beads, perhaps originating from "kori" stones. These glass fragments were joined together with a paste made of finely crushed glass. The seams between the glass fragments and the areas of powder glass are quite smooth, indicating that the powder glass was applied when moist. There is little evidence of grinding, and the bead perforations are highly irregular.

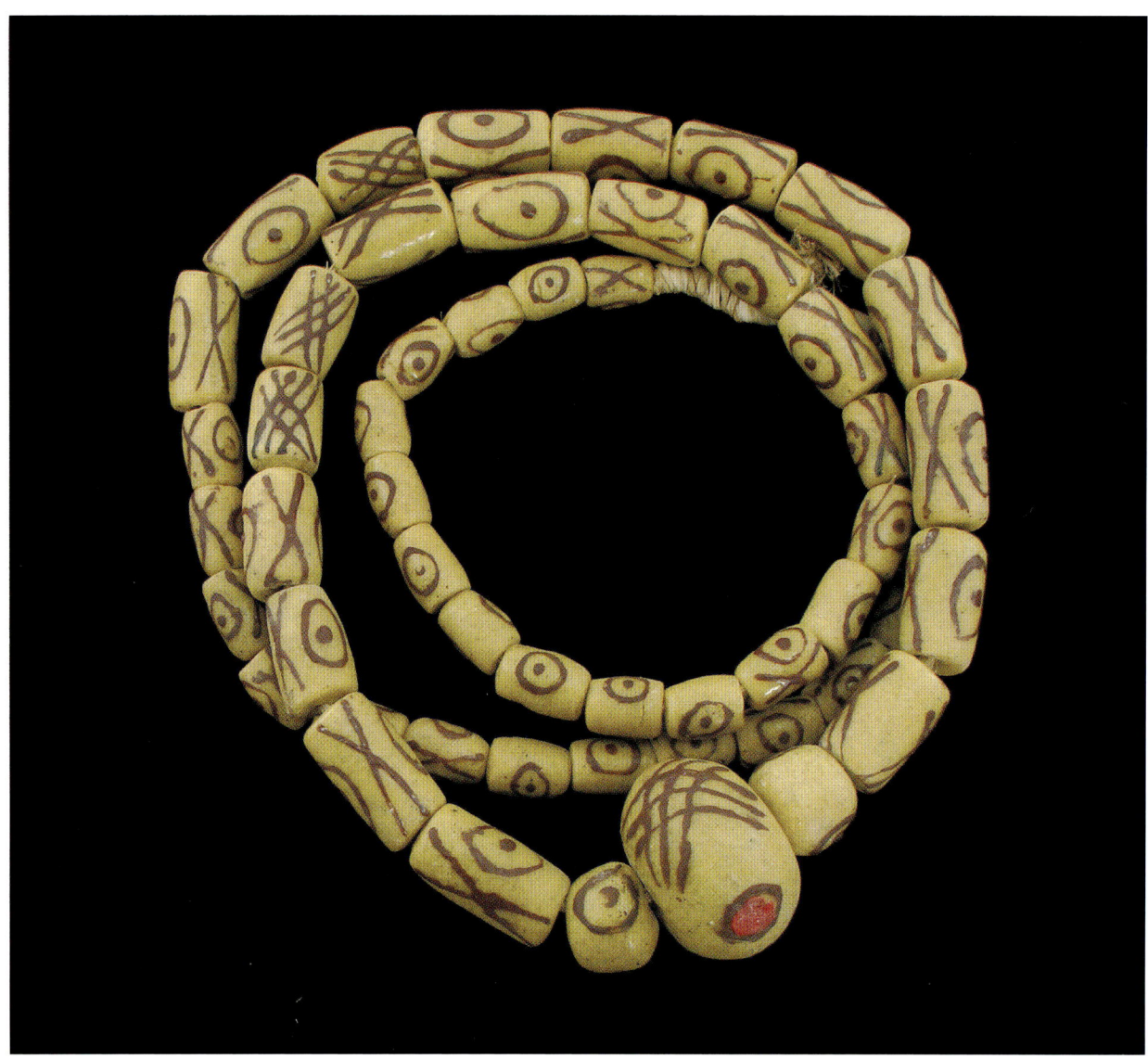

ABOVE *A strand of new Akoso-type powder glass beads, which are not as valuable or as sought after as the originals.*

Powder Glass Coral Imitations

In Nigeria, the most highly coveted red beads are made from coral which had to be imported from the Mediterranean, part of a trade that has been conducted for centuries. In a mural in Ile-Ife the goddess Yemoja is depicted wearing a necklace and bracelets of red coral beads. Yemoja is closely associated with Mammi Wata, the goddess of the ocean and one of the most important juju deities. According to Yoruba tradition, Mammi Wata has the power to save a drowning person, but she may ask a high price in exchange for doing so.

There is an old tradition of making glass imitations of Mediterranean coral. These more easily affordable coral simulations, called Ateyun (Iyun), were produced of powder glass and made in a variety of shapes, always in red. Ateyun beads of the older generation are a rich red in color, and the glass finely textured with a very smooth, polished surface. Later generation Ateyun are of a less intense red color, and they have a grainy texture and a matte surface. Krobo bead makers too produce powder glass coral simulations, using the traditional vertical-mold technique. [97]

Apart from producing a great number of bead types and styles of their own, West African bead makers apply various methods involving lapidary and hot-working techniques, altering and re-working imported European beads,

152 Glass Beads

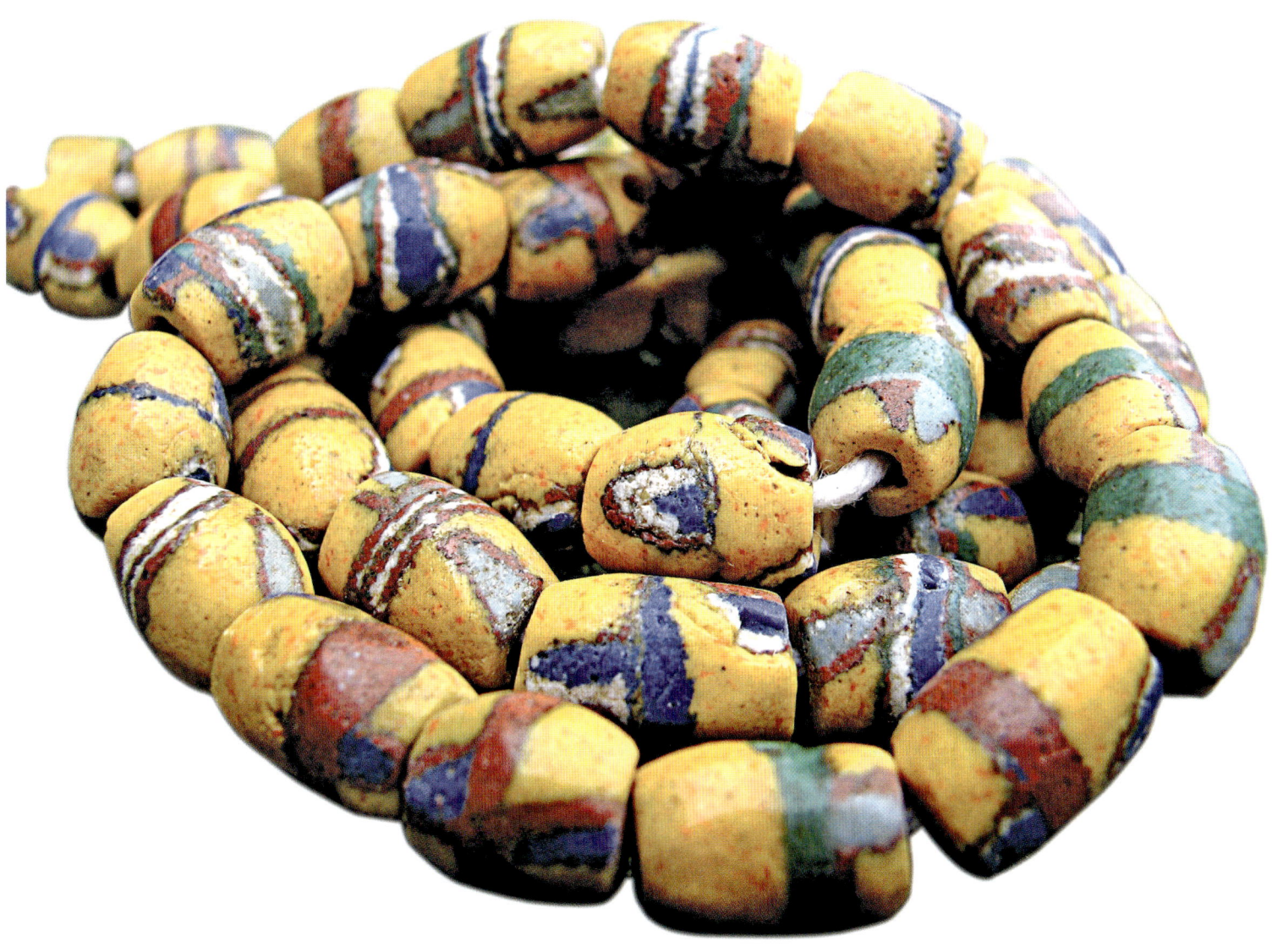

ABOVE *Ashanti powder glass beads dating from the 1970s, with well finished, smooth and glossy surfaces.*

mostly from Venice, in order to better suit local uses. Beveling the ends of cylindrical, spherical and barrel-shaped beads for a smoother fit in necklaces and bracelets is a widely practiced custom. In certain bead types, the trailed decorations were removed by grinding or faceting. Striped cylindrical beads were re-heated and twisted around their axis, converting the stripes into spiraling patterns.

Kano Beads

The so-called Kano beads—highly esteemed in Sudan as waist beads until the 1930s—originated in the city of Hebron (Al-Halil), one of the oldest cities in the Middle East, situated thirty kilometers south of Jerusalem, where glass making has been documented from the early 14th century. Hebron became the main supplier of glass to the Islamic world after the fall of Tyre and Sidon and the destruction of Fustat (old Cairo) in 1168. From Egypt, these beads were sold to many parts of Africa, from the Sudan and Chad to the Gold Coast (present-day Ghana). Peter Francis strongly believed Hebron glass to have been made using deposits from the Dead Sea which contained an impure alkali thought to give the glass its opaque nature. Hausa traders ground the rounded ends of the beads flat so that they would fit better on a strand and brought them to Kano, their largest city—hence the name Kano beads. [98]

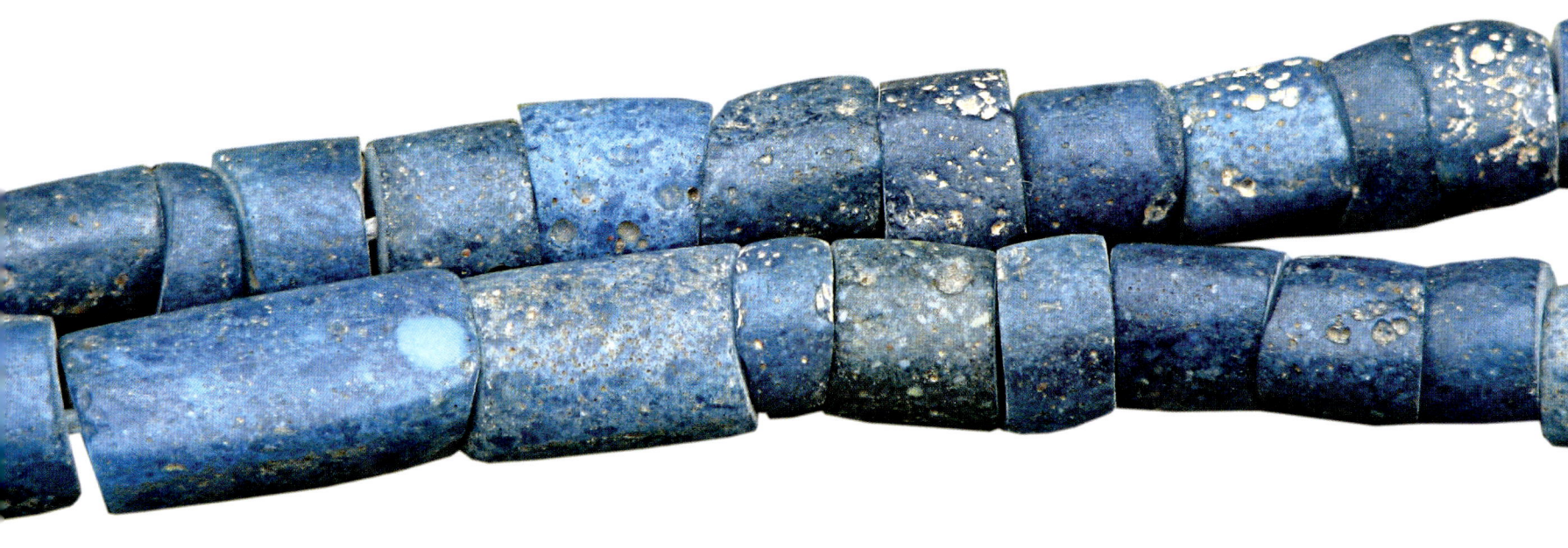

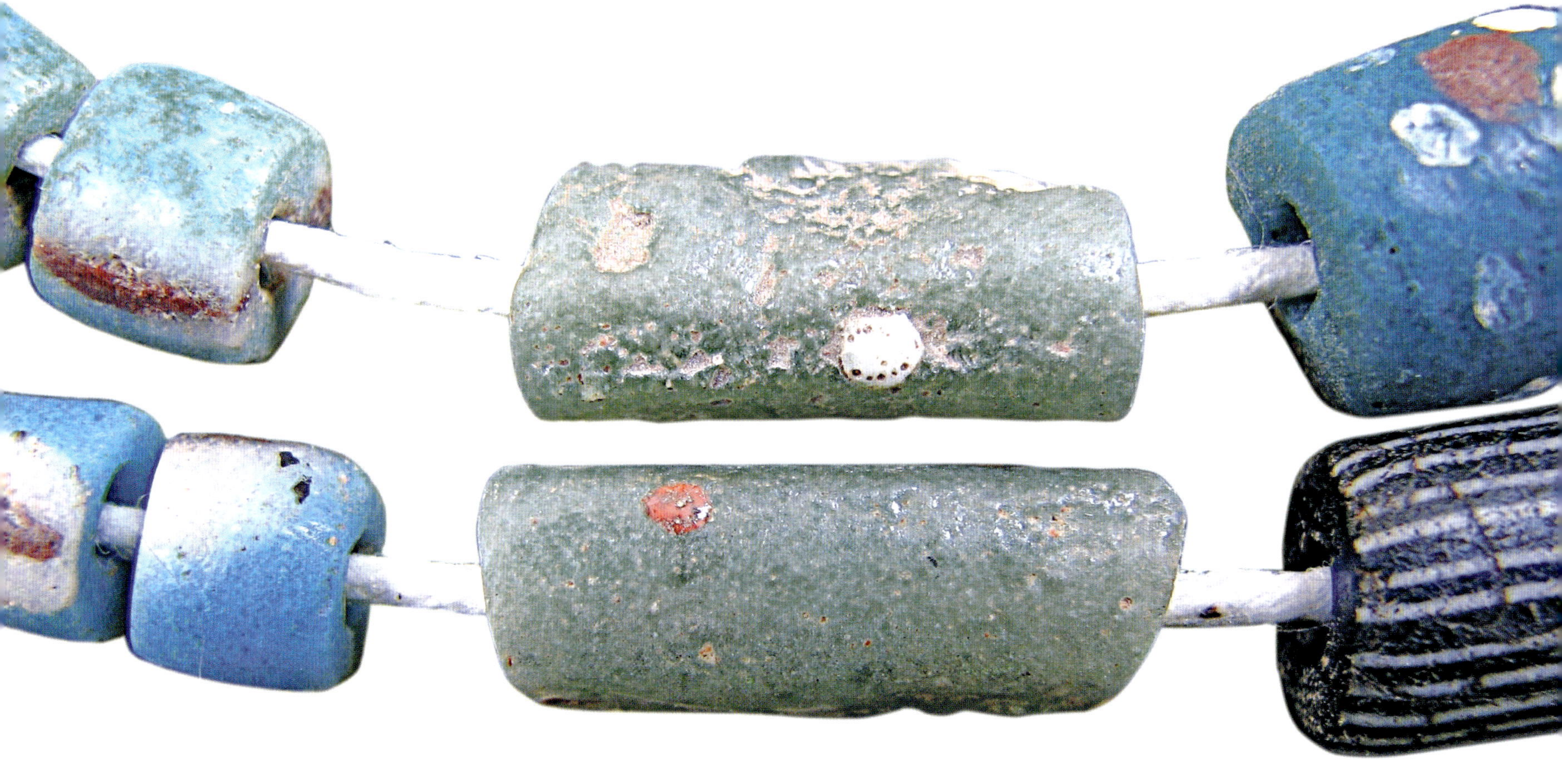

154 ◆ Glass Beads

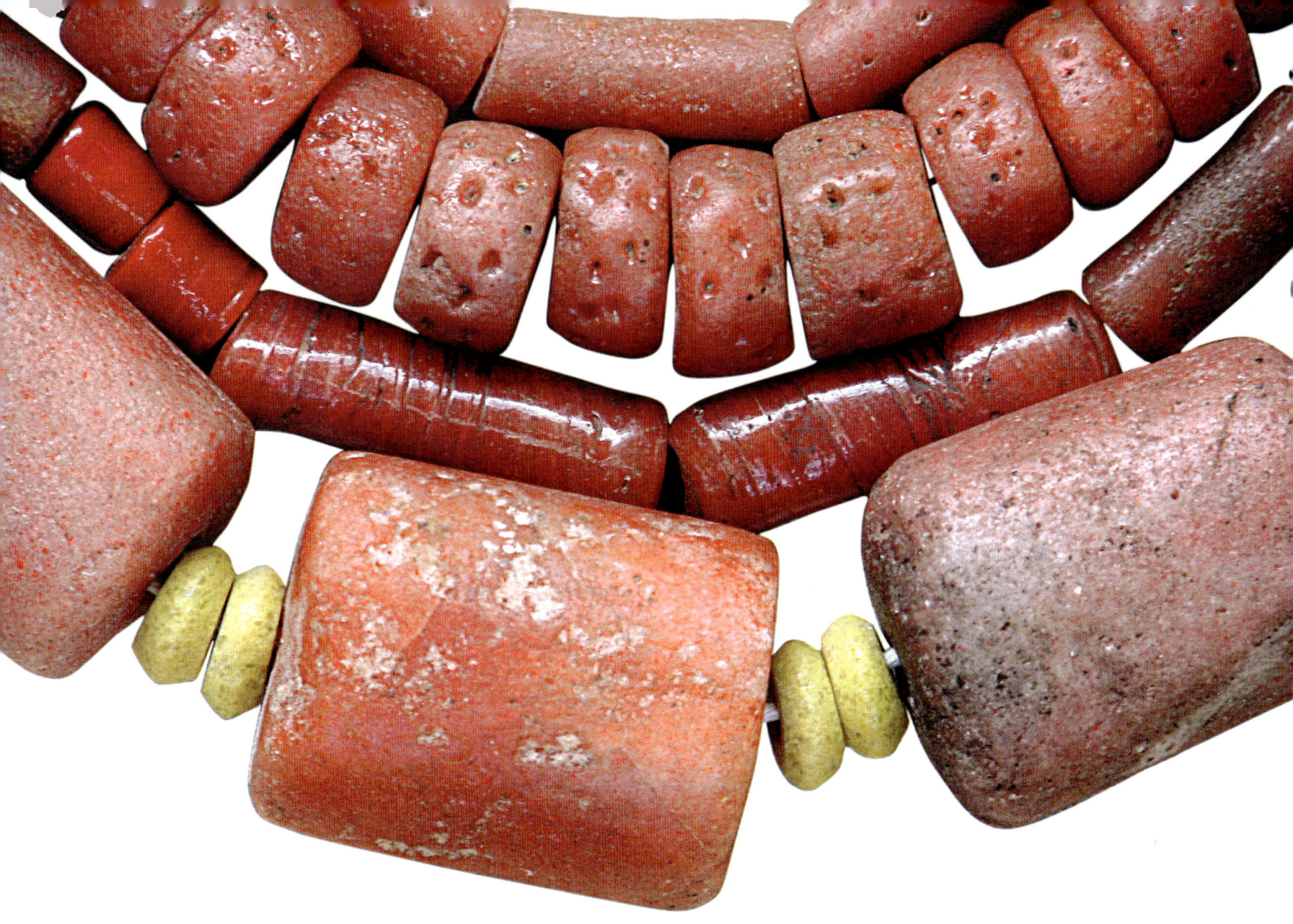

LEFT TOP The beads depicted here were made in horizontal molds and are called Keta Awuazi by the Yoruba of Nigeria. Until the 1940s, Krobo bead makers of Ghana produced similar beads, which they made in vertical molds and called Awuazi.

LEFT BOTTOM Niusisi Koli are green beads that can be slightly translucent. In all probability they were manufactured by Yoruba bead makers, using a moldless horizontal manufacturing technique with powder glass derived from wine bottles. This type of bead manufacture ceased during the 1940s.

ABOVE Imitation Mediterranean coral beads were made in West Africa in a variety of styles. The Yoruba manufactured powder glass versions, called Ateyun or Iyun, in a number of shapes and sizes, and the glass workers of Bida, Nigeria, produced wound glass bead copies of cylindrical shape (depicted here second from bottom).

Glass Beads   155

Mauritanian Powder Glass (Kiffa) Beads

History

According to some scholars, the Hassaniya name for these beads is Murakad. [99] It has been established that Kiffa beads represent a bead type unique to Mauritanian culture and society. The technique of their manufacture is called the wet-core powder glass technique and involves the use of a binder, such as human saliva or gum arabic. The beads are shaped by hand and fired without the use of molds. Archaeological evidence of local glass bead making is documented from Atar, Chinguetti, Nouakchott, Mederdra, Rosso, Aioun and Oualata, sugesting that the manufacture of wet-core powder glass beads in Mauritania might once have been a widely practiced craft. It is believed that the manufacture of Kiffa beads, as they are known today, commenced during the 19th century, because of a revival of centuries-old traditions, and that the beads were made to imitate ancient glass bead types such as Fustat fused rod beads. Some sources suggest that Kiffa beads were made for, and worn by, women of poorer (lower) castes who could not afford to own the more expensive ancient originals. Although no ancient beads resembling Kiffa beads have, to date, been found at archaeological sites or during ongoing excavations, the manufacturing process is said to have originated in Tichitt, an ancient village (8th century) in the vicinity of Tegadoust, and to have spread from there throughout southern Mauritania. [100]

Mauritania used to be part of the ancient Ghana Empire, which lasted from 750 to 1240 CE and encompassed southeastern Mauritania and parts of Mali, growing rich from the trans-Saharan trade in gold, ivory and salt. Koumbi Saleh is believed to have been the empire's capital. Its ruins are located near the town of Kiffa. Glass beads are still being found along the old trade and pilgrim routes in the vicinity of Tegadoust, Oualata, Tichitt and Akrejit, and in the sand dunes that now cover the ruins of Koumbi Saleh. Noted among the bead makers in the vicinity of Kiffa—recognized historically as one of the principal centers of the manufacture of Mauritanian powder glass beads—were the women of the Ehel Sidi Mahmoud family, first mentioned by the French archaeologist Raymond Mauny in 1949. Mauny is credited with having provided the first eyewitness account of their method of manufacture. [101]

Technique

The process of making Mauritanian wet-core powder glass Kiffa beads involves the crushing of glass into fine powder and mixing it with saliva or gum arabic as a binder. In order to build a core for a triangular bead, two blades of stiff grass were fastened together to form a cross shape. The moistened crushed glass was built up around this grass support in a triangular form and smoothed with a razor blade. Decorative patterns were applied with fine needles, using slurry that consisted of finely crushed glass, which was moistened with saliva, or a few drops of gum arabic mixed with water. Contemporary Ghanaian (Krobo) bead makers use a similar method for applying decorative patterns when creating "written" beads. [102] The beads were then covered with a small tin such as a sardine can, and fired on metal plates or flat pottery shards, without the use of molds. When the Swiss ethnographer and anthropologist Jean Gabus visited the last of the Oualata bead makers, Lalla Aicha mint Seyidi, in the 1970s, he observed a slightly different method which was used for making spherical beads. [103]

Originally a Mande agricultural settlement on the periphery of Old Ghana, Oualata later became involved in trade and attracted settlers from the desert and the savannah. In the 14th century, Oualata became a cosmopolitan town dominated by Berbers, but in the 17th and 18th centuries nomadic Arabs sedentarized in Oualata and transformed it again. By the 19th century all the town's free families claimed Arab descent. The scholarly Mande families had begun to disappear in the mid-17th century, but their disappearance was largely a social illusion in that the Arabs who acquired power in Oualata did so by assimilating the elite Mande and Berber families.

Purpose

Kiffa beads were made in small numbers, on commission, for friends and family members or for personal use. The craft of making these beads was considered to be a gift from God and the beads were made in His praise. Every line, dot, circle and triangle mirrored the bead maker's personal interpretation of the universe. Magic, as well as happiness and other emotions, were incorporated and infused in the process of making a bead, always accompanied by a ritual of prayer and incantation. Mauritanian women strongly believed in this magic which offered them powerful protection from the "evil eye," illness and other mishaps. They also considered their beads to be objects that transmitted emotions such as joy and tenderness. Special beads were given names, and their wearers believed that to place such a bead under one's tongue was the most effective method of transmitting its magic to one's body.

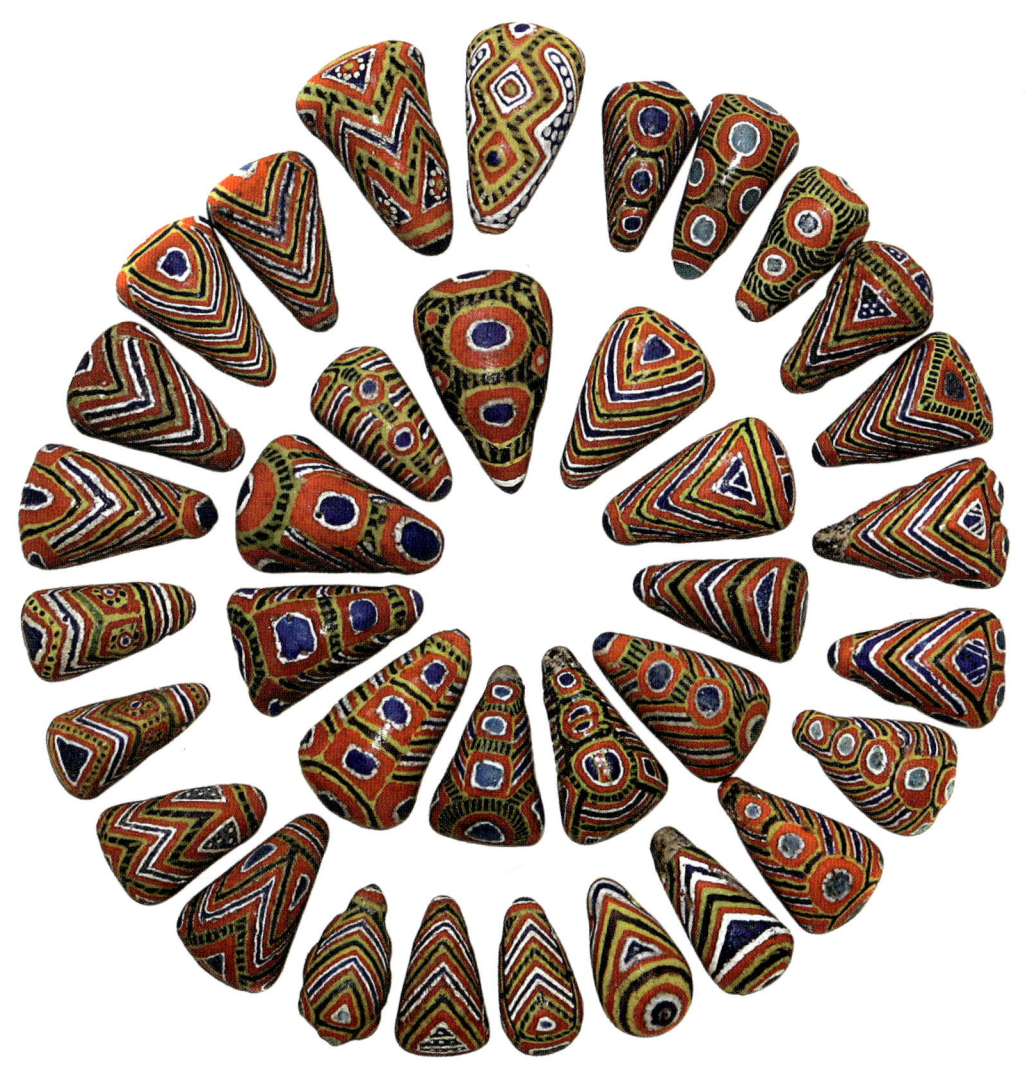

ABOVE *The term Kiffa bead is a fairly recent name coined by bead collectors from the United States during the second half of the 20th century. The name is derived from the town of Kiffa, situated in south central Mauritania, a bead making center, and the place where visitors to Mauritania first found and reported on this style of bead. Polychromatic triangular-shaped specimens such as the types depicted here represent what is probably the most highly valued style among bead collectors today.*

Styles, Shapes and Decorative Patterns

Traditional Kiffa beads can be found in six distinct shapes, the most common being diamond-shaped beads, the great majority of which are either plain red (undecorated), or blue with a great variety of patterns composed of grey or white parallel lines and stripes or dots. A less common variant, called "House of the Turtle" because its decorative pattern resembles a tortoise's carapace, consists of a symmetrical arrangement of squares in red, white, yellow and black. The beads were traditionally worn in a combination of blue, red and a couple of so-called "House of the Turtle" beads. Sewn onto strips of leather or attached to a piece of cloth, these assemblages were worn as bracelets. The shapes and patterns of blue beads are believed to imitate cowry shells, and like them are associated with fertility. Hemispherical or domed beads were occasionally added to bracelets. Their decorative patterns are similar to the beads of the latter group in that they are found in plain red, in blue with parallel lines and with the "House of the Turtle" pattern. Less common versions have white or polychromatic chevron zigzag lines, occasionally in combination with white spots. Plain (undecorated) white specimens are also known.

Triangular Kiffa beads, which technically are pendants, are the most sought after type among collectors. Their shape symbolizes an eye, and the eye motif can be observed repeatedly in their decorative patterns where it is expressed in a great variety of styles on polychromatic, and to a lesser extent on blue specimens. Triangular beads were made in three variants: plain red (red specimens decorated with white spots or with an "eye" pattern are very rare); blue with a number of white spots ranging from one to as many as twenty or more (and less common versions with polychromatic "eye" decorations, or chevron patterns, or no decoration at all); and polychromatic beads with chevron-stripes, circles, dots, "eyes" and triangle motifs, in uncounted variations and combinations. Colors are always applied in the same order, i.e. blue-white-red-yellow-black (green is occasionally substituted for black), a sequence that on traditional beads never varies. Many polychromatic triangular Kiffa beads also have fully or partially decorated reverse sides. Their Hassaniya name is sellkrass or bouzrem and they were traditionally worn plaited directly into the hair or sewn onto bands of cloth or strips of leather, in sets comprised of one blue, one polychromatic and one red triangle-shaped bead which were worn at temple height, one set on each side, complementing each other.

Spherical beads have either powder glass or prefabricated glass bead cores, most of the latter being of European production. Spherical beads were worn plaited into the hair or in elaborate necklaces, combined with stone and glass beads, always in the same color sequence. The Hassaniya term for spherical beads is terlitza.

Conical beads are fairly rare. According to legend the first cone-shaped bead was made by the prophet Souleiman. The Hassaniya name for this shape is khoust el arf, which in literal translation means "imitation of the unique." Other terms are masnoura and nourakad, meaning hand-made. Conical beads can have either a horizontal or a vertical perforation. Beads with horizontal perforations were worn as hair ornaments and are called el veshé. They were strung beginning with a piece of amber at the top, followed by a cone-shaped Kiffa bead, a blue glass bead, and finally a jasper or carnelian bead. Cones with perforations that pass through the bead's base were sewn onto strips of cloth or leather and worn as hair ornaments. Most conical beads have polychromatic decorations consisting of geometrical patterns, dots and "eyes," though plain undecorated white, green and yellow beads have also been documented.

The decorative patterns of cylindrical beads often imitate the styles of beads from other regions, such as Venetian mosaic glass beads. It is not unusual for cylindrical Kiffa beads to have cores, which consist of one, two or even three prefabricated European glass beads. For this reason they are quite fragile and break apart easily. Bead traders who know of this characteristic have used it to their advantage, deliberately breaking or cutting cylindrical beads into several parts and selling these separately. Cylindrical beads were worn in necklaces where, when found as the principal element, they were called bouzrada, a name that is applied to any type of center bead.

The Hassaniya name for beads that have translucent glass cores is melha. [104] The cores of large beads were made from ground fragments of translucent green, and more rarely blue, red, yellow or clear glasses. Blue triangular pendants fashioned from glass are rare. It is interesting to note that a decoration consisting of white spots of powder glass slurry, applied in patterns similar to the blue powder glass counterparts, can be observed on all documented specimens. The green glass cores of smaller beads within this group are often found to fluoresce brightly when exposed to an ultraviolet light source, indicating the presence of uranium which in all probability comes from so-called Vaseline and related bead types produced by the Czech-Bohemian industries before the use of uranium in glass making was prohibited in the early 1940s. The green cores of larger, teardrop-shaped or triangular beads tend to be darker and more opaque, and they are only mildly fluorescent. In the absence of prefabricated beads of the required large sizes, the cores of larger specimens of this type were, in all probability, made of different types of glasses. Their subtle glow is likely due to a composition containing manganese, a mildly fluorescent chemical element commonly found in glasses. The colors of these glass bead cores were usually incorporated into the overall decorative patterns and became part of them.

Diminutive versions of all Kiffa bead types were made specifically for children. These are recognized by their small sizes, most measuring approximately half the size of specimens designed for adults.

New Kiffa Beads

During the second half of the 20th century, environmental changes led to droughts and famine which forced many families in Mauritania to abandon their traditional nomadic way of life in order to survive. While Kiffa beads had become highly desirable objects for collectors in the western world, the art of making them was becoming extinct

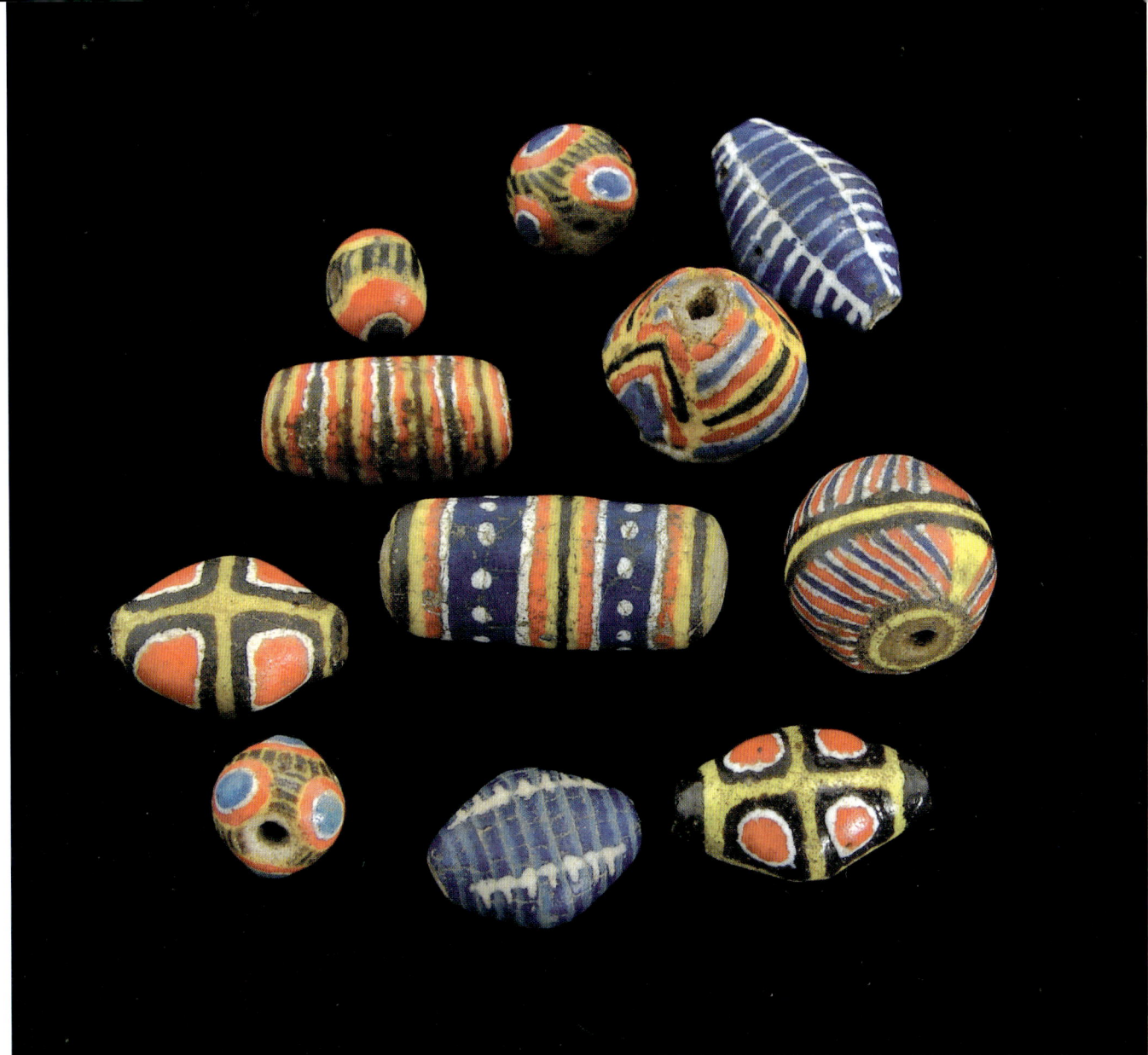

ABOVE *Traditional Kiffa beads were manufactured in six different and distinct shapes. Apart from the triangular versions, there were diamond or lozenge-shaped beads of small sizes and commonly blue or red color, the blue variants usually being decorated with patterns of grey or white parallel lines and stripes or dots. A less common version is called "House of the Turtle" because its decorative pattern resembles a tortoise's carapace. Hemispherical or domed beads belong to this group and are found in combinations with the former, sewn onto leather bracelets. Spherical or oblate beads were made in a great range of sizes and patterns and usually worn plaited into the hair, as were cone-shaped and cylindrical beads, in a variety of styles and sizes.*

in Mauritania. Only a handful of master bead makers, all of well-advanced age, are documented from the 1970s, and reports indicate a noted lack of new apprentices who might have been interested in learning the technique in order to keep the craft alive. Hausa traders were combing the Mauritanian countryside to bring out whatever they could find, regardless of quality. However, as these beads were never produced in significantly large quantities it became increasingly difficult to find them, let alone to find perfect examples. Some traders resorted to offering beads that had been repaired in transit, some more successfully than others. Broken beads were joined together with glue, and damaged or chipped beads which had suffered from decoration loss were touched up with oil paint or nail varnish. Chips and missing chunks were filled in or replaced with a variety of materials ranging from resin and clay to plaster, and then painted.

Glass Beads

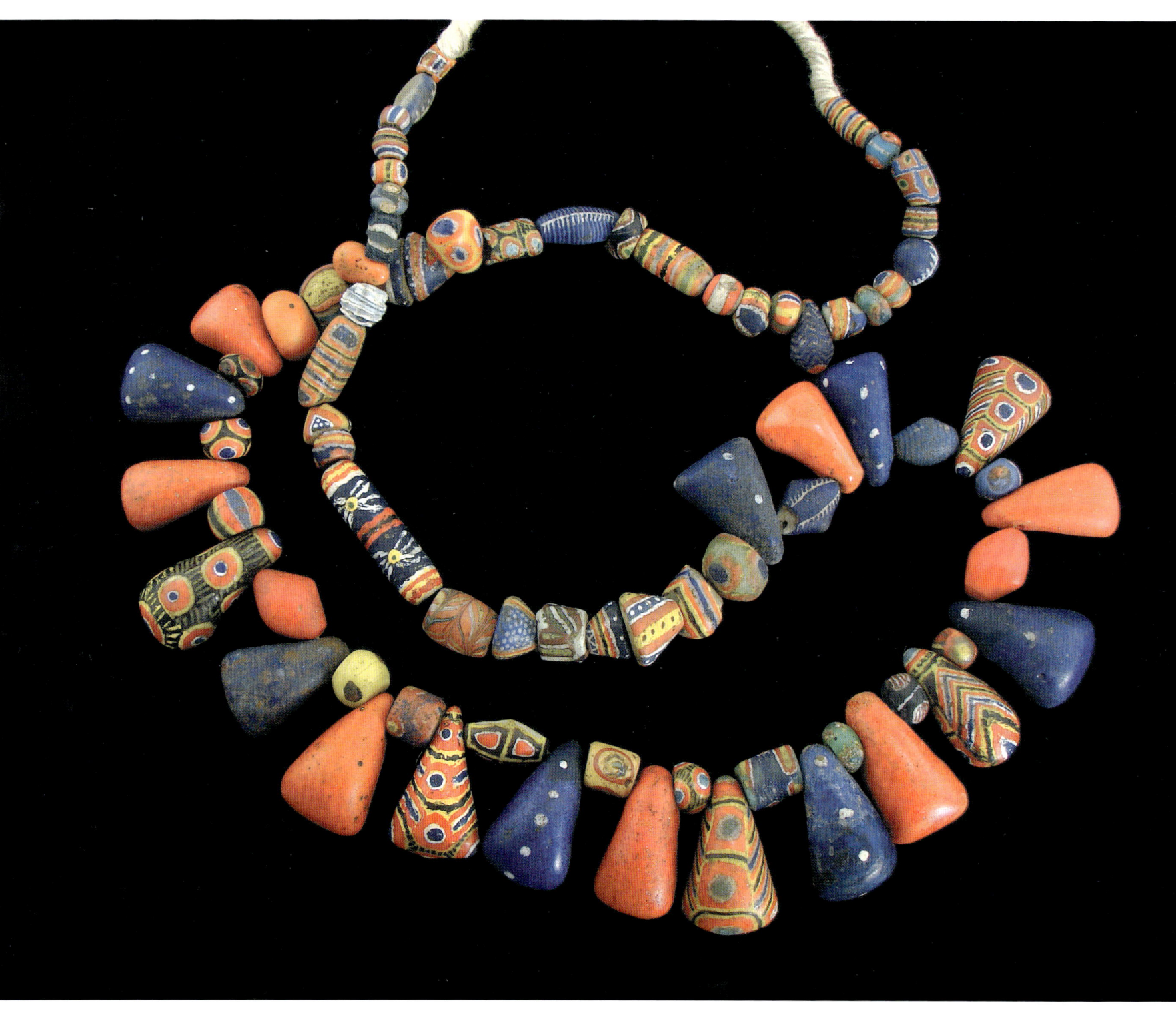

ABOVE AND RIGHT *Three strands of old Mauritanian powder glass Kiffa beads from the collection of Lynn Fisher. These beads illustrate the typical arrangement of market strands. Necklaces of the styles depicted here were not traditionally assembled or worn by Mauritanian women.*

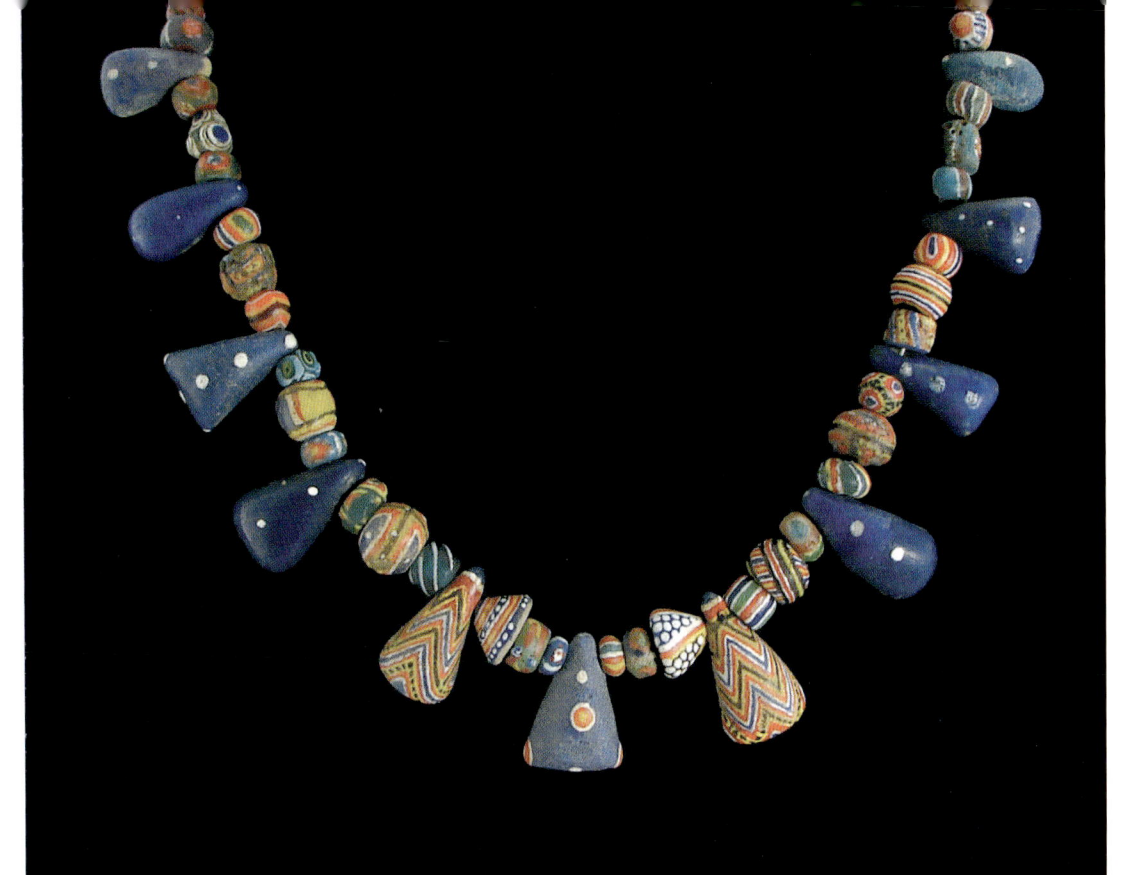
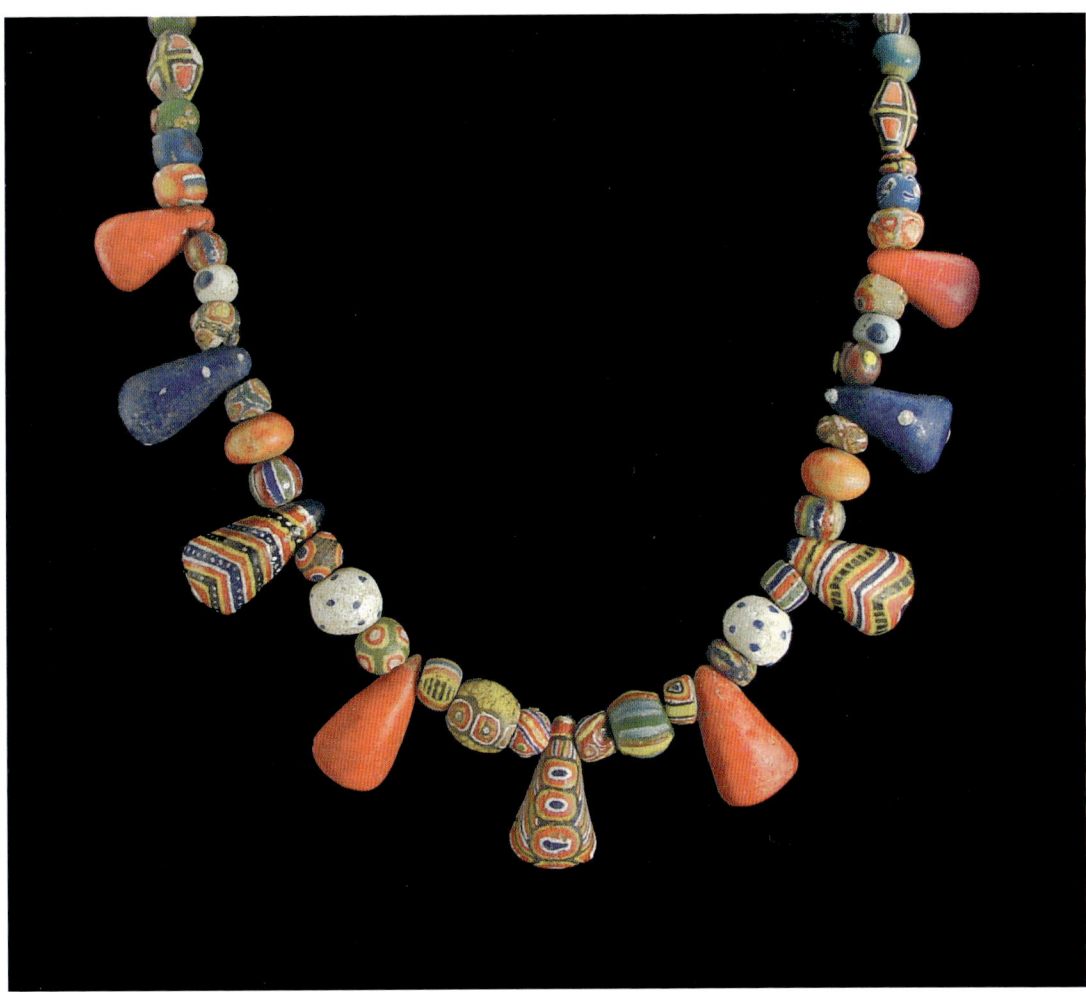

Glass Beads   161

Besides repairing and repainting damaged specimens there have been various attempts at producing imitations. Monochrome European glass beads, which may well have been of the same type as the beads once decorated with powder glass slurries, were ground into shapes that closely resembled red diamond-shaped Kiffa beads. Plastic imitations in a variety of styles have also been produced; the beginnings of a small industry of locally made plastic simulations were reported as early as 1992. [105]

The first attempts to supply collectors' demands by producing new Kiffa beads were noted during the1990s, and the first known organized group of bead makers to realize a potential for profit and external trade appears to have been the Cooperative Nasser. This group, believed to have consisted of a master bead maker and five apprentices, all located in the town of Kiffa, was founded and managed by a non-Mauritanian bead enthusiast and entrepreneur residing in Senegal. Inquiries to a French sister organization about importing commercial kilns have been reported, but by the year 2000 the group could no longer be located. More groups have formed in the meantime, and at present the number of bead makers working in the vicinity of the town of Kiffa is estimated to total about one hundred. Working from their family homes, the women are, in principle, adhering to the traditional methods of manufacture while using new source materials imported mainly from India and China. The glass is crushed in stone mortars or on old grinding stones, but where formerly only a few beads at a time were made per day, now up to one hundred small spherical beads are being produced in one firing process.

The first beads originating from this production were crudely executed and are often described as lacking all the attributes that make traditional Kiffa beads so attractive and appealing. Their brightly colored patterns and commonly mottled or lumpy surfaces lacked detail and gave evidence of poor craftsmanship. After almost two decades of this revival the question remains why contemporary Kiffa beads do not match the high quality and craftsmanship observed in traditional beads. Do the modern bead makers prefer creating new shapes, and applying their own, much simpler, designs, rather than copying the more time consuming traditional decorations of fine lines and intricate patterns? Or is it possible that the old art of creating such intricate decorations has been lost? As modern Kiffa beads are made to order and produced for marketing, it is possible that quantity might be getting priority over quality. Another explanation for the inferior quality of contemporary Kiffa beads may be the bead makers' choice of source materials and tools. Whereas fine needles were once used for applying decorative patterns, present-day use of fairly crude wooden sticks hinders the execution of fine lines and intricate patterns. As changing ways of life have resulted in a change of values, the art of making Kiffa beads has ceased to be a form of worship and present-day bead makers may feel less bound by traditions and less restricted in their creativity. Finally, bead making today is a means of making ends meet in everyday life. Although the town of Kiffa, where most of the bead makers live and work, is the second largest town in Mauritania, the great majority of its inhabitants survive on the traditionally meager subsistence of Saharan settlements, and small scale production and marketing of beads provides but a modest, albeit welcome, additional income. [106]

Indonesian Kiffa Bead Imitations

In the more recent past the Indonesian bead industry has begun to produce its own lamp worked versions of Kiffa beads, in various shapes including stylized triangular pendants and spherical beads, all easily distinguishable from the African-made originals. Lamp worked beads are made using a gas torch for heating a rod of glass (stringer) until it becomes pliable and then winding the soft glass around a metal rod (mandrel). Additional decoration can be added by applying different colored glass (trailing).

Krobo Kiffa Bead Imitations

What were probably the first Kiffa bead imitations originating from Ghana were documented in 2005. They were polychromatic and triangular in shape. Since then a barrel-shaped variant has appeared. The beads are manufactured by Krobo bead makers in the characteristic vertical-mold dry-core powder glass technique, using the Mue Ne Angma method of decoration, where glass slurry is used for the application of decorative patterns with a pointed tool, similar to the method used by Mauritanian bead makers.

Other Kiffa Bead Imitations

Contemporary American bead artists have produced their own versions of Kiffa beads, using a number of dif-

RIGHT *The first efforts at manufacturing new Kiffa beads were documented during the 1990s, but by 2000 the original group of bead makers could no longer be located. New cooperatives have formed in the meantime, and at present there are a number of groups of women who are manufacturing these beads, some at the rate of one hundred small spherical beads per firing.*

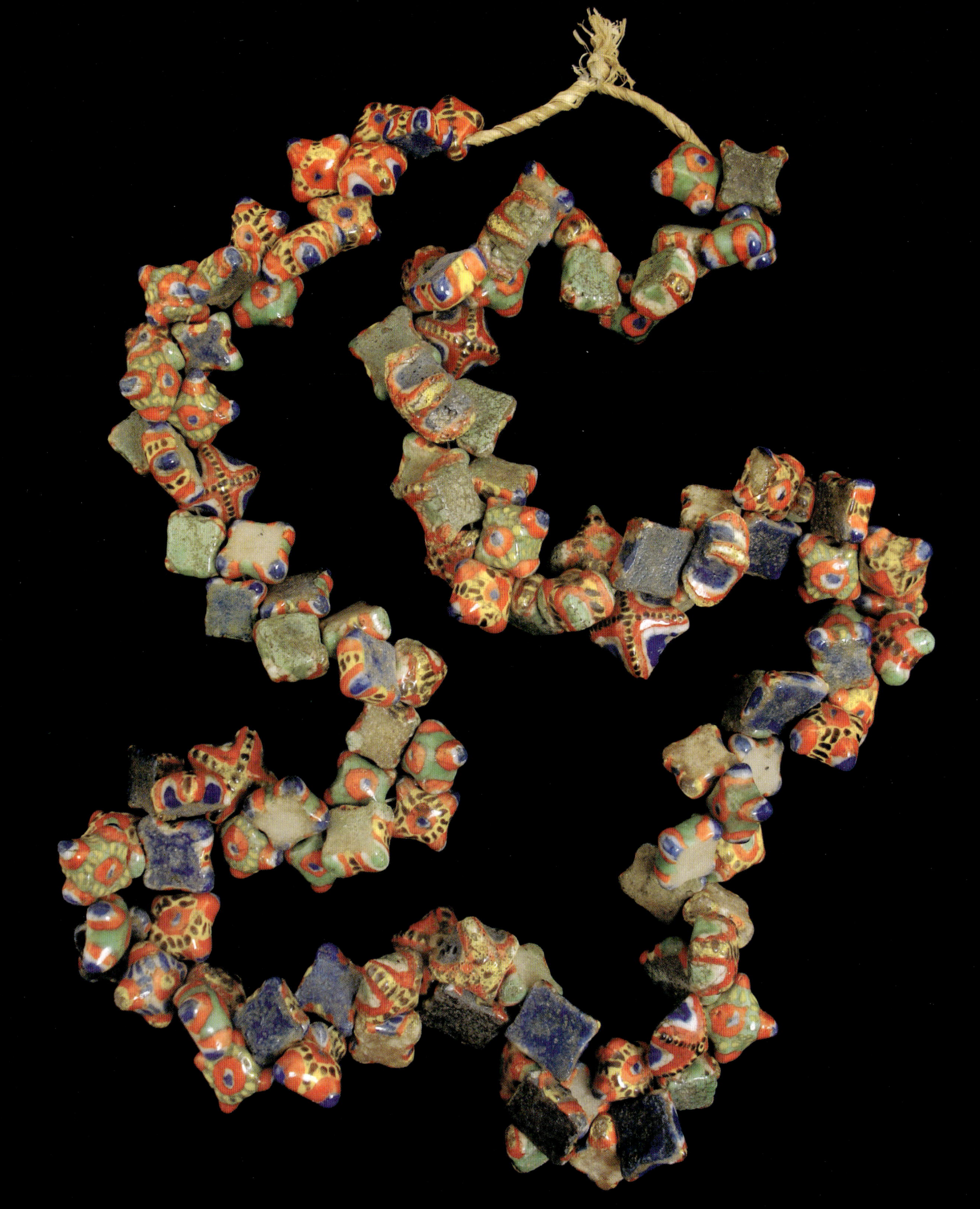

ferent materials. Mike Kury created polychromatic triangular Kiffa beads made of polymer clay in his Homage to Kiffa beads. Patricia Frantz made fine flame worked and trailed glass specimens, and Howard Newcomb presented his triangular examples made from porcelain, at the 3rd International Bead Conference in Washington, D.C., in 1985. [107]

Wound Beads

Bida Beads

The first reference to the glass making industry at Masaga Glass Works in Bida was made by T.J. Bowen, in his "Adventures and Missionary Labours in Several Countries in the Interior of Africa" (1857). Bowen reported that, at the time of his writing, the art of glass bead making was confined to three Nigerian towns, one being located a two days' journey to the west of the Niger. It may well have been Bida, the second largest city in Niger State, Nigeria, located 120 miles from Ilorin, where Bowen was visiting. [108] The first to publish the discovery that glass for the beads and bangles produced by the Masaga guild was actually made at Bida was the German ethnologist and archaeologist Leo Frobenius (1873-1938), who undertook his first expedition to Africa in 1904. [109]

The Masaga glass workers say that they originated in Miram in Egypt, indicating that they were Arabs. They arrived in Bida in the 18th century, settled at Masaga during the reign of Late Etsu Usman Zaki and started their glass works during the reign of Late Etsu Saba. The first glass they produced was called "bikini" and from it they manufactured bangles and beads. On the occasion of his visit to Masaga in 1942, the Austrian-born British anthropologist, S.F. Nadel, who had made his first expedition to the Nupe and other Nigerian peoples in 1934, described the process of glass making from first-hand observation. He reported that the industry was producing the dark brown or black glass locally known as bikini, despite earlier reports that it had ceased. A special domed furnace had been built, with a pit underneath filled with local sand and soda, which was imported from Lake Chad. Later, blacksmiths' slag was added. The furnace had to be heated and kept continuously at high temperatures for three to five days, depending on the quantity of glass being made. The local sand has been described as being rich in a particular element, which Peter Francis, Jr., assumed to have been iron, giving the glass its deep color. Frobenius reported on the making of yellow glass.

LEFT *A triangular, polychromatic imitation Kiffa bead, probably produced by Krobo bead makers in Ghana.*

During colonial times, bottle glass, which was introduced by Europeans, became available and glass derived from broken bottles was soon preferred to the locally made variety. Later writers report on the re-melting of scrap glass or bottles for making beads. Alison Hodge (1981) was the first to document the process of bead making. The old furnace had been widened and the pit beneath it deepened. Broken bottles and beads (for coloring) were melted in a pot. After withdrawing a large gather of glass from the pot, the hot glass was dripped onto three iron mandrels, each held by a bead maker. The beads were shaped with paddles, and glass of a different color was added, using a pair of tongs for making the decorations. [110]

Ceramic Beads

Kazuri Beads

A small factory called Kazuri, the Swahili term for "small and beautiful," produces some of the best-known contemporary beads of Kenyan manufacture. The enterprise was founded in 1975 by the late Lady Susan Wood. Having observed that many women in the villages around Nairobi were single mothers abandoned by their men or widowed by the AIDS epidemic ravaging Kenya, she organized a ceramic workshop, helped by two Kikuyu women. As the cottage industry grew, she made a point of employing single mothers. Less than ten women were working at Kazuri in 1975, but sales have increased considerably since and approximately

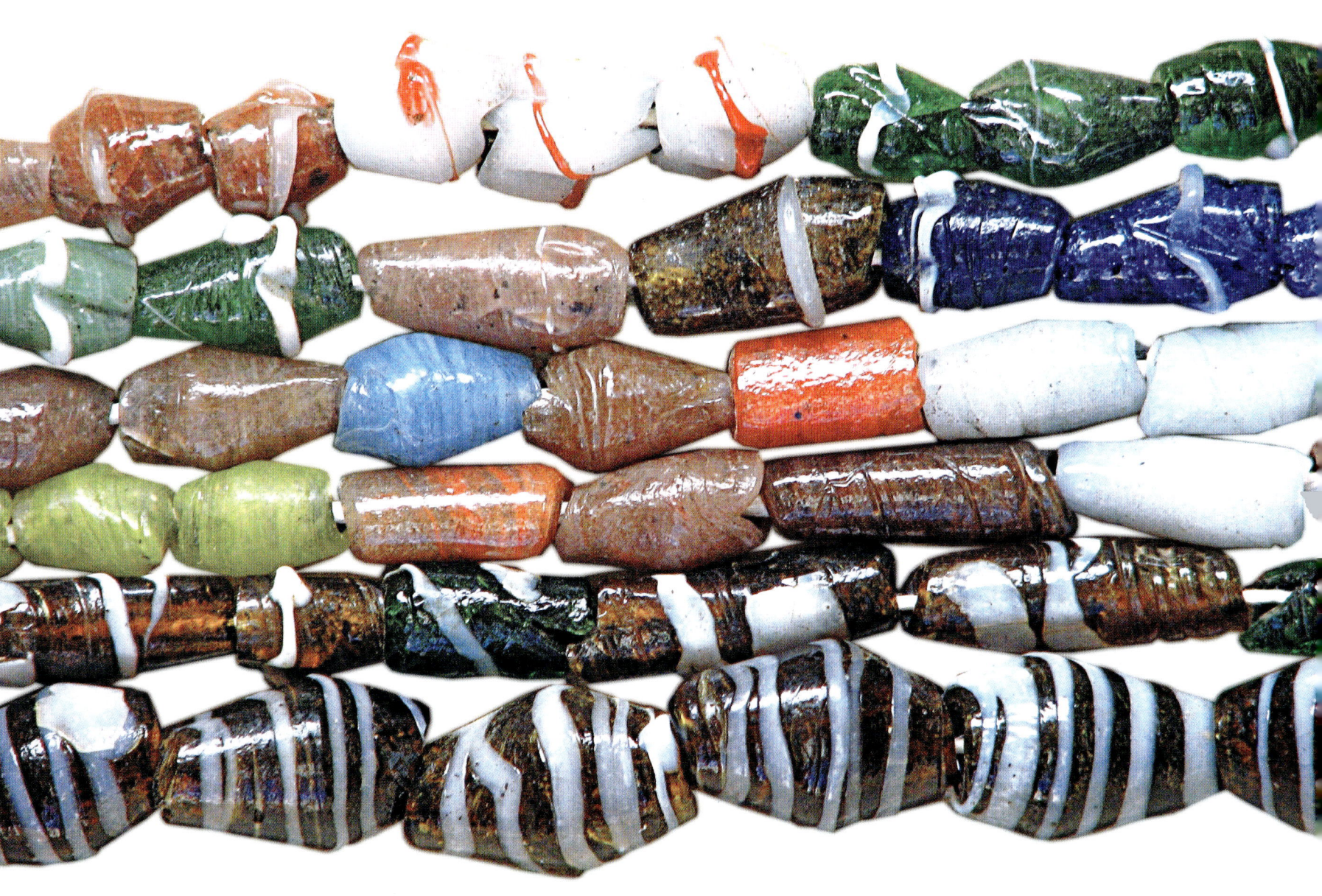

ABOVE *The glass workers of Masaga Glass Works in Bida, Nigeria, produce a wide range of wound beads in a variety of shapes, sizes and decorative styles.*

Glass Beads

two hundred women are employed today. The Kazuri workshop is situated in an area that used to be part of Karen von Blixen's (author of "Out of Africa") coffee plantation, a half-hour drive from the center of the Kenyan capital city, Nairobi. The clay used for the manufacture of a wide range of glazed ceramic beads, jewelry and pottery is drawn from the nearby Ngong Hills. Kazuri beads are being made in a great variety of sizes, shapes, colors and designs, occasionally embellished with fourteen karat gold, and are sought after on the international collectors' market.

Prosser Beads

In Morocco, a special type of clay-ceramic bead called a Prosser is being produced, using machinery that was decommissioned by the Czech bead industry. Prosser beads are made from a secret composition consisting of clay and additives. Around 1840, the British brothers Thomas and Richard Prosser invented a machine for making buttons, and by the 1860s their unique molding technique had been improved to include the production of beads. Typically, Prosser beads have glossy surfaces. Some Prosser bead types have wide and easily discernible seams around their equators, and all have one end which is smooth and glossy and one that is rough and pitted, a distinctive characteristic caused by the manufacturing process. Prosser beads of Moroccan production are commonly small beads of short cylindrical shapes and are produced in a great range of colors.

Faience Beads

Faience typically has a glazed surface and a gritty interior. The glossy (glazed) surface is formed during firing. Although it may at times be difficult to distinguish from weathered ancient glass, the properties of faience are different. Faience is a ceramic material composed of quartz with additions of lime, natron or plant ash, mixed with water to form a paste. It is always shaped when cold. [111] Small objects would be shaped using a mold. When making beads the faience paste was rolled around a string and cut into

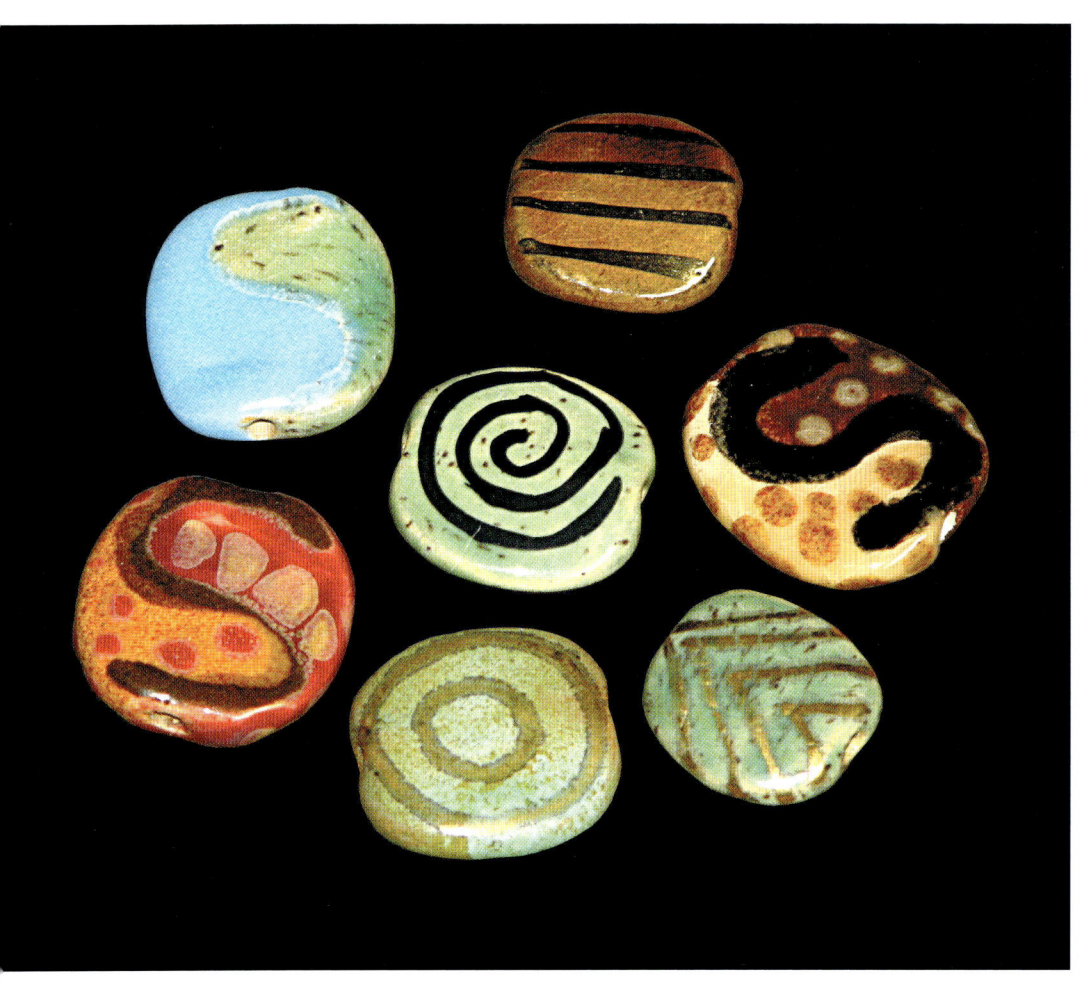

LEFT *Kazuri Beads, an enterprise founded in 1975 by the late Lady Susan Wood in order to create a means of support for single mothers in the vicinity of Nairobi, Kenya, produces a wide range of glazed ceramic beads, jewelry and pottery items from clay collected in the nearby Ngong Hills.*

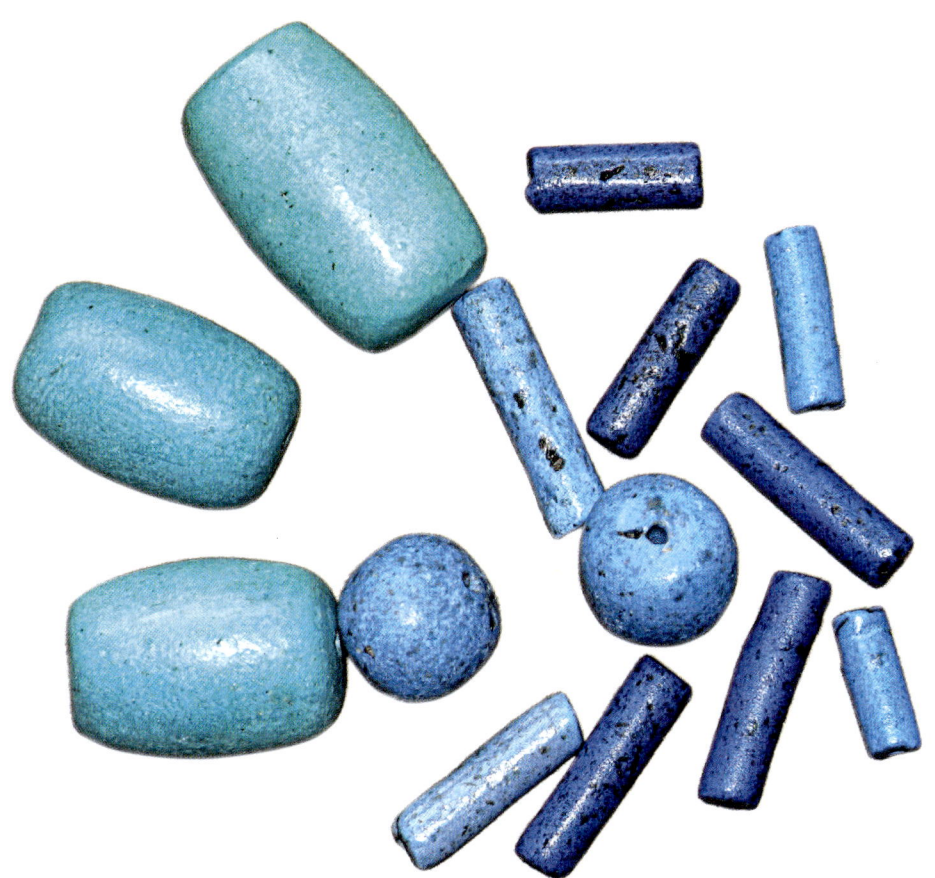

RIGHT *In recent years, North African bead makers have produced mineral-dyed, hand-shaped ceramic beads, some made to resemble amazonite, turquoise and coral, and some in the shape of long thin tubes reminiscent of ancient Egyptian faience (so-called Mummy beads). These beads are commonly combined with saffron-dyed horn or bone beads that imitate amber, and with Prosser and other red glass or plastic beads which are substituted for coral, in necklaces arranged in a style similar to traditional Berber necklaces.*

disks or tubular segments. The string burned away during firing leaving the bead's perforation. By adding metal oxides a range of colors were produced: adding copper salts achieved blue and turquoise hues, cobalt resulted in darker blues, and iron in green.

Faience making is believed to have evolved from the ancient practice of glazing soft stones such as steatite. The process involved the application of a soda-lime-silica coating before firing. When copper was added as a colorant, the surface developed a blue-green hue. Glazed stone beads are documented from as early as the 5th millennium BCE; the earliest glazed stone beads, which are dated to the Badarian period (4500-3800 BCE), were found in tombs located in the vicinity of the modern town of Badari. [112] The tradition of making glazed stone beads and ornaments continues in the villages of Quorna and Deir el-Medina, which are also known for their manufacture of faience beads. Production, mainly for the tourist trade, was revived in the 1920s and is ongoing. The range includes many traditional shapes, such as ankh pendants and beads resembling scarabs.

Egypt has a long tradition of faience production. A depiction which may show faience makers was discovered on a Theban tomb from the 26th Dynasty, which spanned 139 years (664-525 BCE). The material was known as tjehnet or khshdj, the latter being the term used for lapis lazuli.

The earliest evidence of a faience workshop was found at Abydos, one of the most ancient cities of Upper Egypt, where, according to Egyptian mythology, Osiris was buried, as were many other pharaohs. Workshops excavated at Lisht and Kerma in the Sudan date to the Middle Kingdom period (2040-1640 BCE). The tomb of an overseer of faience workers was unearthed at Lisht, and two 19th Dynasty (1295-1186 BCE) faience stelae found in another burial site describe the deceased as a man who held the title "Faience maker of Amun." Large numbers of beads, amulets, scarabs and other ritual and ornamental objects were found from the New Kingdom (1567-1085 BCE), indicating that the zenith of faience production had been reached. Workshops from this period were excavated at Malkata, the palace of Amenhotep III at Thebes, at Amarna and at Qantir. Faience factories were also known to have existed at Naukratis, a Greek settlement in the Nile Delta, at Buto, and at Memphis. Faience continued to be produced for making utilitarian, funerary and ornamental objects until beyond the Roman/Byzantine period which lasted from 640-1517 CE, spanning 670 years. [113]

From the 25th Dynasty (747-656 BCE) onwards, disk-shaped and tubular faience beads were assembled to form masks and shrouds placed on top of the bandages of many mummies. Arranged in a diamond-shaped (net-like) pat-

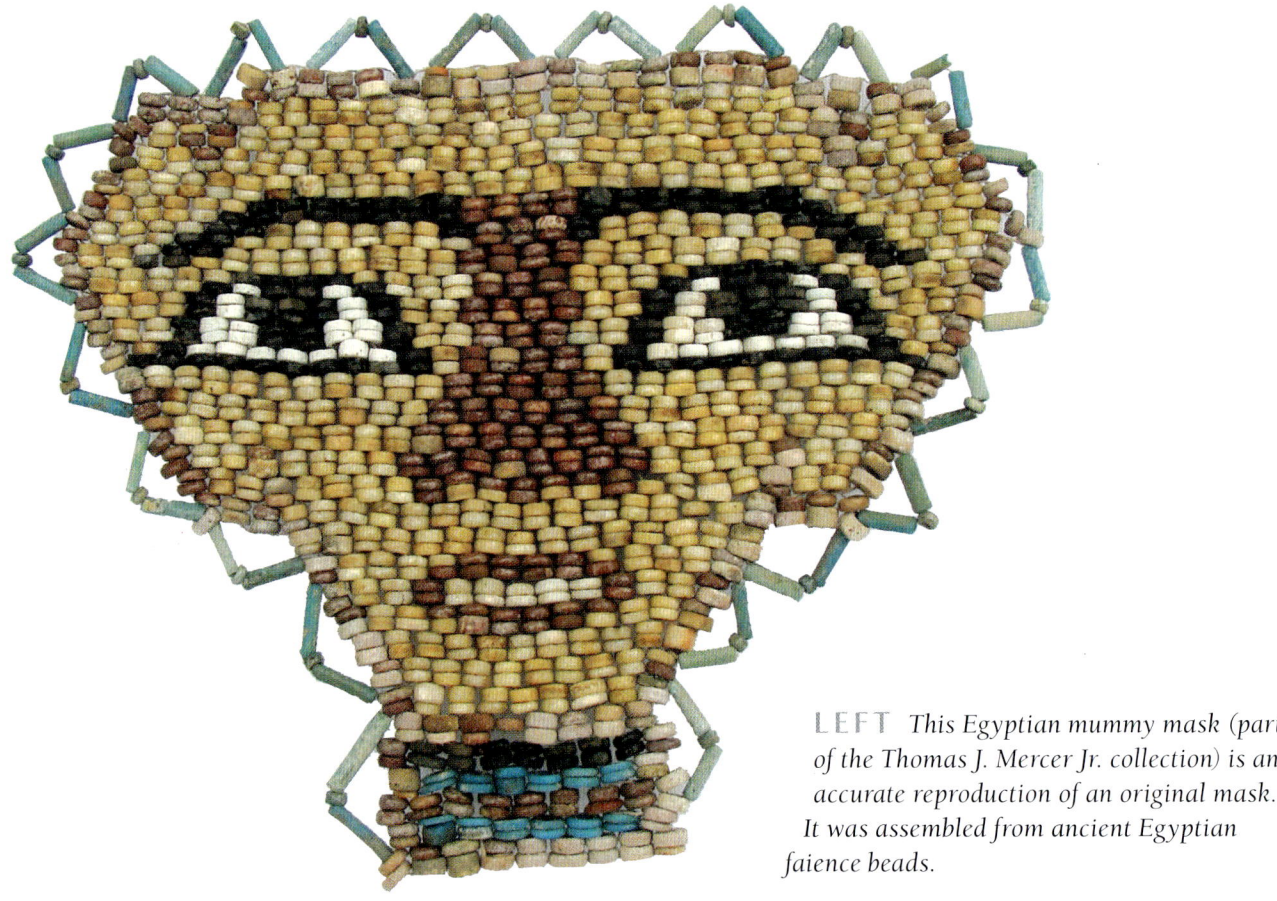

LEFT *This Egyptian mummy mask (part of the Thomas J. Mercer Jr. collection) is an accurate reproduction of an original mask. It was assembled from ancient Egyptian faience beads.*

tern, the shrouds, also called mummy nets, would be composed of a combination of long tubes and short disk-shaped faience beads in the colors blue, turquoise and yellow or tan. The beaded shrouds—believed to derive from the garments worn by goddesses—initially were a simple covering of the body, with winged scarabs and images of the Four Sons of Horus. By the Late period they had incorporated bands of text and a facemask. [114] People who could not afford beaded shrouds were covered with a net of knotted string, or had a netted pattern painted onto the outermost layer of their bandages.

Until recently, faience beads were made to protect not only the dead and the living but also animals used for everyday work such as camels, horses and donkeys. Commonly derived from local quartz stones, which were ground into a powdery substance and mixed with clay and frit, with soda and copper as colorants, the color of these beads is bright blue. Displayed on harnesses they are believed to protect the animal against the "evil eye."

168 Glass Beads

History of Trade in Africa from Antiquity to the Present Day

A 20th Century African Bead Trader's Story

"I am in my mid-thirties and have spent more than half of my time in the United States since my arrival in 1992. I used to work in my brother's hotel in The Gambia, and later in the gem business in what was then Zaire. On my arrival in the United States, I took a job as a cook in a Seattle restaurant where I was introduced to beads by visiting Serahuli traders. I saved some money and bought a strand of chevrons, which I resold a week later for twice the purchase price. I was instantly hooked on the possibility of making profits higher than my weekly wages, but did keep my day job while spending my weekends at flea markets, selling beads and putting aside my profits in order to be able to increase my bead inventory. It took me more than four years to build my house in Gambia. Several years ago, my wife died in childbirth. I have meanwhile remarried and have two children. I travel the US, calling on customers, and I exhibit at shows for approximately six months of the year, driving fifty thousand miles per year. I go back to Africa twice a year and am always home for Ramadan. Although I do like the business, I hope that my son will stay in school and have other opportunities that will not require him to spend so much time away from his family. Because many Serahuli men are traveling traders, our villages are largely occupied by women and children. Boys usually become bead traders when they decide they don't want to continue school. Most often they spend some years in Nigeria and Ghana, where they buy beads in small quantities from people in rural villages, string them and sell to family members and friends, often over the phone, or to their contacts in the United States."

Antiquity

No book about African beads would be complete without mentioning another integral part of African societies—trade and the exchange of trade goods. Africans are often described as being natural traders, and sub-Saharan Africa was indeed characterized by a dense web of trade routes and by the exchange of trade goods. The presence of raw materials, such as iron ore and clay, created a need for the development of local trade, the exchange of local products being especially intense at the borders of ecological zones. The major forces that shaped pre-colonial African societies

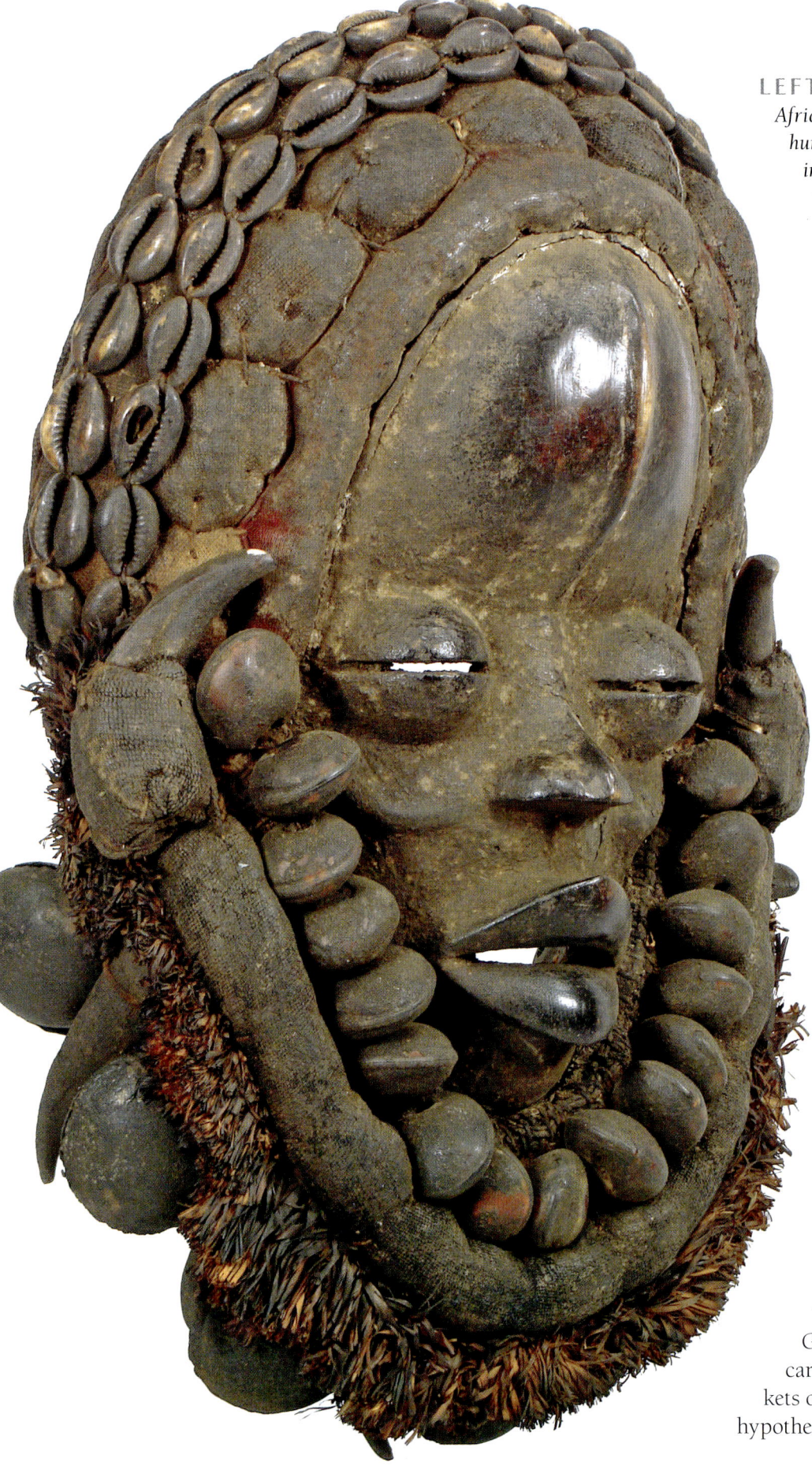

LEFT *The photographs in this chapter illustrate how African-made beads can be used not just to adorn the human figure, but to enhance and embellish carvings, masks and other ritual objects. This mask—with its metal bells and beads made from bone, seeds and cowry shells—is a product of the Poro Society, a secret society that regulates the life of the Dan people in Liberia and Ivory Coast.*

were the impact of ironworking and ensuing trade contacts with more advanced societies. Ironworking was established in Africa with the Phoenicians (ca. 814 BCE). Although the ancient Egyptians were aware of the technique of ironworking, it was not widely used until Egypt was incorporated into the Assyrian Empire in 662 BCE. Ironworking spread across the savannah to the Nok culture, believed to be the oldest organized civilization in sub-Saharan Africa, and from there it was carried eastwards and southwards by Bantu-speaking people over the next seven centuries.

The earliest references to possible contacts between Western Africa and the Mediterranean civilizations are found in classical Greco-Roman literature. The Greek historian Herodotus (484-432 BCE) described the Libyan tribe of Garamantes, who hunted with their chariots, as the Ethiopian "cave-dwellers" in the desert. Rock paintings depicting horse-drawn chariots, the first of which were found in Fezzan in the early 1930s, are associated with these accounts. The paintings, and a number of others, seemed to mark two routes leading from northern Africa to the Niger Bend, and their discovery led to the hypothesis that the Garamantes (or another Saharan people) had carried West African gold and ivory to the markets of Carthage and Rome along these routes. This hypothesis is still found in many histories of Africa, although the existence of paintings alone is not sufficient proof that the desert was ever crossed with chariots—and in fact, no remains of chariots have been found along the suggested routes. However, individual adventurers may well have crossed the desert. According to Herodotus, some youths—members of a Libyan tribe called Nasamones—travelled to the south until they arrived in a swampy area "where they met black men of small statures who took them into their town." This story has been associated with the "little people," a common element in West African oral tradition, describing the original inhabitants of the Niger inland delta.

According to Marinus of Tyre, a Roman merchant called Julius Maternus traveled with the king of the Garamantes to a land called Agysymba where he saw rhinoceros. Since no rhinoceros lived in northern Africa in classical Antiquity, it is assumed that Maternus visited the northern parts of modern Chad. Archaeological evidence of sporadic trans-Saharan contacts between West Africans and Romans has been found in Abalessa and Ahaggar. The German explorer Heinrich Barth encountered and made drawings of many ruined buildings and monuments from Roman times during his travels throughout West and Central Africa in the 19th century. In Djenne-Jeno (Old Djenne), archaeologists found a glass bead of a composition currently known only in south and southeast Asia and dated to the Han dynasty of China (206 BCE-220 CE). A Hellenistic statuette made in Cyrenaica in the 2nd century CE was found in the Republic of Niger in 1976, and a 14th century English bronze ewer was found in Kumasi in 1896. In all probability, these objects ended up south of the Sahara via many intermediaries.

According to a 19th century report from a traveler to the Lower Congo, "The native villages are often situated in groups. Their activities are based upon reciprocality, and they are to a certain extent the complements of one another. Each group has its more or less strongly defined specialty. One carries on fishing; another produces palm wine; a third devotes itself to trade and is broker for the others, supplying the community with all products from outside; another has reserved to itself work in iron and copper, making weapons for war and hunting, various utensils, etc. None may, however, pass beyond the sphere of its own specialty without exposing itself to the risk of being universally proscribed." Referring to the Loango Coast, a kingdom that was situated on the west coast of Africa between the equator and the mouth of the Congo in present-day Gabon, the German anthropologist A. Bastian (1826-1905) mentions a great number of centers of domestic industry. "Loango excels in mats and fishing baskets, while the carving of elephants' tusks is specially followed in Chilungo. The so-called Mafooka hats with raised patterns are drawn chiefly from the bordering country of Kakongo and Mayyume. In Bakunya are made potters' wares, which are in great demand; in Basanza, excellent swords; in Basundi, especially beautiful ornamented copper rings; on the Congo, clever wood and tablet carvings; in Loango, ornamented clothes and intricately designed mats; in Mayumbe, clothing of finely woven mat-work; in Kakongo, embroidered hats and also burnt clay pitchers; and among the Bayakas and Mantetjes, stuffs of woven grass." The French merchant Jean Barbot (late 1600s) notes the trade of Guinean and other locally made cloths and also reports on blue 'coral' beads, called akori, being acquired in Yorubaland and traded for other goods in the Gold Coast (Ghana).

Local and regional exchange systems were connected to extra-regional networks and tied to Asia and Europe through imported goods such as cloth, cowry shells, glass beads and copper and brass items, which were traded for African gold, ivory, hides and slaves. Small trade routes around the Nile Valley had been used for millennia, but travel across the Sahara prior to the domestication of the camel, an animal that can go without food and water for weeks, was difficult. Objects and materials found far from their places of origin today, however, are archaeological evidence of some trade having taken place, particularly in the far west, where the desert is narrowest. The most probable candidates for carriers of the early trans-Saharan contacts are the Berber, nomads residing at the southern edge of the Sahara who left for the north at the beginning of the rainy season, moving through the desert with their camel flocks, following seasonal changes. While staying in their pastures in the northern or central Sahara, these nomads certainly met people who had contacts within the Romans. As the nomads learned to know the value of gold in the Mediterranean world, they may have started bartering it with the peoples of Western Africa for Saharan rock salt and copper. The gold was brought to the north where it was probably exchanged for dates, corn and handicrafts that the nomads could not produce themselves. This type of exchange could not have started properly before the adoption of the dromedary by the Saharan peoples, since horses do not survive well in the harsh conditions of the desert. Camels were more important as beasts of burden than as mounts because they enabled efficient transportation of both large quantities of merchandise and the necessary supplies for crossing the desert—the people usually walked. Customarily, the do-

RIGHT *Among the Luba people of the Democratic Republic of the Congo, feminine beauty and motherhood are venerated, as it is through women that the continuity of the community is ensured. This female figure, with neck and waist beads, is presenting her breasts—an indication of her fecundity.*

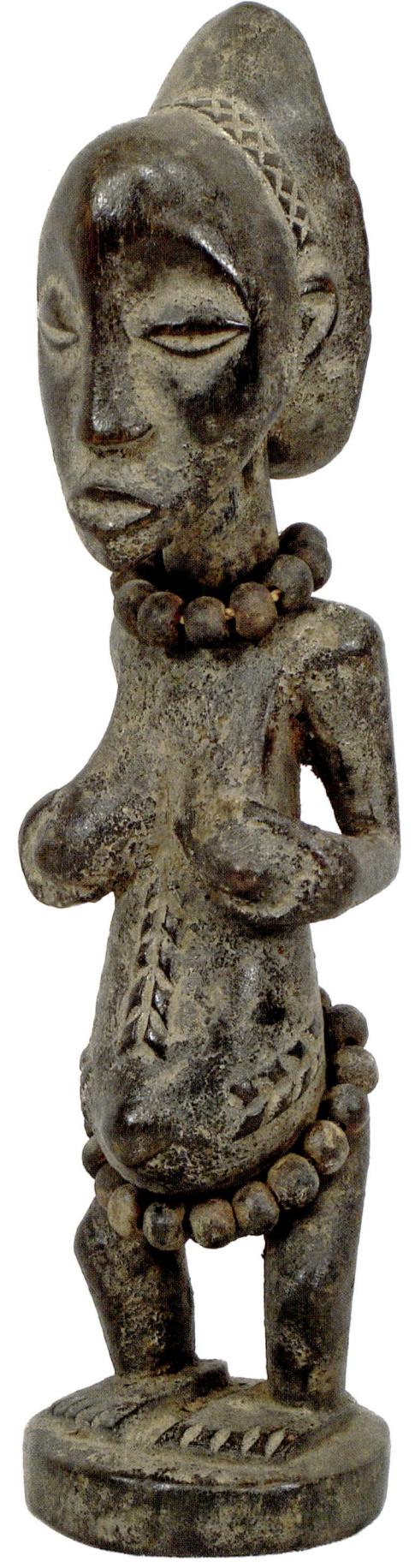

mestication of the dromedary in Northern Africa is dated to the beginning of our era and its introduction is attributed to the Romans, although some scholars suggest that the first domestication may have taken place long before the Roman period. The dromedary originally spread into Egypt from the Middle East during the 8th and 7th centuries BCE.

The Trans-Saharan Trade

The earliest records of the use of domesticated camels by the Berber people date from the 3rd century BCE, but regular trade routes did not develop until the beginning of the Islamic conversion of West Africa in the 7th and 8th centuries. Between the 11th and 15th centuries, West Africa exported goods across the Sahara Desert, and from its seaports to Arabia, Europe, India and China. Pliny mentions a trade involving spices and cinnamon—presumed to have originated in Indonesia—for East African glass and bronze ware, clothing, brooches, armlets and necklaces, adding that this trade depended chiefly on "women's fidelity to fashion."

The first trade route led through the western desert from present-day Morocco to the Niger Bend. Urbanization and state formation had started in the middle Niger valley, independently and without any influence from Mediterranean civilizations. The earliest known settlement in Djenne-Jeno is dated to 250 BCE, and it shows no evidence of northern influence. By 500 CE there already existed large communities which were organized in complex societies and engaged both in regional and long-distance trade with the southern savannah and the desert edge. This development correlates with the proposed date for the adoption of the dromedary by the Saharan nomads, suggesting that increased political centralization was at least partially affected by an external stimulus, since the maintenance of regular long-distance trade requires close cooperation between the different groups involved in it. There are no signs of alien conquest of the middle Niger valley, and it is more likely the accumulation of wealth from regional trade rather than from the still vague trans-Saharan trade which gave birth to the first states in Sudanic West Africa.

The preconditions for large-scale trans-Saharan trade changed radically after northern Africa became part of the Islamic world in the late 7th century CE. The Umayyad caliphate reached from the slopes of the Pyrenees to the banks of the Indus and formed a solid market area with its monetary system based on gold, which was in great demand throughout the Islamic world. Whereas sufficient gold was obtained from local mines in the east, the situation in the western regions was more difficult since there are no gold mines in northern Africa. With the increased volume of trans-Saharan trade in the Islamic period, new cultural influences began to spread across West Africa. By the end of the 11th century, the new religion, Islam, had been adopted in a mainly peaceful conversion in states affected by the caravan trade. Muslims in West Africa are still distinguished visibly by their dress and eating habits. To West African traders, Islam provided uniform standards and measures. To the rulers, the conversion offered political advantages which made diplomatic relations easier, although they had to play a double role in acting as pious Muslims to Arab traders and rulers while fulfilling their duties as divine kings to their own subjects.

After consolidating their power, the Arabs conjoined the trans-Saharan trade to the internal West African commercial network. West African peoples had already established complex states such as Ghana and Gao, and towns like Djenne had some twenty thousand inhabitants. New cities were also founded at the desert edge. Further east, the desert south of Libya was impassable due to its fierce sandstorms and lack of oases. A route leading from the Niger Bend to Egypt was abandoned in the 10th century because it was deemed too dangerous. Until the discovery of the Americas, Mali was the principal producer of gold, which was then traded for salt. African slaves were sent north in large numbers to serve as domestic servants, and African ivory was sought after because it was softer than that from Indian elephants and therefore easier to carve. The Chinese historian Zhao Rugua reports that African ivory was traded to China via Arab merchants in his time (1225), and he comments that the ivory originating from Somalia was preferred to all other varieties.

The cities of the Niger Bend, including Gao and Djenne, prospered, with Timbuktu in particular becoming known throughout Europe for its great wealth. When Sonni Ali, the ruler of the Songhai Empire—situated to the east along the curve of the Niger River—conquered Mali in 1462, he set about developing his own capital, Gao, and the main centers of Mali, Timbuktu and Djenne into major cities which would control a great deal of trade in the region. Important trading centers also developed along the transitional zone between the forest and the savannah, in present-day Ghana and Ivory Coast. Ouadane, Oualata and Chinguetti were the major trade centers in Mauritania, while the Tuareg towns of Assodé and Agadez prospered along a more easterly route in what is now Niger. Muslim traders from North Africa transported goods across the Sahara in large camel caravans numbering on average up to a thousand camels, although there is a record that mentions twelve thousand camels in caravans traveling between Egypt and Sudan.

Very little is known about the volume of trans-Saharan trade during the first centuries of the Islamic period. According to Arabic sources of the time, caravans brought huge amounts of gold to the north annually, with modern estimates putting the total weight between one thousand and three thousand kilograms per year. When the Almoravids, originally a group of Berber nomads from the western Sahara, united Morocco and Andalusia into a single empire in the late 11th century, gold seems to have been transported to the north in great amounts, and after a brief period of stagnation, the trade continued to grow steadily from the mid 13th century until its violent interruption by the Moroccan invasion of Timbuktu in 1591. Leo Africanus (1485-1554), who was born in Granada and educated in Fez, traveled widely in Africa and visited Timbuktu twice, reporting on the city's importance as a trade center during his first visit in 1510. "It is a wonder to see what plentie of Merchandize is daily brought hither and how costly and sumptuous all things be.... here are many shops of artificers and merchants and especially of such as weave linnen and cloth…. the coin of Tombuto is of gold without an stamp or superscription: but in matters of small value they use certain shells brought hither out of the kingdom of Persia, four hundred of which shells are worth a ducat: and six pieces of their golden coin with two third parts weigh an ounce." Long before cotton weaving was a British industry, West Africa and the Sudan were supplying a large part of the world with cotton cloth. In the early 1900s, cities like Kuka, on the west shore of Lake Chad, and Sokota were still manufacturing centers where cotton was spun and woven, skins were tanned, and implements and iron ornaments were produced.

Because the long distance trade helped local economies and supported internal trade, merchants traveling between towns across the Sahara needed places to rest and stock up on food. Food could be purchased at the markets, which relied on local farming communities for their supplies. Small farmers, traders and societies united into stronger trading blocs, often bringing together different cultures under a single authority. Due to the expansion and development of new routes, trades were often conducted between people from different continents, cultures and nationalities who did not speak a common language. The Arab traders isolated themselves in their own quarters, which usually lay outside the local settlements, and because they rarely spoke West African languages, they were dependent on local interpreters and brokers. Large trading centers had their own resident interpreters, commonly located in a particular area of the town. In Agadez this area was aptly named terdjeman—a reference to the profession of its occupants.

Other methods, called silent trade, dumb barter or depot trade, did not require the assistance of interpreters or a common language. A group of traders would leave goods in a prominent position and signal, by gong, fire or drum, that they had done so. Another group would arrive at the spot, examine the merchandise, and deposit the trade goods they wished to exchange. The first group would then return, and either accept the trade by taking the goods the other had left, or withdraw again, leaving the other traders to add to or exchange items in order to create an equal value. The trade ended when the first group of traders accepted the second group's offer and took the goods, leaving its own merchandise for the second group to remove. This method was well established and widely practiced in African countries. Reports written by the Greek sailor Cosmas Indicopleustes, who lived in the early 6th century and traveled to Ethiopia, India and Sri Lanka, document the practice of silent trade in Azania—a name referring to parts of sub-Saharan Africa—where officials from Axum (Aksum in Ethiopia) bartered for gold with beef. Prince Henry of Portugal—often termed "the Navigator" (1394-1460)—mentions this trade in 1415 on the occasion of his occupation of Ceuna, a Spanish exclave on the southern coast of the Strait of Gibraltar, bordering Morocco.

There was no racial discrimination between Arabs and Sudanic West Africans, and many Arab traders took local concubines. Later, separate quarters for the Muslim and non-Muslim populations became common in urban settlements throughout Sudanic West Africa. By isolating themselves, the traders were able to maintain their own culture and practice their own religion. The enclavement increased their security as they could set their own rules and elect their own leaders to represent them collectively to the local rulers, and they could look after the property of those traders who were absent or had died. Outside their trading colonies, Arab merchants followed local laws and customs, but the cultural difference was recognized and the traders were not forced to do things they might find offensive or humiliating. The traders were willing to accommodate local conditions in West Africa because it was the only way to carry on profitable trade.

The West-Atlantic Trade

Portuguese merchants who sailed to the West African coast opened up new avenues for trade between Europe and West Africa, and by the early 16th century a number of European bases had been established on the coast. Old documents give evidence of Portuguese merchants having traded some of their goods to the Yoruba in exchange for akori—highly esteemed blue beads found in Benin that the Portuguese then traded for gold on the Gold Coast (present-day Ghana). Portuguese merchants also conducted a flourishing trade in slaves. West African kingdoms relied on slaves to carry out heavy work. Slaves worked on village farms; the Songhai kingdom used slaves as soldiers. However, slaves were also trusted with important positions, even acting as royal advisers, and one group of slaves, known as the Arbi, served as crafts persons, potters, woodworkers and musicians. Ashanti kings traded gold for slaves to work their mines and farms. The Portuguese, eager to obtain Ashanti gold, opened a trading port at Elmina in 1482 in order to trade slaves for this purpose. The Portuguese bought the slaves from the kingdom of Benin, near the Niger Delta in Nigeria, until the slave trade ban there forced them to search for slaves elsewhere in West Africa. Dutch traders took over their role, and the Dutch dominated the West African and Atlantic slave trade from the 1600s onwards.

Certain trade goods became units of account and developed into a form of currency, such as gold, hides, iron and copper bars, and brass rings. During the late 16th century, one iron bar—these were produced in various European countries but all had the same approximate sizes and weights—was the equivalent of four copper bars. Slaves were valued at twelve to sixteen iron bars. At Goreé, one ounce of red coral cost seven to eight hides. The Denieros pey or kra-kra, introduced by European merchants for purchasing small commodities, was made from gold mixed with a little copper and cut into many shapes. It was commonly used on the Gold Coast (Ghana). The kra-kra money was not counted but weighed. Black and red peas, wood, and taku and damma seeds were used, alongside copper weights which were cast, molded and filed down to bring them in line with those used by the Europeans. Whereas cowry shells were the only standard currency in old Dahomey, the people of Accra commonly used little iron pins or brooches for making payments. During the late 17th century, the Scottish explorer Mungo Park mentions a unit of account measured in gold. Called minkalli, it equaled 10 shillings Sterling. For the weight of one teeleekissi (a black bean, six of which make the weight of one minkalli), a chicken could be purchased; a sheep had the value of three teeleekissi; a bullock cost one minkalli; and a horse from ten to seventeen minkallies. The gold was weighed in small balances. Mungo Park observed that occasionally the beans (teeleekissi) were soaked in shea butter in order to increase their weight, and he noted one instance in which a pebble was ground to resemble a bean.

Because the Portuguese and Dutch governments were unable to colonize West African kingdoms, the slave, ivory, rubber and gold trades remained under the control of the Ashanti, Fon and Congo kingdoms. While there were black slaves in Europe from the decline of the Roman Empire onwards, there was also a substantial trade in white Christians captured by the Moors along the North African coast. When the British government abolished the slave trade in 1807, the West African kingdoms did not cooperate. In order to supply Britain with agricultural products like palm oil, rubber and cocoa, the Ashanti kept the slaves they had captured for the Atlantic slave trade and used them on their farms instead, resulting in the growth of slavery in West Africa. When many of these kingdoms were colonized by the French and British towards the end of the 19th century, slavery came to a slow end, and former slaves became the landless lower classes. While trade with the now wealthier Europeans became of prime importance to West Africa, North African countries had declined in both political and economic importance. The major blow to trans-Saharan trade was the Moroccan War of 1591-2. When Morocco sent troops across the Sahara and attacked Timbuktu, Gao and some other important trade centers, buildings and property were destroyed and many prominent citizens exiled, resulting in a dramatic decline in the importance of these cities. Trans-Saharan trade continued on a reduced scale, but the

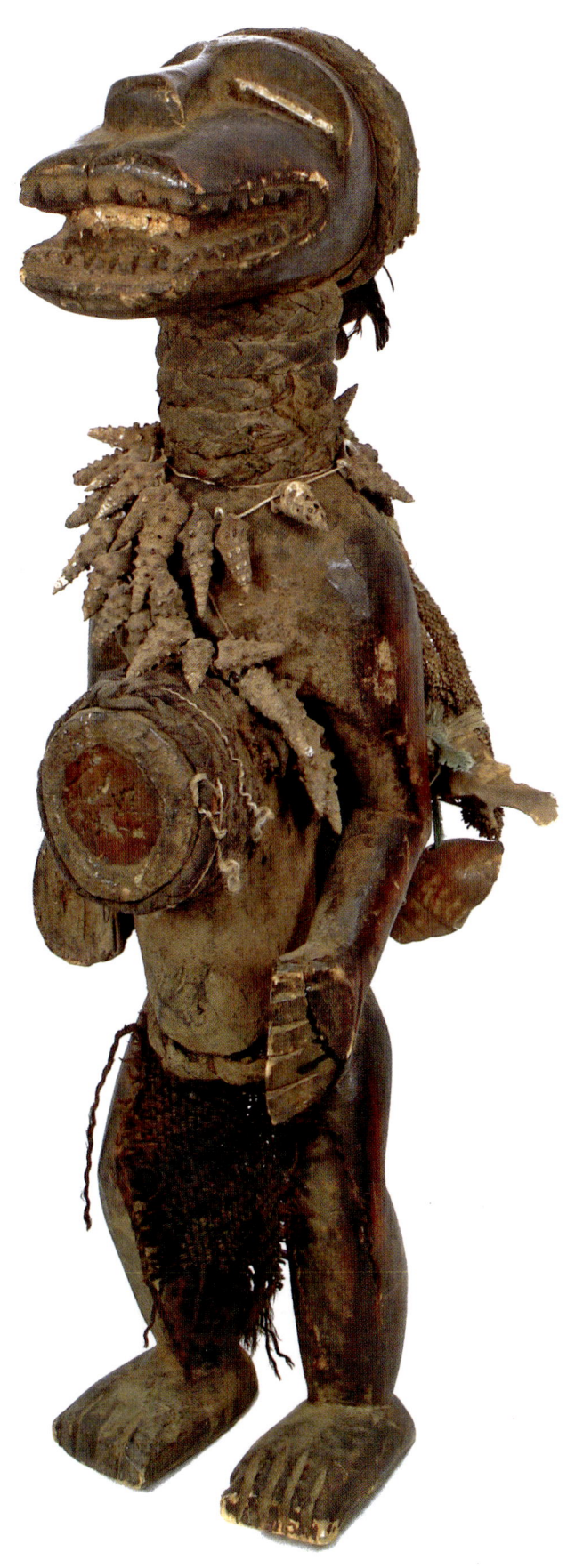

RIGHT *Nkisi power figures like this one are produced by the Kongo people of the Democratic Republic of the Congo. Adorned with shells (including the shells of giant African land snails), bones, feathers and other magical materials, this figure may have been used for divination, although the beads around its neck indicate a protective purpose.*

increasing accessibility of the West African coast after the French invasion of the Sahel in the 1890s and the subsequent construction of railways to the interior led to further decline. The Tuareg Rebellion in the 1990s and the Algerian Civil War caused further disruptions, and many routes are now abandoned or have been closed.

At the beginning of the 21st century, a few tarmac roads cross the Sahara, and a limited number of trucks carry trans-Saharan trade, mainly fuel and salt. Traditional caravan routes are largely void of camels, but shorter routes from Agadez to Bilma and from Timbuktu to Taoudenni are still used regularly. Some Tuareg continue to use the traditional trade routes, often traveling by camel 1,500 miles across the Sahara, on journeys which take six months out of every year. They trade in salt transported in the form of square blocks on the camels' backs.

The Pilgrim Routes

There is no evidence that West African traders crossed the Sahara during Antiquity, but black people were not unfamiliar to the ancient Mediterranean. There were many black warriors, freemen and slaves—mostly Nubians or autochthonous black inhabitants of the northern Sahara—in Egyptian, Carthaginian and Roman societies. Only with the advent of regular trans-Saharan trade during the Islamic period did the first West Africans arrive in the Mediterranean, the vast majority of them being slaves. It is estimated that during the thousand years from the 8th century CE onwards, about 9.3 million black slaves were imported to the north. The total volume of the trans-Saharan slave trade was equal to that of the Atlantic trade, though its annual volume was much lower. Voluntary traffic of West Africans to the Mediterranean began with the adoption of the Muslim faith. The first West African Muslims who visited Mecca in the early 12th century were mainly notables and rulers with the economic means to perform the long journey. The Malian king Mansa Musa became famous for his pilgrimage to Mecca in 1325. He was accompanied by five hundred followers each of whom carried a staff of solid gold, a spectacle which was witnessed by Italian merchants in Cairo. Another equally impressive event was the pilgrimage of Askia Muhammad of Songhai. A caravan of five thousand West African pilgrims is reported to have arrived in Cairo in 1343, having traveled along the most popular route which passed through Oualata and the oases of Tuat, Ghadames and Augila. Another important route crossed the central Sahara through Agadez and Murzuk, and a third route led through Hausaland and Darfur. Having arrived in Cairo, the West Africans joined the official pilgrimage caravan to Mecca organized by the Mamluk rulers of Egypt and later by the Ottoman governors. Important bead making centers were often located at the cross roads of trade and pilgrim routes, and to this day beads can be found in the ruins of old settlements or in clay pots buried in the desert sands for safekeeping many centuries ago, in the vicinity of many once busy and prosperous trading centers.

19th Century

According to one 19th century account, "It was a part of the state system of Ashanti to encourage trade. The king once in every forty days, as is the Adai custom, distributed among a number of chiefs various sums of gold dust with a charge to turn the same to good account. These chiefs then sent down to the coast caravans of tradesmen, some of whom would be their slaves, sometimes some two or three hundred strong, to barter ivory for European goods, or buy such goods with gold dust, which the king obtained from the royal alluvial workings. Down to 1873 a constant stream of Ashanti traders might be seen daily wending their way to the merchants of the coast and back again, yielding more certain wealth and prosperity to the merchants of the Gold Coast and Great Britain than may be expected for some time yet to come from the mining industry and railway development put together. The trade chiefs would, in due time, render a faithful account to the king's stewards, being allowed to retain a fair portion of the profit. In the king's household, too, he would have special men who directly traded for him. Important chiefs carried on the same system of trading with the coast, as did the king. Thus every member of the state, from the king downward, took an active interest in the promotion of trade and in the keeping open of trade routes into the interior."

African Bead Traders

The British-born journalist and explorer Sir H.M. Stanley (1841-1904) remarks, "To buy even a small article you must go to the market; people avoid trading anywhere else. If a man says to another, 'Sell me this hen' or 'that fruit,' the answer as a rule will be, 'Come to the market place.' The crowd gives confidence to individuals, and the inviolability of the visitor to the market, and of the market itself, looks like an idea of justice consecrated by long practice. From the Fish River to Kuka, and from Lagos to Zanzibar, the markets

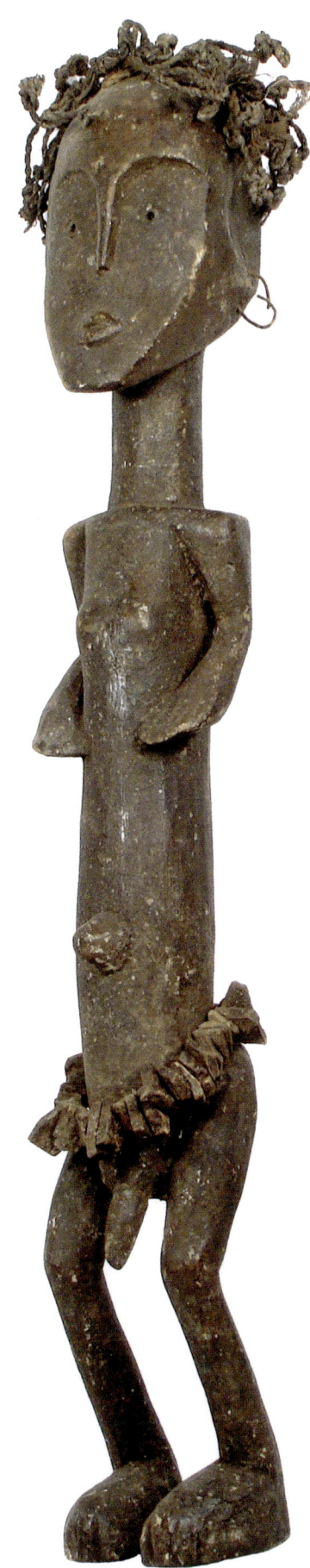

LEFT *This male figure with iron earrings and a waist belt of wooden beads or amulets was probably made by the Nyamwezi people of Tanzania.*

have become great centers of trade, the leading implement to civilization. Permanent markets are found in places like Ujiji and Nyangwe, where everything can be bought and sold from earthenware to wives, from the one to three thousand traders flocked here."

Nothing much has changed, and a great variety of goods, including beads from Europe as well as Africa, are readily available on African markets. It may be discovering the intricate beadwork of South Africa's Ndebele people or the rich adornment and court regalia of Nigerian kings; it may be a visit to the markets of Morocco, Mali, Ghana or Senegal; or it may be an encounter with worshippers reciting the ninety-nine names of Allah on their prayer bead strands—but however it happens, sooner or later every visitor to Africa encounters beads. When Peter Francis, Jr., visited West Africa in the 1980s, he found that the great majority of bead dealers were women, and female owners of bead businesses dominated the markets where locally made beads were sold. Young men, mostly Hausa, often operated the market stalls for their owners. The Hausa are subsistence farmers but some have chosen to develop their skills at weaving, dyeing, tanning leather, and metalworking, and today the Hausa are Nigeria's primary basket makers. They are also traders, some of them quite wealthy, achieving a social status similar to that of powerful Hausa politicians. The Hausa have their own bead trading guild. Guilds are associations of specialists where skills are passed on by training apprentices. Elements of the guild system have been documented in West Africa—there used to be tailoring guilds in Timbuktu; the famous brass and bronze casting industry of Benin was controlled by a restricted group of ironworkers; and the glass and bead workers of Nupe (northern Nigeria) were organized in guild-like groups.

There are two main trading groups in West Africa: the Hausa, operating predominantly in the east, and the Dioula (Soninke), who appear to be concentrated in the western regions. However, there are no defined territories because all bead traders visit all areas and mix constantly. The bead trade in West Africa is well structured, with dealers having their own networks of "runners"—middlemen with established contacts to local suppliers of their own. The Hausa live

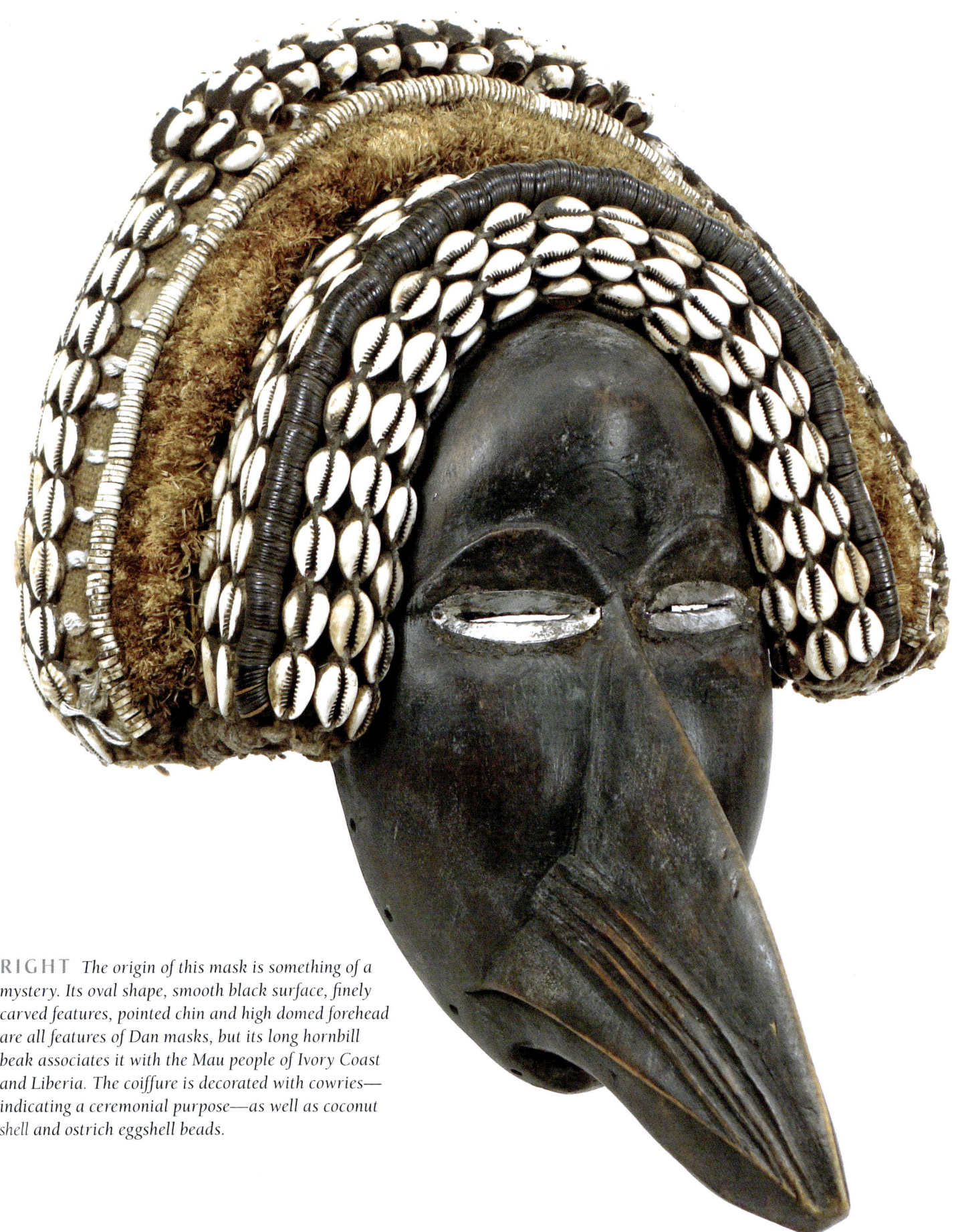

RIGHT *The origin of this mask is something of a mystery. Its oval shape, smooth black surface, finely carved features, pointed chin and high domed forehead are all features of Dan masks, but its long hornbill beak associates it with the Mau people of Ivory Coast and Liberia. The coiffure is decorated with cowries—indicating a ceremonial purpose—as well as coconut shell and ostrich eggshell beads.*

in northwestern Nigeria and southwestern Niger, whereas the majority of Soninke traders originate from the upriver region of The Gambia. Traveling over vast areas, the runners regularly visit their contacts in order to purchase or trade for the beads that have been collected during their absence. These beads are in turn delivered to the dealers. The dealers have established trading routes that they travel at regular intervals, and often have a network of international contacts. When visiting a strange village unannounced, a dealer will find a place in the shade, sit down and wait, sometimes for hours, for word to spread and for people to arrive with beads and other items they wish to sell. Usually the trader is well known, however, because he follows the same routes year after year, and has friends or "brother" dealers nearly everywhere who provide him with free board and lodging in their own homes. All day long he is visited by people, some of whom may have traveled many hundreds of miles hoping for a sale. Good dealers realize they can be vital to their contacts' lives and will often give their them money, thus enabling their contacts to travel home even if they cannot sell their beads.

Most bead traders operating in the United States are Serahuli (also called Seraculeh, or Sarakole) from The Gambia. The Serahuli are related to the Soninke and the Mande, who are descended from the Bafour, and to the Imraguen of Mauritania, the founders of the ancient Ghana Empire (750-1240). The prosperity of the Empire originated from its gold mines, located in Koumbi Saleh, the imperial capital and an important commercial center. Camels facilitated the transport of gold and other products—such as slaves, salt and copper, textiles, beads and finished goods—with the rest of the world. Around 1066, the Soninke became the first sub-Saharan ethnic group to follow the teachings of Muhammad. The Wangara (also known as Wakore) were Soninke clans specializing in trade, Islamic scholarship and law. The Arab geographer and cartographer Al-Idrisi (Abu Abd Allah Muhammad al-Idrisi, 1100-1166), whose world map was used in Europe for many centuries, reports that not only were the Wangara gold merchants, they also exercised a virtual monopoly of the gold trade. Al-Idrisi describes their land as having "flourishing towns and famous strongholds. Its inhabitants are rich, for they possess gold in abundance, and many good things are imported to them from the outermost parts of the earth." The Soninke are distributed across Mali, Senegal, Mauritania, Guinea-Bissau and The Gambia, and many still earn their living by trading, just as their forefathers did in the ancient Empire. Entrepreneurial by nature, they buy and sell a wide variety of items, ranging from gemstones to used cars. Beads make up less than ten percent of their merchandise. Serahuli bead traders say that they have established their own contacts and rarely resort to visiting the markets in Ghana and Nigeria, which are run by Hausa and other, smaller, local ethnic groups.

The Scottish surgeon and explorer Mungo Park (1771-1806) met and commented on the Serahuli of Gambia during his endeavors to map the flow of the River Niger in 1795. "The kingdom of Kajaaga, in which I was now arrived, is called by the French Gallam, but the name that I have adopted is universally used by the natives. This country is bounded on the southeast and south by Bambouk, on the west by Bondou and Foota-Torra, and on the north by the river Senegal. The inhabitants are called Serawoollies, or (as the French write it) Seracolets. Their complexion is a jet black: they are not to be distinguished in this respect from the Jaloffs. The Serawoollies are habitually a trading people; they formerly carried on a great commerce with the French in gold and slaves, and still maintain some traffic in slaves with the British factories on the Gambia. They are reckoned tolerably fair and just in their dealings, but are indefatigable in their exertions to acquire wealth, and they derive considerable profits by the sale of salt and cotton cloth in distant countries. When a Serawoolli merchant returns home from a trading expedition the neighbours immediately assemble to congratulate him upon his arrival. On these occasions the traveler displays his wealth and liberality by making a few presents to his friends; but if he has been unsuccessful his levee is soon over, and every one looks upon him as a man of no understanding, who could perform a long journey, and (as they express it) bring back nothing but the hair upon his head."

21st Century Bead Business

In 1974, B. Drammeh and Saja Tunkara became the first bead traders from The Gambia to set up a business in the United States. Today, the community of Gambian traders in North America amounts to almost one hundred members, and more than five hundred operate in Africa. Many traders travel in West Africa for a couple of months, several times each year, to do business with their contacts and spend time with family and friends. For the rest of the year they tour the United States, carrying their merchandise with them in large vans. Besides exhibiting at venues like the world's largest bead show, held annually in Tucson, Arizona, they regularly visit bead wholesalers, retailers and bead shops up and down the country. They stop at pre-arranged locations—such as hotels, car parks or by the roadside—to meet their private customers, and they visit potential buyers in their own homes by invitation. A number of these traders have established business contacts in, and regularly travel to, Europe, Thailand, China and Japan. They carry a wide range of old and new African-made beads such as brass pendants and necklaces from Ghana and Nigeria; bauxite, granite, gneiss and amazonite stone beads; forged iron necklaces made by the Dogon; and old and new Ghanaian powder glass beads, as well as European beads traded in Africa, which they sell by the strand, and a choice selection of special and rare single beads.

International bead businesses report a growing interest in older brass beads from Ghana and Nigeria, and, especially in Japan, in old Bodom. Contemporary Ghanaian powder glass beads are being shipped in great quantities to both China and Australia, rare Mauritanian powder glass Kiffa and Ghanaian Akoso beads are offered for sale in Thailand, and a great variety of African-made beads of all types can be found in shops in Singapore, Amsterdam, Paris, Melbourne, New York, London, Madrid, Tokyo and Venice. At the beginning of the 21st century, African-made beads are circling the globe.

Notes

Bones, Teeth, Claws and Shells

[1] Francis, *Big Bird, Dinosaur and Eggs*: www.thebeadsite.com/CHI-DINO.html
See also: National Geographic News, 04/15/2004, Mayell. H, *Oldest Jewelry? "Beads" Discovered in African Cave*
http://news.nationalgeographic.com/news/2004/04/0415_040415_oldestjewelry.html
and *Botanical Jewellery at Kew* http://www.kew.org/collections/ecbot/jewel.htm
and *Culture: The Language of Beads*
http://www.travelafricamag.com/content/view/382/56/

[2] Francis, *Beads of the World:* 10
See also: Liu, *Collectible Beads:* 27-29 and Bednarik http://www.chass.utoronto.ca/epc/srb/cyber/rbednarik4.pdf.
and *Totems to Turquoise* (Charles Lovato, an artist from the Santo Domingo pueblo, on heishi - Santo Domingo today is the leading producer)
http://www.amnh.org/exhibitions/totems/contemporary/domingo.php

[3] BBC News 6/22/06, P. Rincon: *Study reveals 'oldest jewellery'*

[4] Fisher, *Africa Adorned:* 30, 42, 127, 162
See also: Liu, *Collectible Beads:* 29
Elizabeth Bennet (Africa Direct), personal communication

[5] Barbot, *A Voyage to New Calabar:* trade/trading, ix, xi-xiv, xxii, xxv, xl, xlii-xlv, lii, liii, liv, lxv, xlvii-lxix, lxxii, lxxv, lxxvi, lxix, lxxvii, xci-xciii, c, cix-cxvii, 1, 2, 4, 7-9, 19-21, 25, 30, 39, 41, 44-47, 50, 51-53, 55-58, 63, 66, 75, 78, 82, 84, 89, 99, 101-106, 275, 297-299, 416-420, 490-492, 641-642, 647-651
See also: Marees, *Description and Historical Account of the Gold Kingdom of Guinea:* 11f, 14-16, 27, 44-57, 48, 56, 58f, 64, 67, 77, 78-87, 105f, 170, 178, 188-97, 202-16, 247, 257f (trade) and Park, *Travels in the Interior of Africa, Vol. 1:* 21-23 (trade) and Wiener, *Africa and the Discovery of America:* 211 (Pacheo Pereira on cowries) and Römer, *A Reliable Account of the Coast of Guinea:* 225 (list of goods and prices) and Barth, *Reisen und Entdeckungen in Nord- und Zentralafrika in den Jahren 1849 bis 1855. Band II, Die Gewerbshtaetigkeit und*

die Handelsverhaeltnisse Timbuktu's: 318f (on currencies and units of account at the time of his stay in the city)

and Levtzion, *Ancient Ghana and Mali:* 120-2 (The Economic Basis of Government) "Cowries as currency were first mentioned by al-'Umari, writing in the 1340s: 'Transactions in the land of Takruer, i.e. Mali, are in cowries'": 121

[6] Barth, *Reisen und Entdeckungen in Nord- und Zentralafrika in den Jahren 1849 bis 185.* Band II, *Aufenthalt in Timbuktu:* 291-303 (on traditions, markets and presents)

[7] Wiener, *Africa and the Discovery of America:* 211f (cowries in Congo)

See also: Hurst Gallery Exhibitions, *Old Money: Currency forms of sub-Saharan Africa* http://www.hurstgallery.com/exhibit/current/OldMoney/OldMoney2.php

and Levtzion, *Ancient Ghana and Mali:* 41 (gold dinars), 120-2 (cowries), 126-7 (Sudan)

[8] Liu, *Collectible Beads:* 29-30, 34

[9] Francis, *Beads of the World:* 109

See also: and: Delaroziere, *Les Perles de Mauritanie:* 18-19 and Francis, *Beads of the World:* 44 and Delaroziere, *Les Perles de Mauritanie:* 36-37

[10] Marees, *Description and Historical Account of the Gold Kingdom of Guinea:* 225, 226-228 (in Benin)

See also: Wiener, *Africa and the Discovery of America:* 237f (Pacheo Pereira on blue beads). " At Rio dos Forcados, in Benin territory, barter takes place, chiefly in slaves, cotton cloth, and a few blue beads with red lines, which they call coris. These things we buy for brass and copper armrings, and all this is of value at the Castle of Jorze da Mina, and our chief's factor sells it for gold to the Negro merchants." Op.cit 253

[11] J. Eicher in: 4, *Beads and Bead Makers; Gender, Material Culture and Meaning,* Ed. L.D. Sciama & J.B. Eicher: 95, 97, 100, 104, 106, 108, 110-11.

See also: Dubin, *The History of Beads* (Concise edition): 10, 30, 32, 35, 47, 63, 72, 74, 75, 83, 90, 92 and Fisher, *Africa Adorned:* 67, 81 (trade in Benin), 230 (Berber beliefs), 259 (Berber hair decoration), 263 (beads) and Delaroziere, *Les Perles de Mauritanie*: 120

General information on coral: http://www.jewelrycentral.com/Target_Coral.asp?c=29255

[12] Fisher, *Africa Adorned:* 230 (beliefs); 259 (hair decoration), 263 (beads)

See also: Liu, *Collectible Beads:* 128-130

[13] Liu, *Collectible Beads:* 43, 134

[14] Liu, *Collectible Beads:* 33

[15] Neuwirth, *Beads from Gablonz:* 332, 333 (2 images of a bead sample card, depicting Snake Beads manufactured by the Redlhamer Bros. glass workshop)

For more information on charms and fetishes see: Römer, *A Reliable Account of the Coast of Guinea:* 159 (Labadi), 238, 240 (fetish makers), 241 (Fante) and

Marees, *Description and Historical Account of the Gold Kingdom of Guinea*: 20, 23, 69, 108 (oaths), 103 (witchcraft), 71 (fish), 144 (leopards, snakes) and Fisher, *Africa Adorned*: 42 (depictions of a Dinka warrior's necklace of carved shell beads and seeds; necklace of a Massai warrior made from the lining of a goat's stomach and a button fashioned from crocodile eggshell; a belt made from glass beads and antelope toe bones, worn by Turkana and Samburu women; a Dinka woman's necklace comprised of ostrich eggshell heishi and stone beads; a Dinka elder's necklace of snake vertebrae, glass beads and cowry shells), 111 (Dogon, Mossi), 115 (Dogon), 128 (reptiles and insects), 140 (Animist bronzes), 36, 87, 15, 108 (charms)and Dubin, *The History of Beads (Concise edition)*: 46-47 (depiction of a Zulu shaman's necklace from S. Africa made of twigs, tortoiseshell, seeds, snake vertebrae, teeth, glass beads and leather and glass beaded amulets)

[16] Fisher, *Africa Adorned*: 36 (antelope), 42 (depiction of a belt made from glass beads and antelope toe bones, worn by Turkana and Samburu women), 65; 13, 16-17, 33, 36, 41-2, 45, 63 (on Turkana people)

[17] Liu, *Collectible Beads*: 33

[18] Fisher, *Africa Adorned*: 68, 75 (enemies'); 75, 134 (leopard's)
See also: Liu, *Collectible Beads*: 43 (lion's)

[19] Fisher, *Africa Adorned*: 48, 53, 55 (Dinka); 96, 121, 142 (bracelets)
See also: Francis, *Beads of the World*: 9, 37-8 and Barbot, *A Voyage to New Calabar*: 114, 152, 154, 189, 225, 237, 275, 282, 673-677, 697-699, 719 (elephants' teeth)

[20] Fisher, *Africa Adorned*: 65, 67 (carvings), 83 (masks)

Amber, Clay and Beads Made from Plant Materials

[21] Fisher, *Africa Adorned*: 230, 283
See also: Delaroziere, *Les Perles de Mauritanie*: 88-91

[22] Francis, *Beads of the World*: 35
See also: Liu, *Collectible Beads*: 35-36 and Delaroziere, *Les Perles de Mauritanie*: 88 and http://www.ambermagic.co.uk/us/about: (formation of, amber around the world, medicinal uses, definition of and testing of amber)

[23] General information derived from Gary Platt's website (www.gplatt.co.uk/map.htm) and from R.V. Dietrich's GemRocks Index (http://www.cst.cmich.edu/users/dietr1rv/Default.htm)

[24] Allen, Amber and its substitutes in: *Bead Journal 2(4): 11-22*.

Ibid. *Bead Journal* 3(2):20-31
See also: Liu, *Collectible Beads*: 36-37 and Francis, *Beads of the World*: 35 and Dubin, *The History of Beads (Concise Edition)*: 11, 32

[25] McIntosh, *Excavations at Jenné-Jeno, Hambarketolo, and Kaniana:* 216, 227-31
See also: Fisher, *Africa Adorned:* 115 and Liu, *Collectible Beads:* 37

[26] Hochberg, *Handspindles:* 10-12
See also: Barber, *Prehistoric Textiles:* ix, xxx, 3-5, 249-259, 299-310

[27] Liu: *Spindle Whorls:* 87-103

[28] For general information on the Kanem-Bornu Empire, see: *http://en.wikipedia.org/wiki/Kanem-Bornu_Empire*
and *http://www.wsu.edu:8080/~dee/CIVAFRCA/KANEM.HTM* and *http://www.blackeconomics.co.uk/earlyad.htm*
For information on tiny clay beads from Mali and their radiocarbon-dating: the information comes from J.& R. Picard of the Picard Trade Bead Museum and African Art Gallery in Carmel Valley, California, USA: *http://www.picardbeads.com/*

[29] Tomalin, *The Bead Jewellery Book:* 17
See also: Wayne's Word, Volume 9 (Number 1), Spring 2000: *Botanical Jewelry* (http://waynesword.palomar.edu/ww0901.htm)

[30] Delaroziere, *Les Perles de Mauritanie*: 101-103

[31] The information pertaining to Flinders Petrie is derived from the website of the Royal Botanic Gardens, Kew www.**kew**.org/collections/ecbot/jewel.htm

[32] Tomalin, *The Bead Jewellery Book:* 8, 70
See also: Wayne's Word, Volume 9 (Number 1), Spring 2000: *Botanical Jewelry* (http://waynesword.palomar.edu/ww0901.htm)

[33] Francis, *Beads of the World:* 42
See also: Delaroziere, *Les Perles de Mauritanie*: 104

[34] General information on plant seeds and their uses in as beads is derived from Wayne's Word, Volume 9 (Number 1), Spring 2000: *Botanical Jewelry* (http://waynesword.palomar.edu/ww0901.htm)

[35] Opper, *Scented Magic Beads in Africa:* 1-26
See also: Gobert, *Tunis et les parfums*: 466-467 and 470-471 and Delaroziere, *Les Perles de Mauritanie*: 121-125
K. Stanfield, personal communication and presentation of a variety of scented past beads as well as of raw materials and ingredients, for examination

[35a] For more information on recycled plastic beads see: http://www.fiema.com/id24.htm

[35b] Initiatives in Uganda producing recycled paper beads
http://www.beadforlife.org/index.html
http://www.papertopearls.org/

Stone Beads

[36]   Lankton, *A Bead Timeline, Volume I*: 9
       See also: Francis, *Beads of the World*: 11, 25, 50-51 (making of stone beads)

[37]   Diamanti J. in Lankton, *A Bead Timeline, Volume I*, 13 and Francis, *Asia's Maritime Bead Trade*: 7, 8 (ancient trade in Carnelians), 175 (traded by Europeans) and Barbot, *A Voyage to New Calabar*: trade/trading, ix, xi-xiv, xxii, xxv, xl, xlii-xlv, lii, liii, liv, lxv, xlvii-lxix, lxxii, lxxv, lxxvi, lxix, lxxvii, xci-xciii, c, cix-cxvii, 1, 2, 4, 7-9, 19-21, 25, 30, 39, 41, 44-47, 50, 51-53, 55-58, 63, 66, 75, 78, 82, 84, 89, 99, 101-106, 275, 297-299, 416-420, 490-492, 641-642, 647-651

[38]   *McIntosh, Excavations at Jenné-Jeno, Hambarketolo, and Kaniana*: 246-247, 248 (stone beads)
       See also: Dubin, *The History of Beads, (Concise edition)*: 47 and Delaroziere, *Les Perles de Mauritanie*: 27-31

[39]   GemRocks Index (http://www.cst.cmich.edu/users/dietr1rv/Default.htm)
       See also: Francis, *Beads of the World*: 108 and Liu, *Collectible Beads*: 12, 18, 22-3 and Fisher, *Africa Adorned*: 65, 115, 137, 160

[40]   Ibid.
       See also: Francis, *Beads of the World*, 109 and Liu, *Collectible Beads*: 18

[41]   Ibid.

[42]   O'Hear, Lantana Beads, Gender Issues in their Production and Use in Beads and Bead Makers; Gender, Material Culture and Meaning: 117-128
       See also: Francis, *Beads of the World*: 46 and Delaroziere, *Les Perles de Mauritanie*: 62-63 and Fisher, *Africa Adorned*: 68-9, 81, 83, 96 (Oba of Benin) and Liu, *Collectible Beads*: 23, 32 and Römer, *A Reliable Account of the Coast of Guinea*: 115 ("… they had neither treasures nor any other precious things, except for their aggreys and concretereés, sc. beads, which no one dared to wear, unless they were those so permitted by the emperor, as a mark of distinction.")

[42a] Harrell J.A, Stone in Ancient Egypt
       http://www.eeescience.utoledo.edu/Faculty/Harrell/Egypt/Stone%20Use/Harrell_Stones_text.htm
       (varieties, quarrying and use of gemstones)

[43]   *GemRocks Index (http://www.cst.cmich.edu/users/dietr1rv/Default.htm)*
       See also: Delaroziere, *Les Perles de Mauritanie*: 61-62 and Liu, *Collectible Beads*: 14 and Francis, *Beads of the World*: 108

[44]   Ibid.
       See also: Delaroziere, *Les Perles de Mauritanie*: 65-66

[45]   Ibid.
       See also: Delaroziere, *Les Perles de Mauritanie*: 63-64

Metal Beads

[46] Levtzion, Ancient Ghana and Mali: 58, 112, 114, 118

See also: Fisher, *Africa Adorned:* 15-16 (Dinka), 17, 109-11, and Hagan & Myers, *Tuareg Jewelery:* 71 and Barbot, *A Voyage to New Calabar:* 97, 101, 111, 272 (on blacksmiths), 89, 90, 101, 516-21, 527, 533, 534 (listing African crafts/trades) and Marees, *Description and Historical Account of the Gold Kingdom of Guinea:* 85, 177, 240 (blacksmiths)

[47] Fisher, *Africa Adorned:* 107 (location), 113 (ancestor cult), 115-6 (symbolism)

See also: Marees, *Description and Historical Account of the Gold Kingdom of Guinea:* 11, 38, 44, 52, 56, 65, 228, 239, 242f, 250 (blacksmiths and iron working)

[48] *INAGINA, the last house of iron* – Film directed by E. Huysecomb, Dept. of anthropology and ecology, University of Geneva, 1997. The film documents one of the last smeltings executed by Dogon blacksmiths in Mali in 1995.

[49] Fisher, *Africa Adorned:* 115, 140, 142

[50] Ibid. 115

See also: Römer, *A Reliable Account of the Coast of Guinea:* 115 (rarer than gold) and Fisher, *Africa Adorned:* 115 (sacred stones, forged iron necklaces)

[51] Römer, A Reliable Account of the Coast of Guinea: 149, 159, 165, 167 (Ashanti trade gold for iron), 228 (source of gold)

See also: Marees, *Description and Historical Account of the Gold Kingdom of Guinea:* 66, 73, 83, 85 (gold mines) and Levtzion, *Ancient Ghana and Mali:* 115-6 (control of gold by Sudanese kingdoms); 17-18, 27-8, 41, 53, 95, 98, 115-16, 137, 152-6, 181, 187, 248 n. 76 (sources and production); 9-10, 134, 146, 150, 157, 164-5, 168-9, 171, 173, 174, 177 (gold trade)

[52] Fisher, *Africa Adorned:* 70, 90

See also: Barbot, *A Voyage to New Calabar:* 527, 528, 541, 542 (on gold working) and: Marees, *Description and Historical Account of the Gold Kingdom of Guinea:* 34, 96, 167, 169, 175 (ornaments)

[53] Barbot, *A Voyage to New Calabar:* xciv, 516, 521, 541, 542, 824 (on goldsmiths)

See also: Marees, *Description and Historical Account of the Gold Kingdom of Guinea:* 65, 68

[54] Fisher, *Africa Adorned: 71, 87, 93, 105, 140*

See also: Römer, *A Reliable Account of the Coast of Guinea:* 34 (gold mining), 152-4 (battles against the Ashanti) and Marees, *Description and Historical Account of the Gold Kingdom of Guinea:* 249 (gold as currency), 19, 59-61 (units of account), 29, 49, 60, 64f, 85f, 106, 191, 249 (gold weights and methods of weighing), and The Ashanti Homepage: http://www.ashanti.com.au/pb/wp_8078438f.html (history, culture, family system, golden stool)

[55] Hagan & Myers, Tuareg Jewelery: 9-11, 33-43

See also: Fisher, *Africa Adorned:* 145, 148-9, 162, 186, 189, 191-5, 198, 202, 214, 217-8, 225

[56] Hagan & Myers, Tuareg Jewelery: 45-61
See also: Fisher, *Africa Adorned*: 186, 194, 210

[57] Hagan & Myers, Tuareg Jewelery: 73-75
See also: Fisher, *Africa Adorned*: 201, 208, 225

[58] Hagan & Myers, Tuareg Jewelery: 109-110
See also: Fisher, *Africa Adorned*: 189, 207-8, 225 (khomissar)

[59] Fisher, *Africa Adorned: 241, 257 (khamsa, Hand of Fatima)*

[60] Fisher, *Africa Adorned: 229, 261, 263*
See also: Hagan & Myers, *Tuareg Jewelery:* 16-32 (on Imazighen), 33-43 (onTifinagh, the Tuareg alphabet) and Levtzion, *Ancient Ghana and Mali*: 136, 140-1 (Maghreb); 6-7, 9, 13, 29, 79, 149, 151 (Sahara); 27, 46, 51-2, 64, 78, 98, 146-7, 160-1, 164 (on the border to Sudan); 124, 126, 146, 160-1, 164 (trade with the Berbers), 126, 131-2, 134, 142, 177 (on silver)
and http://www.al-bab.com/arab/background/berber.htm for general information on the Berbers

[61] Juergen Busch, personal communication

[62] Fisher, *Africa Adorned: 269-71, 285, 291, 294, 296*

[63] Hagan & Myers, *Tuareg Jewelery*: 95
See also: Römer, *A Reliable Account of the Coast of Guinea*: 225 (list of goods and prices, units of account) and Park, *Travels in the Interior of Africa, Vol. 1*: 21-23 (trade) and Barth, *Reisen und Entdeckungen in Nord- und Zentralafrika in den Jahren 1849 bis 1855*: 291f
For information about the Maria Theresia Thaler see: *The Maria Theresa Thaler 1780:* http://www.theresia.name/en/

[64] Fisher, *Africa Adorned: 294-300*

[65] Ibid. 292, 293

[66] Ibid. 17 (popularity), 67, 69 (trade)
See also: Römer, *A Reliable Account of the Coast of Guinea*: 102 (brass), 225 (list of goods and prices)

[67] Fisher, *Africa Adorned: 142*

[68] Ibid. 83 (depiction of a 7 kg bronze collar worn by Yoruba women)

[69] Ibid. 69, 84, 87-8, 105, 109

[70] Barbot, *A Voyage to New Calabar: trade/trading,* ix, xi-xiv, xxii, xxv, xl, xlii-xlv, lii, liii, liv, lxv, xlvii-lxix, lxxii, lxxv, lxxvi, lxix, lxxvii, xci-xciii, c, cix-cxvii, 1, 2, 4, 7-9, 19-21, 25, 30, 39, 41, 44-47, 50, 51-53, 55-58, 63, 66, 75, 78, 82, 84, 89, 99, 101-106, 275, 297-299, 416-420, 490-492, 641-642, 647-651 (trade goods) and Fisher, Africa Adorned: 17 (popularity of); 156 (Fulani); 185 (hair ornaments)

[71] Fisher, *Africa Adorned: 36*
See also: Liu, *Collectible Beads:* 39

Glass Beads

[71a] Spaer M, Ancient Glass in the Israel Museum: Beads and Other Small Objects: 64 (Kom el-Dikra - stone molds)

Ibid. 69 (Gurob)

Ibid. 97/103 (making of fused rod beads)

Ibid. 128 (spot beads)

[72] Barbot, *A Voyage to New Calabar:* 231, 455-467 ("The third sort of false gold, grown pretty common among the Blacks, is a composition which they make of a certain powder of coral glass which they cast.")

[73] Euba, Of Blue Beads and Red: 111-115

See also: Mauny, *Akori Beads:* 210-14 and Kalous, *A Contribution to the problem of Akori Beads:* 61-66, and Willett, *Baubles, Bangles and Beads:* 1-31 and Johnson, *The History of the Yorubas* and Euylemi, *The Living Art and Crafts of Ile-Ife;* 11-18 and Willett, *The Art of Ife, A descriptive Catalogue and Database.* CD-ROM. The Hunterian Museum of Glasgow (The contents of this CD-ROM is based on records made by Frank Willett over a period of 40 years and catalogues all the works of Ife art from Nigerian museums and from museums and private collections in Europe and the USA, with 2200 illustrations and descriptive texts.)

[74] Lankton J.W., O. Akin Ige & Rehren T., Early Primary Glass Production in Southern Nigeria: 111-138

See also: Willett F.Baubles, Bangles and Beads: 1-31 and Davison, Glass Beads in African Archaeology: 243f and Euylemi, The Living Art and Crafts of Ile-Ife: 18f

and Stanfield (Kwesi Amanfrafo) *Yoruba Glass Beads* and *Pacheo's Bead* (website articles)

[75] Wiener, Africa and the Discovery of America: 237f "Estes leuam d'esta casa muitas mercadorias asy como lambes, que he a principal d'ellas, de que ja no noveno item do quarto capitolo d'este Segundo livro falamos, e pano vermelho e azul e manilhas de latam e lencos e coraes e huas conchas vermelhas, que antre elles sam muito estimadas, asy como nos ca estimamos pedras preciosas; isso mesmo val aquy muito ho vinho branco e huas contos azues, a que elles chaman 'coris'. E outras muitas cousas de desvairados modos." op. cit. P.D. Pereira, *Esmeraldo de situ orbis*

See also: Stanfield (Kwesi Amanfrafo), *Pacheo's Bead (website article)* http://tradebeads.net/articles/pacheco.html

"For these (kori beads) they (the African traders) give considerable gold, because they are greatly esteemed by all the Negroes, who put them into the fire, to see that they are not counterfeit, since many are imported that are made of glass, which resemble them greatly, but will not stand the fire test." Quoted from: Wiener, *Africa and the Discovery of America:* 238 op. cit Ramusio, vol. I, fol. 116a

and Francis, *The Aggrey Bead and its Namesakes*

http://www.thebeadsite.com/bnaf-agg.htm

and Landewijk in *The Bead is Constant*: 132-141 (originally published as *'What was the Original Aggrey Bead? (A New Aggrey Bead Hypothesis)* in the Ghana Journal of Sociology Volume 6, No. 2 October 1970; Volume 7 No. 1 February 1971

[76] Pereira, *Esmeraldo de situ orbis, Boletim da Sociedale de Geographica de Lisboa*, 22ser. 1904 quoted in: Römer, A Reliable Account of the Coast of Guinea: 237f

[77] Marees, *Description and Historical Account of the Gold Kingdom of Guinea*: 225

[78] Römer, A Reliable Account of the Coast of Guinea: 26, 115, 156, 160
See also: Euba, *Of Blue Beads and Red*: 109

[79] Lankton J.W., O. Akin Ige & Rehren T., Early Primary Glass Production in Southern Nigeria: 111-138
See also: Davison, Glass Beads in African Archaeology: 243f and Ibid. with Giauque and Clark, Two Chemical Groups of dichroic Glass Beads from West Africa: 645-59 and Shaw, An account of archaeological discoveries in eastern Nigeria: 225-239

[80] Francis, The Aggrey Bead and its Namesakes, http://www.thebeadsite.com/bnaf-agg.htm
See also: Sordinas, *Modern Koli Beads in Ghana*: 75-76 and Bowdich, *Mission from Cape Coast to Ashante*: 268

[81] Stanfield (Kwesi Amanfrafo), Yoruba Glass Beads (website article)
See also: Liu, *Collectible Beads*: 24-25
K. Stanfield, personal communications
U. Mueller, personal communications

[82] Euylemi, The Living Art and Crafts of Ile-Ife: 18f
See also: Stanfield (Kwesi Amanfrafo), *Yoruba Glass Beads*, http://tradebeads.net/articles/niusisikoli.html
and Euba, *Of Blue Beads and Red*: 109f

[83] M. Carey, Powder-Glass Beads in Africa in: Ornaments from the Past: Bead Studies after Beck: 108-113
See also: J. Haigh, *Present-Day Bead-Making in Ghana* in *Ornaments from the Past: Bead Studies after Beck*: 115-117 and Simak, *Contemporary Styles of Krobo Powder Glass Beads*

[84] Barbot, *A Voyage to New Calabar*: 231

[85] (ed. A. Wilson), The Bead is Constant: 7, 11, 20-21, 25, 28, 42, 60, 83, 86, 88, 94-95, 101, 105

[86] J. Haigh, Present-Day Bead-Making in Ghana in Ornaments from the Past: Bead Studies after Beck: 115-117
K. Stanfield, personal communications

[87] K. Stanfield, personal communications

[88] — [92] Ibid.
See also: *The Bead is Constant*: 150-151 for a Glossary of bead names in Krobo-Dangme

[93] Liu, Ahn and Giberson, Bodom and Related Beads: Investigating African powder-glass technology: 28-33
See also: Liu, African-Made Glass Ornaments — Survey & Experimental Results: 52-58 and Stanfield, The Krobo and Bodom: 63-76 and Daaku, Oral Traditions of Adanse

[94] K. Stanfield: http://tradebeads.net/articles/powa1.html

[95] Ibid. http://tradebeads.net/articles/niusisikoli.html

[96] Euba, Of Blue Beads and Red: 109f

[97] Stanfield (Kwesi Amanfrafo), Yoruba Glass Beads (website article)
See also: Liu, Collectible beads: 24

[98] Francis, Hebron as Beadmaker: http://www.thebeadsite.com/MG4-1.htm

[99] Sternberg, Chasing Rainbows: http://www.lapidaryjournal.com/feature/june00str.cfm

[100] Busch, From Powder to Magic – Mysterious Powder Glass Beads from Mauritania: 3-6. Ibid. The Kiffa Bead Tradition in Mauritania
See also: *Delaroziere,* Les Perles de Mauritanie: 82-84 and Ibid. Mauritanian Beads: 24-27

[101] Mauny, Fabrication de perles de verre en Mauritanie
Ibid. Decoration des mains auhenné
See also: Vanacker, Perles de verre decouvertes sur le site Tegadoust: 54-2

[102] Simak E. 2006, Contemporary Styles of Krobo Powder Glass Beads

[103] Gabus, Sahara bijoux et techniques: 121-124
See also: *Delaroziere,* Les Perles de Mauritanie: 84-86 (on Oualata) and Opper & Opper, Rare Mauritanian Kiffa Beads: 33-35

[104] Opper & Opper, Kiffa Beads, Mauritania's Powdered Glass Beads: 1-16 (description of types, shapes and patterns as well as Hassaniya names) and Ibid. Rare Mauritanian Kiffa Beads: 32-35 and Powdered Glass Beads and Bead Trade in Mauritania: 37-44
See also: Busch, From Powder to Magic – Mysterious Powder Glass Beads from Mauritania: 3-6. , Ibid. The Kiffa Bead Tradition in Mauritania and Simak, Traditional Mauritanian Powder Glass Kiffa Beads: *Ornament* 50-54 , Ibid. Mauritanian Kiffa Beads: *Ornament* 60-63

[105] Opper & Opper, An Update on Kiffa Beads: 4-5
K. Stanfield, personal communication
J. Busch, personal communication
D. Nevill, personal communication

[106] D. Nevill, website article: The Modern Day making of Kiffa Beads in the Town of Kiffa http://www.africantradebeads.com/Product_Index/Kiffa/Kiffa-st/kiffa-st.html

See also: Simak, *Mauritanian Kiffa Beads*. Ornament: 60-63
K. Stanfield, personal communication
J. Busch: personal communication

[107] Liu, *Collectible Beads*: 218

[108] Bowen, Adventures and Missionary Labours in Several Countries in the Interior of Africa from 1849 to 1856: 199

See also: Francis, *Glass Beads made in Africa, Part 1:* http://www.thebeadsite.com/bmm-pga.htm

[109] Frobenius, *The Voice of Africa*, Volume 2: 434-437

[110] Hodge, *Nigerian Traditional Crafts*: 72-79

[111] Spaer M, *Ancient Glass in the Israel Museum: Beads and Other Small Objects*: 309 (Explanation of Terms, faience)

[112] *A Bead Timeline, Volume I: Prehistory to 1200 CE*: 19/29 (glazed stone beads in Egypt), 46 (method of making faience explained)

See also: http://www.metmuseum.org/toah/ht/02/afe/ht02afe.htm

[113] Marie Parsons, Egyptian Faience (history of) http://www.touregypt.net/featurestories/faience.htm

[114] Lacovar and Trope, 2004, Carlos Museum at Emory University: http://www.egyptianmuseum.com/article14_emory4.html … "this new custom appears in the Third Intermediate Period, although beadwork garments are known for burials of the Old and Middle Kingdoms. The bead-networks of the Late Period are thought to derive from the costumes worn by goddesses, although they are found on mummies of both sexes. When they initially appeared, they were a simple covering over the body with winged scarabs and images of the Four Sons of Horus worked in. By the Late Period they had incorporated occasional bands of text and a face mask, all executed in painstaking patterns of tiny coloured faience beads."

Bibliography

For African-Made Beads: The Matter of Materials

Appiah, Anthony. "An Aesthetics for the Art of Adornment." in Brincard, Marie-Thérèse. Editor. *Beauty by Design: The Aesthetics of African Adornment*. New York: The African-American Institute, 1984.

Ben-Amos Girshick, Paula. "Brass Never Rusts, Lead Never Rots: Brass and Broadcasting in the Edo Kingdom of Benin." in Herreman, Frank. Editor. *Material Differences: Art and Identity in Africa*. New York: Museum of African Art, 2003.

Blackmun, Barbara Winston. "The Elephant and Its Ivory in Benin." in Ross, Doran H. Editor. Elephant: The Animal and Its Ivory in African Culture. Los Angeles: Fowler Museum of Cultural History, 1992.

Bouzouggar et al. "82,000-year-old shell beads from North Africa and implications for the origins of modern human behavior." **Publication of the National Academy of Sciences** 104(24), 2007.

Burssens, Herman. "Sculpting in Wood, Ivory and Stone." in Herreman, Frank. Editor. *Material Differences: Art and Identity in Africa*. New York: Museum of African Art, 2003.

Drewal, Henry John. "Image and Indeterminacy: Elephants and Ivory Among the Yoruba." in Ross, Doran H. Editor. *Elephant: The Animal and Its Ivory in African Culture*. Los Angeles: Fowler Museum of Cultural History, 1992.

Dubin, Lois. *The History of Beads*. New York: Harry N. Abrams, 1987.

Ebeigbe, S.U. "Coral Beads: Its Significance and Uses in Benin Culture." *Emotan Journal of the Arts*, (University of Benin, Nigeria) vol. 2, 2004.

Eicher, Joanne B. "Beaded and Bedecked Kalabari of Nigeria." in Sciama, Lidia D. and Joanne B. Eicher. Editors. *Beads and Beadmakers: Gender, Material Culture and Meaning*. Oxford and New York: Berg, 1998.

Fisher, Angela and Carol Beckwith. *African Ceremonies*. 2 volumes. New York: Harry N. Abrams, 1999.

Garrard, Timothy F. *Gold of Africa. Jewellery and Ornaments from Ghana*, Cote d'Ivoire, Mali and Senegal in the Collection of the Barbier-Mueller Museum. Germany: Prestel, 1989.

Gessain, Monique. "Jewels of the Bassari Family." in Brincard, Marie-Thérèse. Editor. *Beauty by Design: The Aesthetics of African Adornment.* New York: The African-American Institute, 1984.

Herreman, Frank. Editor. *Material Differences: Art and Identity in Africa.* New York: Museum of African Art, 2003.

Jacques-Meunie in Opper, Marie-José and Howard. "Rare Mauritanian Kiffa Beads." in *Ornament Magazine* 12(3), 1989.

Jereb, James "The Magical Potency of Berber Jewelry." *Ornament Magazine* 13(2). 1989.

Kasfir, Sidney Littlefield. "Ivory From Zariba Country to the Land of Zinj" in Ross, Doran H. Editor. *Elephant: The Animal and Its Ivory in African Culture.* Los Angeles: Fowler Museum of Cultural History, 1992.

Kassam, Aneesa and Gemetchu Megersa. "Iron and beads: male and female symbols of creation. A study of ornament among Booran Oromo (East Africa)." In Hodder, I. Editor. *The Meaning of Things: Material Culture and Symbolic Expression.* London and New York: Routledge, 1989.

Roberts, Mary Nooter and Allen F. Roberts. *Memory. Luba Art and the Making of History.* New York : Prestel/The Museum for African Art, 1996.

Ross, Doran H. Editor. *Elephant: The Animal and Its Ivory in African Culture.* Los Angeles: Fowler Museum of Cultural History, 1992.

Sciama, Lidia D. "Gender in the Making, Trading and Uses of Beads: An Introductory Essay." in Sciama, Lidia D. and Joanne B. Eicher. Editors. *Beads and Beadmakers: Gender, Material Culture and Meaning.* Oxford and New York: Berg, 1998.

Simak, Evelyn. "Traditional Mauritanian Powder-Glass Kiffa Beads." *Ornament Magazine* 29(3), 2006.

Vogel, Susan. *For Spirits and Kings.* New York: Harry N. Abrams/Metropolitan Museum of Art, 1981.

Zahan, Dominique. "Ornament and Color in Black Africa: An Aesthetics for the Art of Adornment." in Brincard, Marie-Thérèse. Editor. *Beauty by Design: The Aesthetics of African Adornment.* New York: The African-American Institute, 1984.

For African Beads: Jewels of a Continent

Africanus L., Cosmographia Dell' Africa, transl. F. Moore, 1738

Ahn P. M. and Giberson D. 2001, Bodom and Related Beads: Investigating African powder-glass technology. *Ornament* 25(2): 28-33

Allen J. D. 1976, Amber and its substitutes, Bead Journal 2(4):11-22

—*Bead Journal* 3(2):20-31

—1996, *Kiffa Beads*, Ornament Magazine 10(1): 76-77

Alpern S. B. "What Africans Got for their Slaves: A Master List of European Trade Goods," *History in Africa*, vol. 22 (1995), 5-43

Arkell A. J. 1973, *A History of Sudan: From the Earliest Times to 1821*, Greenwood Press

Barber E. J. W. 1991, *Prehistoric Textiles*, Princeton Paperbacks

Barbot J. 1746, *A Voyage to New Calabar. Collection of Voyages and Travels, Linot and Osborn* (6 vols.): 455-467

Barth H. 2005, ***Reisen und Entdeckungen in Nord- und Zentralafrika in den Jahren 1849 bis 1855***. Elibron Classics. Adamant Media Corporation—unabridged facsimile of the edition published by Justus Perthes, Gotha, 1859

Bastian A. 1874, *Die Deutsche Expedition an der Loango Küste, nebst älteren Nachrichten über die zu erforschenden Länder.* Jena and London (Trübner and Co.)

Bednarik R. 2006, *Beads, Symbolism and Self-Awareness*, Semiotics Course, Cognition and symbolism in human evolution: Lecture No. 4, University of Toronto

Benouniche Farida 1977, Bijoux et parures d'Algerie. Algiers, Algeria. 45-46

Bowen, T. J. 1981 (orig. 1856) *Adventures and Missionary Labours in Several Countries in the Interior of Africa from 1849 to 1856.* Cass Library of African Studies, Missionary Researches and Travels, No. 3. London: Frank Cass & Co.

Bowdich T. E. 1966 (orig. 1819) *Mission from Cape Coast to Ashantee.* W.E.F. Ward (ed.), F. Crass & Co. London

Busch J. 1994, *From Powder to Magic – Mysterious Powder Glass Beads from Mauritania.* Newsletter of the Bead Society of Great Britain 25: 3-6

—1995 to 1996, The Kiffa Bead Tradition in Mauritania Part 1, Newsletter of the Bead Society of Great Britain 30: 3-8, Part 2, Newsletter of the Bead Society of Great Britain 35: 7-9, Part 3, Newsletter of the Bead Society of Great Britain 45: 3-8

Cirlot J. E. 1971, *A Dictionary of Symbols,* Routledge

Daaku, Kwame Y. 1959, *Oral Traditions of Adanse.* Legon: Institute of African Studies, University of Ghana.

Davison C.C. 1972, *Glass Beads in African Archaeology.* Thesis: University of California, Berkley

Delaroziere M-F. 1984, *Les Perles Mauritaniennes*, Ornament 8(3)

—1985, *Les Perles de Mauritanie.* Edisud

Dubin L. S. 1995, *The History of Beads*, (Concise edition), Thames and Hudson

Du Bois W. E. B. 1915, *The Negro,* New York: Holt

Euba O. 1981/82, Of Blue Beads and Red: The Role of Ife in the West African Trade in Kori Beads, *Journal of the Historical Society of Nigeria* (Dec. 1981-June 1982): 109-127

Euylemi O. 1978, *The Living Art and Crafts of Ile-Ife*, Adesanmi Printing Works, Ile-Ife

Fisher A. 1984, *Africa Adorned*, London: The Harvill Press

Francis P. Jr. 2002, *Asia's Maritime Bead Trade*, University of Hawaii Press

—1999, *Beads of the World*, Schiffer Publishing Ltd.

Frobenius L. 1913, *The Voice of Africa*, Volume 2. London: Hutchinson & Co.

Gabus J. 1976, *Oualata et Geiimaré des Nemadi*. Neuchatel: Baconniere

—1982, *Sahara bijoux et techniques*

Gardi, René (Sigrid MacRae, trans.) 1969, *African Crafts and Craftsmen*. New York: Van Nostrand Reinhold.

Giauque R. D. and Clark D. J. 1971, Two Chemical Groups of dichroic Glass Beads from West Africa. *Man* 6:4 (1971): 645-59

Gobert E. C. 1961/1962, Tunis et les parfums. *Revue Africaine*, Tomes CV no. 466-467, and CVI no. 470-471, Algiers, Algeria.

Gumpert A. 1955, The Once and Future Kiffa. *The Bead Society of Greater Washington Newsletter*, XII (5)

Hagan H. E., Myers L.C. 2006, *Tuareg Jewellery, Traditional Patterns and Symbols*, Xlibris Corporation

Hochberg B. 1977, *Handspindles*. H.& B. Hochberg, Santa Cruz, California

Hodge A. 1981, Nigerian Traditional Crafts. Ethnographic Arts and Culture Series 3. London: *Ethnographica*.

Johnson S. 1921, *The History of the Yorubas*. Lagos 1921

Kalous M. 1966, A Contribution to the problem of Akori Beads. *Journal of African History*, Vol. 7. No.1

Lamb A. 1976, Krobo Powder-Glass Beads. *African Arts* 9(3): 13-39, 93.

Lankton J. W. 2003, A Bead Timeline, Volume I: Prehistory to 1200 CE, *The Bead Society of Greater Washington*

Lankton J. W. & Dussubieux 2006, Early Glass in Asian Maritime Trade. *Journal of Glass Studies*, The Corning Museum of Glass

Lankton J. W., O. Akin Ige & Rehren T., Early Primary Glass Production in Southern Nigeria. *Journal of African Archaeology*, Vol. 4 (1), 2006: 111-138

Levtzion N. 1973, *Ancient Ghana and Mali. Studies in African History-7*. Methuen & Co. London

Liu R. K. 1984, African-Made Glass Ornaments–Survey & Experimental Results. *Ornament* 8(2), 1984

—1995, *Collectible Beads–A Universal Aesthetic*. Ornament Inc. USA

—1978 Spindle Whorls: Pt 1: Some comments and speculations, *The Bead Journal* 3: 87-103

London C. 1965, Safari for Gems, Part Three of 3 Parts: We "Discover" Kwalbite. *Lapidary Journal*.

de Marees P. 1602, Description and Historical Account of the Gold Kingdom of Guinea. Ed. and translated by A. Van Dantzig & A. Jones. British Academy, 1987
Mauny R. 1949, Fabrication de perles de verre en Mauritanie. *Notes Africaines* no. 44. Dakar, Senegal

—1958, Akori Beads. Journal of the Historical Society of Nigeria. Vol. 1 No. 3

McIntosh S. K. & R. J., Excavations at Jenné-Jeno, Hambarketolo, and Kaniana (Inland

Niger Delta, Mali), in the 1981 season. University of California Publications, *Anthropology*, Vol. 20

Meek, C. K. 1971 (orig. 1925), *The Northern Tribes of Nigeria*, Volume 1. London: Frank Cass & Co. (2 vols.)

Meyerowitz E. L. R. 1951, *The Sacred State of the Akan*. London: Faber and Faber

Nadel, S. F. 1951 (orig. 1942), *A Black Byzantium: The Kingdom of Nupe in Nigeria*. London: Oxford University Press

Neuwirth, W. 1994, *Beads from Gablonz*, Vienna: Dr. W. Neuwirth

O'Hear, A. 2001, *Lantana Beads: Gender Issues in their Production and Use. Beads and Bead Makers; Gender, Material Culture and Meaning,* Ed. L. D. Sciama & J. B. Eicher, Berg (Oxford International Publishers), Oxford/New York, 2001

Opper H. & Opper M. J. 1989, *Kiffa Beads, Mauritania's Powdered Glass Beads*. Alexandria, USA

—1989, Rare Mauritanian Kiffa Beads. *Ornament* 12 (3): 32-35

—1992, An Update on Kiffa Beads. *Bead Society of Greater Washington Newsletter* 9, no. 1 (Feb./March): 4-5

—1993, Powdered Glass Beads and Bead Trade in Mauritania. *BEADS* 5:37-44

Opper M. J. 1990, *Scented Magic Beads in Africa.*

Ornaments from the Past: Bead Studies after Beck, Edited for the Bead Study Trust by I.C. Clover, H. Hughes Brock and J. Henderson. The Bead Study Trust: London and Bangkok, 2003

Park M. 1893, *Travels in the Interior of Africa, Vol. 1.* ed. David Price, Casell & Company

Reader J. 1998, *Africa: a biography of the continent*. Penguin Books Ltd.

Robert D. S. 1970, Les fouilles de Tagadoust. *Journal of African History* 9 (4): 471-493

Römer L. F. 1760, *A Reliable Account of the Coast of Guinea*. Selena Alexrod Winsnes, translator. Oxford UP/ British Academy, 2000

Simak E. 2006, Contemporary Styles of Krobo Powder Glass Beads, *Bead Society of Great Britain Newsletter* (84), 2006

—2005/2006. Near Eastern Bone Turned Spindle Whorls, *Bead Society of Great Britain Newsletter* 81/82

—2006, Traditional Mauritanian Powder Glass Kiffa Beads. *Ornament* 29(3):50-54

—2006, Mauritanian Kiffa Beads. *Ornament* 29(5): 60-63

Shaw T. 1970, *An account of archaeological discoveries in eastern Nigeria*. Northwestern University Press Evanston: 225-239

Sordinas A. 1964, Modern Koli Beads in Ghana. *Man*, Nos. 89, 90: 75-76

Springer B. 1509/1902, *Balthasar Springers Indienfahrt, 1505-06,* F. Schulze, Strassburg, 1902

Stanfield K. 2000-2001, The Krobo and Bodom, *Beads* (Journal of the Society of Bead Researchers), Vols. 12-13: 63-76

—(Kwesi Amanfrafo), Yoruba Glass Beads. Internet article

—Pacheo's Bead. Internet article

—Types of Koli Beads among the Krobo. Internet article

Sternberg J., Chasing Rainbows. *Lapidary Journal* 54 (June 2000)

The Bead is Constant (ed. Alexandra Wilson) 2003, Ghana Universities Press, Accra

Tomalin S. 1997, *The Bead Jewellery Book*, David & Charles

d'Ucel J. 1937, *Berber Art*. University of Oklahoma Press, Norman, Oklahoma.

Vanacker C. 1984, Perles de verre decouvertes sur le site Tegadoust. *Journal des Africanists* 54 (2): 54-2

Wiener L. 1922, *Africa and the Discovery of America*. A & B Books, Brooklyn, New York

Wilks I. 1961, The Northern Factor in Ashanti History: Begho and the Mande. *Journal of African History* 2(1): 25-34.

Willett F. 1977, *Baubles, Bangles and Beads*. The Centre of African Studies, Edinburgh University, Feb. 1977

Willie F. 2001, Amulets (Ancient Africa). *Encyclopedia of African History and Culture*. Vol. 1, Ancient Africa. New York: Facts On File, Inc.: Ancient History & Culture

Wood M. 2000, *Making connections: relationships between international trade and glass beads from the Sashe-Limpopo area*, South African Archaeological Society, Goodwin Series 8: 69-79

Index

Abaklé Koli, 131
aberemp nnaasee, 99
Abo, 82, 84, 86
Abyssinia, 109
Acholi, 77
Adai, 176
Adanse, 139
Adjagba, 127, 135
Aedare Mountains, 21
Afghanistan, 88
African Ceremonies, 16
agudee, 99
Agysymba, 171
AIDS, 164
aje ileke, 127
aje Olokun, 127
Akan, 20, 66, 90, 94, 99, 102, 128, 135, 146, 148
Akan metalworking designs
    knife/ekan, 94, 99
    Sankofa bird, 94, 99
    sun disks, 94
    twin crocodile, 94, 99
akori, 127, 128, 171, 174
Akoso beads, 143, 145, 146, 147, 148, 149, 150, 180
    new, 148, 152
Akosu, 145
Akuso, 145
Algeria, 26, 37, 76, 97, 102, 105, 107, 108
    Abalessa, 171
    Ahaggar highlands, 98, 102, 105, 171
    Algiers, 36
    Qued Djebbana site, 26
    Tuat, 176
Algerian Civil War, 176
Al-Idrisi, 179
Allah, 19, 177, 179
Allen, J.D., 59

alternately pivoting stamp technique, 59
Amazon River, 67
Amazons, 74
amber, 17, 22, 35, 37, 42, 53, 54, 57, 58, 59, 158
    African Amber, 59, 61
    amberoid, 57
    Amekit, 53
    antique amber, 57
    Baltic, 15
    bernat, 58
    broken beads, 54
    brown, 53
    Cherry Amber, 58
    cloudy, 53
    copal, 37, 53, 56, 57, 59
    elektron, 57
    imitation, 57, 58, 167
    pressed amber, 57
    River Amber/Ocean Amber, 56
    yellow, 54
amber paste, 73, 74, 76
Ambrose, Stanley, 23
amulet, 15, 17, 19, 20, 33, 37, 38, 42, 44, 46, 49, 53, 73, 74, 88, 90, 98, 102, 110, 113, 114, 115, 124, 167, 177
    Ankh, 115, 167
    kitabe, 99
    suman, 20
ancestor stones, 92
Anglo Gold Ashanti Company, 97
Angola, 20, 26, 36, 46
    Benguella, 26, 36
    Laonda de S. Paola, 124
animism, 92, 103
anklets, 19
anthropomorphism, 66
Anti-Atlas Occidental highlands, 108
aphrodisiac, 73, 74

Appiah, Anthony, 15, 16, 22
Arabia, 31, 67, 116, 125, 172
Arabs, 28, 34, 36, 79, 107, 156, 164, 173, 174, 179
Arbi, 174
Asante, 97, 148
Ashanti, 13, 16, 17, 20, 21, 94, 97, 99, 122, 127, 130, 131, 139, 146, 148, 151, 153, 174, 175, 176
Ashanti gold mine, 97
Ashanti Kingdom/Ashanti Confederacy, 97, 99, 148
Ashanti legends
    Golden Stool/Sika 'dwa, 99
    Okomfo Anokye, 99
    Osei Tutu I, 99
    Sunsum, 99
Ashanti union/Asanteman, 99
Asia, 13, 171
Assyrian Empire, 90, 170
Ateyun, 152, 155
Atlas Mountains, 37
Aures Mountains, 108
Australia, 53, 180
    Melbourne, 180
    Queensland, 53
Austria, 109, 164
Awuazi, 127, 151, 155
Axum kingdom, 90, 174
ayannee, 99
Azande, 44
Azania, 174
Bafour, 179
Bakunya, 171
Baltic Sea, 53
Bamana, 21, 92
Bamileke, 61
Bamun, 36
Bani River, 63
Bantu, 21, 170
Baoule, 66, 116, 122
BaRanga, 21
Barbot, Jean, 31, 127, 131, 171
bark, 73
barrel-shaped, 40, 66, 81, 86, 87, 88, 114, 153, 162
barter, 31
Barth, Heinrich, 31, 36, 171
Basanza, 171
Bassari, 21, 22
Bastian, A., 171
Basundi, 171
batik, 44, 45
Bayaka, 171
BeadforLife, 77

Beckwith, Carol, 16
beeswax, 76
belas, 103
bells, 16, 28, 46, 89, 92, 97, 110, 113, 117, 118, 123
belt, 43, 44, 46, 74, 76, 77, 86, 107
Benin, 19, 20, 21, 33, 35, 36, 46, 85, 87, 117, 118, 127, 128, 146, 174, 177
    Ouidah, 33
    Rio dos Forcados, 127
    Sameh, 134
Bennett-Luther Collection, 61
Benue River, 120
benzoin, 76
Berber, 17, 19, 35, 37, 54, 76, 83, 101, 102, 105, 107, 108, 109, 156, 167, 171, 172, 173
    Ait Atta, 37
    Ait Baha, 37
    Almohads, 107
    Almoravids, 107, 173
    Amazigh, 108
    Chaouia, 108
    Ida ou Semlal, 108
    Kabylie, 108
beveling, 153
bicones, 50, 114, 117, 122, 124, 125, 131, 133, 134, 138, 145, 146, 148, 150
Bida beads, 164
Blackmun, Margaret, 21
blacksmith, 20, 44, 90, 91, 92, 96, 97, 99, 103, 164
Bodom beads, 133, 139, 143, 144, 145, 146, 148, 151, 180
    new, 145, 146
Bohemia, 109
bone, 13, 16, 19, 21, 38, 40, 42, 44, 57, 63, 167, 170, 175
    alligator feet, 44
    animal, 63
    antelope toe bones, 43, 44
    camel, 42
    cattle, 44
    chicken, 38
    deer toe bones, 44
    fish vertebrae, 42, 43
    goat, 42
    human, 63
    python vertebrae, 43
    shark vertebrae, 43, 76
    sheep, 42
    snake vertebrae, 17, 42
    teeth, 17, 20
Booran Oromo, 19
Borneo, 31
Bornu empire, 31

bouzrada, 158
bouzrem, 158
bow drill, 79, 80, 81, 82, 88
Bowen, T.J., 164
bracelet, 13, 16, 22, 44, 46, 97, 152, 153, 157, 159
bride price, 36
Burkina Faso, 36, 66, 69, 103, 129
    Kissi, 129
Bushman, 26
butter, 76
cache sex, 26, 29
camel caravans, 124, 173, 176
camel dung, 57
camels, 73, 168, 171, 172, 173, 176, 179
    dromedary, 172
Cameroon, 31, 36, 44, 46, 67, 113, 117, 118, 120, 124
    Mora Massif, 44
cane, 125, 127
Cape Lopez, 127
Cape Verde, 118, 127
Carthage, 170, 176
caste, 90, 91, 92
cattle dung, 97
cave paintings, 79
Cedi, 139
Cedi Glass Works, 133
celluloid, 57, 58
Celts, 115
Center for Cultural Studies, University of Lagos, 151
Central Africa, 171
ceramic, 13, 61, 122, 129, 164, 166, 167
ceramic colorant, 66, 134, 138, 139, 151
ceremonies
    25th anniversary of King Otumfuo Opoku Ware I, 116
    Dipo ceremony, 131
    Dogon divination rituals, 26
    Ramadan, 169
    The Honor of the Bead, 87
    toru, 80
    Ugie ivie (Festival of Corals), 19, 36
Chad, 31, 68, 117, 118, 153, 171
    Chari-Baguirmi region, 36
chains of memory, 15
chalk, 16, 17, 19, 21
charcoal, 17, 21
charm, 36, 38, 42, 44, 63
chevron beads, 47, 139
    7 layer, 148
    imitation, 70
Chilungo, 171
China, 26, 28, 33, 79, 88, 138, 139, 162, 171, 172, 173, 180

Han dynasty, 171
    Hunan, 88
Christianity, 107, 109, 115, 116, 175
circle-dot motif, 38, 59, 104
circumcision, 16, 90
claws, 44, 124
clay, 15, 16, 21, 37, 38, 59, 61, 63, 64, 65, 66, 68, 69, 70, 77, 122, 131, 132, 134, 159, 166, 168, 169, 171, 176
    polymer, 164
    red, 16, 17
Coca Cola, 133
cocoa, 175
coiled, 122
coins, 37
    Denieros pey, 174
    ducat, 173
    kra-kra, 174
    Maria Theresa thaler, 109, 110, 115
    shilling, 175
collectors, 35, 66, 76, 77, 86, 96, 122, 124, 125, 139, 145, 157, 158, 162, 166
colonization, 148
Columbus, Christopher, 53
coming of age, 131
Comoro Islands, 67
Congo, 15, 20, 26, 38, 47, 57, 171, 172, 175
    Kabongo, 19
    Nyangwe, 177
Congo basin, 67
Coniagui, 22
conical, 113, 158
Cook Islands, 28
Cooperative Nasser, 162
Coptic cross, 107, 115
coral, 15, 17, 19, 21, 22, 36, 37, 38, 74, 76, 87, 127, 128, 152
    black, 36
    blue, 128
    branch coral, 37, 76
    dark red, 35
    imitation, 37, 38, 129, 152, 155, 167
    Ivie ebo, 19
    pink, 35
    red, 19, 174
    red Mediterranean, 15, 36, 37, 38, 87
    round, 37
Coral of Mauritania, 74
corded, 127, 128
cores, 134, 139, 143, 146, 156, 158
Cosmas Indicopleustes, 174
Costa Rica, 67

crescent moon, 110
crosshatching, 50, 145, 148, 150
crown, 13, 19, 115, 127
currency, 13, 26, 28, 31, 33, 34, 36, 110, 124, 174
    minkalli, 175
    teeleekissi, 175
cylindrical, 86, 87, 88, 132, 146, 148, 153, 155, 158, 159, 166
Cyprus, 28
Czech-Bohemian bead industry, 13, 30, 36, 38, 43, 46, 74, 158, 166
Dahomey kingdom, 33, 118, 127, 134, 175
Dan, 170, 178
Dangme, 134
date juice, 139
Dead Sea, 153
deities
    Ama, 92
    Horus, 168
    Kloweke, 131
    Mammi Wata, 152
    Nyami Nyami, 87
    Ogun, 90
    Olokun, 21, 127
    Osiris, 167
    Water Spirit, 21
    Yemoja, 152
de Marees, Peter, 127
democracy, 99
Denkyira, 99
Denmark, 128
dichroic, 127, 128, 130, 131
Dinka, 17, 28, 43
Dioula, 177
disks, 23, 24, 25, 26, 33, 36, 66, 73, 86, 87, 88, 116, 117, 138, 167
diviner, 20, 38, 44, 47, 90, 175
Djaba, Nomoda Ebenezer, 139
Dogon, 20, 21, 26, 66, 81, 82, 91, 92, 96, 97, 180
Dogon creation myths, 20, 92
    Ama, 92
    Nommo, 92
domed, 66, 157, 159
Dominican Republic, 53
douge, 82
dowry, 125
Drammeh, B., 179
drawn beads, 127, 128, 130, 151
Drewal, Henry John, 22
dry-core powder glass technique, 145, 146
    vertical-mold, 134, 148, 162

dumb barter, 174
dye, 44, 54, 58, 103, 134
ear cleaners, 105
earplugs, 87
East Africa, 16, 28, 31, 44, 45, 56, 70, 110, 172
East Asia, 67
Ebeigbe, S.U., 19
Edo, 19
Egypt, 28, 67, 88, 90, 107, 125, 153, 164, 167, 168, 170, 172, 173, 176
    Abydos, 167
    Alexandria, 125
    Amarna, 167
    Badari, 167
    Buto, 167
    Cairo, 176
    Deir el-Medina, 167
    Fustat/Old Cairo, 125, 153, 156
    Gurob, 125
    Kom el-Dikra, 125
    Malkata, 167
    Memphis, 167
    Miram, 164
    Naukratis, 167
    Qantir, 167
    Quorna, 167
    Thebes, 167
    Upper Egypt, 167
Egyptian mythology
    Four Sons of Horus, 168
    Osiris, 167
Ehel Sidi Mahmoud family, 156
elbow-shaped, 132
ellipsoidal, 88, 151
el veshé, 158
enamel, 101, 108, 139
equatorial bands and markings, 54, 61, 67, 117, 134, 138, 145, 146, 148, 166
Erbore, 121, 124
erhu ivie, 36
erinmwin, 21
eshugu, 36
eshu staff, 26
esoro, 85, 87
Ethiopia, 14, 19, 21, 43, 57, 58, 90, 102, 105, 107, 109, 110, 114, 115, 117, 121, 124, 170, 174
    Boorana, 109
    Ethiopian highlands, 109
    Harer, 57
    Omo valley, 124
Euba, O., 151

Europe, 13, 15, 16, 22, 86, 87, 107, 115, 117, 124, 125, 127, 128, 129, 130, 135, 148, 151, 152, 158, 162, 164, 171, 172, 173, 174, 175, 176, 177, 179, 180
evil eye, 22, 28, 36, 37, 38, 42, 44, 74, 105, 110, 125, 156, 168
evil forces, 13, 16, 22, 26, 38, 42, 44, 63, 66, 107, 110, 125
Ewe, 146, 151
executioner, 43
eye beads, 125
    stratified, 125
eye motif, 22, 105, 125, 127, 132, 134, 139, 145, 146, 148, 158
faceted, 74, 80, 153
faience, 166, 167, 168
    Faience maker of Amun, 167
Falasha, 115
    black Jews, 115
Fanta, 133
Fante, 97
fertility, 19, 28, 36, 37, 38, 98, 102, 103, 113, 114, 118, 157
fetish, 20, 29, 38, 46, 63, 66, 92, 97, 99, 117, 132
filigree, 76, 118
Fisher, Angela, 16
Fisher, Lynn, 160
Fish River, 176
flowers, 67, 73
    rose petals, 76
Fon, 175
fossil, 53, 57
four corners of the earth, 98, 103
France, 20, 31, 33, 124, 131, 156, 162, 171, 175, 176, 179
    Corsica, 36
    Paris, 107, 180
    Provence, 36
Francis, Peter, 125, 148, 153, 164, 177
Frantz, Patricia, 164
frit, 168
Frobenius, Leo, 59, 164
fruits, 67, 73, 76
    coconut, 73
Fubara-Manuel, Alate, 19
Fulani, 28, 38, 90, 113, 117, 118
    Wodaabe, 113, 120
fused rod beads, 125, 156
fuwa, 134
Gabbra, 121, 124
Gabon, 127, 171
Gabus, Jean, 22, 156
Gallam, 179
Garamantes, 170, 171
Garden Roller Beads, 131
Germany, 20, 31, 36, 53, 57, 59, 164, 171
    Prussia, 57
Ghana, 13, 15, 16, 20, 36, 38, 43, 50, 59, 66, 67, 73, 82, 84, 86, 90, 97, 114, 115, 116, 118, 122, 125, 127, 128, 129, 130, 131, 134, 139, 146, 148, 151, 153, 155, 156, 162, 169, 171, 173, 174, 177, 179, 180
    Accra, 82, 84, 175
    Akosombo Dam, 82, 145
    Akyem Abompe, 82, 84
    Ampabame Krofrom, 114, 122
    Asokore-Koona, 139
    Begho, 66, 122
    Brong-Ahafo region, 66, 122
    Elmina, 128, 129, 174
    Keta, 151
    Kumasi, 77, 97, 122, 171
    Obuasi, 97
    Odumase-Krobo, 133, 138, 139
Gige beads, 135
glass, 13, 15, 16, 17, 21, 22, 30, 33, 35, 36, 37, 38, 43, 44, 57, 58, 59, 63, 66, 73, 74, 76, 79, 101, 102, 125, 127, 128, 130, 132, 134, 135, 138, 139, 143, 145, 146, 148, 151, 152, 153, 155, 156, 158, 162, 164, 166, 167, 171, 172, 177
    bikini, 164
    bottle glass, 129, 130, 132, 134, 138, 139, 151, 155, 164
    high lime, high alumina, 129
    imitation snake vertebrae, 43
    mosaic, 125, 158
    powder glass, 13, 37, 38, 86, 127, 129, 130, 131, 132, 133, 134, 139, 140, 145, 148, 151, 152, 153, 155, 156, 158, 160, 162, 180
glaze, 166, 167
gold, 28
Gold Coast, 99, 110, 116, 118, 122, 127, 128, 131, 153, 171, 174, 176
gold weights, 99, 102, 122
Great Britain, 33, 36, 87, 88, 99, 124, 164, 166, 171, 173, 175, 176, 179
    Kew botanical gardens, 67
    London, 31, 67, 180
Greece, 53, 57, 74, 115, 170, 174
    Thrace, 74
Greek mythology
    Aphrodite, 28
    the Heliades, 53
griot, 67
guilds, 177
Guinea, 21, 31, 44, 73, 82, 118, 128, 171
Guinea-Bissau, 56, 76, 179

Guinea Coast, 67
Gulf of Guinea, 117
gum arabic, 139, 156
Hausa, 26, 35, 38, 77, 86, 110, 117, 118, 124, 133, 134,
    153, 159, 177, 179
Hausaland, 176
heads of Ife, 116
healing powers, 15, 17, 38, 47, 57, 76, 77, 88, 90, 99, 143
Hebron beads, 146
heishi, 24, 25, 26, 28, 73, 84, 86, 117
Hengme, 134
Hermes of Paris, 107
Herodotus, 170, 171
Himba, 17
Hippocrates, 53
Hodge, Alison, 164
Hodgson, Frederick, 99
Hogon, 20, 82, 91, 92, 97
honey, 139
horn, 54, 57, 58, 59, 167
Horn of Africa, 110
Huguenots, 20
Hungary, 109
hunter, 26, 38, 42, 171
Hutu, 92
Ife Kingdom, 127
Igbo, 21, 28, 34, 46, 117
Igbo Bugs, 118
Iljaw, 117
Imam/baluster bead, 114
Imraguen, 179
Inagina, 97
incense, 73
incision, 59, 64, 66, 105, 108, 118
India, 26, 28, 31, 33, 66, 79, 80, 88, 90, 138, 162, 172, 173,
    174
Indian Ocean, 28
indigo, 103
Indonesia, 162, 172
Indus, 173
inlay, 67, 72, 88
Islam, 36, 64, 67, 74, 103, 109, 114, 115, 122, 125, 153,
    172, 173, 176, 179
Israel, 26
    Hebron/Al-Halil, 153
    Jerusalem, 153
    Skhul Cave, Mount Carmel, 26
Italy, 13, 37, 176
    Genoa, 36
    Gulf of Naples, 36
    Sardinia, 36

Venice, 13, 28, 38, 152, 180
ivory, 15, 16, 17, 19, 20, 21, 22, 36, 42, 44, 46, 49, 50, 122,
    124, 156, 170, 171, 173, 175, 176
    elephant, 46, 49, 50
    imitation - hippopotamus teeth, 46, 49
    imitation - warthog tusks, 46, 49
Ivory Coast, 19, 36, 44, 66, 97, 116, 122, 170, 173, 178
Iyun, 129, 131, 152, 155
Jacques-Meunie, 22
Jaloff, 179
Japan, 59, 180
    Jomon, 59
    Tokyo, 180
jeff-lekk, 92
Judaism, 115
juju, 152
Julius Maternus, 171
Kabylie Mountains, 108
Kajaaga, 179
Kakongo, 171
Kalabari, 19
Kalahari Desert, 15, 16
Kanem-Bornu, 13
Kanem kingdom, 66
Kano beads, 146, 153
kaolin, 17, 65, 66, 69, 134
Karo, 21
Kashin Zomo, 134, 138
Kazuri beads, 164, 166
Kente, 135
Kente cloth, 135
Kenya, 13, 15, 19, 23, 43, 44, 45, 57, 109, 117, 164, 166
    Enkapune Ya Muto rock shelter, 13, 23
    Nairobi, 164, 166
    Ngong Hills, 166
    Rift Valley, 13
Keta Awuazi, 127, 151, 155
khoust el arf, 158
khshdj, 167
Kiffa beads, 13, 125, 139, 156, 157, 158, 159, 162, 164, 180
    American, 162
    House of the Turtle, 157, 158, 159
    imitation, 162
    Indonesian, 162
    new, 158, 162
Kikuyu, 43, 164
kings
    Akhenaten, 125
    Amenhotep III, 167
    ancient, 90
    Ashanti king/Asantehene, 16, 99, 174, 176

Askia Muhammad, 176
Bornu, 31
divine, 20, 90, 127, 173
Emir of Ilorin, 87
Ewe, 146
Igbo, 46
Kalala Ilunga, 20
Kuba, 26
Late Etsu Saba, 164
Late Etsu Usman Zaki, 164
Mamluk, 176
Mansa Musa, 176
Menelik II, 109
Nigerian, 177
Nkongolo Mwamba, 19
Oba of Benin, 19, 21, 36, 46, 51, 87
Osei Tutu I, 99
Otumfuo Opoku Ware II, 16
pharaohs of Egypt, 167
Sonni Ali, 173
Tutankhamon, 125
Tuthmosis, 3, 125
Wangara, 97
West Atlantic coast, 90
Yoruba, 127
knotty, 127, 128
Koli beads, 127, 128, 130
Kongo, 175
Kori beads, 36, 127, 128, 151
    imitation, 130
kori stones, 127, 151
kpo, 145
Krobo, 13, 127, 128, 130, 131, 132, 133, 134, 138, 139, 140, 145, 148, 151, 152, 155, 156, 162
Kroboland, 134, 135, 151
Kuba, 17, 26
!Kung San, 16
Kury, Mike, 164
Kwau, 127, 135
Lake Chad, 66, 164, 173
Lake Turkana, 43
Lake Volta, 82, 146
lamp worked beads, 162
languages
    Akan, 97, 122
    Arabic, 53, 105, 107
    Ateger, 44
    French, 107
    Hassaniya, 156, 158
    Nahuatl, 57
    shilha, 107

Swahili, 164
Tamachaq, 102, 105
Tamazight/Amazigh, 108
Zenete, 108
Lantana, 85, 86
lantshoong, 26
lapidary beads, 129, 130, 151, 152
Latvia, 53
leather, 13, 16, 17, 33, 91, 92, 98, 99, 103, 105, 118, 122, 157, 158, 159, 177
leaves, 67, 73
    cassava, 134
    myrtle, 76
Lebanon, 53
    Sidon, 153
    Tyre, 153, 171
Lego, 44
Lele, 26
Leo Africanus, 173
Liberia, 44, 118, 170, 178
Libya, 31, 90, 107, 124, 170, 173
    Augila, 176
    Cyrenaica, 171
    Fezzan, 170
    Ghadames, 176
    Murzuk, 176
Life in Africa Foundation, 77
lime, 166, 167
Lithuania, 53
Loango, 171
loops, 92, 97, 118, 146, 148, 150
lost wax casting technique, 13, 44, 94, 113, 115, 116, 117, 122
lozenge-shaped, 157, 159, 162
Luba, 15, 16, 17, 19, 20, 46, 172
Luo, 43
Maasai, 15
Madagascar, 57
Mafooka hat, 171
Malabar Coast, 31
Malawi, 36
Malaya, 67
Maldive Islands, 28
malekmapyeem, 26
Mali, 1, 3, 20, 21, 26, 36, 38, 61, 64, 65, 66, 76, 79, 81, 82, 83, 88, 92, 96, 103, 123, 129, 139, 156, 173, 176, 177, 179
    Bambuk and Bure regions, 20, 97, 179
    Bandiagara Escarpment, 92
    Bandiagara Plateau, 81, 82, 92
    Bondou, 179

Djenne, 63, 64, 66, 79, 80, 122, 139, 172, 173
Djenne-Jeno, 61, 63, 64, 66, 171, 172
Gao, 129, 173, 175
Hambarketolo, 63
Kaniana, 63
Mopti, 79
Niger Bend region, 79, 81, 92
Segou, 79
Taghaza, 97
Taoudenni, 176
Timbuktu, 31, 36, 79, 173, 175, 176, 177
Zobora, 64
Mande, 90, 122, 156
Manding Empire, 92
mandrel, 125, 162, 164
manganese, 158
Mangbetu, 44
Mantetje, 171
Marco Polo, 28
Marinus of Tyre, 171
market, 176, 177, 179
Masaai, 26
Masaga Glass Works, 164, 165
mask, 15, 16, 46
    Dan, 170
    Dogon, 92
    Igbo, 28
    ivory, 20
    Kuba, 17
    maskettes, 116
    minyaki, 46
    mummy, 167, 168
masnoura, 158
Mason, Dr. J. Walter, 26
matched beads, 134
Mau, 178
Mauny, Raymond, 156
Mauritania, 13, 22, 33, 43, 54, 59, 67, 72, 74, 76, 88, 107, 125, 129, 131, 139, 156, 157, 158, 159, 160, 162, 173, 179, 180
    Aioun, 156
    Akrejit, 156
    Atar, 156
    Chinguetti, 156, 173
    Foota-Torra, 179
    Kiffa, 156, 157, 162
    Koumbi Saleh, 129, 156, 179
    Mederdra, 156
    Nouakchott, 156
    Ouadane, 173
    Oualata, 156, 173, 176

    Rosso, 156
    Tegadoust, 156
    Tichitt, 156
Mayumbe, 171
Mayyume, 171
McEwan, Frank, 87
McIntosh, S.K and R.J., 63
medicines, 17, 36, 77
    lunar paste, 57
Mediterranean, 36, 102, 152, 170, 171, 172, 176
melha, 158
Mende, 19
mergaf, 102, 113
Mesopotamia, 13, 63
metals, 13, 15, 20, 21, 22, 44, 57, 76, 90, 123, 177
    aluminum, 14, 24, 82, 121, 124
    brass, 13, 15, 17, 20, 24, 28, 54, 67, 72, 89, 92, 98, 99, 108, 110, 113, 114, 115, 116, 117, 118, 120, 122, 124, 127, 171, 174, 177, 180
    bronze, 110, 116, 117, 118, 120, 122, 124, 171, 172, 177
    cobalt, 167
    copper, 13, 15, 20, 21, 24, 54, 67, 72, 90, 98, 99, 101, 110, 114, 118, 119, 120, 122, 124, 127, 167, 168, 171, 174, 179
    gold, 13, 16, 17, 20, 36, 73, 76, 90, 94, 97, 99, 103, 110, 111, 116, 118, 122, 124, 127, 128, 131, 148, 156, 166, 170, 171, 173, 174, 175, 176, 179
    iron, 13, 15, 16, 17, 20, 21, 34, 44, 66, 82, 89, 90, 91, 92, 96, 97, 99, 110, 116, 118, 122, 124, 134, 164, 167, 169, 171, 174, 175, 177, 180
    metal oxides, 167
    nickel, 110, 113, 114, 115
    silver, 13, 20, 35, 37, 54, 57, 67, 72, 73, 74, 76, 97, 98, 99, 101, 102, 103, 105, 107, 108, 109, 110, 113, 114, 115
    white metal, 104, 113, 114, 115, 122
    zinc, 20
Meteyi, 127, 151
Mexico, 57
micaceous luster, 127, 128
Middle East, 13, 66, 127, 129, 153, 172
milk, 58
mint Seyidi, Lalla Aicha, 156
mirrors, 38, 74, 132
Miti Metee, 127, 134
Mohs, Friedrich, 79
Mohs hardness scale, 79, 86
mojo bag, 44
molded beads, 43, 122, 131, 134, 138, 139, 145, 146, 148, 151, 166
    horizontal mold, 127, 151, 155

vertical mold, 134, 148, 151, 152, 155
monochromatic, 134, 162
Moors, 175
Morfia, 125
Moroccan War, 175
Morocco, 16, 35, 37, 42, 54, 57, 58, 76, 83, 88, 97, 101, 102, 107, 108, 166, 172, 173, 174, 175, 177
    Ceuna, 174
    Draa Valley, 37
    Fez, 173
    Grotte des Pigeons, 16
    Sidjilmassa, 97
    Tiznit, 108
Mozambique, 31
mpatea, 99
Mue Ne Angma, 132, 139, 140, 162
Muhammad, 179
mummy, 167, 168
Mummy beads, 167
Murakad, 156
Mursi, 14
museums
    Florida Museum of Natural History, 44
    Musée de l'Homme, Paris, 26
    Natural History Museum, London, 26
myrrh, 76
Nadel, S.F., 164
Namibia, 17, 88
    Swakopmund, 88
Nasamones, 171
National Geographic Magazine, 63
natron, 166
Ndebele, 177
Ndembu, 21
necklace, 13, 15, 16, 17, 19, 20, 21, 22, 28, 29, 33, 37, 38, 40, 42, 43, 44, 47, 50, 57, 63, 66, 67, 73, 74, 76, 77, 82, 83, 85, 87, 89, 90, 91, 92, 97, 99, 101, 102, 110, 113, 114, 118, 123, 129, 152, 153, 158, 160, 167, 172, 180
Netherlands, 33
    Amsterdam, 31
Newcomb, Howard, 164
New York Stock Exchange, 97
Niger, 31, 87, 103, 117, 171, 173, 179
    Agadez, 98, 103, 173, 174, 176
    Assodé, 173
    Bilma, 176
Bend, 170, 172, 173
Delta, 33, 63, 79, 139, 171, 174
Nigeria, 13, 15, 19, 21, 31, 35, 42, 44, 46, 53, 77, 86, 87, 90, 110, 116, 117, 118, 119, 120, 124, 125, 127, 128, 129, 130, 131, 134, 146, 151, 152, 155, 164, 165, 169, 174, 177, 179, 180
    Ameki Foundation, 53
    Bauchi plateau, 90
    Benue State, 120
    Bida, 155, 164, 165
    Gando, 31
    Ife, 127
    Igbo-Ukwu, 129
    Ile-Ife, 128, 152
    Ilesha, 129
    Ilorin, 86, 87, 164
    Ita Yemoo, 128
    Kano, 31, 110, 153
    Katsina, 90
    Kuka, 31, 173, 176
    Kwara state, 86
    Lagos, 33, 176
    Masaga, 164
    Niger State, 164
    Old Oyo, 87
    Olokun Grove, 128
    Onikroga, 129
    Orun Oba Ado, 128
    Oyo, 127, 146
    Sokoto, 90
Niger River, 63, 79, 87, 97, 164, 173
Niger Valley, 19, 172
Nile Delta, 167
Nile Valley, 90, 171
Niusisi Koli, 151, 155
nkisi power figures, 26, 175
Nkrumah, President Dr. Kwame, 146
Nok, 90, 170
nomads, 14, 102, 108, 113, 120, 156, 158, 171, 172, 173
North Africa, 17, 28, 63, 73, 79, 107, 167, 170, 171, 172, 173, 175
nourakad, 158
nsaknnee, 99
Nubia, 90, 176
Nubian Desert, 88
Numidia, 107
Nupe, 164, 177
nuts, 13, 66, 67
    almonds, 74
    kola, 20, 122
nyama, 91
nyamakalaw, 91
Nyamwezi, 177
oblate, 45, 59, 88, 159
Obuoso, 135

ochre, 16, 17, 21
Okata, 138
Ologo, 131, 138, 145
Olokun cult, 129, 130
Omo River, 21
Omo Valley, 14
Opper, M.J., 73
oral tradition, 129, 134
Oromo, 19, 20, 109
Ottoman Empire, 176
Out of Africa, 166
ovoid, 108, 117, 122
Oyo Empire, 87, 117, 127
painted beads, 37, 70, 159
paper, 77
Paper to Pearls, 77
Park, Mungo, 175, 179
patina, 21, 22, 50, 81, 122
pendant, 13, 17, 20, 26, 36, 38, 40, 44, 46, 49, 51, 57, 67, 72, 81, 87, 88, 90, 91, 92, 94, 97, 98, 102, 103, 105, 108, 110, 113, 117, 118, 122, 123, 125, 135, 138, 158, 162, 180
    Agadez cross, 98, 103, 105, 107
    breast-shaped, 103
    Croix du Sud, 108
    ear cleaners, 105
    engagement, 114
    face, 116
    flower-shaped, 135
    Hand of Fatima, 76, 107, 108
    Igbo Bugs, 118
    ingall, 99
    Khomissar, 98, 105
    phallic, 114
    Star of David, 108, 115
    star-shaped, 135, 138
    tagmout, 108
    Tcherot, 98, 99, 105
Pende, 20, 46
Pereira, Pacheo, 127
perforation, 26, 29, 36, 44, 57, 59, 66, 67, 73, 76, 77, 79, 80, 81, 82, 85, 88, 117, 127, 128, 134, 135, 138, 151, 158, 167
perfumes, 73, 74, 76, 77
    ambergris, 74, 76
    Indian, 76
    orange essence, 76
    rose essence, 76
    rose water, 74
Persia, 173
Persian Gulf, 36

Petrie, Sir Flinders, 67
phallic beads, 117
phenolic resins, 57, 58
Phoenicians, 90, 170
Pieters, Sid, 88
pilgrims, 176
plant ash, 166
plants, 67, 73, 77
    bamboo, 73
    coffee, 166
    corrigiola, 76
    geranium, 73
    Job's tears, 67
    nut grass, 74, 77
    seed ferns, 53
plaster, 122, 159
plastic, 37, 38, 54, 57, 59, 76, 77, 162, 167
    casein, 57, 58
    cellulose-based, 58
    phenolic plastics, 57, 58
Pliny, 13, 172
Podokowo, 44
Poland
    Gdansk, 57
polychromatic, 157, 158, 162, 164
polyester, 57, 58
polystyrene, 57
porcelain, 36, 128, 164
Poro Society, 170
Portugal, 26, 28, 31, 33, 34, 36, 87, 116, 124, 127, 128, 174, 175
pottery, 21, 59, 63, 99, 132, 156, 166, 171, 174
Powa beads, 127, 134
prayer beads, 57, 67, 114, 177
    musbaha, 105, 114
priest, 16, 17, 20, 38, 44, 46, 90, 99, 132
Prince Henry of Portugal, 174
Prosser beads, 166, 167
Prosser, Thomas and Richard, 166
pyramidal, 76, 120, 134, 138
Pyrenees, 173
queens
    Hatshepsut, 125
    Maria Theresa, 109
Quran, 20, 98, 113
radiocarbon dating, 66, 129, 130
raffia, 17, 84, 86
Redlhamer Brothers, 43
Red Sea, 59, 90
repousse, 99
resin, 73, 74, 159

Rhodesia, 87
rings, 37, 80, 92, 97, 99, 108, 110, 117, 118, 120, 124
Roberts, Allen F., 19
Roberts, Mary Nooter, 19
rocker technique, 59
Romania, 124
Romans, 13, 36, 67, 115, 167, 170, 171, 172, 175, 176
Römer, L.F., 128
roots, 73
royal court, 15, 16, 35, 36, 46, 85, 87, 127, 177
rubber, 37, 175
runners, 177
Rwanda, 92
saffron, 42, 54, 58, 76, 167
Sahara, 28, 59, 90, 97, 102, 108, 162, 170, 171, 172, 173, 175, 176
Sahel, 176
saliva, 156
salt, 13, 97, 122, 156, 171, 173, 176, 179
Sambara, 43, 44
Samburu, 15, 21
sand, 122, 134, 156, 164
Sao civilization, 66, 68
Sarakole, 179
Saudi Arabia
    Mecca, 176
scarab, 167, 168
scented paste beads, 43, 73, 74, 76, 77
Schreger Lines/Lines of Retzius, 50
seed beads, 133, 138
seeds, 13, 15, 17, 20, 66, 67, 73, 74, 76, 170
    damma, 174
    drift seeds/sea beans, 67, 73
    Job's tears, 67, 74
    Kekeore/coffee bean, 67, 73
    Lead tree, 67
    Mucuna, 67
    rosary pea/crab eye, 67, 74
    sea heart, 67
    seed pods, 67
    taku, 174
Segi beads, 127, 128, 130
sellkrass, 158
Senegal, 21, 74, 76, 92, 116, 118, 127, 162, 177, 179
    Bambuk and Bure regions, 20, 97, 179
    Foota-Torra, 179
    Goreé, 174
Senegal River, 97, 179
Senufo, 19, 26
Seraculeh, 179
Serahuli, 169, 179

Serawoolli, 179
Seymour, Art, 139
shaman, 38
shea butter, 175
shell, 13, 15, 16, 17, 19, 20, 21, 22, 26, 37, 38, 105, 128, 173
    African land snail, 26, 175
    Arca, 34, 36
    bivalve, 59, 61
    clam, 26, 86
    coconut, 25, 73, 178
    Conus, 17, 19, 33, 36
    cowry, 13, 17, 19, 20, 26, 28, 29, 30, 31, 33, 34, 36, 43, 73, 74, 110, 127, 157, 170, 171, 174, 178
    hippo tooth, 36
    Nassarius, 16, 26
    ostrich egg, 13, 16, 23, 24, 25, 26, 28, 86, 178
    palm nut, 73
    tortoise, 17
    white, 16
    white coral, 31
Shona, 87
Sierra Leone, 44, 56, 118
silent trade, 174
silica, 167
silversmith, 90, 97, 101, 103, 105, 114
Simak, Evelyn, 20, 22
Sinai, 88
Singapore, 180
sintering, 134
skhab, 73, 74, 76
slag, 164
Slave Coast, 33, 36
slave trade, 13, 31, 33, 34, 36, 124, 127, 131, 171, 173, 174, 175, 176, 179
slurry
    clay, 66, 69
    glass, 132, 139, 156, 158, 162
smelting, 82, 96, 122
soda, 164, 167, 168
Somalia, 57, 173
    Ras Hafun, 31
Songhai, 13, 91, 173, 174, 176
Soninke, 124, 177, 179
Souleiman, 22, 158
South Africa, 26, 42, 67, 97, 177
    Blombos Cave, 26
    Sofala, 90
    Transvaal, 67
South America, 63
Southern Africa, 16

Spain, 107, 174
  Andalusia, 173
  Catalonia, 36
  Granada, 173
  Madrid, 180
spangling, 54
spherical, 66, 74, 76, 97, 108, 113, 114, 117, 122, 124, 132, 135, 153, 156, 158, 159, 162
spices, 73
  cinnamon, 172
  cloves, 74, 76
  nutmeg, 74, 76
spindle whorls, 59, 61, 62, 63, 64, 65, 66, 122
spirals, 33, 69, 124, 135, 153
spot beads, 125
spruing, 122
Sri Lanka, 31, 174
Stanley, H.M., 176
stencil, 59, 66
stone, 13, 15, 16, 20, 21, 38, 59, 63, 64, 66, 79, 80, 87, 91, 97, 125, 158, 162, 167
  agate, 37, 87, 88, 101
  amazonite, 76, 79, 83, 88, 167, 180
  amethyst, 88
  basalt, 80
  bauxite, 79, 82, 84, 86, 180
  biotite, 80
  boehmite, 82
  carnelian, 21, 22, 80, 87, 88, 99, 158
  chalcedony, 79, 86, 87, 88
  chert, 86
  diamond, 79
  feldspar, 79, 80, 88
  gibbsite, 82
  gneiss, 79, 80, 81, 82, 180
  granite, 79, 80, 81, 82, 180
  greenstone, 79
  hematite, 80
  Hombori marble/granitoid stone, 80
  hornblende, 80
  igneous, 80
  jasper, 79, 85, 86, 87, 88, 158
  kaolinite, 82
  lapis lazuli, 88, 167
  metamorphic, 80
  metasomatized, 88
  meteorite, 20
  microcline, 88
  muscovite, 80
  onyx, 88
  pegmatites, 88
  Pietersite, 88
  quartz, 77, 79, 80, 82, 86, 87, 166, 168
  red shale, 134
  Riebeckite, 88
  rock crystal, 88
  ruby, 88
  sandstone, 79, 80, 92
  sapphire, 88
  serpentine, 87, 88
  silicate-bearing, 59
  steatite, 167
  talc, 79
  turquoise, 88, 125, 167
Strait of Gibraltar, 174
stringer, 162
sub-Saharan Africa, 13, 20, 73, 123, 169, 170, 174, 179
Sudan, 17, 38, 43, 62, 66, 67, 68, 69, 90, 153, 167, 172, 173
  Darfur, 176
  Kerma, 167
  Lisht, 167
Sudanic style, 79
Switzerland, 156
Sylla, Sarakata, 94
synthetic resins, 57
  bakelite, 57
  novalak, 57
  resolan, 57
Syria, 13
tabular, 122, 138
tagelmoust, 103
talisman, 16, 19, 20, 38, 42, 44, 57, 63
Tanzania, 57, 177
  Ujiji, 177
  Zanzibar, 176
tapered, 66, 79, 127
tattoos, 15
teeth, 38, 44
  alligator, 44
  crocodile, 38, 44, 47
  human, 44
  leopard, 38, 44
  lion, 38, 44, 47, 124
Tehe Koli, 127, 151
Tellum, 82, 92
telsum, 110
Teranja Bead Works, 132, 138, 139
terlitza, 158
termite mound, 77
terracotta, 59, 66
Terrazzo, 139
Tetteh, Ransford, 132, 138, 139

textiles, 44, 45, 66, 99, 132, 139, 179
Thailand, 180
Thebes, 167
The Gambia, 118, 169, 179
The History of Beads, 15
the Indies, 31
the Netherlands, 124, 127, 174, 175
    Amsterdam, 180
Third International Bead Conference, Washington, D.C., 164
Thomas J. Mercer, Jr., collection, 168
time periods
    Pennsylvanian period, 53
    Cretaceous period, 53
    Miocene period, 53
    Paleolithic period, 16, 79
    Middle Paleolithic period, 16
    Upper Paleolithic period, 16
    38th millennium BCE, 16
    11th millennium BCE, 59
    10th millennium BCE, 59, 63
    Neolithic period, 38, 79
    7th millennium BCE, 63
    6th millennium BCE, 13
    5th millennium BCE, 90, 167
    4th millennium BCE, 16
    3rd millennium BCE, 63
    21st century BCE, 167
    17th century BCE, 167
    16th century BCE, 13, 125, 167
    15th century BCE, 13, 125
    14th century BCE, 13
    13th century BCE, 13, 125, 167
    12th century BCE, 125, 167
    11th century BCE, 167
    9th century BCE, 90, 170
    8th century BCE, 167, 172
    7th century BCE, 90, 167, 170, 172
    6th century BCE, 167
    5th century BCE, 90
    Bronze Age, 53
    3rd century BCE, 64, 90, 92, 171, 172
    2nd century BCE, 92
    1st century BCE, 13, 125
    2nd century, 130, 171
    3rd century, 171
    4th century, 107, 115
    5th century, 53, 170
    Middle Ages, 36
    6th century, 64, 172, 174
    7th century, 79, 167, 172, 173
    8th century, 64, 79, 156, 172, 176, 179
    9th century, 125
    10th century, 64, 125, 131, 173
    11th century, 13, 92, 107, 116, 127, 172, 173, 179
    12th century, 64, 66, 122, 125, 153, 176, 179
    13th century, 28, 66, 81, 90, 107, 116, 156, 173, 179
    14th century, 28, 153, 156, 171, 176
    15th century, 64, 66, 92, 116, 127, 172, 173
    16th century, 28, 31, 33, 36, 64, 66, 81, 87, 97, 109, 127, 128, 167, 173, 174, 175
    17th century, 20, 31, 87, 99, 118, 120, 124, 127, 131, 156, 174, 175
    18th century, 31, 33, 79, 109, 118, 122, 128, 146, 156, 164
    19th century, 13, 31, 34, 36, 58, 79, 86, 87, 94, 97, 109, 110, 116, 118, 120, 123, 139, 146, 148, 156, 164, 166, 171, 175, 176
    20th century, 13, 15, 26, 30, 36, 38, 43, 46, 56, 57, 59, 63, 64, 73, 79, 80, 82, 86, 87, 88, 97, 99, 101, 109, 116, 117, 127, 128, 130, 131, 132, 134, 135, 138, 139, 140, 145, 146, 148, 151, 153, 155, 156, 157, 158, 162, 164, 166, 167, 169, 170, 171, 176, 179
    21st century, 26, 53, 77, 97, 162, 176, 180
Tiv, 113, 117, 120
tizerzai, 108
tjehnet, 167
Togo, 117, 146, 151
Toloy, 92
trade beads, 13, 14, 86, 116
trader, 28, 34, 36, 88, 102, 108, 124, 133, 153, 158, 159, 169, 173, 174, 176, 177, 179
trading companies
    British East India Company, 31
    Compagnie du Senegal, 31
    Danish West India and Guinea Company, 128
    Dutch East India Company, 31
    Royal Africa Company, 33
trailed patterns, 139, 146, 148, 153, 162, 164
transfer technique, 66, 69
trans-Saharan trade routes, 79, 97, 102, 124, 156, 171, 172, 173, 175, 176
tree resin, 53, 57
trees, 67, 73
    Aquilaria agallocha, 74
    coconut palm, 73
    conifers, 53
    deciduous, 53
    Dentarium microcarpum, 76
    evergreen, 67
    Ficus benjamina, 74
    Lead tree, 67

Mastic, 74
tropical broad-leafed trees, 53
triangular, 22, 67, 76, 110, 125, 156, 157, 158, 159, 162, 164
tsakati, 138
Tuareg, 97, 98, 99, 102, 103, 107, 109, 173, 176
blue men, 102
Tuareg Rebellion, 176
tubular, 66, 81, 113, 120, 127, 128, 130, 167
Tunisia, 73, 74, 107
Tunis, 36, 74
Tunkara, Saja, 179
Turkana, 43, 44
Uganda, 67, 77
Gulu, 77
Kampala, 77
Umayyad caliphate, 173
United States of America, 13, 58, 67, 86, 107, 117, 124, 138, 139, 157, 162, 169, 179
Denver, Colorado, 61
New York, New York, 107, 180
Seattle, Washington, 169
Tucson, Arizona, 179
Washington, D.C., 164
Upper Volta, 28, 66
uranium, 158
Vaseline beads, 158
Venetian beads, 132, 135, 139, 146, 148, 152
7-layer chevrons, 148
chevrons, 13, 47, 169
greenhearts, 146, 148
imitation chevrons, 70
King beads, 138, 146, 148
lamp work beads, 134, 140
millefiori, 13, 139
mosaic glass beads, 158
red whitehearts, 146, 148, 150
vines, 67, 73, 74
virginity, 132
Voices for Global Change, 77
Volta River, 33
von Blixen, Karen, 166
Wakore, 179
Wangara, 97, 179

wax, 44, 122
weapons, 90, 171
ax, 16
firearms, 20, 90
musket, 13
swords, 99
West Africa, 13, 14, 19, 28, 30, 31, 33, 34, 36, 38, 43, 46, 54, 59, 63, 64, 66, 67, 73, 81, 88, 90, 97, 102, 110, 117, 122, 124, 125, 127, 128, 131, 143, 148, 151, 152, 155, 170, 171, 172, 173, 174, 175, 176, 177, 179
West Atlantic coast, 90
Western Sahara, 59
wet-core powder glass technique, 134, 139, 143, 145, 146, 151, 156
Wilhelm, Gebhardt, 58
Willett, F., 127
Wolof, 90, 92
wood, 13, 16, 36, 37, 38, 44, 46, 64, 66, 67, 73, 74, 171, 174, 177
African mahogany, 67
agalloch, 76
ebony, 67, 72
euclea, 67
Wood, Lady Susan, 164, 166
wool, 57, 74
wound beads, 155, 164, 165
yams, 134
Yeboah, Daaku Kwame, 139
Yoruba, 13, 20, 22, 26, 34, 35, 59, 97, 110, 111, 117, 118, 127, 128, 130, 151, 152, 155, 174
Yorubaland, 33, 86, 127, 151, 171
Zagba, 127, 135
Zaire, 26, 44, 46, 169
Zambezi River, 87
Zambia, 21, 36
Sokota, 173
Zanzibar, 56, 57
Zhao Rugua, 173
zigzag patterns, 59, 125, 127, 158
Zimbabwe, 36, 87, 131
Mapungubwe, 131
zoomorphism, 66
Zulu, 17

Acknowledgments

From Lois Dubin

A very special thank you to Niangi Batulukisi for her research assistance and for directing me to important sources of information.

From Evelyn Simak and Carl Dreibelbis

We would like to thank Saibo Tunkara (Tunkara and Brothers, United States and The Gambia), Haji Tunkara and Abdul Touray (Touray Beads, United States and The Gambia) for their firsthand information concerning the present-day bead trade; Jürgen Busch (Kiffa Beads, Moroccan/Berber Beads) and Kirk Stanfield (Powder Glass Beads, Yoruba Beads, Bead Trade) for information shared concerning bead types and styles.

Many thanks to Elizabeth Bennett (Africa Direct, Inc.) for making this book possible.

Any unintended errors contained in these pages are ours alone, and not the product of anyone who assisted us.

Publisher's Note

This book exists because of the incredible generosity of several people, whose joint efforts brought this book to fruition:

Evelyn Simak is an indefatigable researcher, who brings to her subject not only passion and scholarship but also grace and humor which make working with her a joy.

Carl Dreibelbis collaborated in the writing, and also kindly let us photograph his superb collection of Bodom and Akosu beads, which are some of the finest anywhere.

Lois Dubin's enthusiasm delighted us all, and her fascinating introduction provided the ideal entry point to the chapters that follow.

Mark Donato's photographs caused us to gasp when we first saw them... and we are still gasping.

Sally Luther edited copy with enthusiasm and care.

Mayapriya Long, of Bookwrights, designed this book with sensitivity and an artist's eye.

Jacob Liechty coordinated production, from proofing and indexing through design and printing. His fingerprints are on every page.

◊ ◊ ◊

Africa Direct, Inc. had its beginnings in 1994, when Sara Luther and I took our three still-at-home children and moved to Africa for a year. We drove fifteen thousand miles in a used camper which had been crudely converted from an old panel van, and saw a great deal of Southern Africa.

Selling African art has been our business since 1995. Our website, www.africadirect.com, lists more than sixteen thousand items. We are among the biggest sellers of African art, trade beads and ethnic jewelry on eBay, and are major supporters of eBay Giving Works charity auctions.

We also publish books on African art, beads and jewelry, and are interested in receiving manuscripts for review.

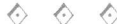

Elizabeth Bennett, President
Africa Direct, Inc.

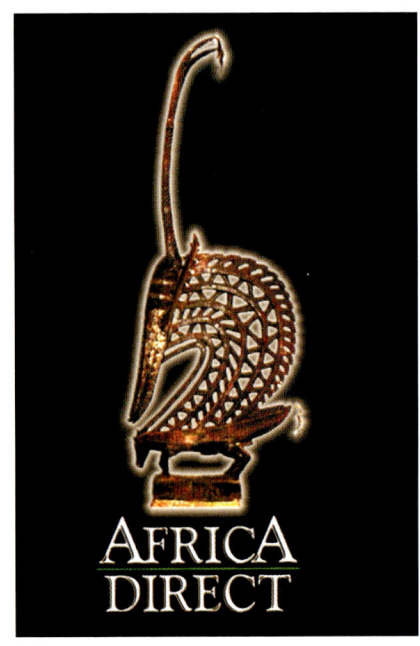

Books Published by Africa Direct

Yoruba: An Art of Life
by Daniel Mato, Ph.D., and Chelsea Cooksey
Introduction by Moyo Okidigi, Ph.D.

Zulu Beadwork: Talk With Beads
by Hlengiwe Dube

Kuba Textiles and Design
by Elizabeth S. Bennett and Niangi Batulukisi, Ph.D.

Museum Exhibits Available from Africa Direct

Yoruba: An Art of Life

African Beads and Beadwork
Opening South Dakota Art Museum, 2010